Padre Junipero Serra. 5-615
Founder of the California Missions.

Story of the

MISSION SANTA CRUZ

by

H. A. van COENEN TORCHIANA, LITT.D., LL.D., 1867–

[handwritten: Henry Albert Willem]

PAUL ELDER AND COMPANY
SAN FRANCISCO, CALIFORNIA
1933

Copyright 1933
by
H. A. van Coenen Torchiana

To

The Memory of My Sister,

Aimée Elise Begemann Torchiana,

Widow of Reverend Simon Begemann, D.D.,

Directrice of the Military Hospital at Paramaribo,

Suriname, Netherlands West Indies,

Bearer of Knight's Cross of the Order of Orange Nassau,

Who Devoted to the Afflicted

Her Life unto Death,

Paramaribo, 1924,

This Book is Dedicated.

Publications by the Author

BOOKS

Holland, the Birthplace of American Liberty

Tropical Holland, Java and Other Islands

California Gringos

Story of the Mission Santa Cruz

BROCHURES

The Future Trade

The Netherlands is Right

Good Citizenship in Pacific Relations

A Constructive Criticism

Interest in American Estates

Insulinde and American Business

Author's Note

The story presented to the reader in this volume is a history of the Mission of Santa Cruz in California. There are two methods of making such a presentation; that is to prepare an account of a series of events and actions which bear on the Mission only, or on the other hand to surround the picture with a frame of the acts and events affecting the country as a whole.

The latter method has been selected here, for to follow the former often leads to a presentation which is barren and sometimes incomprehensible to the average reader, who is not particularly versed in Mission history.

The broader method makes it possible to project on the screen of history an image of the times rather than a table of events.

In the story that follows, it will be seen that Santa Cruz was isolated. Early world travellers in their chronicles often fail to mention this particular Mission, but as the Missions in Alta California were all operated under one system and very much the same circumstances, it has been considered advisable to reproduce the impressions of those observers who visited adjoining Missions, even though they did not go to Santa Cruz.

Wherever data on Santa Cruz exists having historical value, this has been given, but if the data is lacking, it has been supplemented by information left us by historians or travellers describing other Missions.

The assistance and encouragement given by Carl I. Wheat, Esquire, Chairman of the Committee on Publication of the California Historical Society of San Francisco; by Dr. Owen C. Coy, Professor in American History at the University of Southern California; by Professor William Hawley Davis, Editor of the Stanford University Press; by Mr. Robert Ray, Librarian of the San Francisco Public Library; by Father P. J. McGrath, of the Santa Cruz Parish, and by Mr. Leon Rowland, City Editor of the Santa Cruz News, are hereby gratefully acknowledged.

The map found on page 118a of this book is a copy of one which Miss Narcissa L. Parris (now Mrs. Clinton Veerkamp, of Placerville), a native of Santa Cruz County, prepared for her thesis for the degree of Master of Arts in History at the University of California entitled, "The Early History of the Santa Cruz Region;" the map at the end of the book was prepared by Dr. H. E. Bolton, of the History Department of the University of California, for his great work, "Anza's Expeditions." I appreciate their permission to reprint the maps here.

Introduction

"California, the Child of Spain!" This oft-repeated phrase has come to be regarded as the true definition of the parentage of our great State. In general this may be entirely acceptable, for California is rich indeed in her legacy of Spanish romance.

However, the serious student of history cannot accept this definition as an unqualified basis for study of the Hispanic institutions of California in 1848 without being led into many errors. The California that came into the possession of the United States in 1848 by the Treaty of Guadalupe Hidalgo was not in reality the child of Spain but more exactly the grandchild of Spain, the direct child of Mexico. To be sure, the child was in many ways the "very image" of the grandparent, and this has caused many to forget an important intervening link in the genealogical table.

For a quarter-century or more the institutions and customs of Spain were modified under the régime of Mexico, that new nation torn from Mother Spain by a process of revolution, under circumstances which presaged possible violent changes in the institutions of the older order. It is remarkable that more revolutionary changes did not occur, and that many of those which did come about were merely the putting into execution of ideas inherently a part of the evolved Spanish policy.

The fact remains, however, that the California of 1846 was not the California of 1822, and even less was it the California of 1800-1810, when the Spanish régime in the province was at its height. The Missions, the pride and glory as well as the economic support of California, had fallen from their position of power. In 1846 their vast fields, where thousands of cattle had been herded by neophytes, had passed into the hands of retired officers and soldiers, or were even more firmly held by newly-arrived *gringo* owners.

Around each of the Missions, except those in complete ruin, centered a group of villages of ex-neophytes who in some cases had combined with the *gente de razon* to form *pueblos*. While similar in many characteristics to the *pueblos* of Spanish California, these newer institutions were governed by laws enacted and administered by an entirely different government. This fact has often been overlooked in the superficial approach which assumes that institutions bearing the same name and having many similarities are therefore identical.

The so-called "Spanish Grants" were another inheritance from an earlier day. The name as generally used implies that those numerous large private estates had been granted by the King of Spain to his loyal subjects. The fact is, however, that only a small part of these lands were granted under Spain, all but a score or so of the remaining six to eight hundred grants having been given by Mexican Governors. The land policy taken over by the American pioneers was therefore essentially Mexican.

Students and readers of history are therefore greatly indebted to studies such as the present one made by Dr. H. A. van Coenen Torchiana on Branciforte, or Santa Cruz, the origin of our present city of Santa Cruz. Dr. Torchiana is an attorney of note, and it is interesting to know that he was led into this study to meet the requirements of a case at law. The volume is not, therefore, the exercise of a mere academician, but has already served a useful historical purpose. It is only by relying upon detailed studies of such institutions that the historians of California and the Hispanic American field are enabled to make valid generalizations. It is hoped that this scholarly work by Dr. Torchiana will be followed by others until every phase of the interesting subject of California history is accurately recorded in readable form.

OWEN C. COY, Ph.D.
Professor of History at the University of Southern California, and Director of California State Historical Association.

TABLE OF CONTENTS

BOOK I

PROLOGUE (Continued)

BOOK II

(The Missions Existing at the Time of the Founding of Santa Cruz)

THE STORY

BOOK III

THE STORY (Continued)

BOOK IV

THE STORY (Continued)

BOOK V

EPILOGUE

BOOK VI

ILLUSTRATIONS

ABBREVIATIONS USED IN NOTES

Am. Antiq. Soc.—American Antiquarian Society.

App.—Appendix.

Arch.—Archives.

Archb. Arch.—Archbishop's Archives.

B. C.—Bancroft Collection.

Bib. Nac.—Refers to National Library.

Cal.—California.

Cal. Arch. M. & C.—California Archives, Miscellaneous and Collected.

Cal. Arch. LR (or Leg. Rec.)—California Archives, Legislative Record.

Col.—Collected.

Dc.—Documentary.

D. S. P. (or Dep. St. Pap.)—Departmental State Papers.

Ex. Doc.—Executive Documents.

Fr.—Fray.

Id.—Same.

M. A.—Mexican Archives.

Mil.—Military.

Miss.—Miscellaneous.

M. S.—Manuscript.

Noticias—Refers to Noticias de la Nueva California by Fr. F. Palou or M. Venegas, as indicated.

p.—Page. *pp.*—Pages.

Prov. Rec. (or PR)—Provincial Records.

Prov. St. Pap. (or PSP)—Provincial State Papers.

Rep.—Report.

S. A.—Spanish Archives.

Sac.—Sacramento.

Sec.—Section.

Sta. Barb.—Santa Barbara.

Sta. Cruz—Santa Cruz.

St. Pap. (or SP)—State Papers.

U. C.—University of California.

U. S. S. C.—United States Supreme Court.

Vida—Refers to Relacion de la Vida del Padre Junipero Serra.

Vol.—Volume.

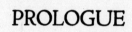

PROLOGUE

BOOK I

CHAPTER I

Why the Names California and Santa Cruz?
The Romantic History of the California
Missions

BOOK I
Chapter I

Why the Names California and Santa Cruz?
The Romantic History of the California Missions

OF the known history of all the countries which are prominent in today's world, that of California has, perhaps, the latest beginning. This is the more astonishing, for the State now looming so large on the Pacific horizon, appealing so much to the imagination and hopes of millions of people elsewhere, is the sixth in the North American Union in number of population (about five and one-half million) and the third in the value of its exports, even outstripping the much older and more highly industrialized State of Pennsylvania with its ten million inhabitants.

Of its history little if anything is known before the middle of the eighteenth century, though the name was vaguely mentioned two centuries earlier.

There are several theories as to the derivation of this name, which first appeared in the official records of 1524.[1]

One is that the word was coined by Indians, who showed an explorer snow-white heaps upon a knoll, calling them *cal y forno;* the *cal* meaning lime and *forno* meaning an oven or kiln.[2]

Venegas in his *Noticia de la California* mentions the theory that the name was derived from *calida fornax,* or hot furnace, and applicable to the prevailing heat;[3] but inasmuch as the heat in California was far less than that experienced elsewhere by the *Conquistadores,* this theory seems to have little to sustain it.

Bancroft countenances the suggestion that the name might have been derived from the Indian *kali forno,* signifying "high hill," as well as "sandy coast," or "native land," though he comes to the conclusion that the derivation given by Dr. Edward Everett Hale is the correct one.[4]

Jules Marcou in his Notes of 1878[5] declares that Cortes classified the lands of the Indies in *tierra fria, tierra templada, tierra caliente* and *tierra california.*

---

[1] Cortes, Carta Quarta VII; Lorenzana, p. 349, Notes.
[2] Richman, California under Spain and Mexico, p. 365.
[3] Perhaps also applicable to the Indian *temescal,* underground sweat or hot house, universally used by the California Indians for medical purposes.
[4] Bancroft, History of California, Vol. I, p. 64, et seq.
[5] Marcou's Notes upon the First Discoveries of California and the Origin of Its Name, Washington, 1878.

Dr. Edward E. Hale advances a totally different theory.[6] He ascribes the name to an Island, appearing in a famous book of fiction, "Amadis de Gaula," written by Vasco de Lobeira in the Portuguese language in the 14th or beginning of the 15th century. It was translated into Spanish by Garci Ordóñez de Montalvo, who added a new book (a fifth volume), which he entitled "Las Sergas de Esplandián" or "The Adventures of Esplandian—Son of Amadis." In this book is described the Amazon "Calafia, Queen of the Island of California." It mentions the island[7] "California" as situated very close to the Terrestrial Paradise, peopled by black women, without male companions, who lived like Amazons. It was a good yarn, assuring the credulous readers that the women were armed with weapons of gold, that their half-tame riding beasts wore harnesses of gold, etc.[8]

This romance, like many others of similar nature, was a favored book in Spain, as well as in "the Indies" or New Spain.

Besides the tales of the Amazons and of the Straits of Anian, mentioned hereafter, there were a good many others current of a phantastic nature—for instance, one called "The Seven Golden Cities of Cibola" (see Appendix No. 1), which seven cities were presumed to be somewhere in the mysterious north of the Rio Grande; there was another about a rich province of "Quivira;" also one of a Rio Oro and Rio Plata (Gold and Silver Rivers).

These stories so excited the colonials in New Spain that in 1543 their importation in the Colonies was prohibited by Charles V, as that kind of literature proved rather harmful to the enthusiastic, excitable and gullible hidalgos *outre-mer*.

It is astonishing over what large territory these fairy tales prevailed, and how long they persisted; they were prevalent elsewhere as well as on the Rio Grande, and even a good many years afterwards (1618) Sir Walter Raleigh, the English discoverer, firmly believed in the existence of one of

---

[6] First published in Am. Antiq. Soc. Proceedings, April 30, 1862, pp. 45-53.

[7] Until the middle of the 18th century, California was believed to be an island.

[8] Dr. Hale was a distinguished author and preacher. He read the old Spanish novel in 1862. How, when and why the name California was applied to the peninsula, believed by Fortun Jimenez, one of Cortes' lieutenants, to be an island, when he landed in 1533 on Baja California, remains a mystery. When Cortes landed at La Paz on the Bay of Santa Cruz, in 1535, he did not mention the name of "California" in his reports, and so far as is known never used this name in any of his writings.

these marvels—El Dorado[9] on the Orinoco—by the discovery of which he hoped to save his head from the block; but of course he failed.

The *Conquistadores* evidently mixed poetry with business and military enterprise, throwing a glamor over the geography and history of the country, and the name California was given to the whole northwest of the new discoveries, having for a long time no definite geographic meaning.

The English equivalent for the Spanish words, Santa Cruz, is of course Holy Cross, and the Spanish discoverers and pioneers, being devout Catholics, gave the name Santa Cruz, like that of Santa Maria, to many places in the "Spanish Indies" or the Americas.

Santa Cruz, the subject of the present essay, is a modern seaside resort in the State of California, with a permanent population of about 15,000, while many times that number abide there during the summer season, and on holidays.

Situated[10] on the northern shore of the famous Bay of Monterey, it is known for its salubrious climate, being sheltered against the fogs and winds, prevalent on the opposite side of the Bay, and has modern streets, good hotels, and bathing pavilions.

Historically it is the successor of the Mission of Santa Cruz, the Pueblo de Figueroa, the Pueblo of Santa Cruz, as well as the Villa of Branciforte.

Of the original Mission buildings there is very little left. Earthquakes and the elements partly destroyed the church and other buildings, which the Indian neophytes erected under the direction of the Padres, and neglect did the rest. Behind the present church one still can find part of an old wall, built of great blocks of local chalk rock. It probably surrounded a court. Somewhat below, there is also the trace of a foundation,—possibly of the blacksmith shop.

The old Plaza,—now known as the "Upper Plaza" on Mission Hill,— is still there, faced by the modern Catholic church, erected in September 1891, partly on the site of the Mission church; by one of the old residences, a relic of the padres' time; by the Holy Cross Orphanage and School for Girls; and by the Holy Cross Parish Grammar School and High School.

---

[9] El Dorado was originally the name of the gilded king, who was supposed to receive a coat of gold dust every morning, which he washed off every evening in a lake, until it became a regular treasure house. Afterwards the name was applied to localities in various parts of the Americas, where it was fancied great treasures were to be found. It covered many a dream place.

[10] It has considerable manufacturing, a large canning and lumber industry and is the center of an important cement industry and of an area of chicken ranches, dairying, vegetable growing (mostly artichokes) and flower and bulb raising.

In School Street, which runs into the Plaza, there are two old adobe residences in a good state of preservation. The larger one, formerly the residence of the Corporal of the Mission Guard, belongs to the Neary family of Santa Cruz. The smaller building, separated by a party-wall five feet thick, still belongs to the Rodriquez family, old Spanish residents of that neighborhood, and formerly was the home of the subordinates of the Corporal. In the rear, rambling old gardens suggest the charm of the Mission days, and a gnarled fig tree reminds one that the padres brought to each new settlement the mission fig, the mission olive and the mission grape.

On the opposite side of School Street were located the buildings in which the girls and young women neophytes were housed. Between the two rows of houses ran a diverted stream. School Street runs into a small street on the brow of Mission Hill, overlooking the San Lorenzo Valley. It is said to be the first street laid out in Santa Cruz.

There are still fruit trees north of the hill on which the present church stands, which were planted soon after 1791, now much gnarled and twisted of limb, but still bearing some pears and apples. They are scattered on different lots, part of the old Mission orchard near Mora and Quintana Streets, where Father Quintana was murdered by Indian neophytes in 1811. For a long time the spot was avoided by the superstitious natives.

Recently a smaller replica of the old Mission Church was erected on the corner of School Street and the Plaza. Though not situate on the exact spot of the old church, it is but two hundred and fifty feet from it and is built on ground immediately adjoining the former institution. Its erection was made possible through the enthusiastic and energetic devotion of Father P. J. McGrath and the generosity of one of his parishioners, Mrs. Richard Sullivan Doyle, a member of the Phelan family, a devout member of the Mother church and a public-spirited citizen of Santa Cruz, living a greater part of the year with her family at the old and stately Phelan estate overlooking the Bay of Monterey.

A plaque reading "Mission Santa Cruz, Founded September 25, 1791, Destroyed January 9, 1857, Restored November 1931" is attached to the church proper, which has an arched doorway with pilasters at each side and flaring buttresses at each corner. The tower, with a circular belfry, is at the southern corner, and a long archway and corridor have been erected to the side, with three or four of the quarters which the friars occupied. In this space are safely housed the magnificent vestments used by the early missionaries in their church celebrations, which are only worn now on solemn occasions.

An old iron bell has been placed in the circular-shaped dome with its open belfry, which had hung for years in the old Catholic chapel built at Aptos sixty-five years ago by Don Rafael Castro, patriarch of the branch

PRESENT CATHOLIC CHURCH AT SANTA CRUZ

RESTORED MISSION AT SANTA CRUZ
(Through the generosity of Mrs. Richard Doyle)
Over the door is a motto, "O Crux Ave Spes Unica."
(Hail, thou Cross, our only hope.)

of that family on the north side of Monterey Bay. The bell is not the original one of silver which was given by Don Rafael, but is one brought from San Francisco after early-day thieves had stolen the original.

Padres in brown or gray monk's cassocks no longer walk around, but the parish priest and his assistants may be seen walking in the gardens, meditating and saying their prayers, and the gentle Sisters of Charity move about in dark blue gowns and wide-spreading white caps, and the flavor of the old Mission days still clings to the spot.

The story of the Mission of Santa Cruz never attracted as much attention as that of the more prominent Missions, although it is well worth the study of historians as well as laymen.

While in Upper California and elsewhere in the Spanish Provinces there was a constant struggle between the representatives of the Church and those of the State, this struggle, for obvious reasons, was nowhere more acute than in the Santa Cruz-Branciforte region. It even continued and was aggravated after the separation of Mexico from Spain. That neither the Mission of Santa Cruz nor the Villa Branciforte ever responded in growth and development to the expectations of their founders is due in no small degree to this struggle. As in most other Mission districts, the founding Fathers soon realized that the sacerdotal Mission should be kept at a distance of several miles at least from the temporal presidios or civil pueblos. When it happened that they were placed in close proximity, the religious establishment was removed as soon as possible to a more remote location.

In Santa Cruz this remedy was impossible, for the Mission was firmly established before the Villa Branciforte was thought of. They remained close neighbors; and the Villa,—semi-civil and semi-military in character,— did not even have the temporizing influence of a presidio commander, generally a commissioned officer of fine character and broad tolerance.

Although climatically and topographically better located than almost any other Mission, either in Baja or Alta California, Santa Cruz Mission was not on the main road, El Camino Real. The route from the Mission San Carlos and the Presidio at Monterey towards the Mission and the Presidio at San Francisco did not lead by Santa Cruz, but by the way of the Pueblo of San Jose and later by San Juan. The Santa Cruz Mission was off the beaten path, a link of the Mission system of Alta California, both spiritually and economically, but not a link in the main chain.

Like that of the other Missions, its story is a bit of that great Mission romance, described repeatedly in prose and poetry by churchmen and laymen alike, for the history of the Missions in Alta California is one of high hopes and endeavors, of bold undertakings and accomplishments, and unselfish devotion. In it are revived tales of Knighthood in Flower, of the Teutonic Knights of the Cross, launched by the Holy See against the heathen in East Prussia, of Christian monks, devout and fearless, carrying the message of the Cross and the benefits of civilization to the barbarians living beyond the Pale.

The stage on which this historic drama was played was an inspiring one; it covered a stretch of four hundred miles along the coast of the present State of California,—a coast unsurpassed for its beauty even by that of Southern Italy. Here 70,000 primitive Californians dwelled, ranging from a state of upper savagery to that of lower barbarism, those dwelling around the Santa Barbara Channel being the most advanced.[11] About 66,000 more,[12] mostly living in savagery, were scattered over other parts of the State. For about two decades this stretch of four hundred miles, separated by a thousand miles from the nearest place of effective reinforcement, was held by a small Spanish force of between one hundred and two hundred men.

In this history we read once more of commanders of noble birth and old lineage who shared the hardships of the trail with small bands of mounted men-at-arms under their command; of leaders who thoroughly recognized the motto *noblesse oblige;* of cuirassed soldiers, who made long rides into the wilderness and continued on foot hundreds of miles with unflagging courage after their mounts had perished from fatigue, hunger and thirst; of priests who accompanied the troops as chaplains, diarists, cartographers and scientific observers, but always carrying the message of Bethlehem into the unknown wilds of the far northwest; of courageous friars, who mounted horses and mules especially reserved at the Missions for that purpose and pursued the fleeing, "backsliding" neophytes to bring them back into the fold, thereby saving, as they fully believed, their souls from the punishment of everlasting hell; of monks wearing tunics of deerskin as protection against the arrows of the very Indians to whom they came to bring salvation. It is a tale of sublime heroism, devotion and sacrifice, and inasmuch as it is a very human tale, it is inevitably mixed with those other well nigh universal human traits,—greed of power, longing for wealth, and the atavistic instinct of the strong to oppress the weak and defenseless.

We read about great feudal-ecclesiastical estates, carved out of the wilderness, some sheltered under the stockaded walls of the presidios, and all protected by military guards, teaming with a busy population, with live stock and domestic industries, bringing abundance and security, where

---

[11] See, Charles E. Chapman, History of California, the Spanish Period, p. 11, et seq.
[12] See, Handbook of the Indians of California, Bulletin 78, Bureau of American Ethnology, Government Printing Office (1925).

formerly only starvation and perils existed; we read of the sudden rise and equally sudden fall of a Spanish-Indian civilization on the shores of the Pacific Ocean; and we likewise read about adventurers, whose conscientious feelings towards the Indians were as elastic as their energies were prodigious.

For those who can bring before them a vivid picture of the conditions existing in the Iberian Province under Roman rule and later in Europe generally during the tenth to the fifteenth centuries, prior to the development of the powerful city governments and the crystallization of national feelings, it is easy to imagine that the hand of time in California in the latter part of the eighteenth and beginning of the nineteenth centuries had slipped back to the middle ages, if indeed not to earlier times. In the western and northern Spanish-Americas, the white man's civilization was again at a period when, through the agencies of the military religious orders, such as the Hospitalers or the Knights Templar, it sought to conquer with sword and cross the unbelievers' country, and when the Teutonic Knights created their estates on the heathen shores of the Baltic.

Here in the northern and western Spanish-Americas we see in modified form a revival of the medieval condition of the three estates—the Lords Spiritual, the Lords Temporal and the Commoners of Old England, with the institution of villainy attached; social and political distinctions, known on the continent of Europe as the clergy, the nobility, the burghers and the serfs. The prototypes of the Lords Spiritual and clergy were the Guardians of the Colleges, the Fathers-presidente, the priests and Brother Missionaries. The Lords Temporal were the Spanish Commanders in the field, many of them with illustrious, historic names, who later became the owners of great haciendas and ranches; the Commoners were represented by the Colonists in the secular pueblos; while the villains or serfs were the neophyte Indians.

Conditions of Medieval Europe again present themselves to our minds when reading about the neophytes—the baptized Indians. Prior to the advent of the Cross, they lived close to the starvation line (except in some favorable locations like the Santa Barbara Channel country) and they exchanged their freedom for shelter, food and spiritual salvation, laboring mightily thereafter on the Mission grounds or the small fields allotted to them.

Many of the so-called freed men or half-freed men of Europe likewise attached themselves voluntarily to the soil of the great convents and monasteries, obtaining protection, security and substance from the hands of their ecclesiastical overlords and escaping a far worse fate.

In the militant Fathers we are reminded of the medieval Bishops in Arms, protecting their spiritual and temporal rights with the sword, and of the Abbots presiding over the monasteries of Friesland—men equally famous for their moral purity and their physical courage, who, clad in knightly armor, led their brawny brothers into the thick of battle.

In the Spanish mothers we find the first pioneer mothers of the west, the forerunners of those brave American mothers who came in the prairie schooners across the plains, the Rocky and Sierra Nevada Mountains. For the first thirty years there were barely one thousand "whites" in Alta California, and even later three thousand was the limit. These women faced the loneliness of countries far away from civilization; they bore large families, and still they found the time to introduce Castillian gracefulness in their new surroundings.

The story of the founding, maintenance and abandonment of the Mission of Santa Cruz follows the natural law of bloom, growth and decay. It is the story of one of the many scenes in a great drama of the colonization of Spanish-America by the *Conquistadores* and their successors. This scene cannot be understood unless we have at least an elementary knowledge of the whole play, for the story of any particular Mission is not a detached story but must forever remain framed in the general history of early Alta California.

The flavor of romance which still clings to the colorful Mission period has induced many authors to devote ability and unending toil to the general story. Exhaustive academic, as well as short popular works, are to be found in almost every western library, and yet there is hardly a subject about which more erroneous impressions are clinging to the mind of the average reader than to this very much written-up history. Whether the reader dwells outside of the State of California and has only been a casual visitor to the still existent Mission buildings of California, or is a permanent resident of the State and lives within a stone's throw from one of the spots hallowed by Mission history, these impressions seem to persist.

There is a similar lack of understanding as to Spain's endeavors in all the lands north of the Rio Grande.

An endeavor therefore first to dispel some of these errors seems not to be out of order.

CHAPTER II

The North American Civilization not entirely of
Teutonic but partly of Spanish origin; The
California Indians and the Duration
of the Mission Period.

BOOK I

Chapter II

*The North American Civilization Not Entirely of Teutonic But
Partly of Spanish Origin; the California Indians and the Duration
of the Mission Period*

THE early history of the United States seems to have been written
in isolation, for as viewed by our Nordic historians, it is the story of
that small part of the Republic situate between the Atlantic and the
Allegheny Mountains and north of the Gulf of Mexico.

It is true that the Dutch and English, the Swedes and the Germans
brought to our northeastern shores a civilization of pure Teutonic origin,
and the idea of individual liberty cradled in the German forests. These
ideas are amongst our most valued heritages.

But to Spain is due the credit of bringing to these shores another great
civilization of Gothic and Roman origin, the Roman ideals predominating.

Our American civilization is the hybrid flower of these two great cultures, and this hybridization has given to the American people a mode of
thought at once practical and enlightened with a strong leaning towards
high intellectual and aesthetic ideals.

This civilization, accentuating the desirable as well as the less desirable qualities of both parents, is for foreign observers so often difficult to
interpret.

The British who first settled in Virginia, and the Pilgrim Fathers,
when they arrived off the coast of Massachusetts in 1620, and the Dutch,
when they entered the Hudson River aboard the "Halve Maen," were
decidedly late comers.

It has always been the desire in every country to glorify the dominant
race at the expense of other groups of the population.

The stories of the first British settlements in Virginia, of the Knicker-
bockers and the Patroons on the Hudson, of the Pilgrim Fathers and the
famous Rock, have been highly colored and idealized, while the efforts of
the early Spanish pioneers have been almost obliterated from the historical
view of young America.

Almost a century before the advent of the white man on the Coast of
North Carolina or on the rock-bound coast of Maine, the Spanish advance
agents had planted the standard of Castile on North American soil.
Guzman, Becerra, Cabrillo and many other Spaniards wrote their names
in the Book of Fame long before the Nordic settlers were ever heard of.

In the year 1512 Ponce de Leon, sailing from Puerto Rico, discovered Florida.

In 1519 Cortes began the conquest of the countries discovered by Córdoba and Grijalva the two previous years. It was only a short time before the Pacific Ocean was reached, other lands discovered and people subjugated.

For centuries the Spanish sphere of influence was the only one which stretched from the Atlantic to the Pacific, and from the sub-tropics far to the north, encompassing Florida and all the States now known as the Southwest and West, and a part of the so-called Southern States of the Union. It finally came in conflict with the three other European cultural influences which have left deep marks on this Republic.

When an American of today speaks about missions and missionaries, he thinks of the work of Christian denominations in countries like India, China, Korea, etc., or he may think of the missionary labors in the different churches amongst our Indians, the one bright spot on the dark record of the treatment of the North American Indians by the whites.[1]

Such missionaries are engaged in spiritual work, sometimes fortified by worldly benevolence, for instance when educational or medical missionaries are sent out, but this conception does not apply to the founding of the Spanish Missions in Alta California.

The primary purpose of establishing the Missions in Alta California and elsewhere in the Indies was not religious. To civilize a barbarous people and convert them to the Catholic faith meant the rescue of savages from future perdition, but it was not the policy or intention of the government to found the Missions solely for the religious benefit of the natives;[2] they were not established by order of the dignitaries of the Catholic Church, but by order of the political power in Madrid and its subordinates in New Spain (Mexico).

In ordering the establishment of Missions in connection with the contemplated presidios, the Spanish Crown did not seek primarily aggrandizement, but rather to make herself strong in order to insure retention of that which was claimed by her in ownership;[3] she wanted to strengthen her title to this ownership through the erection of physical symbols of possession and by colonization, for which the Missions would form excellent temporary nuclei. This would also make the cheap labor of the converted Indians available, and likewise secure control of the Strait of Anian, whenever definitely located.

---

[1] Helen Hunt: A Century of Dishonor, p. viii of preface.
[2] James, In and Out of Old Missions, p. 84.
[3] Chapman, The Founding of Spanish California, p. 50.

Spain little thought that this would be one more case in which man proposed but fate disposed, for it was only through the very heroic efforts of the early Spanish missionaries, soldiers and settlers that the invasion so feared by the mother country was made possible. This province, prior to these efforts, was practically bare of any supplies so direly needed by an invading army. The country was far removed from the base of supplies. The provisioning of the invading force was next to impossible with the small sailing ships then in existence. From the land side the province was inaccessible to foreigners on account of both the rugged mountains and the deserts situate along its boundary, and furthermore all land routes were situate in Spanish territory. Even the first Spanish-Mexican expeditions nearly starved to death, notwithstanding the efforts of sailing vessels from Mexico to supply the small forces moving along the coast. Subsequent wealth, created especially by the missionaries and by the settlers, made this rich province a juicy plum, offering all necessary substance to a fighting force and thereby defeating the very purpose of the creation of these settlements.

The Indians of California, known now and partly through the later Mission period as "Digger Indians," did not belong to the "Digger" tribe. There was no such Indian tribe. Digger was simply a name of derision or opprobrium. These poor Indians were "only good to dig in the dirt," in accordance with the viewpoint of later white settlers—the so-called gringos.

Neither did they belong to an Indian nation, like the Aztecs or the Yaquis in old Mexico, or the Yumas, Apaches, Sioux, etc., of the North-west. They belonged to twenty-one[4] different linguistic tribes, some savages, some barbarians, who hardly ever took the trouble to visit one another; they were inferior to the general run of American Indians, and spoke all kinds of dialects, one tribe not being able to understand the other. They were not all friendly with one another, and sometimes actually hostile.

Their origin is obscure. Some authorities believe that they were left by a great Aztec migration from Asia into Mexico, which passed by the way of California and which left some of the least desirable elements behind; others think that they are degenerate Asiatics, descendants of mariners and women thrown on this coast from shipwrecked junks; still others believe that they are weak offshoots of the Esquimaux tribes to the North; others again declare that they had no connection with other Indians whatsoever, etc. Sometime this point will be definitely settled, but today it is still open to discussion.

---

[4] Alfred L. Kroeber, Indians of California.

There must have been about 70,000 between San Diego and San Francisco in Alta California.

Linguistically, they were divided from the present northern line of California, near Eureka, to the southern boundary, near San Diego, into the following groups: Athapascan, Weitspekan, Cutumian, Quoartean, Wishoskan, Chimarikan, Tanan, Yukian, Pujunan, Kulanapan, Moquelumnan, Shastan, Copehan, Costanoan, Mariposan, Esselenian, Salinan, Chumaschan, Shoshonean and Yumen.

The Mission period of Alta California is often spoken of as having covered a long stretch of years, but it was not a long one. As history goes, it was a very short one. Much was accomplished in so short a time.

The first Mission—the Mission of San Diego—was founded in 1769; the last Mission—San Rafael—in 1817. Already thirty-six years after the founding of the first Mission, the threat of secularization, or disestablishment, was rearing its head, and even before 1805 there had been strong rumors and indications of such a possibility. Several of the Missions were founded after the Fathers knew that their work might be ended at any time.

The Mission of Santa Cruz, founded in 1791, seven years after the death of the great leader, Father Serra, was partly confiscated or secularized in the year 1834. The Mission was under the administration of the padres only forty-three years, and during all these years the very existence of it and of other Missions was seriously threatened.

The northwest of America in general, and California in particular, have known several "waves" of influence. There has been the period of the Mission Fathers, of the trappers, of the miners, of the cattle men, of the wheat growers, of the orchardists and the vineyardists, and of the intense farming on smaller tracts, justified by the growth of manufacture and commerce in the West. These different periods had no sharp lines of demarcation; often they overlapped one another; sometimes several of the former were still in evidence when the newer one already forged ahead; many merged almost automatically and painlessly; others died a violent death; some vanished without hardly leaving a trace, but the Mission period was one of the transitory conditions, which is in a class by itself.

It is unique, because it was the first white man's wave which rolled over California; it is unique because, though small compared with its successors, it left its indelible impression on the State; and it is further unique because of its great accomplishments and the high moral purpose and devotion which incited a good many of its participants.

CHAPTER III

Spain's Title to California and her purpose
in establishing the Missions.

BOOK I

Chapter III

*Spain's Title to California and Her Purpose in
Establishing the Missions*

IN years gone by a legal title to foreign lands was considered sufficient. Moral considerations hardly entered the situation. Such title was acquired by discovery and exploration, by conquest, by treaty, or by a combination of two or three of these means.

To base the Spanish claim to the far-flung Western lands, and especially Alta California, on discovery or exploration was a doubtful procedure.

While some early Spanish navigators, especially Vizcaino, had sailed along the Coast and some landings and minor explorations had been made at widely separated points little was known of the interior. The existence of the two great rivers, the San Joaquin and Sacramento, was not suspected, nor that of the expansive interior valleys, nor of the high Sierra Nevada, nor even of the real Bay of San Francisco. A land expedition sent in 1769 to relocate the Bay of Monterey, visited by Cabrillo in 1542 and very much overestimated and misrepresented by him, passed this bay twice without recognizing it, and the little bay, now known as Drake's Bay, or the whole surrounding indentation of the coast, was thought to be the Bay of San Francisco.

Spain could hardly maintain her claim to title by conquest, for her armies or bands of armed men had never conquered or even visited the land or the inhabitants of Alta California. Neither could she claim that she had conquered California indirectly, as a dependency or province of some central nation which she had subjected.

Alta California lay "out of doors," self-sufficient and undisturbed in its savage state and politically unattached to any other country.

She could not have obtained title by treaty, for no treaty was ever made by Spain with anyone who had a shadow of right to these lands, and in Alta California proper there was not even a semblance of centralized authority with whom a treaty could be made.

On what then did she base her claim to all the lands of the Indies?

On the Papal Bull of Demarcation, dated May 9th, 1493, by which Pope Alexander VI, as arbitrator, endeavored to put a stop to the constant strife for far-distant lands, between two children of the Church—the sovereigns of Spain and Portugal—and established a line of demarcation about three hundred miles west of the Azores Islands. To the Spanish all lands west, to the Portuguese all lands east of this line were assigned. The far-sighted Pope was deeply interested in the religious welfare of the native inhabitants of the countries involved, and the Spanish sovereign was urged to send out "only tried, learned and skilled men, who fear God and can instruct the inhabitants in the Catholic faith, teaching them good morals."

The modern mind is intrigued with the thought that any ruler could seriously believe that his rights to far-away lands could be established by the grant of the head of a church and by his order to civilize and Christianize the inhabitants thereof, when neither the Pontiff nor the Church had any title whatsoever to such lands.

But the Pope was convinced, and many agreed with him, that he, as Vicar of Christ on earth, held all the lands of the earth as a kind of fief, granted to him by the celestial power. He assumed the divine right to dispose of all lands not discovered or occupied by Christian powers, as his best judgment dictated.

The Spanish Crown accepted the grant, and all that was deemed necessary to perfect the title was to visit the shore, as Balboa did, plant the cross and unfurl the royal standard.

Such a course would hardly be followed today by the leader of any church, least of all by the Pontiff at Rome, but this did not happen in the twentieth century, but in the year 1493, when other notions of what was right and wrong prevailed.

The possibility that other countries—the Netherlands, England, France or Russia—would later decline to recognize such a title as valid was not even considered.

Even if Spain, in accordance with the notions of those days, had acquired title by this Papal Bull, such title—so far as the legal Indian owners were concerned—was nothing more nor less than a permission, as against Portugal, to commit an international trespass.

For almost three centuries (1492-1770) little was done to strengthen this supposed legal title to Alta California into an equitable title, by giving assistance to the religious, moral, ethical, political, economic or industrial evolution of the native race or races living there.

In 1602 Sebastian Vizcaino visited San Diego and the open roadstead at Monterey, but evidently the reports of his visit aroused no active interest in Spain and for one hundred and sixty years longer nothing further was done.

Suddenly Spain's title was not only questioned, but actually threatened, by Russia, England and France.

Carlos III was then Spain's able King and he acted with energy. He realized that not only the British were pressing against the Louisiana borders, but that the Russians were seriously threatening his domain on the Pacific Coast, while between the two points an extended frontier had to be held against the constant menace of hostile and warlike Indians.

To ward off this last danger, he ordered the strengthening of a long line of presidios and missions from the Gulf of Mexico to the Gulf of California. Louisiana and Florida followed, and Gaspar de Portola, the Governor, sent to Baja California in the fall of 1767, was given orders to exercise the greatest vigilance against the Russians, seeking to establish themselves along the coast of the Pacific Ocean.

Spain still hoped that somewhere in the North a through passage from the Pacific to the Atlantic might be found, and anxiously desired to control it, for it would give her possessions in "the Indies" great additional value.

To appreciate this anxiety we must consider the geography of those days.

For a long time the continent of North America, as we know it today, was unknown to Europeans. Marco Polo's book (A. D. 1477)[1] announced to the western world that a great mass of islands, as many as 7,459, formed a screen between the east coast of Chin (China) and Europe. A large island, known as Zipangu (Japan), was reported to lie 1,500 (?) miles from China's coast, while the Philippines and the Moluccas, now part of the Netherlands East Indies, formed the other groups.

North America was considered by the Spanish authorities as an Asiatic Archipelago, part of this mass of "out-lying islands," mentioned by Polo. The early Papal Bulls do not even mention America by name, but speak of "the Indies and other islands." Only slowly it dawned on the Spanish authorities that they had to do with a continent.

When in 1622 the "Herrera" Map (Kaspar van Baerle) was published, and in 1625 the "Purchas" (Briggs) Map, and in 1628 the Drake "World Encompassed" Map (by Hondius), California was shown as a large island. By that time the conviction had gained ground that there was a continent of North America besides only islands as thought before, but still the belief persisted that somewhere in the North a good navigable passage existed across the continent. This mysterious passage was indi-

---

[1] This book was dictated by Marco Polo, the famous Venetian traveller, while a prisoner of war at Genoa in the years 1298-99. He was born in 1254 and began his first great journey in 1269. He returned in 1295 after spending most of his time at the Court of Kublai Kahn. He died in 1324 and his manuscript was published long after his death. The first printed copy appeared in 1559.

cated as the "Strait of Anian," the Island California was presumed to be situated at its western outlet.

In 1700 Father Eusebio Francisco Kino,[2] after extensive exploration, concluded that California was not insular but peninsular, attached to the Continent, but it was not until 1746 that the Jesuit missionary, Father Fernando Consag, sent by his provincial, Cristóbal Escobar, to the mouth of the Colorado River, finally and definitely proclaimed California a peninsula. This in no way stopped the quest for the famous Strait of Anian, which was now believed to be much further North, connecting the Gulf of the St. Lawrence with the Pacific Ocean.

"California"[3] was then a subdivision of New Spain (Mexico) with a more or less definite boundary on the West and South, but extending quite indefinitely towards the East and North. It was subsequently divided for administration purposes in two divisions: *Baja* or *Antiqua* California (Lower or Old California, now a part of the Republic of Mexico and generally indicated as the California peninsula) and *Alta* or *Nueva* California (Upper or New California, and now a part of the State of California). At first California belonged directly under the Viceroy, residing at Mexico City, but subsequently (1776) became part of a new jurisdiction, known as the Commandancia General Provincias Internas—the frontier provinces.

In Spain, ever since the defeat of the Moors and the taking of Granada, religious fervor had run high, but this was closely interwoven with the ambition for world empire and conquest, and the secular power dominated the situation.

This was the policy of King Ferdinand and Queen Isabella; their grandson, Charles I (Emperor Charles V), had two main aims, to make Spain a powerful nation and to extend the Catholic Faith—but the former was always paramount.

The King had derived his vast power in church matters from the *Regio Patronato,* which originated at the beginning of the sixteenth century, when Ferdinand was King of Aragon, and on behalf of his insane daughter, Jane (the mother of Charles V, who became King of Spain,

---

[2] Father Kino was born at Trent, Austrian Tyrol, in 1640. He was a professor of mathematics at the University of Ingolstadt, in Bavaria, became a Jesuit and went to Mexico in 1680. He visited California as a cosmographer in 1683 with Isidro Otondo y Antillon.

See also: The Padre on Horseback, a sketch of Eusebio Francisco Kino, S.J. Apostle of the Pimes, by Herbert Eugene Bolton (1932).

[3] California is indicated on the old maps sometimes as California, again as New Albion, or as the Isles of Carolinas.

Emperor of Germany, overlord of the Netherlands, etc., etc.), Regent of the Kingdoms of Castile and Leon.

At his request, and in reward for services rendered to Christianity, especially against the Moors in Spain, Pope Julius II issued a Bull, dated July 28th, 1508, by which the concession was made "that no church, monastery, or pious institution should be erected or founded in the islands and places already acquired, or in others yet to be acquired, without the consent of King Ferdinand and Queen Jane . . ." etc.

Thus the right of Regal Patronage *(Jus Patronatus)* was bestowed on the Crown, with the consequence that in all Spanish-America, not even a Bishop could erect a chapel, oratory or mission, or found a monastery or convent without the expressed order of the King of Spain as General Patrono, or of his Viceroy as Vice Patrono, or his deputies, the Governors, Vice-Governors, etc. The King named all the ecclesiastical dignitaries of whatever position. The Church could only acquiesce.

The Church certainly had no reason to be proud of her position under the Laws of the Patronato, but continued to acquiesce, for history had taught the Popes that it was dangerous to interfere with the wishes of powerful Catholic Monarchs. The sack of Rome in May, 1527, by the troops of His Most Catholic Majesty of Spain was never forgotten. Rome had been sacked before—by the Vandals under King Genseric in 455, by the Goths under Alaric—but neither of these invasions compared in ferocity with that of 1527, when the Spanish and German troops of Charles V, under command of the Constable de Bourbon, entered the eternal city and Pope Clement VII was forced to flee from the Vatican to save his life.

Rome had learned its lesson, which was never forgotten until modern times struck these shackles from the Church.

The Church of Christ in the Indies was therefore the handmaiden of the State, not the State of the Church, and the religious conversion of the Indians was a subordinate part of the policies of the State.

Neither the Spanish nor the Mexican Government went to any expense for the sake of Christianizing the Indians; the Viceroy drew on the Pious Fund (see Appendix No. 1) to pay the cost of the expeditions for the conquest and occupation of the new territory.

The Council of the Indies, established in 1511 by King Ferdinand, was perfected by Charles V in 1524. It superintended all the colonial affairs; all regulations originated there under a two-thirds vote of the members and required the approval of the King. All colonial officers were accountable to this Council for their policies and actions. While the Crown wanted exploration, conquest, wealth and increase of territory, the Church wanted spiritual conquest, salvation of souls, and increased power for their missionary orders. There were also the inevitable soldiers, adventurers and settlers, who cared little for the State and less for the Church; plunder of the natives and the acquiring of wealth without toil was uppermost in their minds.[4]

The missionaries, though themselves often ambitious to extend the territory, power and wealth of their orders, stood many a time between the natives and the authorities, the colonists and adventurers, shielding them from oppression and rapacity wherever possible.

While much humanity was contained in the Laws of the Indies, regarding the treatment of the natives, men at war or on the path of conquest generally show little care for the rights of the inhabitants of an invaded country. Quite often the Indians found their only refuge in the humanity which remained in the clergy.

The priest, therefore, came with the soldier, not the soldier with the priest. One carried the sword, the other the cross; both looked for victory, the soldier for material gain, the priest for a spiritual triumph, but a statesman in counsel or a soldier in the field, as representative of the Crown, always had the final word.

The Mission Fathers and their superiors were far from being free moral and religious agents. The most humble ecclesiastical servitor, who labored under the Mission system, as well as the *Padre-presidente,* yes, even the Guardians of the Colleges at Mexico City, in charge of vast missionary efforts, were each subject in all material matters to the secular powers, who saw to it that the Mission Fathers did not forget this. Presumably free as far as purely spiritual matters were concerned, the secular authorities and commanders had rather vigorous ideas as to the scope of their authority, and acted accordingly.

[4] Blackmar, Spanish Institutions of the Southwest, p. 53.

CHAPTER IV

Alleged decadence of Spain; supposed inferiority
of the Colonial System.

BOOK I

Chapter IV

Alleged Decadence of Spain; Supposed Inferiority of the Colonial System

THOUGH the field of the Spanish occupation included the present
States of Florida, Louisiana, Texas, New Mexico, Arizona and
California, besides Mexico, Central and South America, many still
believe that Spain was permanently "decadent" when she exercised dominion over this tremendous territory and when she undertook the further
subjugation of Alta California. Nothing is further from the truth.

Spain had for a long time suffered from an unfortunate policy of
over-expansion, outside of her legitimate sphere of activities. Had she
been satisfied to develop her own resources and those of her colonies
outre-mer, she would have remained a powerful and wealthy nation. But
instead of this she followed imperialistic policies in Europe and was
engaged in endless war, resulting in crushing defeat on the seas, when her
great Armada was destroyed by the combined efforts of the English and
Netherlands fleets in the Channel; in a series of defeats on land, when the
despised Republican burghers of the Netherlands fought the heroic struggle
of the eighty years war in the Low Lands, and her fight for possessions in
Italy was a continual drain on her resources.

During the times of the Conquistadores, gold and silver had flowed
liberally from her American Colonies into the King's Treasury. It was
this flow of precious metal, plundered mercilessly from the natives, which
enabled Charles V and Philip II to occupy an outstanding position in
European politics and persist in imperialistic ideas, wasting their treasures
and many lives in foreign wars. It became the settled policy of the Council
of the Indies and of the *ministros general de Indias,* who not seldom dominated the Council, to have the royal treasury in each Audienca spend as
little as possible on the needs of the district, in order that as much as possible could be remitted to the treasury of the Vice Royalty—in casu
Mexico—enabling the latter in turn to make important annual remissions
to Madrid.

After the establishment of the Bourbons in 1700 on the Spanish
throne, and notwithstanding several wars with England, less was spent in
foreign conquest, and much improvement took place at home.

Charles (Carlos) III succeeded King Ferdinand in 1759. Ferdinand,
who briefly participated in the Seven Years' War, was by nature a peace-

loving monarch, establishing libraries and academies, encouraging the arts and sciences, and leaving a well-filled treasury. There were fifty warships under the Spanish flag.

Spain had recovered from the ill-effects caused by the prodigious influx of gold and silver from New Spain, which for a while made all productive labor at home unprofitable, and from the difficulties caused by the expulsion of the Moors and Jews. By the expulsion of the former, Philip II had driven out a great army of excellent agricultural laborers and artisans; by the expulsion of the latter, some of its most learned and progressive citizens.

But as long as Spain was a great colonial empire, she could not remain satisfied with developing her home resources only. The law of nature is growth, and that law applies politically as well as in other fields. The Persian and Roman Empires had to submit to this law, and so did Russia later, when she moved to and across Siberia and reached the Pacific; Great Britain feels the effect of this rule today, and realizes that stagnation in her efforts will mean death to her Empire. Fortunate indeed are the countries like the United States and Russia, which find unoccupied lands right at their borders with which to satisfy this inevitable urge, and unfortunate are those expanding empires, like Germany and Japan, which are differently situated.

The home wants being satisfied, it is no wonder therefore that the interest in the Spanish colonies received a new impetus, and with this came a desire for a more liberal policy. California was soon to feel this change of attitude.

It had remained for a long time untouched by the Spanish colonial exertions, being situated on "the border and far beyond," but now the great triumvirate, Galvez, de Croix and Serra, came together and planned the "reduction" of California.

Neither Visitador Jose de Galvez, nor Viceroy de Croix, nor Father Serra, the new Franciscan missionary, all of whom became deciding factors in the history of California, nor any of the other Spanish commanders or Mission fathers, showed any signs of the alleged decadence of the Spanish race, but on the contrary developed an amazing amount of energy, fortitude and virile strength.

Though the Spanish Colonial Archives, disclosing a system second to none in the world, are open to inspection and research, the opinion persists in northern countries, that it was far inferior to the English or Dutch systems.

The systems are different, based upon the different philosophies and ideals. In the Spanish system, patterned largely after the Colonial system of Rome, the efforts of the State were paramount. The Netherlands and English efforts in the American Colonies were mostly left to the individual enterprise of the Colonists or otherwise to that of the Patroons, concessionaires, delegates, proprietors, etc., who after appointment by the home countries were left very much to their own devices.

Each system has its merits, but even while the Indians, when reduced, found themselves in a condition of peonage or half-slavery, they were not driven from their homelands or killed, but received more consideration and fared better under the Spanish system than under the Nordic direction, where dealing with the Indians too often meant massacres or at least a sanctimonious plundering, unchecked by governmental policies.

While the right of the Indians to the land by occupancy and the law of alienation, subject to confirmation by the conquerors, was acknowledged in theory by all the discovering nations in North America—Spain, France, the Netherlands and England—Spain alone remained true to this theory.

"We command," said the Spanish King, "that the sale, grant and disposal of lands be executed with such attention that the Indians be left in possession of the full amount of lands belonging to them, together with their rivers and waters; and the land which they shall have drained or otherwise improved, etc., and must in no case be sold.

"Grazing estates are ordered to be located apart from the fields and villages of the Indians. No such lands shall be granted in any parts or places where any damage can accrue to the Indians.

"The King's solicitors are to be the protectors of the Indians and plead for them and no gifts or sales of land shall be made except with an eye to the benefit of the Indians."

By the concluding paragraph of the King's Order all the lands are "reserved to us (the Crown) clear of any incumbrance, for the purpose of being given as rewards or disposed of according to our pleasure," but only, as is once more reiterated, "after distributing to the Indians what they may justly want to cultivate, sow and raise cattle, confirming to them what they now hold and granting what they may want besides."

It is interesting to note that the Netherlands, in its Colonial land policies, in the Far East (Java and other islands)[1] later followed a land system, somewhat similar to the Spanish one, and the prosperity of the inhabitants in the Netherlands East Indies is largely due to this.

---

[1] See H. A. van Coenen Torchiana, *Java and Other Islands*, University of Chicago Press, 1924.

CHAPTER V

The Period of Exploration

BOOK I

Chapter V

The Period of Exploration

I N Chapter III we saw that Governor Portola, of California, received
the order in 1767 to protect the rights of Spain in Alta California.
Little was known of these lands to the north.

The earliest positive information of the Bay of Monterey, on the
north shore of which is situated the present city of Santa Cruz, is contained in a report made by the early Spanish navigator, Juan Rodriguez
(Cabrillo).[1]

On the 27th of June, 1542, he sailed from the Port of Navidad. He
returned after an absence of ten months, having gone to Cape Mendocino
and back fifty years after Columbus discovered America, and long prior
to the arrival on this coast of the French, Dutch and English. (See Appendix No. 1.)

This expedition, like Coronado's in the interior of the American Continent, and Villalobos' to the Philippines, was part of the general Spanish
policy of expansion.

George Davidson (United States Coast and Geodetic Survey, pp.
210-211) translates the report of Cabrillo's ships creeping up the coast in
1542 as follows:

"Saturday on the eleventh (November 11, 1542) they were coasting
with a southwest wind, and continually they were looking for el Rio de
Nuestra Senora, and did not find it, but a great range of mountains very
high, with many trees, to which they gave the name of Las Sierras de
San Martin, and they are in 37½ degrees, and at the termination of them
at the northwest it forms a cape which is thirty and eight degrees, and
they named it the Capo de San Martin."

"The position where Cabrillo anchored was most likely under Pt.
Santa Cruz at the northwestern extremity of the Bay of Monterey, as he
described the shores as "steep and scarped," and impossible to effect a
landing from the terrible surf breaking on the beach, no doubt from a
heavy southernly swell common at this day in the wet season, and which
has given the roadstead of Santa Cruz to the east of this an unenviable
reputation as a safe anchorage in winter.[2]

---

[1] Account published by the Hackluyt Society of London.
[2] Alex. S. Taylor, First Voyage to Coast of Cal., Hayes, Mission Book I, p. 49, B.C.

"On Friday following, which was the 16th of November, 1542, when day dawned, we found ourselves at the entrance of a very large bay that appeared to have an anchorage and a river emptying into it (Salinas River). . . . The shore is covered with pine trees down to the sea, and we gave it the name of Bay of Pines or Pine Bay."[3]

The curtain of history then drops. No attempt was made to discover any new shores pertaining to the northern half of the Pacific Ocean by Spain for a period of fifty-seven years, though in 1578 Sir Francis Drake, while sailing along the coast of California observed the same wooded mountains that Cabrillo had noticed.[4] This voyage, though interesting, is not germane to the present subject.

Sebastian Vizcaino was a trader who was first heard of in 1593, when he applied to Viceroy Luis de Velasco for a pearl fishing permit in the Gulf of California. The permit was granted to "fish for pearls, cod, sardines," etc., on the coast of the South Sea, from la Navidad to California. This permit was to continue for four years, but thereafter it was to be limited to a district of ten leagues on the California coast.

On the 26th of November, 1597, Viceroy Count de Monterey forwarded to King Philip II a memorandum from Vizcaino asking that he be allowed to explore the Gulf of the Californias. Philip's son, King Philip III, became interested, and on the 27th day of September, 1599, a royal cedula was forwarded from Madrid to the Count de Monterey. The order required the Viceroy to undertake a new discovery in California, and the latter appointed Sebastian Vizcaino as Captain-general.[5]

On Sunday, May 5th, 1602, at five o'clock in the evening, Vizcaino sailed from Acapulco for—as he wrote the King—"the discovery of the harbors and bays of the coast of the South Sea as far as Cape Mendocino." (See Appendix No. 2.)

There were four vessels, of which the San Diego, also called the *la Capitana,* was the flagship. It was the custom, at that time, to give several of the ships two names. On the *San Diego* was Vizcaino, called general, and his son; three Carmelite Fathers, Andres de la Asumpcion, Antonio de la Ascencion, and Tomas de Aquino; besides a cosmographer, commissioned and petty officers, and two civilians who went along as counsellors, and also the chief pilot, Francisco Bolanos. The second ship was called the *Santo Tomas,* or *La Admiranta.* On this ship sailed Captain Toribio Gomez de Corban, as commander (called the "admiral"), and

[3] Account published by the Hackluyt Society of London."
[4] Dr. S. H. Willey, Historical sketch of Santa Cruz Co., p. 1.
[5] C. E. Chapman, A History of California, the Spanish Period, pp. 128-138.

various other officers. The *Tres Reyes,* a smaller ship called a *barcolongo,* was commanded by Sebastian Melendez, with Antonio Flores as pilot; while a fourth ship, not named, but called by the Spaniards a *lancha,* is described as a long boat for the purpose of exploring shallow water and narrow inlets. The expedition consisted of about two hundred persons.

These ships and these men, according to Torquemada,[6] formed one of the most brilliant forces ever raised in New Spain for such a purpose. The ships were provisioned for eleven months.

On May 19th the port of Navidad was reached, and three days later the voyage was resumed. The ships passed up the coast, and after various landings, vicissitudes and mapping different points on the coast, they arrived, on November 10th, 1602, at San Diego.

Vizcaino in his diary, in Chapter XI, speaking of this port, states: "On Sunday, November 10th, we arrived at a port which is the best found in the whole South Sea, as it is protected on all sides and has good anchorage . . . On the 12th of said month, which was the day of the glorious San Diego, the general, the admiral, religious (see Appendix No. 3), captains, ensigns and almost all the men went ashore. A hut was erected, and holy Mass was said to celebrate the feast of San Diego."

Proceeding north, they discovered and named several points on the mainland, islands and straits, and finally on the 16th day of December, 1602, at seven o'clock in the evening, they dropped anchor in the port of Monterey.

In his diary Vizcaino describes his approach and entry of the harbor as follows: "The ships found themselves near a very high and white ridge of mountains, but reddish towards the skirts, covered with woods. This they called the Santa Lucia Range. This is the usual landmark of ships coming from China. Four leagues from there a river falls into the sea among rocks, after a precipitate course from some high and white mountains. This river is called Carmello. Two leagues further is a noble harbor, there being between it and the said river a wood of pine trees, six miles in breadth, and at the entrance of the harbor a cape, called Point Pine."[7]

The port was called Monterey in honor of the Viceroy.

The next day Vizcaino directed preparations to be made for the Carmelite Fathers Andres de la Asumpcion and Antonio de la Ascencion to say Mass on shore during their stay there. The altar was erected under a large oak close to the seaside, and within twenty paces of it were some springs, affording plenty of excellent water.

---

[6] Monarquia Indiana, tomo i, lib. v. cap. xlv, 694-695.
[7] Vizcaino's *Diario,* XI.

All the ships' company were sickly, scarcely one in perfect health, and very few able to do duty. The master of the flagship and his mate were not able to stir themselves in their beds, and the master and mate of the captain's vessel could hardly stand on the deck. A number of the sailors, soldiers and boys were very ill; sixteen had died before their arrival in this port; there was a shortage of sailors for going forward, and supplies were becoming exhausted because of the length of time spent in coming. A conference was called to consider what should be done, and it was decided that the *Santa Tomas* should return as a messenger to the Viceroy of New Spain with a record of the discoveries, carry back those who were most ill, and ask for further supplies of men and provisions in order to make a perfect discovery to the entrance of California. (For a long time it was supposed there was a wide strait, which was called the entrance to California, terminating at Cape Mendocino and the Gulf of California, and the land lying between it and the Pacific Ocean forming a large island.)

Accordingly the *Santa Tomas,* under command of Admiral Toribio Gomez de Corban, with Pilots Pasqual and Balthasar, and the sick, together with Father Tomas de Aquino, having been put on board, and everything being ready for departure, sailed out of the harbor on December 29th, 1602. Owing to lack of wholesome food, of medicines and facilities, the voyage was a great hardship. Twenty-five died on the way or soon after reaching port; and only nine, among whom were the Commander, de Corban, and Father Tomas, survived the hardships.

It will astonish present dwellers of Monterey and Santa Cruz to hear what Vizcaino wrote about the weather: "In making the preparations necessary the men labored under great difficulties while taking on wood and water, because of the extreme cold, which was so intense that Wednesday, New Year's Day, 1603, dawned with all the mountains covered with snow, and that the hole from which we were taking water was frozen over more than a palm in thickness."[8]

The climate must have changed a great deal since that time or it must have been an extremely cold winter, for seldom is there any snow in that locality, and then only for a few hours.

To return to the harbor of Monterey, where the *San Diego* and *Tres Reyes* remained, Father Antonio de la Ascencion wrote:[9] "They took in

---

[8] Vizcaino, Diario, capp. XIV.

[9] Sources of information are not lacking as to the Vizcaino expedition of 1602-3; for, besides the account written by Father Ascension, taken from his diary kept during the voyage, the information gathered by Father Torquemada; the various official documents; and the letters written by Vizcaino, there are two journals: one dealing with the juntas—(councils) and the other, a general diary, sometimes referred to as "the Vizcaino Diary."

wood and water. This is an excellent harbor and secure against all winds. Near the shore are an infinite number of very large pines, straight and smooth, likewise oaks of proper size for building ships. Here also are rose trees, firs, willows and poplars; large clear lakes, fine pasture and arable lands; wild beasts, particularly bears of an uncommon size, are found here, and a species of horned cattle resembling buffalo, about the same size, others as large as wolves, and shaped like stags, with skins resembling those of pelicans, with long necks and horns on their heads as large as those of stags, their tails being a yard in length and a half a yard in breadth, and their hoofs cloven like those of an ox.

"The country also abounds in deer, rabbits, hares, and wild-cats, buzzards, geese, ducks, pigeons, partridges, thrushes, sparrows, gold finches; cranes and vultures are also found here, with another kind of bird the size of a turkey, and the largest seen during the whole voyage, being seventeen spans from the tip of one wing to that of the other. Along the coast are great numbers of gulls, cormorants, crows, and seafowl. In the rocks are a great number of cavities in which are found a large shellfish, with conque shell equal to the finest mother-of-pearl (aulon, the Indian name, or sea-ear, haliotis).

"The sea abounds with oysters, lobsters, crabs, etc., also sea wolves and whales. This harbor is surrounded with villages of Indians, a well-looking, affable people, and very ready to part with everything they have They are under some form of rule. Their weapons are bows and arrows They expressed a great deal of concern when they perceived the Spaniards were going to leave them, which happened on the 3rd of January, 1603, when the captain's vessel and tender sailed out of the harbor."

Vizcaino, on the *San Diego,* sailed north, and must have reached about the present Oregon line of 42 degrees, though de Aguilar, commanding the *Tres Reyes,* reached 43 degrees. The return trip of each vessel was full of hardship and suffering. The *San Diego* found relief at Mazatlan, and finally reached Acapulco on March 21st, 1603; while the *Tres Reyes* had reached Navidad on February 26, 1603, where the remaining crew was paid off and returned to Mexico, having been absent about eleven months.

About three years later, King Philip III, moved by fear that Spanish ships might be beset by pirates, privateers or other enemies, issued a new decree on the 19th day of August, 1606. He desired the establishment of a safe half-way port between the Philippine Islands and Acapulco, where his ships could put in to obtain further supplies and especially to combat the much-dreaded scurvy, the cause of which was then unknown.

This decree is so remarkable that it is given in full:

"DECREE OF KING PHILIP III.

By the KING, DON PEDRO de ACUNWA, Knight of the Order of St. John, my Governor and Captain General of the Philippine Islands and President of my royal Audience there.

"You are hereby given to understand that Don Luis de Velasco, my late viceroy in New Spain, in regard to the great distance between the Port of Acapulco and those islands, the fatigue, hardship, and danger of that voyage, for want of a port where the ships might put in, and provide themselves with water, wood, and masts, and other things of absolute necessity, determined to make a discovery, and maps, with observations of the harbors along the coast from New Spain to these islands, and ordered this service to be performed in a ship called the San Augustine (was wrecked near the entrance of San Francisco, in 1595, the loss of which at that time prevented the same discovery), and the Count de Monterey, who succeeded him in that government, having the same opinion of the inconveniences of that voyage, and the same zeal for removing the difficulties by pursuing the discovery intended by Don Luis de Velasco, wrote to me concerning it, and was of opinion that small vessels from the harbor of Acapulco were the fittest, and that in the discovery might be included the coasts and bays of the Gulf of California and of the fisheries for pearls; to which in my letters of the 27th of September, 1599, I ordered to be answered that the discovery and making maps with observations of that coast and bays along it, having appeared to me highly convenient, it was my will he should immediately put it in execution, without troubling himself about that of California, unless occasionally.

"Agreeably to this, he appointed for the conduct of the enterprise, Sebastian Vizcaino as an experienced navigator, particularly acquainted with the voyage in question, and in whom he placed entire confidence, and, having furnished him with two ships and a tender, well provided with all necessaries for a year, he immediately embarked with a suitable number of seamen and soldiers, and an able cosmographer, skilled in making maps in order that the ports and places discovered might be set down with the greatest clearness and accuracy. Having with him orders and instructions how he was to proceed, and what he was to do, he put to sea from Acapulco harbor on the 5th of May, 1602, according to the advice sent me by the Count de Monte Rey and Sebastian Vizcaino, who, after several letters, the last of which was on the last day of April, 1605, informed me that he had been eleven months on the voyage, and that from the same harbor he had begun to sound and take draughts off the coast, harbors, creeks and bays as far as the 27th degree, with all necessary precision and exactness, and that from the 26 to 45 he did no more than keep within sight of land, so that he was not able to make such particular observations as he had done till the 27th degree.

"Soon after many of the people fell sick, and, the weather being very unfavorable, he could only observe that the coast as far as 40 degrees lies northwest and southeast, and that in the other two degrees, which make up the other forty-two, it lies almost north and south. He added that between the mouth of the Gulf of California to 37 degrees he met with three very good harbors on the continent. These are: San Diego in 32d degree, which is very spacious, being capable of containing navy ships, and at the same time affording both water and wood; another contiguous to it but small; and the third, called Monterey, was still better and more convenient for the China galleons and for the relief of ships in their voyage to and from the Philippine Islands.

"Monterey is situated in 37 degrees north latitude, and its wood and water are preferable and are in greater plenty than at the other place named. It is well sheltered from all winds, and along its shores are great numbers of pine trees fit for masts. It lies very conveniently for ships returning from the Philippine Islands to put into, thus, in case of storms, avoiding the necessity of making for Japan, as they have several times done, and expending great sums of money. Besides, they usually have sight of the coasts of China, which is an additional benefit, as by knowing where they are they will not, as formerly in case of bad weather, make for Japan or those islands, as the same winds which would carry them thither bring them into this safe harbor. They further say that the climate is mild and the country covered with trees, the soil fruitful and well peopled, and that the natives are so tractable, kind and docile in temper that they will be easily converted to the Christian religion, and become subjects of my holy crown. Their chief subsistence is on the spontaneous products of the earth, and the flesh which they catch in hunting, of which there is a remarkable plenty. Their clothing is of the skin of sea wolves, which they have a very good method of tanning and preparing, and they have abundance of flax, hemp, and cotton.

"And the said Sebastian Vizcaino carefully informed himself of these Indians and many others whom he discovered along the coast for about eight hundred leagues, and they told him that up the country there were towns, and SILVER AND GOLD,[10] whence he is inclined to believe that great riches may be discovered, especially as in some parts of the land

---

[10] It will be noted that it was believed that there was gold and silver in California. Or possibly this belief was only a devoted wish originally repeated to justify the heavy expense of the expedition and to arouse the further rapacity of the Spanish Monarch.

veins of metals are to be seen, and the time of their summer being known, a further discovery might be made of them by going within the country. The remainder may be discovered along the coast as it reaches beyond 42 degrees, the limits specified to the said Sebastian Vizcaino in his instructions.

"He came to Japan and the coast of China and he could not return by the route of California, as I sent orders he should be directed, on account of a great mortality among his people, and the decay of the provisions, which obliged him to hasten his return. And the cosmographer, Andres Garcia de Cespedes, having made his appearance in my royal council of the Indians, together with the narratives and draughts which were sent with a separate plan of each harbor of those discovered by the said Sebastian Vizcaino, and having in council heard the report of the cosmographer, and considering how much it concerns the security of ships coming from those islands (Philippine Islands), in a voyage of no less than two thousand leagues on a wide and tempestuous sea, that they should be provided with a port where they might put in and furnish themselves with water, wood, and provisions, that the said port of Monterey lies in 37 degrees, nearly half way the voyage, having all the good qualities which could be desired, it seems to me that all ships coming from those islands, as they make the coast of California, should put into this port (Monterey), and there refit and provide themselves.

"In order to the beginning of a design of such utility, and that it may be publicly known, I have, by another commission of this date, ordered and directed the Marquis de Monte Carlos, my present viceroy of the said province of New Spain (Mexico), that he use all possible care and diligence to find out the said General Sebastian Vizcaino as the person who made the discovery, he having coasted all along from Acapulco to Cape Mendocino. In case he be not living, to make the like inquiry after the commander of his ship, and that, on his being found, he immediately prepare to go to these islands, taking care to carry with him his chief pilot, and that of the said commander. And that his going on this desirable service may be with all convenient dispatch, I have also ordered the said marquis that the ships which are to be sent to said islands be of the usual form hitherto used, there being little appearance that you have any ships ready of two hundred tons, as they are to be, agreeable to new orders which I have issued relating to them, on account of the shortness of time, and which nominates as commander of said ships Sebastian Vizcaino, and for his captain he who was with him at the discovery of the said port, if they are both living. In case either of them be dead, the survivor to be commander in chief, and for the first pilot the person who was in that post under Sebastian Vizcaino, or under his captain, in order that, having the ships under their charge, they may at their return consider the best manner of making a settlement at the said port of Monterey, and thus introduce the touching at that port, and carefully instruct the pilots and sailors on the necessary particulars of the voyage, especially two persons well qualified, whom you are hereby ordered to send from those islands with the said General Vizcaino, on his return, that they may be acquainted with the said port and may return general and commander of the ships, which are to go from Acapulco to those islands in the year 1608. Sebastian Vizcaino is to conduct the settlement of the said port, to whom and his sea captain and the two others referred to it is my will and pleasure that you in all things show all possible countenance and regard.

"It is also my will that they receive the pay which other generals and commanders have received in said voyage, and that it be paid them in the usual form and manner. And that the premises may obtain the end desired, I charge you to assist and aid them with the utmost care and diligence, as I promise myself from your prudence and zeal, and that you acquaint me with what shall be performed.

"Dated at San Lorenzo Real, on the 19th of August, 1606."

The contemplated voyage, however, was very likely never made, for when Father Junipero Serra first landed in Monterey he wrote to an associate: ". . . Our joy increased still more when, on the great feast of the Pentecost, June 3rd, close to the same shore, and under the same oak tree where the Fathers of Vizcaino's expedition had celebrated, we built an altar. . . ."

Again the curtain drops for another sixty-odd years. We find that the religious orders, through their Guardians, Presidents and other Missionaries, in conjunction with the secular authorities, are this time the leaders in the drama to be enacted in the Californias.

CHAPTER VI

The Mission Fathers go to the Front.

BOOK I

Chapter VI

The Mission Fathers Go to the Front

A GREEABLE to the injunction contained in the Bull of Pope Alexander IV, priests were sent out with each exploring expedition. Unfortunately these men—especially in the beginning—belonged to no specific order and some of the older writers describe them as "greedy, lustful and insolent." Even Cortes, never squeamish, protested against their character, and it was therefore a relief when more worthy members of the various missionary orders took their places. The new Padres soon became the friends and advocates of the Indians, and in 1512 one of the Dominican Fathers, Antonio de Montesino, personally protested to the King regarding the treatment of the Indians. The Vicar of the Dominicans, Pedro de Cordova, went to New Spain in the same year, and never tired of defending the rights of the natives until death silenced him in 1521.

Often there was strife between the friars and the civil authorities, chiefly on account of the management of the Indians, and also between the secular clergy and the friars. Quarrels between the Franciscans, who came to New Spain in 1523, and the Dominicans were rather frequent, while the advent of the Jesuits in 1572, the Carmelites in 1585, and the Benedictines in 1592 added to the confusion.

The Franciscan Fathers played the largest part in the spiritual conquest of New Spain until the advent of the Jesuits, with the Dominicans a close second.[1] In spite of all conceivable hardships, including revolts accompanied by murder, the Jesuits by 1644 had established thirty-five Missions in New Spain, mostly in Sinaloa and Sonora.

In 1681 a beginning was made by the Jesuit Order, under Father Francisco Eusebio Kino, to explore Baja California with the idea of establishing Missions there.[2] Lower California was not then, nor is it now, a very prepossessing country. It was largely sand, rocks, rugged mountains, wastes and thorns, due to want of water and shade. Only the rich pearl fisheries in the Gulf of California were of value. (See Appendix No. 1.)

Father Ugarte, professor of philosophy in the Jesuit College of Mexico City, became interested and consented to act as treasurer of the enterprise.

---

[1] Bancroft, The North Mexican States, p. 116, Vol. 1.
[2] Father Kino accompanied Admiral Atondo y Antillion in 1683 on his expedition to Baja California.

47

This gave a great impetus to the undertaking. Many wealthy Mexicans made large contributions, thus founding the Pious Fund, which later became so famous as a bone of contention between the ecclesiastic and lay authorities.

There proved to be a major difficulty to overcome. A royal decree forbade expeditions to California. However, when the size of the embryo Pious Fund justified the belief that no demands would be made upon the royal treasury, Moctezama, the Viceroy, granted a permit to Father Juan Maria de Salvatierra, *Visitador General* of the Jesuit Order, and Father Eusebio Kino to proceed with the enterprise, to enlist and pay military men, and appoint and discharge officers—in one word, to administer Baja California.

The mother Mission and Presidio was established at Loreto in October, 1697 (see Appendix No. 2), and other Missions followed. The Pious Fund grew through liberal donations and the government interested itself more and more in the missionary endeavors.

The Jesuits divided the natives of Lower California into three main groups: the Pericues, the Monquis and the Cochimies or Laymones. Each of them was divided into sub-branches. They were a tall, erect, robust and well-made race; their color was dark and they mutilated and disfigured themselves, as savages often do. They had no houses or tepees and the men were quite naked, as were also the women of some of the tribes. All were infested by filth and vermin.[*]

Their food consisted of roots, seeds, wild fruit and the flesh of the deer, wild cats, rats, mice, owls, bats, and even snakes, lizards and caterpillars. They lived promiscuously, the men seeming to have no preference for particular females, hence there was no jealousy. They had nothing which might be called a government, nor any system of faith which could be called religion; they stood very low in the scale of human beings; yet they were not vicious or cruel. They were savages without anything approaching even barbaric civilization.[*]

There were no roads on the entire peninsula and the communication between the Missions was maintained by following horse trails.

The members of the Jesuit Order were simple-hearted, honest, devoted men, who labored manfully to better the lot of the natives, and for themselves at best they lived a hard, isolated life.

---

[*] See Introduction page 5 et seq. of Marguerite Eyer Wilbur's translation of Father Sigismundo Taraval's Journal, published by the Quivira Society at Los Angeles (1931).

[*] Father Jacob Baegert, a German Jesuit, who lived for several years amongst them describes them in his Nachrichten von der Amerikanischen Halbinsel California as dull, awkward, rude, unclean, insolent, ungrateful, lying, thievish and lazy with reasonings and actions of children.

The enterprise did not prove a worldly success. In 1730 the Missions were already on the decline (see Appendix No. 3), having only half the number of former neophytes, though gauging the success by the object in view: the conversion of souls to Christ, and considering the salvation of a soul of more importance than the most outstanding worldly accomplishment, then, of course, this enterprise was a success indeed.

That some of the leaders in California Antiqua and elsewhere courted secular and political power, as well as ecclesiastical authority, is natural. That the Order often did acquire and exercise such power is of course well known.

The unlimited power granted to Salvatierra and Kino held in it the seed of destruction. All kinds of charges were brought against them, including abuse of power by the successors of the original founders of the Missions.

Charles of Spain, the most Catholic King, reigning over a country which he had largely recuperated after more than one hundred years of stagnation, suddenly turned against them. The storm broke loose in 1767, when arrangements were perfected to arrest and deport every professed Jesuit from the Spanish dominions.

The blow was complete, for the Order was most ruthlessly, often cruelly, executed. There were then fifteen Missions in Baja California from Cape Lucas, in the south, to Santa Maria near the mouth of the Colorado River, in the north. These were San Jose del Cabo, Santiago de los Coras, Nuestra Sinora del Pilar or Todos Santos, Nuestra Sinora de los Dolores or La Pasion, San Luis Gonzaga, San Francisco Javier, San Jose Comondu, Purisima, Guadalupe, Sta Rosalia Mulege, San Ignacio, Sta Gertrudis, San Francisco de Borja, Sta Maria, and Loreto, the headquarters of the spiritual conquest, which became the capital of the province where the Governor resided.

At the time of their expulsion there were sixteen Jesuits in the province—fifteen priests and one lay brother; of these, eight were Germans, six Spaniards, and two Mexicans.

Thus it was that Lower California lost its Jesuit missionaries. The story of their expulsion is pathetic and has aroused the sympathy and indignation of many impartial writers.

There have been during all these years the usual charges and countercharges between the clergy and the lay authorities. When, for instance, a great revolt had broken out amongst the Pimas, of Pimeria Alta, under the leadership of an Indian who went by the name of Don Luis, Governor Parrilla claimed that the cause of the outbreak was the ill treatment and gross oppression of the Indians by the Jesuit missionareis; but the famous missionary, Father Kelly, countered by saying that it was the weak position of the Governor towards the chief which had made the latter overwhelmingly conceited, and therefore disdainful of Spanish rule. The quarrel grew in intensity, for the settlers took, as usual, different positions, as their interests dictated, and once more the old disharmonies between the sacerdotal and lay authorities had their innings.

But, for all that, the Jesuit Order had, like the others, many great members laboring in the outlying provinces who shed lustre not only on their own religious organization but on the Spanish name in general. There were, for instance: Father Marcos, of the "Seven Cities" fame; Father Augustin Rodriguez, known for his travels in New Mexico; Father Larious, of the Coahuilla travels; Father Juan Maria Salvatierra, to whom was due the permanent settlement in Baja California; and Father Eusebio Kino, who explored the Gila and Colorado Valleys, and established a chain of Missions in Altar-River Valley; he spent a lifetime on the frontier and wrote the chronicles, Favores Celestials;[5] also Fathers Ignacio Keller and Jacobo Sedelmayr, who did heroic work amongst the Moquis; Father Fernando Consag, who make his famous voyage to California Baja in 1746; Father Miguel Venegas and Father Tarabel, both mentioned elsewhere in connection with the "Venegas Noticia de la California," which was translated in English (1759), in Dutch (1761), in French (1767), and in German (1769-1770), and many other worthy priests.

These Jesuit Mission Fathers never hesitated to take great personal risks and made explorations in countries where dwelt Indians of a quite different breed than the submissive Indians of California Alta.

There were, for instance, the Seri Indians, the Moquis, the Pimas, the Yaquis, the Topocas, and other war-like tribes, scattered throughout Sonora, Colorado-Gila country, Sinaloa, Pimeria and other regions little explored except for the efforts of these undaunted missionaries.

Jose de Galvez was sent as *Visitador* General (inspector general) to the "Indies" in 1761. He was born at Velez-Malaga in October, 1729, of poor parents. They managed to send him to the University of Alcala, where he graduated as a lawyer. He became a brilliant advocate, private secretary to the Marquis de Grimaldi, and member of the Council of the Indies. Before that he had been one of the secretaries of the Marquis de Duras, the French Ambassador[6] and had absorbed many of the liberal French ideals then budding.

[5] Bolton's Father Kino's Lost History, its discovery and value, p. 17.
  Richman, California under Spain and Mexico, p. 387.
[6] Biographie Universelle (Michaud), Paris, 1856

In 1764 he was vested with almost supreme power, and in 1766 his position was strengthened by the arrival in Mexico City of Carlos Francisco de Croix, a member of an aristocratic Flemish family, as Viceroy to Mexico. De Croix was entirely in sympathy with Galvez.

It was now proposed that into the hands of the Franciscan Brotherhood—men avowed to "poverty, chastity and obedience"—with a somewhat meagre military organization to aid them, there should be placed the seemingly impossible task of "reducing" to profitable and intelligent citizenship the horde of Upper California Indians, a race far below the other tribes of American aborigines.

The Franciscans, though organized like all the other Orders for the purpose of supporting the Church, did not, like the Jesuits, so openly and entirely subordinate the interests of their country to that of their Order, and therefore had far more the confidence and support of the State.

As early as 1503 the Franciscan Order had founded the College of San Domingo. As the Spanish conquests increased, the Order constantly founded new establishments, and largest and most important in the Americas being the College of San Fernando in Mexico City.

This organization was in excellent condition to replace the Jesuits, with whom there never had existed an overly cordial relationship.

To Don Jose de Galvez almost unlimited powers were given. After the royal order banishing the Jesuits had become effective, Marquis de Croix tendered to the Franciscan College at Mexico City the Missions in Baja California. The College accepted them and twelve Franciscans took the place of the banished Jesuit Fathers. After a short delay the padres arrived at the Mother Mission of Loreto, where Gaspar de Portola, the new Governor of California, had preceded them.[7]

At first the Franciscans were placed in charge only of the spiritual welfare of the inhabitants and of the church buildings. This soon proved impractical. Upon the arrival of Don Jose de Galvez in July, 1768, at Loreto, all Mission property was therefore turned over to the Franciscans for administration. It having become necessary to place someone in charge of the missionaries in Alta California as Father-*presidente,* the unanimous choice of the College fell upon Father Junipero Serra.

When Galvez and Serra met, a strong friendship, based on mutual respect, sprang up between the two men, and they worked together in complete harmony and sympathy.

Portola's and Serra's orders from *Visitador* General Galvez, who was primarily concerned with the occupation of Alta California, were explicit:

---

[7] H. I. Priestley, Jose de Galvez, *Visitador General* to Spain, p. 245.

"Occupy and fortify San Diego and Monterey, for God and the King of Spain."

Thus began the founding of the Missions of Alta California.

Serra was a remarkable man, and is the outstanding religious figure in the great Alta California Mission drama.

It is much easier to understand the devotion of these Franciscan Fathers and their *Presidente* in Alta California when one contemplates the causes of the founding of their great Order.

Pope Innocent III was one of the most ambitious—and able—men who ever sat on the Papal throne. The Crusaders, under Baldwin of Flanders and of Hainault, with the assistance of the Venetians, under their half-blind Doge Dandolo, had won the Byzantine Empire for Rome. Innocent was establishing the Papal authority over far frontiers. Kings visited Rome as vassals. Peter, King of Aragon, Count of Barcelona and Lord of Montpellier, swore allegiance in the Basilica of St. Peter, and voluntarily made his kingdom tributary to Rome. With the exception of Philip Augustus of Swabia and Otto of Brunswick, all the kings of Christendom became vassals of the See of Rome. The Crusaders were gathering again, but Innocent, fearing at that time a possible disaster if a crusade against Jerusalem would again fail, kept the warriors in Europe to serve the needs of the Papacy. The Jerusalem crusade could wait.

In southern France a new cult had spread, first among the humble, later among the high nobles like the Count of Foix, the Viscount of Bearn, and even Raymond VI of Toulouse, descendant of the Great Raymond, one of the main leaders of the First Crusade. The Provincials and Gascons, who accepted this cult, had some Moorish blood in their veins and had learned much of the Arab philosophers. They were known as "Cathars," or the pure, and were aroused against the luxury-loving and worldly high clergy of that time.

Raymond of Toulouse was excommunicated by Innocent III in 1208, whereupon the Papal Legate sent there was murdered in a personal quarrel.

Innocent now called for a Crusade against these heretics. The Crusaders were placed under command of Simon de Montford. The town of Beziers was stormed and seven thousand women and children, who had taken refuge in the Church of the Madeleine, were butchered.

Peter, the King of Aragon, notwithstanding his former submission to the Pope, indignant at the outrage, took the field against de Montford, but was defeated and slain in 1213. The Pope now withdrew the Teutonic Knights from Palestine and sent them amongst the pagans of Prussia to convert them, sword in hand, while in Spain another crusade was launched against the Moslems. The sword had been drawn to exterminate heretics in the home countries of Europe, and for several centuries thereafter other Popes and monarchs would follow this bloody ideal.

It was under these conditions that monks appeared amongst the peasants without sanction of their superiors. They fomented a silent rebellion in the Church, taking pity on the poor people of the countryside, comforting them and giving them their sympathy. One of the leaders of these kindly spirits was a man from Assisi, who tended the lepers, helped the down-trodden and lived, like Christ, amongst the simple country folk, giving a helping hand where he could, and often assisting in the hard manual labor of the little farms.

The people called them the "jongleurs of Christ," and loved them. By their poverty (see Appendix No. 4) they protested against the growing wealth of the clerics, and were known as the Franciscans or Gray Friars.[8]

Francesco was born in 1182 in the town of Assisi, in Italy. As his father had traded and made a fortune in France, they baptized the boy "Francesco," or "Francis." Like St. Augustine, and so many of the former and later saints, he had at first lived a gay and prodigal life, until he was caught in a war with a neighboring town of Perugia and kept in jail for one year. There he had ample time for meditation and his whole viewpoint was changed. He became a penitent, donated his worldly goods to the Church and did many benevolent deeds.

Afterwards the same St. Francis went with the European army on the first Egyptian crusade, and in September, 1221, the apostle of poverty and gentleness appeared before Al' Kamil, the victorious sultan, at Cairo.

He died in 1226. During his life the growth of the Order which he had founded was extraordinary. He began his active labors in 1208 or 1209, when the Church gave its sanction to the "Seraphic Saints," and ever since the Franciscans have been benefactors of mankind. Ten years after it was founded there were five thousand members. In 1223 the Order was confirmed by a Papal Bull, and two years after St. Francis' death (1228) his canonization took place. Fifty years later the Order counted 200,000 members, with 8,000 colleges and convents.

The Franciscans had an overwhelming influence in the early history of the Americas, for Juaro Perez de Maschina was a Franciscan friar, while Queen Isabella of Spain, as well as Columbus, were members of the Third Order of St. Francis. In Alta California they were the first founders of the white man's civilization.

Father Serra had much in common with St. Francis, both as to earnest persistency and devotion.

---

[8] Harold Lamb, The Flame of Islam, p. 277.

When the name of Father Serra is spoken, true history, free from sectional bigotry, raises an ancient and benign face, and her eyes light with soft radiance, for such history, so often viewing with a sarcastic if not a sardonic smile, the heroics of pseudo great men, holds out to Father Serra the final laurels in the history of the west.

While each nation, and for that matter each age, has its own conception of God or Gods, the Padre's conception of the Deity will forever illuminate the pages of California history.

Serra was born in the village of Petra, on the Island of Majorca or Mallorca, in the Mediterranean Sea, on December 24, 1713, his parents, Antonio Serra and Margareta Ferron, being laboring people. (See Appendix No. 5.) He was baptized on the day of his birth and received the name of Miguel Joseph. He retained this name at his confirmation in the parent church of the same village where he was born.

In his early youth he frequently attended the Church and Convent of San Bernardino in his native village, and learned to chant in Latin. From there his parents took him to the City of Palma in order that he might devote himself to higher studies. There a devout priest, a beneficiary of the Cathedral, took a friendly interest in him, teaching him to recite the Divine Office and encouraging him to study philosophy. Finally, on the 14th day of September, 1730, his often-expressed and dearest wish was gratified, and at the age of sixteen years, nine months and twenty-one days, he was allowed to take the habit as a novice in the Convent of Jesus, outside the walls of Palma.

He distinguished himself as a young student, and at the age of eighteen years had taken his final vows, and was soon elected teacher of philosophy at the Convent at Palma.

On becoming a monk on the 15th day of September, 1731, his baptismal name of Miguel Joseph was changed to Junipero, for he felt a great admiration for one of the first followers of Saint Francis, a devoted and quaint lay brother called Junipero. He had been of a whimsical nature and was known as the "Jester of the Lord," but he was, on account of his great charity and many other virtues, a favorite of St. Francis, who once exclaimed, "I wish I had a whole forest of such Junipers!"

Three other young monks were studying at the same convent at the same time—Palou, Crespi and Verger—all destined to leave their marks on the world.

The University of Palma conferred on Junipero the Degree of Doctor of Sacred Theology, and he was appointed John Scotus Professor of Philosophy, at the University. Yearning for missionary work in a foreign field, he departed for Cadiz in 1749, where a great body of missionaries were gathered, chiefly destined for Mexico. The four friends—Junipero Serra, Juan Crespi, Francisco Palou and Rafael Verger—sailed on the same ship.

Arriving at Vera Cruz, Serra did not find the promised conveyance, and impatient to start his work, he walked all the way to Mexico City.

For nineteen years after their arrival in Mexico the four young monks worked under the control of the San Fernando College of their Order, all the time preaching and founding Missions. Part of this time Serra worked among the Indians at Sierra Gorda and elsewhere, and his fame as a zealous, inspired missionary spread.[9]

Finally in 1767 three of the friends had a chance to go to California, Verger remaining behind at the college.

In the Francisco College at Santa Barbara an old daguerreotype may be seen, taken from the painted portrait of Father Serra at San Fernando in Mexico City. It shows a face full of sadness and spiritual tenderness, also great energy and singleness of purpose. Monuments have been erected in his honor, both at Monterey, and in the Golden Gate Park of San Francisco.

The order of Galvez to occupy and fortify San Diego and Monterey had of course to be executed within the limits of the Spanish laws and policies in the Indies, which were under the King's immediate control. Those affecting the general government, municipal organization, military control, administration, treatment of the natives and religious establishments had little in common with the laws of the other colonies in America, except perhaps in a few respects the French.[10]

The land belonged by right of conquest to the Crown, but the natives had a right of occupancy, and on becoming Spanish citizens they acquired a more complete title. As it was the policy to "reduce" the natives to the conditions of citizens as speedily as possible, a great number of laws were enacted and Regulations and Royal Decrees promulgated to bring this about.

The laws gradually became so numerous that in 1665 it was found necessary to condense them into a code. At the instance of Carlos II the famous *Recopilation de Leyes de Los Reinos de las Indies* was compiled, comprising a digest of the *cedulas, Reglamentos,* etc., issued at different times for the government of the American possessions. This code covered the military, political and fiscal affairs of Spanish America.[11]

---

[9] Palou's Life of Junipero Serra, English translation by C. Scott Williams, with introduction and notes by George Wharton James.

[10] Blackmar, Spanish Institutions of the Southwest, p. 63.

[11] Schmidt, Civil Law of Spain and Mexico, p. 95.

Prior to 1665 all laws enacted in Spain applied equally to the colonies, but it was now provided that all laws designated for the Indies should be definitely proclaimed as such by the "Council of the Indies." This remained the rule until 1810, when all new laws made in Spain were again enforced in the American Colonies, without special enactment.

Military, religious and civil steps were now taken by the government to extend her authority in the still wild and unexplored lands of her domain. Military, by the establishing of the presidios; the religious by founding the Missions; and the civil by creating as soon as possible pueblos and villas (towns and villages). That these steps were bound to bring confusion and dissensions is obvious, though the alliance between State and Church in these enterprises was less difficult to regulate than it would be today, many of the statesmen and soldiers being hardly less fervid in their religious enthusiasm than the regular churchmen themselves.

When a new place was formally taken possession of, it was done in the name of the Church, by religious ceremonies, and in the name of the King of Spain by unfurling the royal standard, planting it side by side with the Holy Cross.

When a presidio, which was a crude fortress, was established, it guarded the Mission in its immediate vicinity, and sent military guards to the outlying Missions, and eventually to the pueblos in its district.

As soon as the Indians had become confessing Catholics, partly civilized and self-supporting, the Missions were to be changed into pueblos, the Mission church into a regular parish church, and the Mission Fathers were to give way to the secular clergy. The whole political structure was built with the object in view of eventually secularizing, that is disestablishing, the Missions. That the Franciscan Fathers had not and could not have much sympathy with this probable ending of their endeavors is only natural. Theirs was consecrated work; they were mainly interested in the saving of the souls of the Indians, and to save souls effectively they had to have establishments. For themselves they wanted little; for, like the Dominicans, Capuchins and Augustinians, they belonged to the Mendicant Orders, eschewing personal property, but they were zealous in the interest of their organizations.

In 1783 there existed three Franciscan missionary colleges in New Spain: Guadalupe de Zacatecas for Durango, Santa Cruz de Queretaro for Sonora, and San Fernando de Mejico for Alta California; eventually four Mission sub-jurisdictions corresponding with the Presidio jurisdictions were formed:

MISSION SANTA BARBARA, THE QUEEN MISSION OF CALIFORNIA ALTA

JURISDICTION OF SAN DIEGO

Presidio of San Diego; Mission of San Gabriel Arcangel (founded in 1771); Mission of San Juan Capistrano (founded in 1776); Mission of San Diego (founded in 1769); and Mission of San Luis Rey (founded in 1798).

JURISDICTION OF SANTA BARBARA

Presidio of Santa Barbara; Mission of Santa Barbara (founded in 1786); Mission of La Purisima (founded in 1787); Mission of San Ines (founded in 1804); Mission of Buena Ventura (founded in 1782); Mission of San Fernando (founded in 1797); Pueblo de la Reyna de Los Angeles.

JURISDICTION OF MONTEREY

Presidio of Monterey; Villa of Branciforte (founded in 1797); Mission of San Juan Bautista (founded in 1797); Mission of San Carlos (founded in 1770); Mission of Nuestra Senora de Soledad (founded in 1791); Mission of San Antonio (founded in 1771); Mission of San Miguel (founded in 1797); and Mission of San Luis Obispo (founded in 1772).

JURISDICTION OF SAN FRANCISCO (1776)

Presidio of San Francisco; Pueblo of San Jose de Guadalupe; Mission of San Francisco Solano (founded in 1823); Mission of San Rafael (founded in 1817); Mission of Santa Clara (founded in 1777); Mission of San Jose (founded in 1797); and Mission of Santa Cruz (founded in 1791).

Besides the Missions proper there were outlying chapels, called *asistencias*—generally located near one or more Indian villages *(rancherias)*. These *asistencias* were sometimes called *visita,* and with the rancherias were called *pueblos de visita,* and were visited regularly by the Padres.

The missionaries serving Alta California were all called *Frater,* writing Fr. before their name, but as they attained priesthood were generally called Padres, and wrote, in addition "P" before the Fr. In the whole California history, down to 1854, not one lay brother *(laico)* appears amongst the missionaries.

CHAPTER VII

Account of Expedition to Monterey;
Fr. Crespi's Diary.

The Santa Cruz Mission Site viewed for the
first time by white men.

BOOK I

Chapter VII

Account of Expedition to Monterey — Fr. Crespi's Diary —
The Santa Cruz Mission Site Viewed for the First Time
by White Men

GALVEZ, the great colonizer of the Californias, had reached Lower California on the 5th day of July, 1768. He had sailed from San Blas on May 24th, where he had established a supply depot for the Californias and a base for Sonora operations. He was driven back and forth by contrary winds and it took him forty days to cross the narrow Gulf of California and land at La Paz. He was met by Fernando Xavier Rivera y Moncada, the captain of the presidio at Loreto. He had three immediate problems to solve: the establishment of Indian pueblos, the colonization by Spaniards, and the expedition to Monterey.

There were numerous Indian settlements in Lower California, the spiritualities of which, formerly in charge of the Jesuits, were in charge of the Franciscans until 1772, when they were transferred to the Dominicans; the temporalities were in charge of the military; but the neophytes or native clientage, naked, half fed, suffering from syphilis brought by the Spaniards, had for the most part deserted and were wandering in the mountains.

The military commissioners had wasted the Mission estates; the great resources of precious metals and pearls, which the Jesuits were supposed to have hidden, were non-existent. There was nothing but some very much-diminished pearl fisheries, and everything was in a miserable state.

Galvez acted with vigor. He gave the missionaries temporal powers; ordered the restoration of the Mission system, brought supplies and clothing, and established besides the Missions *pueblos formales,* or regular towns.

He endeavored to induce Spanish colonization by offering Crown lands and military rights,[1] but the peninsula of Lower California was largely a desert, offering little attraction to settlers. However, it was the expedition to San Diego and Monterey which appealed especially to him, and he wanted to make haste, for the Russian Bear, ever since Bering had discovered the Straits named for him and coasted along the American

---

[1] Decreto de Colonizacion en Baja California, 1768 (B.C. Prov. St. Pap. Vol. 1, pp. 61-66).

mainland, had established a string of outposts on the Aleutian Islands, stretching for one thousand miles towards America.

An expedition of two hundred and twenty-five men, including Indian auxiliaries, in four divisions—two by sea and two by land—was organized.

By that time San Blas, situated on the west coast of the mainland and separated from Alta California by the Gulf, had become the naval base for the northwest, and several transports were plying between that port and San Jose del Cabo and Guaymas.

Galvez ordered the *Laurentana,* the *Sinaloa* and the *Concepcion* to bring supplies from San Blas to La Paz on the opposite east coast of the Peninsula, while the *San Carlos* and the *San Antonio* (or *Principe*) were each directed to take a division of the expedition from La Paz.

In addition the *visitador* requested donations from the peninsular churches at La Pasion, San Luis and Todos Santos of elaborate and costly vestments and silver church utensils, such as censers, candlesticks and chalices, placed there by the Jesuits.

On January 9th, 1769, the *San Carlos,* a tiny craft of only two hundred tons, sailed for San Diego loaded with church furniture, with oil, dates, wines, meal, fish, maize, lard, garlic, flour, cheese, hams, chocolate, and a number of other supplies, including hens and live cattle, and one thousand pesos in money. This vessel had reached La Paz early in December, but had been so battered by storms in the Gulf that it had to be unloaded, careened and reconditioned. Galvez on the *Concepcion* accompanied the *San Carlos* to Cape San Lucas, at the southern end of California Baja and saw the ship round the Cape and sail north.

Captain Vicente Vila, an Andalusian, was commander, Jorge Estorace was mate, Alferez Miguel Costanso,[2] cosmographer and diarist, Pedro Prat, surgeon, Lieutenant Pedro Fages (who was later to become one of California's best Governors) commanding twenty-five volunteers of the Catalan company serving in Sonora; Father Hernando Parron, one of Serra's Franciscans, was chaplain, and there was a crew of twenty-three sailors and a cabin boy, besides four cooks and two blacksmiths.

The *San Antonio* sailed on February 15th, under command of Juan Perez, with Miguel del Pino as master's mate, and Chaplains Juan Viscaino and Francisco Gomez. This ship was even more heavily provisioned than the *San Carlos.*

Both of them had a difficult passage. Scurvy, the curse which beset all ocean-going vessels during that time, exacted an appalling toll of human life, no efficient anti-scorbutic having been discovered.

---

[2] See Diary of Miguel Costanso, Publications of the Academy of Pacific Coast History, Vol. 1, No. 4, p. 61. (Quoted in following chapter.)

The *San Antonio* (or *Principe*) was forty-five days at sea; the *San Carlos,* misled by errors in latitude and adverse winds, took one hundred and ten days to reach the northern port, now reached in a few days by modern steamers; and the supply ship, *San Jose,* simply disappeared and was never heard of again.

En route many died on the *San Carlos,* and the balance of the crew, with few exceptions, were sick.

In the meantime the two land divisions were getting ready to start.

Of the first Rivera y Moncada was commander. This division was gathered at Santa Maria de los Angelos, the most northerly of the California Baja Missions, and at Velicata, a post eighteen leagues further north—two hundred cattle, thirty-eight horses, one hundred and fourteen mules, pack saddles, leather bags, wine and all kinds of supplies. It started on the 24th day of March, 1769, guided by the cosmographer, Jose Canizares, twenty-five *cuirassed* men (*soldados de cuera,* so-called after their leather jackets) from the garrison at Loreto, forty-two of the Christianized Indians from the old Missions, equipped with sapper tools like shovels, pick-axes, etc., to clear a path when necessary, and three muleteers with one hundred and eighty-eight mules and horses made up the expedition, which was joined by Padres Juan Crespi and de Lasuen, the former becoming the historian of the expedition.

Bravely the cavalcade rode away from Velicata towards the north. Mounted on fine horses, the *soldados de cuera* led the way. They were clad in their leather jackets and chaps or aprons, the latter fastened to the high pommels of the Spanish saddles and protecting their lower limbs against Indian arrows, as well as thorns of the brush or spines of the cactus. They carried shields of bullhide on their arms, with lances at rest.

They were like the knights of old, riding "into the blue"—the unknown beyond—true pathfinders, carrying the Royal Standard of Spain into wilds of California Antiqua which had only been visited once by a white man, Father S. J. Link, and only for a part of the way; thence farther to the north. Gentle, lovable, learned Father Crespi and his colleague carried the cross and salvation to the wild inhabitants of the mysterious lands.

There were of course pack trains of loaded mules to be guarded, Indians driving the *caballada*—the exchange saddle horses and extra mules—as was the Spanish wont.

On May 13th they reached the high ground, from which they could see the Bay of San Diego. They had suffered great hardships, especially due to a shortage of water, the Peninsula being mostly desert, and also because of insufficient fuel for the campfires. They camped on the high ridge very near the present boundary line between the United States and

Mexico, and next day they met the sea party, opposite the point where the ships were anchored in the Bay.

Finally, the last of the divisions, which had started on March 9th from Loreto, reached San Diego overland on June 30th, after a march of six weeks. Don Caspar de Portola, a Catalan cavalry officer, forty-seven years of age, was in command. He was an able, easy-going, popular man, though a brave and taciturn officer. He ruled the country as civil and military governor, and was a newcomer, having only arrived the previous year, while Captain Fernando Xavier Rivera y Moncada, commanding the garrison at Loreto, had been long in the country.

The last division consisted of ten *cuirassiers,* under command of Sergeant Jose Francisco de Ortega, forty-four Christianized Indians, four muleteers with one hundred and seventy mules, and two servants.

Governor Portola had been joined on May 5th by Father Junipero Serra, the president of the new establishment.

On his arrival the Governor found that the *San Antonio* had anchored in good condition on April 11th, but that the *San Carlos* had not reached the port until sundown April 29th, had had a terrible voyage, scurvy had claimed many victims, and the condition of her crew was "ghastly." (See Appendix No. 1.)

Portola's account to the Viceroy,[3] sent on July 4th, stated that "of the sea divisions, all without exception, seamen, soldiers and officers, are stricken with scurvy, some wholly prostrated, some half disabled, others able to rise but without strength; the dead number thirty-one."[4] While Father Crespi, writing to the guardian of the College of San Fernando in Mexico City, says that "on June 22nd, twenty-three persons (two of them Catalan *cuirassiers*) have died."[5]

On July 16th, 1769, the Mission San Diego de Alcala was dedicated, and nearby the Presidio of San Diego was founded. Thus were laid down the cornerstones of the first civilization in Alta California.

Under instructions from Galvez, Portola left two days prior to the dedication (July 14th) to rediscover the Bay of Monterey, while Father Serra remained at San Diego.

Governor Portola was accompanied by Captain Rivera with twenty-six soldiers "in leather jackets;" Lieutenant Fages, with six volunteers from

---

[3] Chapman, History of California, Spanish Period.
[4] Diary of Gaspar de Portola, Vol. 1, No. 3, p. 57, Publications of the Academy of Pacific Coast History.
[5] Many Indians had deserted or died during both land expeditions. Of Portola's 44 Indians, only 12 reached San Diego.

Catalonia; Engineer Costanso, seven muleteers and fifteen Christians from Lower California, besides Fathers Gomez and Crespi, while in the advance guard rode Sergeant Ortega and his scouts. In addition were the usual pack trains of mules, saddle horses, etc. (See Appendix No. 2.)

Father Crespi's diary now becomes of great interest for those who study the history of the Santa Cruz Mission.

After describing the route north from San Diego, and stating that the soldiers, when they first saw the Salinas Valley, believed they were looking upon the ocean, he says that six days later they reached Monterey, where Portola could not see anything which resembled the much-talked-of and anticipated harbor; so he continued his search north.

On October 7th the expedition must have neared a point now known as Castroville, from whence it proceeded on the following day to a river, called by them the River of the Bird. Father Crespi writes:

"Sunday, October 8.   After Mass we administered the holy viaticum to the sick man of last night, and to another who had also become worse, and today the latter likewise received the holy oils, nevertheless they are continuing the journey on litters which have been made for them. In the same way nine more are going who are almost crippled with the same disease, the scurvy, although not so badly as the two mentioned. After this tender and devout ceremony we left the place about eight in the morning, going north through hills higher than the preceding. At each bay formed by the land there was a lagoon of greater or lesser magnitude, which made it necessary for us to make many detours.

"After traveling five hours, covering four leagues, we came to the large village which the explorers had told us about. We found it abandoned, contrary to our expectations; for when we set out from the lake of Santa Brigida de las Grullas, we saw near the camping place several arrows and little darts thrust in the ground, with some mussels at their feet, which the Indians, either in the afternoon or the night of the preceding day, had fixed in that spot without allowing us to see them. These signs of peace convinced us that we should find them friendly, and that they would allow us to treat with them at their village, but the fear of these poor creatures caused them to desert and burn it as we found it. We all regretted this circumstance, because we need them greatly, especially to acquire information of the country, and to accompany the explorers in their reconnaissance to find good camping places, and to serve as interpreters in the villages which are newly met with, so that they may not do what the others have done.

"We halted on the bank of the river which the explorers had discovered not far from the burned village, which was near its very verdant and

pleasant plain, full of cottonwoods, alders, tall oaks, live oaks, and other
species not known to us. We saw in this place a bird which the heathen
had killed and stuffed with straw; to some of our party it looked like a
royal eagle. It was measured from tip to tip of the wings and found to
measure eleven spans. For this reason the soldiers called the stream Rio
del Pajaro,[6] and I added the name of La Senora Santa Ana. I could not
make observations on account of the fog.

"Monday, October 9. This day was devoted to rest on account of
the sick, who are giving us anxiety, and in order to give an opportunity to
explore for the next two marches.

"Tuesday, October 10. About eight in the morning we set out northwest. We could not make the march as long as was intended, because the
sick men were worse, and each day their number increased, so we must
have traveled but little more than one league, over plains and low hills, well
forested with very high trees of a red color, not known to us. They have
a very different leaf from cedars, and although the wood resembles cedar
somewhat in color, it is very different, and has not the same odor; moreover, the wood of the trees that we have found is very brittle. In this
region there is a great abundance of these trees, and because none of the
expedition recognizes them they are named redwood from their color.
We stopped near a lagoon[7] which has much pasture about it and a heavy
growth of the redwoods. In this march many tracks of animals resembling
those of domestic cattle have been encountered, and there is some discussion
as to whether they may not be buffalo. Some very large deer have also
been seen, which they call stags to differentiate them from ordinary deer.
The droppings of some mule-like animals have also been found. Bands
of them have been seen, and it is said that they are long-eared and have
short, flat tails. In the lagoons many cranes are also seen. The explorers
say that near here they have seen many chestnut trees which are in flower,
and they brought some few nuts, which we tasted, and they truly are
chestnuts,[8] the only difference noticed being that they have a thicker shell
than those of Spain.

"Wednesday, October 11. During the night the sick became worse
and others have been prostrated, for which reason the commander ordered
a halt. We two said Mass this morning to the Most Holy Patriarch San

[6] Still called Pajaro River. Camp was near Watsonville. The route from this point
to Soquel Creek (El Rosaria), reached on October 16th, is difficult to trace with
minute precision, but the explorers evidently ascended Corralitos Creek and swung
round some distance to the north, for they crossed Soquel Creek a league from the
coast. Their route was close to the present highway from Watsonville to Soquel,
near Santa Cruz.

[7] College Lake or Pinto Lake, evidently.

[8] Buckeye nuts, perhaps.

Jose, for the recovery of the sick and the success of the expedition. We gave the viaticum and the holy oils to three more, the ones that are most seriously ill. The commander determined that while we were resting for the sick, the explorers should go out and examine everything as far as possible, so as to have that done. With this object Sergeant Ortega set out with eight soldiers, each one taking three mules for relay, for the animals have become very thin from the cold.

"Thursday, October 12. The sick men appear to be somewhat better this morning. We commended them to Nuestra Senora del Pilar, and in her honor we named this place the Lagoons and Chestnuts of Nuestra Senora del Pilar. I took the latitude, as the sun allowed itself to be seen, and it was thirty-seven degrees and thirty-five minutes.

"Friday, October 13. Nothing special happened this day, nor is there any change in the condition of the sick.

"Saturday, October 14. This afternoon the explorers returned. The sergeant reported that he had gone ahead twelve leagues without getting any information of the harbor that we are looking for, and that he went to the foot of a high white mountain range.

"Sunday, October 15. We two said Mass, commending to God the sick persons, who were feeling rather better. For this reason the commander decided that we should start, as we did, setting out northwest through a valley grown with redwoods, and over hills all covered with chestnuts. After half a league's travel we came to an arroyo with a good volume of water;[9] it seemed to be very much boxed in, with many trees along its banks, cottonwoods, alders, and willows, but there is no plain near by to make use of that water. We traveled only a league and a half on account of the fatigue of the sick persons, and we halted in a valley near another small lagoon which I named Santa Teresa[10] because it was her day. The place has good pasture, and we had found the same along the road.

"Monday, October 16. We set out in the morning from this place, to the northwest, following the valley of the preceding day, and going afterwards through the thickest growth of chestnuts and redwoods, of which there are many extremely large ones. After traveling half a league we crossed the arroyo that I spoke of in the preceding journey, because it is very near the beach, and the range of hill which follows, which has good pasture, although it has just been burned by the heathen, who do not permit themselves to be seen. The march lasted three hours and a half, during which we traveled only two leagues because of the sick, but the poor creatures are slowly recovering. We stopped on the bank of a small stream,

---

[9] Corralitos Creek.
[10] Apparently in Pleasant Valley, Santa Cruz County.

which has about four varas of deep running water. It has on its banks a
good growth of cottonwoods and alders; on account of the depth at which
it runs it may be that it cannot be utilized to water some plains through
which it runs. It was named El Rosario del Beato Serafin de Asculi.[11]

"Tuesday, October 17. We set out about nine in the morning to the
west-northwest, and traveled over good land well covered with grass and in
sight of the seashore, although it was about a league away, and having the
redwood trees still with us. We traveled for three hours and made about
two leagues, during which we found three arroyos, two of them with running water, one with a buey of water, and all with plains of good land and a
heavy growth of cottonwoods and alders in their beds.

"At the end of the day's march we turned to the west. Not far from
the sea we came to a large river,[12] which, in the place where we crossed it,
must have been about eighteen varas wide, and which in the center reached
to the bellies of the animals. It is one of the largest that we have met with
on the journey. In its bed there is a thick growth of cottonwoods and
alders, and it has good meadows for raising crops by irrigation. It is not
far from the shore, and according to what the explorers say, it empties
into an estuary of a bay. We made camp on the other side of the river,
the descent and ascent of which cost some trouble to clear and made a
passage. Besides the growth along the river there are many redwoods. Not
far from the stream we found a good patch of ground that is not burned,
and it is a pleasure to see the grass and the variety of herbs and roses of
Castile. This river was named San Lorenzo. We did not find a single
heathen on it, nor did we see one in the whole day's march.

"Wednesday, October 18. About eight in the morning we started,
taking our way along the coast, which runs to the west-northwest, over high
hills precipitous on the side towards the sea. Five hundred steps after we
started we crossed a good arroyo of running water which descends from
some high hills where it rises. It was named Santa Cruz.[13] Afterwards we
crossed some large mesas of good land which could easily be irrigated with
the water of this stream. The mesas, which end in cliffs at the sea, must
be about one league wide, extending to some hills at the foot of the mountains. We traveled three hours and a half, but only made two leagues,
during which we descended and ascended four deep watercourses carrying
running water which empties into the sea. Only in the watercourses are
any trees to be seen; elsewhere we saw nothing but grass, and that was
burned. About halfway on the march we left the redwoods behind us. We

---

[11] Soquel Creek, Santa Cruz County.
[12] Santa Lorenzo River.
[13] At Santa Cruz.

Portola's Route through the Santa Cruz Region

stopped at the fourth arroyo, which ends in an estuary; it was named Arroyo de San Lucas,[14] but the soldiers called it Las Puentes, because it was necessary to bridge it with poles and earth before it could be crossed."[15]

From there the expedition went to Half Moon Bay (half way between Santa Cruz and San Francisco) and saw a giant new tree which they named Palo Colorado. From Half Moon Bay they sighted the Farallones, Point Reyes and Drake's or Cermenos Bay, which they recognized, and made up their minds that they must have passed Monterey after all.

Ortega, the famous scout, so highly praised by Father Crespi, went north and soon returned with the news that Point Reyes could not be reached via the coast line, for an almost land lock bay, with a narrow entrance, blocked the approach. On November 4th the bay was reached at Palo Alto, and in their endeavor to circle the bay they went as far as a point where Haywards is now, and then returned to Point Reyes and Monterey.

Before leaving Point Pinos[16] they erected on its southern side a large wooden cross, partly as a memento of their sojourn there, and partly to attract the attention of the expedition by sea, in case of its reaching the same place. On the cross was cut the legend, "Dig at the foot of this and you will find a writing," and at its foot accordingly they buried a brief account of their journey. Its text is set forth in the diary of Father Crespi as follows:

"The overland expedition which left San Diego on the 14th of July, 1769, under the command of Don Gaspar Portola, Governor of California, reached the channel of Santa Barbara on the 9th of August, and passed Point Conception on the 27th of the same month. It arrived at the Sierra de Santa Lucia on the 13th of September, entered that range of mountains on the 17th of the same month, and emerged from it on the 1st of October; on the same day caught sight of Point Pinos, and the harbors on its north and south sides, without discovering any indications or landmarks of the Bay of Monterey. Determined to push on further in search of it, and on the 20th of October got sight of Point Reyes and the Farallones, at the Bay of San Francisco, which are seven in number. The expedition strove to reach Point Reyes, but was hindered by an immense arm of the sea,[17] which, extending to a great distance inland, compelled them to make an enormous circuit for that purpose. In consequence of this and other

---

[14] Coja Creek.
[15] Bolton, Crespi, Misisonary Explorer, 1769-1774, pp. 210-216.
[16] John T. Doyle, Memorandum as to the Discovery of the Bay of San Francisco. Worcester, 1874.
[17] Bay of San Francisco.

difficulties, the greatest of all being the absolute want of food, the expedition was compelled to turn back, believing that they must have passed the harbor of Monterey without discovering it. Started on return from the Bay of San Francisco on the 11th of November, passed Point Ano Nuevo on the 19th, and reached this point and harbor of Pinos on the 27th of the same month. From that date until the present, 9th of December, we have used every effort to find the Bay of Monterey, searching the coast, notwithstanding its ruggedness, far and wide, but in vain. At last, undeceived and despairing of finding it, after so many efforts, sufferings, and labors, and having left of all our provisions but fourteen small sacks of flour. We leave this place today for San Diego. I beg of Almighty God to guide it; and for you, traveler, who may read this, that He may guide you, also, to the harbor of eternal salvation.

"Done in this harbor of Pinos, the 9th of December, 1769."

Immediately following this Father Crespi gives the latitudes of various places on the trip, taken by the engineer of the trip, Don Michael Costanso. Then this further comment:

"If the commanders of the schooners, either the *San Jose* or the *Principe,* should reach this place within a few days after this date, on learning the contents of this writing, and of the distressed condition of this expedition, we beseech them to follow the coast down closely toward San Diego, so that if we should be happy enough to catch sight of them we may be able to apprize them by signals, flags, and firearms of the place in which succor and provisions may reach us."

On the other side of the point they erected another cross, and carved upon its arms, with a razor, these words:

"The overland expedition from San Diego returned from this place on the 9th of December, 1769, starving."

Portola's expedition returned to San Diego in a half starving condition, on the 24th day of January of the following year, six months and ten days after the days of departure.

CHAPTER VIII

Account of Expedition to Monterey
Engineer Miguel Costanso's Diary
and Father Serra's Letter.

BOOK I

Chapter VIII

Account of Expedition to Monterey — Engineer Miguel Costanso's
Diary and Father Serra's Letter

THE diary of Miguel Costanso,[1] the engineer of the party, describes the country.[2] His diary from Saturday, September 30, 1769, to Friday, October 20, 1769, is as follows:

"Saturday, September 30. We proceeded for another three and a half leagues, down stream,[3] to the northwest and west-north-west. The hills gradually became lower, and spreading out at the same time, made the canyon wider; at this place, in sight of two low points formed by the hills, it extends for more than three leagues. The soil was of the same quality as that we have mentioned above—treacherous footing, full of fissures that crossed it in all directions, whitish in color, and scant of pasture.

"From our camp[4] we could hear the sound of the ocean, but we could not see the shore. Therefore, desirous of knowing on what part of the coast we were, and convinced that we could not be very far from the desired port of Monterey, and that the mountain range which we were leaving behind was assuredly that of Santa Lucia—as we inferred from the account written by Father Torquemada, which treats of the expedition and voyage of General Sebastian Vizcaino, and from the sailing directions of the pilot Cabrera Bueno—our commander resolved that the scouts should set out promptly to explore the coast and the mouth of the river.

"They returned saying that the river emptied into an estuary[5] which entered the canyon from the sea; that the beach, bordered by sand-dunes, had been seen to the north and south, the coast forming an immense bay, and that, to the south, there was a low hill covered with trees like pines which terminated in a point in the sea.

"On hearing this news some began to suspect that we might have left behind us the port we were seeking, by reason of the great circuit we had

---

[1] Costanso had in his possession the "Manuel of Navigation" of the famous galleon pilot Cabrera Bueno (printed in Manila in 1734), and he consulted this valuable document whenever on the coast or sea.

[2] The diary of Portola gives a much less detailed account. Portola, G., Diary of Gaspar de Portola During the California Expedition of 1769-1770, in publications of the Academy of Pacific Coast History, Vol. I, No. 3, pp. 31-89.

[3] Salinas River.

[4] The party on its return trip camped here December 11th.

[5] Bay of Monterey.

made in passing through the mountain range, which we traversed in a northeasterly and northerly direction until we descended to the canyon which permitted us to resume the road along the beach towards the northwest and west-north-west. They added that the Punta de Pinos, which appeared to the south, was a strong indication of it, for it is one of the landmarks given in the sailing directions for the Port of Monterey. They also stated that the large bay, about which the scouts gave particulars, was, without doubt, the one that lay between the Punta de Ano Nuevo and the above-mentioned Punta de Pinos.

"These reasons somewhat worried all of us, and to these could be added the fact that we were above 36 degrees 30 minutes north latitude; so it was considered a most necessary measure to reconnoiter this point before undertaking anything else.

"(Through the same canyon 3½ leagues. From San Diego 158 leagues.)

"Sunday, October 1. We approached somewhat nearer the beach, following the course of the river for about a league.[6] Some of the officers afterwards went with the engineer to examine this beach. There they observed the large bay which the scouts had seen. Its northern point, which ran a considerable distance into the sea, bore northwest at a distance—in their judgment—of eight maritime leagues; the southern point, which formed the hill of pines, bore southwest by south. They did not see the mouth of the estuary because it does not enter and join with the sea where they were, but very much farther to the north.

"It was not possible to observe the meridian altitude of the sun with the octant to determine the latitude of the place, because the coast prevented a clear horizon either to north or south.

"(Through the same canyon, 1 league. From San Diego 159 leagues.)

"Monday, October 2. The scouts set out in the morning with a great desire to reconnoiter the Punta de Pinos, convinced that they would not fail to find the port of Monterey, which we imagined had been left behind. As it was not possible yesterday to observe the meridian altitude of the sun on the shore, this calculation was made in the camp by means of the gnomon. . . . The latitude of the place was therefore 36 degrees 44 minutes.

"Tuesday, October 3. The scouts returned in the afternoon and said that they had not seen a port, either to the north or south of the Punta de Pinos; they did see, however, a small bay[7] lying between the said Punta de

---

[6] Novemberr 26th, the party again camped here after returning from San Francisco and before going to Carmel Bay.

[7] Carmel Bay.

Pinos and another point[8] farther to the south. This bay had a stream[9] flowing into it from the mountain range, and an estuary into which the stream emptied. Farther on, the rocky coast extended to the south-south-west; its impenetrable ruggedness obliged them to turn back, and they believed that the steep cliff they had in sight was the same that had obliged us to leave the shore, and to pursue our way through the mountains.

"Wednesday, October 4. Our commander, somewhat confused by those reports, determined to call a meeting of his officers to consider what action was most suitable in the present exigency. We drew attention to the scarcity of provisions that confronted us; to the large number of sick we had among us (there were seventeen men half crippled and unfit for work); to the season already far advanced; and to the great sufferings of the men who remained well, on account of the unlimited work required in looking after the horses, and watching them at night, in guarding the camp, and in the continual excursions for exploration and reconnaissance. The meeting was held after we had heard the Mass of the Holy Ghost, and all the officers voted unanimously that the journey be continued, as this was the only course that remained, for we hoped to find—through the grace of God—the much-desired port of Monterey, and in it the packet *San Jose,* which would relieve our needs; and, if God willed that in the search for Monterey we should all perish, we would have performed our of the undertaking upon which we had been sent.

"Thursday, October 5. The scouts sent out early in the morning to examine the country so that we might continue our journey.

"Friday, October 6. The scouts returned in the afternoon with very pleasant news. They had found a river (valley),[10] of great verdure and with trees of Castile, and they believed that they had seen another point of pines to the north (it was afterwards known, however, that they had been deceived, because it was very foggy). They likewise saw tracks of large animals with split hoofs, and thought they might be bison; and a populous village of Indians who lived in huts covered with thatch, and who, according to what they said, must have numbered over five hundred souls. . . .

"Saturday, October 7. We proceeded for two leagues over the plains, where we experienced delay in crossing two swampy ditches[11] which we found on our way. We had to fill them with earth and fascines[12] so that our pack animals and horses could pass.

---

[8] Point Lobos.
[9] Carmel River.
[10] Pajaro.
[11] Most probably the Tembladera and Mora Cojo Slough.
[12] Fascines are bundles of sticks or brush.

"We pitched our camp[13] between some low hills near a pond, where we saw a great number of cranes—the first we had seen on this journey. . . .

"This place was given the name of Laguna de las Grullas.

"(To the Laguna de las Grullas, 2 leagues. From San Diego 169 leagues.)

"Sunday, October 8. We continued our way over the hills that were higher than those we were leaving behind; in every depression of the land there was a pond of greater or lesser extent, which obliged us to make many circuits. After marching for four leagues we arrived at the village of which the scouts had given us information; contrary to our expectations, we found it deserted. . . . This circumstance we all regretted, as we needed them greatly . . . chiefly to obtain information in regard to the country, and to accompany the scouts in their explorations, from which we hitherto derived great advantage. We pitched our camp on the bank of the river discovered by the scouts, not far from the village, which stood near the river bottom. This was verdant and pleasant, covered with poplars, elders, and tall white oaks, live oaks, and another kind of tree that we did not know.

"Here we saw a bird that the natives had killed and stuffed with grass; it appeared to be a royal eagle; it was eleven palms from tip to tip of its wings. On account of this find we called the river the Rio del Pajaro.[14]

"(To the Rancheria del Pajaro, 4 leagues. From San Diego 165 leagues.)

"Monday, October 9. The short and cloudy days did not give the scouts opportunity to examine the country, especially as we arrived somewhat late at the camping-place. This obliged us to rest here in order to give the scouts time to make their explorations. They left early in the morning and were given the day for this purpose.

"They examined the country for (a distance equal to) two days' march of the pack animals, and returned without any information of importance, . . . which greatly depresses us, considering the scarcity of the provisions and the embarrassment caused by the sick, who could not shift for themselves, the number of the ailing increasing every day.

"Tuesday, October 10. We left the Rio del Pajaro and proceeded for one league over level ground, not being able to continue the march farther, as the sick were already exhausted, falling down from their mules. We halted near a small pond formed between some low hills . . . a place with plenty of water and pasture.[15]

---

[13] This camp was to the north of the Moro Cojo Slough. The presence of the hills would disqualify a site near Castroville previously identified.

[14] Recrossed November 24th, on the return trip.

[15] Camped here again November 23rd.

"(To the Canada de Lagunilla del Corral, 1 league. From San Diego 166 leagues.)

"Wednesday, October 11. The sick were in such a serious condition and so near the end, that, the sacrament having already been administered to several of them, we realized it would be exposing them to the possibility of dying on the road if we did not give them some respite and quiet. Our commander resolved, therefore, that they should rest at this place, and that we should proceed as soon as they felt better. In order to save time, however, and to obtain information about the port of Monterey, which we all believed to be near, he ordered a party to set out, and to advance as far as the animals—they were growing very thin from the cold—could go. The sergeant of the presidio with eight men set out on this exploration, each one taking three mules as remounts.

"Thursday, October 12. Nothing happened today; the sick felt somewhat better.

"Friday, October 13. Nothing of importance.

"Saturday, October 14. We are anxiously awaiting the scouts, who returned in the afternoon. The sergeant[16] reported that they had travelled about twelve leagues without having learned anything of the port for which we were searching, and that they had reached the foot of a high white mountain range.[17]

"Sunday, October 15. We set out from the Laguna del Corral—a name given to it on account of a piece of fence that was constructed between the lake and a low hill in order to keep the animals penned by night with few watchmen. We marched very slowly, so as to cause the sick as little distress as possible; we contrived to carry them on side saddles, as the women in Andalusia travel. We proceeded for a league and a half, and halted near another small pond[18] in the bottom of a narrow and very pleasant little canyon, with plenty of firewood and pasture.

"The road was somewhat difficult. We directed our course to the north-northwest, without withdrawing far from the coast, from which we were separated by some high hills very thickly covered with trees.[19] They were the largest, highest, and straightest trees that we had seen up to that time; some of them were four or five yards in diameter. The wood is of a dull, dark, reddish color, very soft, brittle, and full of knots.

"This canyon was given the name of La Lagunilla.

"(To La Lagunilla, 1½ leagues. From San Diego 167½ leagues.)

---

[16] Sergeant Oretga, the famous scout and pathfinder.
[17] Ben Lomond mountains.
[18] Probably Valencia Lagoon.
[19] Redwood trees. That these trees are "full of knots," is of course a mistake.

"Monday, October 16. From La Lagunilla we came to the bank of a stream of good water, at a distance of two leagues to the west-northwest, travelling in sight of the sea. On our road there were two bad places over which we had to make a way. The first of these was a deep gully thickly grown with brush; the other, a ditch in which, to descend and ascend its sides, we had to open a path.

"This place was afterwards called El Rosario."[20]

"(To El Rosario, 2 leagues. From San Diego 169½.)

"Tuesday, October 17.[21] At a distance of two leagues from El Rosario we forded a river considerably swollen; the water reached to the girths of the animals. The descent to the river, and the ascent after we forded it, gave the pioneers much work in clearing and opening a way through a thicket that covered the river bottom. The same thing had been done at another stream which we had crossed shortly before.[22] We pitched our camp on the right bank of the river, which was named San Lorenzo."[23]

"(To the Rio de San Lorenzo, 2 leagues. From San Diego 171½.)

"Wednesday, October 18. We continued to follow the direction of the coast—west northwest—over high hills which were steep on the side towards the sea. The shore is practically without beach on the whole stretch of two leagues over which we travelled. There were three bad places in as many canyons[24] where we had to make a road. These canyons contained running water in very deep ditches, over which it was necessary to lay bridges of logs covered with earth, and fascines, so that the pack animals could cross. We pitched our camp[25] on a low hill near the shore, on the eastern side of a canyon which extended from the mountain range, and contained a stream of good water.

"This place was called Las Puentes."[26]

---

[20] Soquel Creek. November 22nd, the party camped again on Arroyo del Rosario.

[21] Portola's diary for the sixteenth and seventeenth is as follows: "The 16th, we proceeded for two hours, and halted on the banks of a river where there was very good pasture." "The 17th we traveled for two hours and a half; part of the way through a rough canyon between mountains and remainder on a good road. We found many watering places and two rivers. We halted beside one of these rivers, close by the sea, where the pioneers declared it would be possible for small ships to be sheltered to the northward." Portola G., Diary of Gaspar de Portola during the California Expedition of 1769-1770 in Publication of the Academy of Pacific Coast History. Vol. 1, No. 3, p. 37.

[22] This may have been the Rodeo Gulch.

[23] The name "San Lorenzo" means Saint Lawrence. This river was so named because it was discovered on St. Lawrence day. It flows today through the City of Santa Cruz.

[24] The canyons were probably those of the Meder, Baldwin, and Coja Creeks, immediately north of Santa Cruz.

[25] Near the mouth of Laguna Creek.

[26] Camp site again November 21st.

"(To Las Puentes, 2 leagues. From San Diego 173½ leagues.)

"Thursday, October 19. The march we made on this day was toil-some on account of the many ravines we came upon—there were seven or eight of them, all of which gave the pioneers much work, one especially because of its depth and the ruggedness of its sides. Into this fell the mule that carried the kettle, and for this reason the place was named the Barronco de la Olla.

"The coast turns more to the northwest, and is everywhere precipitous, excepting at the outlet of these ravines, where there is a short stretch of beach. To our right there were some whitish barren hills[27] that filled us with sadness, and there were days on which we missed the comfort of seeing natives.

"We halted on a very high hill and in sight of the white mountain range, which the scouts had discovered, where some clumps of pines could be seen. At the foot of the low hill, to the right and left, ran some streams containing plenty of water. Today we travelled for two leagues and a half.

"This place was given the name of Alto del Jamón.[28]

"(To the Alto del Jamón, 2½ leagues. From San Diego 176.)

"Friday, October 20. As we set out from the camp a very long slope presented itself; this we had to ascend after crossing the stream which flowed at the foot of the hill to the north. It was necessary to open the way with the crow-bar, and in this work we were employed the whole morning. We afterwards traveled a long distance along the backbone of a chain of broken hills, which sloped down to the sea. We halted on the same beach at the mouth of a very deep stream[29] that flowed out from between very high hills of the mountain chain. This place, which was named Arroyo or Canada de la Salud, is one league or a little more from Alto del Hamon. The coast in this locality runs northwest by north. The canyon was open towards the north-northeast, and extended inland for about a league in that direction.

"From the beach a tongue of land[30] could be seen at a short distance, west by north. It was low, and had rocks which were only a little above the surface of the water.[31]

---

[27] Ben Lomond mountains.

[28] Alto del Jamón was near Scotts Creek and was again the camp of the party on November 20th.

[29] Waddell Creek. The present coast highway between Santa Cruz and Half Moon Bay.

[30] Punta de Ano Nuevo.

[31] They remained in camp due to a storm until October 23rd, then went on up the coast leaving what is now Santa Cruz County behind.

"(To the Canada de la Salud, 1 league. From San Diego 177 leagues.)"[32]

From here the party marched until they came to San Francisco Bay, still believing that Monterey Bay was to be reached.

"Saturday, November 11. The commander decided to call together his officers in order to resolve jointly upon the course that should be suitable to adopt in the present circumstances . . . and resolved to return in search of the port of Monterey."[33]

Turning again to Miguel Costanso's diary to follow the return march, he states that the expedition entered the Santa Cruz country November 20th, crossed the San Lorenzo River November 22nd, and reached their old camping place November 26th.

"Monday, November 20. From the Punto de Ano Nuevo west to the Alto del Jamón, a distance of four leagues.

"(To the Alto del Jamón, 4 leagues. From the Estero de San Francisco 24½ leagues.)

"Tuesday, November 21. On this day's march we travelled for two leagues—as far as the place called La Puentes, where we halted.

"During these days we killed many geese; it was impossible to estimate the number of flocks of these birds which were seen at every step, so no lack of food was felt in the camp.

"(To Las Puentes, 2 leagues. From Estero de San Francisco 26½ leagues.)

"Wednesday, November 22. We forded the Rio de San Lorenzo without stopping there, and continued the day's march as far as the Arroyo de Rosario, a distance of four[34] leagues from the Alto del Jamón.

"(To El Rosario, 4 leagues. From the Estero de San Francisco 30½ leagues.)

"Thursday, November 23. This day's march brought us to the Laguna del Corral, a distance of three leagues and a half from El Rosario.

"(To the Laguna del Corral, 3 leagues. From the Estero de San Francisco 33½ leagues.)

"Friday, November 24. From the Laguna del Corral the scouts set out to examine the country with renewed care, as the road which it was necessary for the animals and men to follow extended somewhat inland. We halted one league farther on than the Rio del Pajaro, near a pond which was called Laguna del Macho.

[32] Costanso, M., The Portola Expedition of 1769-1770, etc., Vol. II, pp. 76-93, No. 4.

[33] Costanso, M., The Portola Expedition of 1769-1770, Diary of Miguel Costanso, in Publications of the Academy of Pacific Coast History, Vol. II, No. 4, p. 113.

[34] Six leagues.

"(To the south of the Rio del Pajaro, or to the Laguna del Macho, 2 leagues. From the Estero de San Francisco 35½ leagues.)

"Saturday, November 25. With the object of examining the coast with minuteness and care, we rested at the Laguna del Macho.

"The scouts returned at night without any important information. They only said that they had found out that the tracks which we had seen on the way to the port of San Francisco were not those of bison, but of very large deer, of an extraordinary appearance;[35] they had seen a herd of twenty-two near the shore. They said that these animals had high branching and heavy horns; that their color from the breast to the chin was white, the rest of the body a light chestnut, excepting the hind quarters, which likewise were white.

"Sunday, November 26. From the Laguna del Macho we came to our old camping place at the river which was thought to be the Carmelo,[36] a distance of five leagues and a half from the Laguna del Macho.[37]

"(To the Rio Carmelo, 5½ leagues. From the Estero de San Francisco 41 leagues.)"[38]

The party continued on around the bay and camped at the mouth of the Carmel River. Still not knowing that the outline of the bay had been carefully followed, the party returned to the Salinas River, and from here continued its march until it reached San Diego (January 24, 1770).

Wonder is often expressed that the expedition failed to find the bay, or rather the harbor, of Monterey, but to anyone familiar with the numerous bays and locked harbors of the coast of Lower California and the eastern shore of the Gulf of Mexico it does not appear so strange. They were accustomed to the Lower California coast line, and expected to find a sheltered harbor like at San Diego, but the Bay of Monterey, viewed from one angle only on the landside, looked to them like an open roadstead.

The expedition crossed Santa Cruz County twice from one end to the other; twice passed over or near the spot where the Cross was afterwards

---

[35] Probably elk.

[36] Salinas River.

[37] November 27th, the party marched on around the Bay and pitched their camp in sight of the Punta de Pinos. November 28th saw the camp pitched at the mouth of the Carmel River. The party remained there until December 10th, when it broke camp, reaching the old camping place on September 30th on the Salinas River, December 11th. Following the river it continued the march south. (Early History of the Santa Cruz Region, by Narcissa L. Parrish, a thesis in manuscript form.)

[38] Costanso, M., The Portola Expedition of 1769-1770, Diary of Miguel Costanso, in Publication of the Academy of Pacific Coast History, Vol. II, No. 4, pp. 161-327; see also Vol. I, pp. 91-159.

erected, but without suggesting the establishment of a Mission. When they returned and reported to Father Serra, the latter, after due reflection, expressed the opinion that they had passed the Bay of Monterey without recognizing it, and he was determined to find the place.

On his return to San Diego, Governor Portola found things in a bad condition. Up to February 11, 1770, there were fifty deaths—thirteen of them Catalonians of Fages' command. The Indians around San Diego were of the Yuma tribes, inclined to robbery, and a brush had taken place between the soldiers and the natives. Three Yumas and one Spaniard (shot through the throat with an arrow)[39] had been killed, while Father Vizcaino was shot through the hand.

Both Portola and Crespi wrote to the Viceroy and to the *visitador* that Monterey could not be found, and was an illusion, but as a consolation they also stated that they had found a much better harbor, the great land-locked Bay of Saint Francis.

Supplies running low, the Governor sent Rivera back to Lower California for succor. He departed on February 10th, 1770.[40]

The Fathers began a series of supplication services, and on the 19th a sail was sighted, while on March 23rd, the *San Antonio,* under command of Perez, sailed into port.

Their distress being relieved, Portola, Fages and Crespi, with twelve soldiers and five Christian Indians, once more took up their march north on April 17th. On the previous day, the *San Antonio* had likewise gone north with Perez, Serra, Costanso and Prat on board, all bound for Monterey. They arrived on May 31st, and found that the land party had arrived on the previous 24th.

Father Serra announced his arrival to his collaborator, Father Palou, in an historic letter which reads as follows:

"My Dear Friend: On the 31st of May, by favor of God, after a tedious and perilous voyage of a month and a half, the packet boat *San Antonio,* commanded by Captain Don Juan Perez, anchored in this beautiful Bay of Monterey, the same unchanged as it was left by the expedition of Don Sebastian Vizcaino, in the year 1603. It was a great consolation for me to be here, and the pleasure I felt increased with the news I received that same night, which was that the land expedition had arrived eight days previously, and with it Father Juan Crespi, all in good health. Our joy increased still more when, on the great feast of Pentecost, June 3rd, close by the same shore, and under the same oak tree where the

---

[39] August 15, 1769.
[40] He returned to San Diego in July with eighty mule-loads of provisions and some live stock.

San Carlos—Prisidio de Monterey, 1770

SAN CARLOS MISSION

Fathers of Vizcaino's expedition had celebrated, we built an altar, and the bell having been rung, and the hymn 'Veni Creator' intoned, we erected and consecrated a large cross, and unfurled the royal standard, after which I sang the first Mass which is known to have been sung at this point since 1603. I preached the same Mass, and at its conclusion we sang the 'Salve Regina' before a lovely image of our Blessed Lady, which had been placed above the altar; the statue was presented by His Excellency. Our celebration terminated with the singing of the 'Te Deum,' after which the officers took possession of the land in the name of the King of Spain. During the celebration a salute of many cannons was fired from the ship. To God alone be honor and glory. It is not for me to judge why this harbor was not found by the first expedition. It was a year last May since I received a letter from the land of Christians. Let me know the names of the reigning Pope, the canonization of Blessed Joseph Cupertino and Serafino Asculi, that I may mention it at the canon of the Mass, also if the canonization of Blessed Joseph Cupertino and Serafino Asculi has taken place; if there be any dead for whom we may pray. In a word, let us know whatever could be of interest to poor hermits sequestered, cut off from the society of men. I earnestly solicit you to send us two more missionaries, who, with the four here, will securely establish the Mission of San Buenaventura in the Channel of Santa Barbara, the land being better adapted to the purpose than San Diego, Monterey, or any other port yet discovered. I would not wish that for want of missionaries this Mission should be retarded. In truth, as long as Father Juan and I can stand, we will not be separated; for me it will be the greatest of trials to remain eighty leagues distant from another priest.

"Our supply of candles has run out here, as well as in San Diego; nevertheless, tomorrow we are going to celebrate the feast and procession of Corpus Christi, in order to chase away as many little devils as there may be found in this land. Write to the Visitor-General concerning the discovery of this harbor.

"Mission of San Carlos of Monterey, June 13th, Feast of St. Anthony of Padua, 1770.

"Your friend and companion,

"Father Junipero Serra."

A few years later Father Palou joined his friend, Father Serra, on one of his travels from San Francisco to Monterey. Following largely the route of Portola,[41] he came across the place where subsequently the Mission and the City of Santa Cruz were located. He wrote that he had found six

---

[41] Bancroft, History of California, Vol. I, pp. 234-235.

sites which he had deemed suitable for Missions. These were in the valley of San Pascual, near the modern city of Hollister, in the "plain of the great estuary," where the cross was left on San Francisquito Creek, in the vale of San Pedro Regalado, and that of San Pedro Alcantara between Spanish Town and Pescadero, *on the River San Lorenzo* at Santa Cruz, and on the River Pajaro at Watsonville.

"God grant," he wrote, "that in my day I may see them occupied by Missions, and in them assembled all the Gentiles who inhabit their vicinities, and that none of the latter die without holy baptism, to the end that the number of the children of God and of His Holy Church be increased, and also of the vassals of our Catholic Monarch."

With the founding of the Mission of San Carlos Borromeo de Monterey and the establishment of the Presidio on June 3, 1770, the Sacred Expedition of Galvez was ended. Portola's task was accomplished.

Word was sent by letter, carried by *cuirassier* Joseph Velasquez, to Viceroy Croix.

Portola turned the command over to Fages, and with Costanso and Perez sailed on the *San Antonio* to San Blas, landing there on August 1st. The Viceroy received word of his arrival on August 10th, prior to the receipt of the message carried overland by Velasquez.[42]

---

[42] Portola was promoted to a colonelcy and in 1776 was made Governor of Puebla, New Spain. He retired in 1784 and returned to Spain, at the age of 61.

CHAPTER IX

The Founding of the Missions (1770-1791)

BOOK I
Chapter IX

The Founding of the Missions

1770-1791

THE Mission of San Carlos Borromeo, known as the Carmel Mission at Monterey, was thus founded in 1770; it took twenty-one years before the Mission of Santa Cruz, on the same Bay, came into being, notwithstanding that Fathers Palou and Serra, already in 1774, pointed out the ideal location and advantages of the site.

When the news of the founding of the second Mission reached Mexico City there was great rejoicing. Both the State and the Church were happy; the taking possession of the country and the civilization of the savage race had begun. Great fiestas were organized; everyone participated.

But neither the authorities in Spain nor in Mexico City realized in what a perilous position their representatives in California were at the time of this merrymaking.

The history of the next twenty years is a story of struggle and heroic achievement. With admirable fortitude the Mission Fathers withstood the many hardships and dangers involved in all pioneering. These were shared not only by the military commanders, the officers and soldiers, but by the colonists, men, women and children, alike.

Anyone acquainted with the early history of the West knows that the sunbonnet of the pioneering mother covered as courageous a head as the helmet or sombrero of the bravest man. The padres, often as gentle as women, showed no less courage than the soldiers.

Until his death the indefatigable Father Serra was the mainspring and support of it all, the very exemplification of spiritual force, the embodiment of "the Mission-idea amongst the Indians." Many will read with awe and wonder the almost incomprehensible fervor of the Father President. Baptizing Indians was his passion; the saving of one soul was unspeakable joy. When he first attempted baptism at the San Diego Mission, the parents in sudden terror snatched their baby from under the Father's very hand, raised to sprinkle the papoose's face. Tears rolled down his face, as he believed that some unworthiness in himself had caused this contretemps, and he suffered accordingly.

This unbridled enthusiasm had its drawbacks, for it often carried him to great extremes. Setting out early in July, 1771, from Monterey, with an escort of eight soldiers and three sailors, in addition to a few Indian workmen, to found the mission of San Antonio de Padua, he arrived at the desired spot full of ardor. He had the Mission bells hung on a live oak tree, and after ringing them shouted: "Come, Gentiles, come to the holy Church. Come and receive the faith of Jesus Christ!"

His companion, Father Pieras, reminded the enthusiast that as yet there was no church; that there was not a Gentile within hearing, and that it would be well to stop the noise and go to work.[1]

This extreme zeal also explains the words of the Presidente when he heard of the murder of Padre Jayme at San Diego, where the latter met his martyrdom of torture at the hands of the Indians:

"Thanks to God that land is now watered; now the conversions of the Dieguenos will be effected."

Subsequently he wrote to the Viceroy and to the Guardian of his College that he was not discouraged, but only envied the happy (!) death of the Padre, which the latter had merited! (1775).

A curious old engraving shows him high above a motley group of listeners, holding in one hand a blazing torch, in the other a stone. While preaching he would violently beat his heart with a stone, or lacerate his flesh with a chain, or scorch it with a torch, illustrating the tortures of hell, in which he so firmly believed. This seemed to have a marked effect on the Indians, who answered by lamentations and prayers.

Serra's life was often darkened by collisions with the military and civil authorities. He was a single-hearted man with a great moral purpose—conversion of the Indians—and with small tolerance for the mixed motives of the political administrators. He has been accused of being arbitrary. His enemies called it pride and self-will, though all agree that this was never shown in his relation with the Indians or in his spiritual functions.

The "Sacred Expedition of Galvez" having ended with the founding of the second Mission, Father Serra was now burning with zeal to establish not only the one more Mission originally intended, but several more.

Matias de Armona had succeeded Portola as Governor of California. Already in August, 1770, Father Serra, entirely disregarding the views of everyone familiar with the conditions existing, and the fact that every new venture required extra military forces, while no more men at arms were available, had so importuned the Governor to proceed that de Armona sug-

[1] Palou, Vida, 122.

gested that in his opinion the vehement desire of his Reverence, in the face of the dearth of troops, was "a temptation of the evil one."

However, Serra's desires prevailed, and on November 12th, 1770, both Galvez and the Viceroy wrote Serra and Palou that five additional establishments (San Gabriel Arcángel, San Luis Obispo, San Antonio de Padua, Santa Clara and San Francisco de Asis) were to be started in California Alta, and that ten friars would be sent out.

San Antonio de Padua (near the present town of Jolon) and San Gabriel Arcángel (a few miles from Los Angeles) were founded in 1771. In that year both Viceroy de Croix and *Visitador* Galvez were recalled to Spain, de Croix to become captain general of the Kingdom of Valencia, Galvez *ministro universal* of the Indies.

In December, 1771, San Carlos Mission was, for various reasons, moved away from the Presidio of Monterey and re-erected in the Carmelo Valley.

The following year Mission San Luis Obispo de Tolosa was established, while all the Missions of Lower California were transferred from the Franciscans to the Dominicans, and the division line between the two apostolical jurisdictions was fixed fifteen leagues south of San Diego by a *concordato* dated April 7th of that year, thereby eliminating friction between the two ecclesiastical jurisdictions.

Unfortunately this did not bring peace amongst the quarreling ecclesiastical and secular authorities in the new land of Alta California.

When Governor Portola had returned to lower California in July, 1770, Lt. Don Pedro Fages was appointed *commandante-militar* of Alta California.

In his excessive zeal Father Serra appeared to have been importunate, if not unreasonable. Being on the ground, knowing conditions, and being responsible for the safety of the Missions and the general order in the territory over which he ruled as Vice-Governor, and having the courage of his convictions, Fages quite often discarded instructions to assist the missionaries in "whatever is necessary in order that the sovereign intentions of His Majesty may be realized." He mistrusted the Indians; in fact, a military party under the Commander himself had been stoned on the coast, and it had been necessary to kill a few of the Indians, to put an end to the attack.

The Padres themselves could not go any distance without an armed escort, hence Fages had good reason for caution, though the manner in which he handled the controversy must have often been offensive to the Father President and the missionaries.

Fages was not unmindful of the fact that the Bay of San Francisco should be further explored, and so on March 20th, 1772, he organized another expedition under his and Father Crespi's leadership, with fourteen soldiers and an Indian servant. On this trip the Bay was circled as far as the southeastern shore of San Pablo Bay. They reached there March 29th at a site near Berkeley; Crespi called it "una Baia Grande Redonda." They also saw the San Joaquin River, then called the Rio Grande de Nuestro P. San Francisco; on April 5th the party was back at Monterey. Point Reyes had of course not been reached, although that was the goal.

Don Felipe Barri had meanwhile succeeded Don Matias de Armona as Governor of the Californias, and Fages reported to the former, in the fall of 1772, that the desertions from the ranks which had recently taken place were largely due to the Mission Fathers, who protected the deserters in the San Diego church, which was regarded by them as a sanctuary.

The Mission Fathers countered that due to lax discipline the military were wont to capture the Indian women with the lasso, and this had given rise to tumult in the *rancherias,* as well as the infecting of the Indians with dreaded blood diseases, which had caused such a havoc in Lower California.[2]

In 1772, when conditions had reached the starvation point (see Appendix No. 1), and the differences of opinion had become acute, Fr. Serra took ship from San Diego to San Blas, toiled on foot from San Blas to Guadalajara with only an Indian boy as companion and guide, fell seriously ill with fever, but finally reached Mexico City in February, 1773.

It must not be thought that Fr. Serra's extreme zeal was shared by all the lay church people, or by the missionary colleges, who were in favor of a conservative course. Many had different views from Serra, and amongst those was the Guardian of the Franciscan College of San Fernando, the famous Fray Rafael Verger. He considered it necessary to moderate Serra's ardent wishes, notwithstanding the great respect he had for "the learning and beautiful endowments" of the spiritual leader in California Alta.

Fray Verger considered it unsound to proceed too fast, and therefore opposed the simultaneous founding of so many Missions as the Presidente insisted upon. But under the *Patronato* it was the Viceroy who held the final decision, and Serra concentrated his efforts on him.

The new Mexican Viceroy, Don Antonio Maria Bucareli y Ursua, Knight Commander in the Order of St. John, was an illustrious man.

---

[2] See Palou's *Vida and Noticias;* also charge of Padre Jayme of San Diego.

Descended both on his father's and mother's side from noted families, he was a man of broad sympathies and great experience. Prior to coming to Mexico, he had been Governor General of Cuba. He, as well as the Guardian of the College of San Fernando, received Fr. Serra with open arms.

Serra placed his grievances before the authorities in two memorials, containing in all thirty-three representations, dated respectively March 13th and April 22nd. One of his main complaints was against Fages, who meddled with the management of the neophytes, protecting his soldiers in their illicit relationships with Indian women, refusing to punish soldiers who were of notoriously loose conduct, and inclined to treat the Padres as subalterns.

The decree of the authorities was that on the demand of the Padres the soldiers could be relieved of guard duty at the Missions for irregularities, without the necessity of specifying the same; that a missionary in the management of his Missions stood in *loco parentis ("a que un padre de familia")* toward the neophytes, and therefore had the right of discipline; was the sole judge in all matters ecclesiastical; and the Mission letters were not to be intercepted by the Comandante.

Serra's difficulties being cleared up, he returned to California. He had also succeeded in convincing the Viceroy that it was impractical to supply the Alta California Missions by overland route, via Guaymas.

Guaymas is the most northerly of the four principal harbors on the west coast of Mexico—Guaymas, Mazatlan, San Blas and Acupulco. It is situate on the Gulf of California, while the other three face the Pacific Ocean. Prior to, and during the early Mission period, Guaymas was often used as a port of refuge for Spanish ships threatened by pirates, while later, and before the railroad traversed Arizona, goods shipped from California around Cape San Lucas were transferred here to light draft sternwheel steamers, which paddled up the Gulf and the shallow Colorado River as far as Yuma. Today it is a harbor with some shipping, but especially famous for its fishing, turtles abounding here.

This "overland" route ran only partly overland, the theory being that goods would be forwarded from Mexico City to Guaymas, then shipped across the Gulf to San Luis Bay, and from there on overland to Alta California by packtrain, via Velicata, San Diego, Santa Barbara, Monterey to San Francisco. The four main objections of Father Serra were:

First: that the transport would be 800 miles by land and 200 miles by sea, and often a very stormy sea, and it might take two years before a shipment would arrive.

Second: that the expense would be prohibitive, for it would take 1,500 mules, 100 horses and 100 guards and muleteers.

Third: that the passing and repassing of the packtrains, taking in consideration the character of the men usually engaged in this work, would brutalize the Indians and spread further dreaded diseases, retarding the spiritual conquest.

Fourth: that in journeying to and fro along the Santa Barbara Channel, the soldiers would debauch the native women, or the native women would corrupt the soldiers, and "it would be a miracle if thus the Indian men were not changed from quietude and docility into tigers."[3]

Father Serra considered the port of Mazatlan likewise too far north. This harbor was once a famous rendezvous for smugglers and pirates, for whom it was particularly well situate at the entrance of the Gulf. Today it is a rather prosperous city, being a division point on the international railroad between California points and Mexico City via Guadalajara.

Acapulco, which has been recently connected with the City of Mexico by a modern automobile road, was considered too far south, and his choice therefore fell on San Blas, which choice was approved by the Viceroy. (See Appendix No. 2.)

There was already in existence an excellent road between the capital and this harbor. This slave-built highway, paved with small, fitted cobblestones, started in the main street of San Blas, ran for endless miles over hot plains and high mountains, and was on each side flanked by stone fences to prevent stampeding of the pack animals by brigands. It finally terminated at Vera Cruz, for it was mainly used to carry treasure, protected by a heavy military guard, from the west seaboard to the east, whence it was transshipped to Spain.

True, the yearly galleon sailing from Manila, loaded deep with gold, silver, spices, silks and what not, usually planned to put in at Acapulco, whence a similar road led east, but sometimes these and other ships were compelled to find safety from storms or buccaneers in the harbor and under the guns of San Blas.

Lying at the mouth of the Santiago River, near the towns of Compestella and Tepic, it had at one time a population of over thirty thousand. The "forwarder of supplies" (we would call him now "the general business—traffic manager") resided here. It was here that all the Mission bells which afterwards called the Indian neophytes of California to or from labors or church, were cast in the foundry of the town, and it was decided

---

[3] B. C. Arch. Sta. Barbara, Vol. 1, p. 240.

that here all supplies were to be shipped to the California Missions by sailing vessels.

On instructions from Mexico City, Juan Jose de Escheveste, forwarder of supplies at San Blas, drew a plan in 1773 for the government of the Californias, political-military, as well as financial. This plan was adopted (see Appendix No. 3); it went into effect in January, 1774; both Californias were placed under one Governor, residing at the capital, Loreto. He received a salary of 4,000 *pesos*. California Alta was provided with one captain, three sergeants, eighty-two soldiers, eight mechanics, two storekeepers and four muleteers. The total expenditure for both Californias was to be about 120,000 *pesos* a year, of which Alta California, which had to have a Vice-Governor in the person of a Commandant, had the lion's share. The moneys were to be found out of the proceeds of the Pious fund, the salt-works near San Blas, a special subsidy from the King and the Royal Treasury.

The year 1774 proved to be an eventful one for California.

On May 9th the ship *Santiago* relieved the extreme distress existing at San Diego.

Serra had returned to Monterey on May 13th on the same ship.

Nine days later Captain de Anza arrived overland from his Presidio at Tubac (New Mexico), at San Gabriel Mission.

On May 23rd, Captain Rivera y Moncada arrived at Monterey; on the 25th Fages was replaced by Rivera. In the beginning the missionaries were greatly rejoiced by that change, but the new military commander proved, from the standpoint of the Padres, no great improvement on Pedro Fages.

Captain Don Juan Bautista de Anza, Sr., well-known Indian fighter of northern Sonora, who in 1739 fell on the battlefield against the Apaches, left a son, his namesake, who became still more famous than his father. In 1772[4] we find him commanding the Presidio of Tubac, New Mexico; he was then about fifty-seven years old and was the Bayard, the Chevalier *"sans blame ni reproche"* of the northern front of Mexico—a brave, prudent and energetic commander.[5] The younger de Anza, like his father, had urged the establishment of a route via the Gila-Colorado River Country to the North-west. Finally he obtained permission, after offering to pay the expenses himself, and started, guided by the Indian, Sebastian Tarabel, on the first expedition. This was largely in the way of a military recon-

---

[4] Richman, California under Spain and Mexico, p. 413.
[5] An extensive treatise containing several of the diaries has been published by Dr. Herbert Bolton, The California Expedition of Anza (5 vols.) U. C. Press.

naissance. On January 8th, 1774, he left Tubac, reaching Monterey April 18th, and returning to Tubac on May 26th, proving that the road was feasible. His course took him from Tubac to the Gila Colorado Junction; from there to the San Jacinto Mountains, and then northwest to San Gabriel Mission. The first part of the trip lay over deserts, lava beds and mountains, but it was the stretch between the Colorado and Gila, through the hills of sand to the Sierra Madre of Southern California, which brought the greatest hardships.

In the same year, Rivera, complying with the instructions of Viceroy Bucarelli to make a correct survey, commanded an expedition toward the Bay of San Francisco. Returning, the party crossed the San Lorenzo River (near the present city of Santa Cruz) on December 11th, 1774, and Father Palou's diary (he was the historian of the expedition) reads:

"After crossing this[6] and traveling a short space, we reached the San Lorenzo River, which is quite large and has a deep bed; its water reached the stirrups. The entire bed is lined with poplars, willows, alders, small poplars and other trees, and near the crossing, close to the mountains, there is much redwood timber. This site is suitable, not only for a pueblo, but even for a city, for it lacks nothing that is necessary, having good land, water, pasture, fire wood, and timber, all at hand and in abundance, and close to the beach of Monterey Bay. In fact, the settlement could be placed a quarter of a league distant from the bay and still have all the advantages mentioned.

"The river once crossed, we continued on our way over some mesa of arable land, gradually moving away from the beach to a distance of about one league from it. In the passage of two leagues of our way we came upon three arroyos, all having plenty of running water, and with their banks lined with a good growth of poplars, alders, willows, and some small live-oaks. All three streams came from above, from which it would be easy to make use of them to water the mesas of good land which they crossed on their way to discharge on the beach. Above the ridge runs the high range, which is peopled with redwood timber . . ."[7]

De Anza's success created a sensation, and after being promoted to Lieutenant Colonel of Cavalry as a reward for his achievement, he was commissioned by the Viceroy to lead a much larger expedition to Alta California, for the special purpose of founding the Mission and Presidio of San Francisco, and bringing settlers to California. It was to be the first "overland" trek to the Golden Gate. There being no settlers to be had in Tubac, he went to the little town of San Miguel Horcasitas, the place where the

---

[6] This refers to the arroyo of Santa Cruz identified as Majors Creek.
Palou, Fr. F., Noticias de la Nueva California, Tomo III, p. 209.

Governor of Sonora resided. After travelling around himself and sending word to the different pueblos that soldiers with families and some civil colonists would be enlisted, the colony slowly gathered at Horcasitas, while the horse herd and pack animals were cared for at Tubac.

Unfortunately, before a start could be made, the Apaches swooped down on Tubac and ran off most of the animals, and at Horcasitas a stampede caused the loss of more horses and mules.

Finally, on September 29th, the march started, with inferior and many overloaded animals, on the first leg of the journey two hundred miles to Tubac, which was reached on October 15th.

On October 23rd, 1775, de Anza set out from Tubac with a large company: three padres, Francisco Garcés, Pedro Font and Thomas Eciarc (Eixarch or Eisarch); two officers, Alférez Don Joseph Joachin Moraga and Sergeant Juan Pablo Grijalva; ten soldiers of the Presidio as escort to return with de Anza; twenty-eight other soldiers; twenty-nine wives of soldiers; one hundred and thirty-six persons of both sexes, belonging to the soldiers and to four volunteer families; fifteen muleteers; three servants of the padres; three cowboys; four of the Commander's servants; five Indian interpreters of the Indian tribes; and a commissary (Vidal); two hundred and forty persons all told.[8] Father Font makes computations which show that this figure is not exactly correct, and it is generally reported that several babies were born during the march and that one woman died shortly after they started. There were six hundred and ninety-five mules and horses, and three hundred and fifty-five cattle, mostly beef, to be killed on the way for food.

En route[9] praise to the Sacrament was sung each morning, after which camp was broken; likewise religious services were held at the end of each day.

After almost unbelievable hardships and the display of heroic fortitude, coupled with extreme humanity and consideration of the commander, who proved to be a great leader and frontiersman, and no less courage of the padres, the party arrived safely at San Gabriel Mission, in California, on January 4th, 1776. There it was learned that the Mission at San Diego had been burned in an Indian uprising on the night of November 5th, the previous year, and that Fray Luis Jayme had been killed. He had been seized, dragged away, and beaten to death. When his body was found, it was pierced with eighteen arrows and, as usual, had been horribly mutilated.

See Bolton's "Anza's California Expeditions," Vol. 3, pp. 1-2.
The course of the second expedition, though diverging here and there, was in the main the same as the first.

De Anza reported to the Vice-Governor of Alta California, Rivera y Moncada, who, supposedly from mixed personal and public motives, opposed the founding of the Presidio and the Mission San Francisco. He got into a quarrel with de Anza, and about the same time managed to get himself excommunicated on account of forcibly seizing an Indian named Carlos, who had claimed the privilege of asylum in a storehouse used for church purposes at San Diego, after the Mission church was burned down.

De Anza returned to Tubac, turning over to Lieutenant Moraga the actual founding of the San Francisco Mission and Presidio, which was finally accomplished. (See Appendix No. 4.)

Rivera y Moncada remained at Monterey until February, 1777, when Governor Felipe de Neve, appointed Governor on March 4th, 1775, removed his residence from Loreto to Monterey, and Rivera went to Loreto to assume the lieutenant governorship. (See Appendix No. 5.)

Don Teodoro de Croix (*caballero del orden Teutonico*, etc., etc.), a nephew of the former Viceroy of that name, a man of noble Flemish birth, had been appointed *Gobernador Comandante General en Jefe* of the Provinces of Sinaloa, Sonora, Californias and Nueva Vizcaya, a new *comandancia* general; in other words, *Comandante* General of the *Provincias Internas* or frontier provinces—that tier of northern provinces from Sonora to Texas, with Arispe, Sonora, as capital. Governor de Neve was directed by the Viceroy to report directly to de Croix at all times.

De Neve, who received the active support of de Croix, was ordered on December 25, 1776, "to establish various Missions, strengthening the line of communication between Loreto and San Francisco; to determine the practicability of maintaining the overland communication through a chain of posts from Los Angeles to Mexico City, via the Gila and Colorado Rivers, and especially to distribute lands to colonists and soldiers, in the hope of making the Province independent of subsidies of the royal treasury, and finally to endeavor to gain the Indians by "attention, love and gifts, and not by rigor;" also to settle if possible the usual bitter quarrels between the State and the Church, the former being represented by Governor Barri, the latter by Father Mora, President of the Dominicans. He had reached Monterey on February 3rd, 1777, where he learned of the new government measures which had been put into effect concerning Alta California.

In the meantime de Neve had advised the establishment of three more Missions and a presidio on the Santa Barbara Channel, and likewise had encouraged the third step of "reduction," to wit, the establishment of pueblos.

On November 29th, 1777, he caused the Pueblo de San Jose to be founded, and the Pueblo in Los Angeles in 1781, while during his period or shortly thereafter, five Missions were started: San Juan Capistrano, 1777; San Buenaventura, 1782; Santa Barbara, 1786, and Purisima Concepcion, 1787.

In the meantime it was found that the *reglamento* formulated by Jose de Echeveste needed some revision. Governor de Neve was invited by de Croix, in 1778, to make suggestions for its improvement. On June 1st, 1779, he submitted to de Croix a new *reglamento,* which was approved by the latter and subsequently by the King, under the hand of Jose de Galvez, Ministro de Las Indias, on October 24th, 1781.

Article 15 of the *reglamento* was adverse to the Mission plan, but the College of San Francisco, by its determined opposition, succeeded in nullifying its provisions to a very large extent.

On July 12th, 1782, de Neve was promoted to inspector general of all the troops under de Croix, and Pedro Fages became Governor of the Californias.

The years from 1776 to 1782 were filled with the usual bickerings and quarrels between the sacerdotal and military-civil authorities.

Outstanding was the quarrel between de Neve and Serra. The latter had been given for ten years the right of the sacrament of confirmation *(faculted de Confirmar)* by special order of the Pope, accompanied by "instructions." Father Serra made liberal use of this right, confirming before the end of 1778 about nineteen hundred neophytes as members of the Church.

The Governor, as representative of the *Patronato Real,* demanded that the documents granting the right be submitted to him for inspection, to ascertain if the Royal approval *(pasé)* had really been granted.[10] In this particular case the Viceroy of New Spain had also to affix his pasé.[11] Both requirements had been complied with, the latter on September 19th, 1776, but the documents did not reach Serra until 1778, when brought to San Francisco in September by the *Santiago.*

It was a long-drawn-out quarrel, reflecting little credit on either.

By 1780, twenty-five hundred persons had been confirmed, this number including about one hundred *gente de razon.*

Another cause for friction was the civil status of the Indians.

In 1776, Padre Antonio de los Reyes, about to become Bishop of Sonora, was requested by the Viceroy to give an opinion on the question of providing civil status for the Indian. He advised adherence to the plan

[10] Bancroft, History of California, Vol. I, p. 326.
[11] Engelhardt, Vol. II, p. 320.

of "reduction," mercifully applied by Cortes, rather than the Mission system. He suggested that the Provinces be each divided into *Custodia* districts. In the principal town of each district a *hospicio,* for six or more padres should be established under a director, reporting to the *comisario*-general. These padres should preach the faith in Spanish pueblos and mining camps, and the Indian *rancherias* (villages or hamlets).

Manuel de la Vega, the Franciscan *comisario*-general, had suggested four of these *custodias,* the one for Alta California to be located at San Gabriel.

In his famous paper[12] Father de la Vega stated:

"In all the *Provincias* the Indians should retain their natural liberties without obligation to perform community labor, or render personal services to the missionaries or secular judges. . . There should be put in effect the instruction of *Visitador* General Galvez, that lands be granted to the Indians in severality. . . . To the padre of the Mission there should belong only the garden of the Mission. The Indians should be compelled to live in pueblos of fifty or more families; one missionary priest should reside in each. . . ."

The idea of the *custodia* was therefore radically opposed to that of the Mission. The three Missionary Colleges of St. Francis brought united protest against this, but on suggestion of Bishop Reyes were overruled. However, the scheme was postponed and finally abandoned.

The differences of opinion continued. In December, 1778, de Neve began to enforce the so-called Alcalde law of the Indies, and instructed the padres at San Diego and San Carlos to have their neophytes choose two alcaldes and two *regidores.*

The natives were entirely unprepared to accept responsibility or exercise authority, and the padres, realizing this, protested against the folly, though they had to obey.

The consequences were as foreseen by the missionaries, for the new officials over which the padres had lost authority simply considered their office as a badge of unrestrained license.

Still, during all the quarrels, the missionaries had steadfastly carried on, and the founding of the Mission San Francisco de Asis and the Presidio of San Francisco was accomplished under the direction of Lieutenant Joseph Joachin Moraga, a capable officer, who had been second in command of the famous second de Anza expedition from Tubac to California. (See Appendix No. 6.)

Father Juan Crespi had died on the first of January of that year, and on August 25th, 1784, he was followed by Father *Presidente* Serra, who died as he had lived, simple of faith and pure at heart.

---

[12] S. A. Madrid, Bib. Nac. MS. No. 2550.

Shortly before his death Father Serra had been distressed by reports that the Franciscan Fathers, who had accomplished so much in Alta California, were to be displaced by the Dominicans. That this report had good foundation is shown by the fact that Bishop Antonio de los Reyes, of Sonora, a lay cleric, officially advised the new *Comandante*-general de Neve[13] to take this step on December 13th, 1783, half a year prior to Serra's death.[14] Even seven years earlier (September 16th, 1776), the Bishop had cited the Bull of Pope Innocent XI, dated October 16th, 1686, directing the reduction of Mission Indians to *pueblos formales.*[15]

Serra's funeral was an imposing one. The body was covered with *rosas de* Castilla, which he loved so much, and which were often mentioned in the diaries of the padres; it was guarded by soldiers with lighted candles, and was borne amid singing about the plaza to the church, in the presence of marines (Captain Jose Canizare's ship happened to lie at anchor before Monterey), men at arms, monks and Indians.[16]

Palou wrote a full report of the funeral to Guardian Sancho at Mexico City.

It may well be believed that Serra's heart broke under de Neve's regime, for while it appears that the fathers often grasped for the temporalities, the secular authorities appeared to be inclined to make an excessive, if not offensive, use of the powers granted to the temporal officers under the *Patronato,* interfering in purely spiritual matters.

At the death of his close friend, Serra, Palou, who had been President ad interim when Serra went to Mexico, became President *pro temporo,* in accordance with the expressed wishes of the friars. He had announced his plans to retire, but remained until a new President could be appointed and had taken charge, which was not until September, 1785. In the meantime he engaged in writing the life of Serra.[17]

A worthy successor to the labors and policies of Father Serra was Padre Fermin Francisco de Lasuen, born about 1720 in Vitoria, Spain, in the Basque Province of Alava. He had blessed Rivera's expedition in 1769, had served for two years (1773-1775) at San Gabriel, then for a year at San Juan Capistrano, and until 1785 at San Diego. He was less stern, less exalted than Serra, but full of piety and religious zeal. Upon

---

[13] De Croix had been promoted in that year to Viceroy of Peru.

[14] L. Sales, Noticias de la Provincea de California, pp. 71-75.

[15] The great Viceroy Antonio Bucareli, who had always taken an intense interest in Alta California and who was the great official figure standing behind the colonization plans of the Province, had died on April 9, 1779, after 14 years of service in the Colonies. Alta California owes him a great debt of gratitude.

[16] Palou's Vida de Serra, pp. 271-305.

[17] English translation by C. Scott Williams, published by George Wharton James, with notes (1913).

his death in 1803 he had served thirty years as missionary in California, and had been President for eighteen years.

He gave the Missions a prudent and wise administration, and they prospered under his able guidance.

Though more conciliatory than Father Serra, he soon had trouble with the State authorities. The Missions had been requested to furnish the Governor with inventories and statistics, and de Neve had ordered in 1782 that no padre be accorded a military escort save when visiting a presidio or *rancherio* to hear confessions.

After de Neve's departure the duty fell on Pedro Fages to enforce these orders, with the results to be expected. Criminations and recriminations filled the air, until on September 26th, 1785, Governor Fages determined to submit the matter to the Viceroy at Mexico City. The result was a kind of compromise judgment.

The Mission Fathers were sorely beset with difficulties. There was the ever-threatening danger of the *Custodia;* the obligatory presence of the Indian *alcaldes,* and *regidores,* who were often worthless and offensive; the fear of the *reglamento,* and the constant menace of the Pueblos, where the Indians—and white settlers—in accordance to Father Lasuen, "with their scandals and libertinism were a constant danger to the adjoining Missions."

Governor Fages, who besides his official troubles had many domestic ones, was relieved in May, 1790, but the formal transfer was not made until April 16th, 1791, to Antonio Romeu by Jose Joaquin de Arrillaga, the Lieutenant Governor of Lower California, at Loreto.

Fages had been in Monterey for more than seven years and was fifty-six years old. When he left, there were in Alta California nine Missions, four Presidios—San Diego, Monterey, San Francisco and Santa Barbara—besides two Pueblos—one at San Jose with a population of eighty, and one at Los Angeles with one hundred and forty people.

Governor Romeu arrived at Monterey on October 13th, 1791, but was sickly and died on April 9th, 1792. He was buried at San Carlos Mission, Monterey.

An epoch had now arrived when the history of California was to take a new course and loom larger on the international horizon.

Russia had never ceased to claim its right to California, holding that it belonged naturally to the Russian Empire, inasmuch as it was supposed to have been peopled from Siberia.

Already in 1769 and 1771 it was learned in Madrid that a Russian official of the Navy, Tscherikow, had made an exploration voyage from Kamtchatka towards America.

The Spanish Government, still hoping to make the whole coast safe for the galleons from Manila, which at stated times navigated along the Western shore, and likewise wishing to make California a haven of rest for the ships' crews, sometimes near death from scurvy and hardships encountered, decided that prompt action was necessary.

Consequently, in the beginning of 1774, Juan Perez, a trusted and energetic navigator, who had been at San Diego, but was then stationed as naval officer at San Blas, was ordered to proceed with his ship, the *Santiago,* up the coast to 60 degrees latitude, and take possession—by planting crosses, etc., in the name of the Spanish King (Carlos III). He stopped at San Diego to put Father Serra on shore; went to Monterey, where Fathers Crespi and de la Pena joined him as chaplains and diarists, and surveyed the coast from Mendocino to Queen Charlotte Island in latitude 55, though nowhere was it possible to make a landing, nor was 60 degrees latitude reached. The usual hardships, caused by scurvy, were experienced on this voyage, and though no physical symbols of Spain's authority had been placed on shore, she considered that her title had been strengthened by discovery and exploration.

The *Santiago* sailed again from San Blas on the 16th of March, 1775, this time under command of Lieutenant Bruno Heceta, with the small schooner *Sonora,* thirty-six feet over all, which came under the command of Lieutenant Bodega y Quadra, after its first commander, Juan de Ayala, had been transferred to the San Carlos. Bodega discovered the mouth of the Columbia River and reached 58 degrees latitude.

Perez, who had accompanied the *Santiago* as *piloto,* found on one of the islands along the coast a bayonet and sword in possession of an Indian; it must have been obtained from the Russians, but there was no other sign of them.

Learning that Captain James Cook had been promised a grant of Parliament of twenty thousand pounds if he could locate the famous Straits of Anian, and that he was preparing two ships, the *Resolution* and the *Discovery,* for the trip, the Spanish Government laid plans for another expedition from San Blas to the North, but for several reasons this did not get under way until the 11th day of February, 1779. Two frigates, the *Princessa* and the *Favorita,* built respectively at San Blas and Lima, set sail under the command of Lieutenants Ignacio Artego and Bodega y Quadra.

On July 1st they reached a latitude of 60 degrees, but on account of scurvy were compelled to return, anchoring before San Francisco on September 15th.

Meanwhile Captain Cook had visited the northwest coast, and had met his death at the hands of the Kanakas in the Hawaiian Islands.

Finally Captain George Vancouver arrived in Monterey, in November, 1792, the year after the founding of the Santa Cruz Mission on this Bay.

Internally a new era had also been dawning, and under Governor Diego de Borica, a sagacious ruler, who took charge in May, 1794, many of the old policies of California passed into history. The new Mission of the Holy Cross was the first religious establishment to be reared under the new order.

Before describing the founding of the Mission of Santa Cruz and its subsequent history, it may be well, in order to understand fully the event, to consider the condition and the importance of Alta California in general, and the Missions which had come into existence in the last twenty-one years in particular.

BOOK II

CHAPTER X

Facts generally applicable to all Missions in Alta
California after their foundation.

BOOK II

Chapter X

Facts Generally Applicable to All Missions in Alta California
After Their Foundation

WHAT were these Missions really and how were they operated?
We have seen that the lands "in the Indies" had all been
granted by the Pope as a feudal fief to the Crown of Castile in
sovereignty. The King held the land in private dominion until he granted
it to others. The Missions, being instruments of State, were not granted
any of the land they occupied, this remaining the property of the government, the theory being that these lands would eventually belong to the
natives, whenever they should be fitted to profit by their possession.

When we read that the Missions occupied vast stretches of land, both
for grazing and agricultural purposes; that the territory of one Mission
joined that of the other; that the Missions had possession of all the known
land along the Coast in Alta California, except that which was held in the
presidio boundaries, or incorporated in the villas or pueblos, it should be
understood that this was only a temporary occupancy, at sufferance, to be
terminated at the will of the government.

Subsequently the Spanish—and later its successor, the Mexican Government—did grant large ranchos occupied by the Missions to private
settlers (not Indians); the latter Government, under the Mexican Colonization Law of 1824 and the subsequent regulations of 1828.

The Mission system itself was fundamentally simple and efficient.
The friars in charge of each Mission were directly responsible to the
Father President; he in turn to the Guardian, President of their College
in Mexico City. A purchasing officer, the *procurador,* was the fiscal officer
of the Guardian; he always remained in Mexico City. It was he who purchased the supplies to be sent out, which were paid for from the regular
stipends derived from the Pious Fund, from the returns of the drafts
given by the presidio commanders for goods furnished, and later from
selling produce to ships visiting the coast.

There was also a general agent at San Blas attending to the shipping—
the forwarder of supplies.

There were, therefore, only a few functionaries, but they had large
and direct responsibilities.

That part of the income supporting the Missions derived from the
Pious Fund continued until Spain began to withdraw property and cash

from it to finance its war against Portugal and England. Later Mexico followed this course of plunder. During the revolutionary times, the bills of exchange on the Government issued by the presidio commanders remained unpaid, and as the Missions' costs mounted higher and higher, bankruptcy and ruin threatened them.

From the Pious Fund the Government allowed $1,000 to be appropriated for the establishment of each Mission, including construction of buildings, church accessories, agricultural implements, etc. The neighboring Missions were ordered to contribute what they could of livestock, vestments and altar accessories. Each of the Fathers was entitled to a stipend of $400 a year. This was paid to the College *sindico,* who from this money purchased the articles desired by the friars. Much of the allowance, often one-half, was used for transportation costs. Actual money hardly ever reached the friars from Mexico. The padres were therefore paid the same salary, or less, than a sergeant, and often this modest stipend was, for various reasons, withheld by the authorities.

Sometimes the Fathers obtained some small cash contributions for saying Mass, from the soldiers or colonists, all of which went into the Mission fund. For themselves they retained nothing.

From the earliest days it had been established that no religious should be permitted to dwell alone in a town, castle, or parish church, but must reside in his convent. If he should be stationed elsewhere, he must live in company with another friar in order to strengthen and fortify him to battle with the flesh.[1] Therefore there were always two priests assigned to each Mission. This rule, for obvious reasons, was considered especially essential in frontier Missions.

Scholastic teachers, through the Mission period, and especially in the beginning, were very scarce. The Fathers, as messengers of the Gospel, taught the Christian Catholic faith; they had in addition to take care of the moral and physical welfare of their charges, just emerging from savagery. There was, at least in the beginning, no money to pay for books, necessary articles for schoolrooms, or traveling expenses to bring teachers from Mexico City or Spain.

Without permission of the Government, the Superior in Mexico City could not send a third assistant, much less a lay brother.

The Government constantly complained about the expense, and as a means of relieving the Pious Fund, which showed a deficit, Governor Borica suggested to the Viceroy, on November 16th, 1797, that if it was

---

[1] Letter of Fr. Pedro Callejas to Viceroy Branciforte, dated October, 1797. Engelhardt, Vol. 2, p. 541.

necessary to maintain two missionaries at each Mission (the authorities had endeavored to reduce the number to one at each post), then the two together should only receive the stipend of one.

This was vigorously and rightly opposed by the Guardian of the College of San Fernando, to which the California friars belonged. Fortunately, Fr. Miguel Lull, the Guardian, was successful in this opposition.[2]

The construction plan of the Missions was more or less uniform. As a rule the buildings were placed in the form of a hollow square. The church proper was the front, the quarters of the priests and the houses of the Indians forming the wings. These quarters were generally colonnaded with a series of semi-circular arches, all covered with red tiles. As in most Spanish or Moorish structures, there was a court, called a *patio,* in the center, which was often landscaped with gardens, walks, a fountain, etc. Upon this court opened all apartments and quarters, including workshops, storehouses and schoolrooms.

Most Mission churches had one or more towers, in the belfry of which the Mission bells were placed. Santa Cruz Mission had only one. The domes were reached by a series of steps at each "corner" of the half dome, giving easy access to the surmounting cross.

In building these structures there was often a shortage of hardware, especially nails, and wooden pegs and rawhide were resorted to for fastenings.

Both in facades and campaniles the Missions showed great variance in details. While there was likewise a good deal of variety in the columns used, the diversification in the detail was not any greater than in the arches themselves. This showed as well in span as in form, but all were kept within the boundaries of good architectural taste.

Heavy and massive buttresses were provided for most of the Mission churches and other principal buildings. These were obviously employed to minimize the danger of earthquake shocks, which did so much damage.

While the Mission architects were dominated by one common style, within this style many variations were used.

The term "Mission style," so liberally used to indicate a certain kind of heavy furniture, is rather misapplied, for there was comparatively little household furniture in the modern sense of the word, and what there was, was manufactured principally of material close at hand, such as rough lumber, raw hide, tanned cowhide with the hair on it, etc., and was very

[2] Engelhardt, Missions and Missionaries of California, Vol. II, p. 543.

simple indeed. "Mission style" is simply a name applied for commercial purposes.[3]

At the Missions the girls from about eleven years old upward, the single women and wives whose husbands were absent, passed the night together in a separate building. Matrons were in charge and the place was called *Monjerio* or nunnery. This was necessary on account of the actions of many of the white men and because, according to Indian custom, unmarried women were the public property of the men of the tribe. The girls remained under tutelage until they married, marriage being blessed in the church, and the new couple assigned an adobe dwelling. The girl, however, was free to accept or repel the suitor for a husband.[4]

That this method of handling the Indian women was wise is proven, for after the secularization of the Missions these women generally fell back into a degrading condition.

Instruction in ecclesiastical matters was given in Castilian, as soon as the Indians could be made to understand. This was necessary, for a number of languages were spoken in the different *rancherias* or native villages, making it frequently impossible for Indians of neighboring places, meeting at the Missions, to understand one another. Many Fathers learned several of the dialects, enabling them to talk to the natives in their own idiom.[5]

The missionaries, standing *in loco parentis* towards the neophytes, managed the Mission Indians as "a father would manage his family," and exercised authority in accordance to the existing notions of parental authority.

The daily routine was about as follows: At sunrise the bell called to church all the adults and children over nine years of age. Holy Mass was celebrated by one of the Fathers, whilst the other recited aloud the prayers and the *Doctrina* with the Indians. At the conclusion the *Alabado* was sung in accordance to a melody which was the same at all the Missions. During certain seasons of the year, instruction in Spanish followed the celebration of the Mass. All then took breakfast. This consisted of *atóle*,[6] a kind of gruel made of corn or grain which had been roasted before it was ground. It was prepared in large iron kettles. Every family sent in bark or earthen vessels for its share, which was ample. The girls and young men took their meals in their respective quarters. After breakfast,

---

[3] George Wharton James, In and Out of the California Missions, p. 342.
[4] Engelhardt, Missions and Missionaries of California, Vol. II, p. 260.
[5] Id. p. 248.
[6] Derived from the Aztec word *atolli,* or *atlaolli.*

which lasted about three-quarters of an hour, the men and larger boys went to the work assigned in the field, among the live-stock or in the shops. The girls and single women found occupation under the care of the matron. At noon the Angelus Bell announced the time for dinner. This was served in the same manner as the breakfast, but consisted of *pozóle*,' a gruel to which meat, beans, peas, lentils, or *garbanzos* were added, according to the seasons and the means of the Mission. Two hours were allowed for the meal and for rest. At two o'clock work was resumed, one of the missionaries encouraging the neophytes by his words and example. At about five o'clock work ceased, and the whole population went to church for the recitation of the *Doctrina* and religious devotions. On these occasions the Father would add an instruction in Spanish or Indian, as appeared expedient for his polyglot audience. As usual, the *Alabado*' concluded the exercises. At six o'clock supper was served in the shape of *atóle*. The remainder of the evening was passed in various amusements, which the Indians enjoyed with much latitude, being permitted to indulge in the pastimes of their savage state "as long as decency and Christian modesty were not offended."

Besides the *patios* there were private walled gardens at every Mission, mostly with waving palms, fountains, olive and fruit trees. Connected with the Missions were broad vineyards and orchards.

The friars were forced, by their very situations, to entertain many strangers, which they did royally. Travelers' rooms were kept at each Mission. A man might ride from San Diego to Monterey and afterwards to San Francisco, and be a guest each night at a Mission, where he and his horse were taken care of without charge, and if necessary he could get a free mount from the Mission herds.

It is small wonder that a departure from the hard and ascetic rules of living, originally preached and practiced, finally came about, though not without objections, for sometimes a *Presidente* tried to discourage this "worldliness." A zealous one, ascertaining that the friars occasionally rode in the crude Mission carts instead of walking or riding a mule, had all the carts burned. At another time it was found that the friars, to the scandal of their superior, were so luxurious that they carried silver watches and used stockings and shoes instead of sandals. The watches were confiscated and that kind of footgear prohibited.

' Derived from the Aztec word *pozoatl*.
' Praise of the Sacrament.

Still, no matter how conservative the leaders **were**, the natural consequences of the march of events could not be stopped entirely, and conditions were bound to change materially.

The military gradually lost much of their early religious fervor and devotion, and the ecclesiasts became administrators of large and prosperous estates, their attention being increasingly taken up with worldly considerations.

CHAPTER XI

Life at the Missions.

BOOK II
Chapter XI

Life at the Missions

MISSION life must have been a strange existence, even viewed from the standards of a century and a half ago. It was probably somewhat like the one existing under the patriarchal rule of the ancient Jews.

Many accounts have been given, but perhaps it will be best to give the impressions of an educated foreign eye witness who visited the Missions.

The famous French navigator, Jean Francois Galoup de la Perouse, had sailed from Brest, France, on the 11th day of August, 1785, with the frigate *La Boussole*. A second vessel, *l'Astrolabe,* was in charge of M. de Zangle. The object of the voyage was scientific observations.

They entered the Harbor of Monterey on the 14th of September, 1786, where they were received by the Spanish transports *La Princesa* and *La Favorita*. After that they were invited by Presidente de Lasuen and the other Mission Fathers to visit the Mission and thoroughly study the methods in vogue.[1]

De la Perouse was entertained at the Mission San Carlos, on the south side of the Bay of Monterey, sixteen years after its establishment. In 1798 his description of his voyage around the world was published in two volumes. What he wrote about San Carlos is equally applicable to the surrounding country and its inhabitants; and these conditions must have likewise prevailed at the soon to be established Mission at Santa Cruz, on the north side of the Bay.

The following abstract from his book is, for our purposes, most illuminating:

"The Bay of Monterey, formed by New Year's Day Point to the northward, and Cypress Point to the southward, is eight leagues[2] across at its entrance in that direction, and nearly six in depth to the eastward, where the lands are low and sandy. The sea rolls in to the very foot of the dunes of sand with which the coast is skirted, with a noise which we heard at above a league distance. The lands to the northward and southward of this bay are elevated and covered with trees. Ships intending to

---

[1] La Perouse, Voyage, etc., tom. II. Cap. i, 16.
[2] 1 league = 3 statute miles (U. S.).

113

put in here must keep the south shore aboard, and after doubling Cypress Point, which stretches out to the northward, they will see the presidio, and may drop anchor in ten fathoms[2] of water within and behind this point, which shelters them from the sea breezes.

"The Spanish ships that intend making a long stay at Monterey are accustomed to approach within one or two cables"[4] length of the shore, in six fathoms of water, where they moor to an anchor which they bury in the sand of the beach. They are then sheltered from the south winds, which are sometimes very strong, though not dangerous, as they blow off shore. We got soundings all over the bay, and anchored four leagues from the land in sixty fathoms of water, over a bottom of soft mud. But the sea is very heavy there, and ships can only remain a few hours at such an anchorage, while waiting for daylight or the clearing of a fog. At the full and change of the moon it is high water at half-past one, and the tide rises eleven feet; as the bay is very open, its drift is almost imperceptible; I never knew it more than half a knot an hour. I cannot describe the number or familiarity of the whales that surrounded us. They were continually blowing at the distance of half a pistol shot, and occasioned a very disagreeable smell in the air. This was an effect unknown to us, but the inhabitants informed us that the water blown by whales always had that quality, which spread to a considerable distance. But it would doubtless have been no new phenomenon to the fishermen of Greenland or Nantucket.

"The coasts of Monterey Bay are covered by eternal fogs,[5] which render it difficult of approach, though in other respects there scarcely exists a bay more easily entered, for there is no sunken rock a cable's length from the beach, and if the fog is too thick, there is anchorage everywhere, till a clear interval exposes distinctly to view the Spanish settlement, situated in the angles formed by the southern and eastern shores.

"The sea is covered with pelicans, but it appears these birds never go above five or six leagues from land, so that navigators who perceive them during a fog will be certain they are within that distance. We saw them for the first time in this bay, and I have since learned that they are very common on all the coast of California. They are called by the Spaniard alcatras.

---

[2] 1 fathom = 6 feet.
[4] 1 cable length = 720 feet (U. S.).
[5] This applies to some extent to the southern shore of the Bay, near the present city of Monterey, but very much less to the northern shore near Santa Cruz.

"A lieutenant colonel, who resides at Monterey, is Governor of both the Californias.[6] Though his government is eight hundred leagues in circumference, his real command extends but to two hundred and eighty-two soldiers of cavalry, who garrison five small forts and furnish detachments of four or five men to each of the twenty-five Missions, or parishes, into which Old and New California are divided. These little guards suffice to keep in subjection about fifty thousand wandering Indians, spread over this vast extent of the American continent, and of whom nearly ten thousand have embraced Christianity. These Indians are generally small and feeble, and afford no proof of that love of independence and liberty which characterizes the northern Indians, to whose arts and industry they are strangers. Their complexion very nearly resembles those negroes whose hair is not woolly; that of this nation is long, and very strong, and they cut it four or five inches from the roots. Several of them have beards, while others, according to the missionaries, never had any, though it is an undecided point in the country itself.

"The Governor,[7] who had traveled much in the interior, and had lived with the savages during fifteen years, assures us those who had no beard had extracted it with bivalve shells, used as pinchers. But the President of the Missions, who had resided in California an equal length of time, maintained the contrary. Thus travelers are wholly unable to form a decision, and as we cannot assert what we have not witnessed, we must acknowledge we only saw beards on one-half of the number of adults, some of them having it so thick as to have made a respectable figure, even in Turkey or the environs of Moscow.

"These Indians are very adroit in the use of the bow, and killed the smallest birds in our presence. It is true, their patience in getting near their prey is inconceivable. They conceal themselves while creeping up to it, and rarely pull the bow till within fifteen paces.

"Their industry in hunting is still more surprising. We saw one of them crawling on all fours with a stag's head fixed on his own, as if he were browsing the grass, and performing his part so well that all our hunters would have fired at him at a distance of thirty paces, had they not been apprised of that maneuver. Thus they approach a herd of stags within reach and kill them with their arrows.

"Loretto is the only presidio of Old California on the eastern coast of that peninsula. Its garrison consists of fifty-four cavalrymen, and furnishes detachments to the fifteen following Missions, of which the functions are

---

[6] Lower and Upper California.
[7] Pedro Fages.

performed by the Dominican monks, who have succeeded the Jesuits and Franciscans. These last, however, remain in undisturbed possession of the ten Missions of New California. The fifteen Missions of the Department of Loretto are San Vicente, San Domingo, El Rosario, San Fernandez, San Francisco de Borgia, Santa Gertrude, San Ignacio, La Guadalupe, Santa Rosalia, La Concepcion, San José, San Francesco Xavier, Loretto, San José de Cabo Lucar, and Todos los Santos. About four hundred Indian converts, collected round their fifteen parishes, are the only fruit of the long apostleship of the various religious orders, who have successively undertaken this painful duty. In the history of California by Father Venegas, we may read an account of the establishment of the fortress of Loretto, and the various Missions it protects, whereby, comparing their past conditions with that of the present year, it is evident that their progress is very slow.

"As yet there is only one Spanish village. It is true, the climate is unhealthy, and the Province of Sonora, which forms the boundary of the Mar Vermejo, or Red Sea, to the eastward, and California to the westward, is much more attractive to the Spaniards, who find there a fertile soil and abundant mines—objects far more important in their eyes than the pearl fisheries of the peninsula, which require a considerable number of slaves who can dive, and these often very difficult to procure.

"Yet North California, notwithstanding its great distance from Mexico, appears to combine infinitely greater advantages. Its first settlement, which is San Diego, commenced only on the 26th of July, 1769, and is the presidio most to the southward, as that of San Francisco is the most northerly. This last was constituted on the 9th of October, 1776; that of Santa Barbara's Channel in September, 1781, and Monterey, now the capital and seat of government of both Californias, on the 3rd of June, 1770. The roadstead of this presidio was discovered in 1602, by Sebastian Vizcaino, commodore of a small squadron equipped at Acapulco, by order of the Viscount of Monterey, who was Viceroy of Mexico. Since that epoch the galleons, on their return from Manila, have sometimes put into this bay to procure refreshments after their long runs; but it was not till the year 1770 that the Franciscans established their Mission there. They have now ten, comprehending five thousand one hundred and forty-three converted Indians. The following table will show their names, dates, number of baptized Indians, and the presidios on which they depend. I will here observe that with the Spaniards presidio is a general name for all forts, whether in Africa or America, placed in the middle of a country of infidels, and implying that there are no other inhabitants than the garrison, which resides within the citadel.

Parishes	Presidios on which they depend	Date of their foundation	Number of Indians converted
San Carlos	Monterey	June 3, 1770	711
San Antonio	Monterey	July 14, 1771	850
San Luis	Monterey	Sept. 1, 1772	492
Santa Clara	San Francisco	Jan. 12, 1777	475
San Francisco	San Francisco	Oct. 9, 1776	250
San Buena Ventura	Santa Barbara	May 3, 1782	120
Santa Barbara	Santa Barbara	Dec. 4, 1786	...
San Gabriel	Santa Barbara	Sept. 8, 1771	843
San Juan Capistrano	San Diego	Nov. 1, 1776	544
San Diego	San Diego	July 16, 1769	858
			5,143

"The piety of the Spaniards[8] has, at a heavy expense, kept up these Missions and presidios to the present time, from no other motive than to convert and civilize the Indians of these countries—a system far more praiseworthy than that of avaricious individuals who seem invested with national authority merely to commit with impunity the cruelest atrocities. The reader will soon perceive that a new branch of commerce may procure to Spain more solid advantages than the richest mines of Mexico, and that the salubrity of the air, the fertility of the soil, the abundance of furs, for which they have a certain market in China, give this part of America the most important advantages over Old California, whose unwholesomeness and infertility cannot be compensated by a few pearls collected from the bottom of the sea.

"Before the Spaniards settled here, the Indians of California only cultivated a little maize, and almost entirely subsisted on fishing and hunting. No country abounds more in all sorts of fish and game. Hares, rabbits, and stags are very common, otters and sea wolves as abundant to the northwards, and they kill in winter a very large number of bears, foxes, wolves, and wild cats. The coppices and plains are full of little gray crested partridges,[9] which, like those of Europe, flock together, but in covies of three or four hundred. They are fat and very well flavored.

"The trees are the habitation of the most charming birds, and our ornithologists stuffed many varieties of the sparrows, blue jays, tomtits, spotted magpies, and troupiales. Among the birds of prey were the white-headed eagle, the large and small falcon, goss hawk, sparrow hawk, black vulture, great horn owl, and the raven.

"The waterfowl found on pools and on the seaside were the mallard, the gray and white yellow-crested pelican, goelands of various kinds, cor-

---

[8] Pious Fund, see supra.
[9] Now called California quail.

morants, curlews, ring-necked plover, small gulls, and herons; and we killed and stuffed a promerops, which most ornithologists have thought to belong to the old hemisphere.

"The fertility of the soil exceeds conception. All sorts of leguminous plants are in great perfection, and we enriched the gardens of the Governor and Missions with various seeds we brought from Paris. They were perfectly well preserved, and will increase the stock of their enjoyments.

"The harvest of maize, barley, wheat, and peas can only be compared to those of Chile, a fertility of which the European husbandman can form no adequate idea. Its medium product of corn is from seventy to eighty fold, and the extremes ninety and one hundred. Fruit trees are as yet very scarce, but the climate is perfectly adapted to them, being nearly that of our southernmost provinces in France. At least the cold is never more severe, though the heats of summer much more moderate,[10] in consequence of the perpetual mists, which fecundate the earth with constant moisture.

"The forests contain the pineapple, fir, cypress, evergreen oak, and western plane tree, all thinly sown. A greensward, very pleasant for walking, covers the earth within them, and they have openings of many leagues, forming vast plains amid the surrounding forests, and abounding in every sort of game. The soil, though very fertile, is sandy and light, owing, I imagine, that excellence to the humidity of the air, as it is very ill watered. The nearest stream to the presidio is at a distance of two leagues; it is a rivulet which runs near the Mission of San Carlos, and called by the ancient navigators Rio de Carmel. This distance from our ships was too great for us to water there; we got it from the ponds behind the fort, though the quality was indifferent, hardly dissolving soap. The Rio de Carmel, which furnishes a salubrious and agreeable beverage to the missionaries and their converts, might, with little labor, be made to water their garden.

"It is with the liveliest pleasure that I describe the wise and pious conduct of these monks, who so fully correspond with the object of their institution, though I shall not conceal what I deem reprehensible in their internal administration. But I declare that, good and humane in their individual capacity, they temper the austerity of the rules laid down by the superiors of their orders with the mildness and benevolence of their private character. I confess that, more attached to the Rights of Man than theology, I should have wished them to combine with the principles of Christianity a legislation calculated to make citizens of a race of men, whose

---

[10] It is clear that La Perouse was only acquainted with the Coast Ranges and not with the interior valleys of California.

condition scarcely differs from that of the negroes of our colonies, in those plantations which are conducted with most mildness and humanity.

"I am perfectly aware of the extreme difficulty of this new plan. I know these men possess few ideas, still less steadiness, and, if their conductors cease to consider them as children, run away from those who have had the labor of instructing them. I know, too, that reasoning is almost lost upon them, and that an appeal to their senses is necessary, and that corporal punishment with a double proportion of rewards has hitherto been the only means adopted by their governors. But it is possible for men influenced by ardent zeal and possessed of extreme patience to demonstrate to a small number of families the advantages of a society founded on the rights of nations, to establish among them the institution of property so engaging to the rest of mankind, and by this order of things to induce everyone to cultivate his field with emulation, or devote himself to some other species of industry.

"I allow the progress of this new mode of civilization would be very slow, the necessary labor of it very painful and tedious, and the scenes of action of very remote distance, so that the applauses due to the person who would devote his life to deserve them would never reach his ears. Nor am I afraid to confess that mere humanity is an inadequate motive to undertake the office. The enthusiasm to which religion gives birth, and the rewards she promises, can alone compensate the sacrifices, the tediousness, the fatigue, and the risk of this mode of life. I only wish that the austere, though charitable and pious, individuals I met with on these Missions, possessed a little more of that true spirit of philosophy.

"I have already declared with freedom my opinion of the monks of Chile, whose irregularity appeared to me a general scandal to their order. I shall with equal truth portray those truly apostolic individuals who have quitted the lazy life of the cloister, to encounter every kind of fatigue, of care and of solitude. I shall, as usual, give the narrative of our own adventures by relating their history, and placing before the reader all we saw or learned during our short stay at Monterey.

"We anchored on the 14th of September,[11] in the evening, two leagues off shore, within sight of the presidio and the two ships that lay in the harbor. They fired a gun every quarter of an hour to apprise us of the place of anchoring, which the fog might conceal from us. At ten o'clock at night the captain of the corvette *La Favorita* came on board in his longboat and offered to pilot our ship into harbor. The corvette *La Princesa* also sent her longboat with a pilot on board the *Astrolabe*. We then learned that these two ships were Spanish and commanded by Don Estevan Mar-

---

[11] 1786.

tinez, Lieutenant of Marine of the Department of San Blas, in the Province of Guadalajara. The Government keeps a small navy in that port, under the orders of the Viceroy of Mexico, consisting of four corvettes of twelve guns, and a schooner, whose particular destination is the victualing the presidios of North California. It was these same ships that performed the last voyage of the Spaniards on the northwest coast of America. They are also sometimes sent as packet boats to Manila, to carry with promptitude the dispatches of the court.

"We had got under way at ten in the morning, and anchored in the road at noon, where we were saluted by seven guns, which we returned. I then sent an officer to the Governor with a letter of the Spanish Minister delivered to me before my departure for France. It was unsealed, and addressed to the Viceroy of Mexico, whose jurisdiction extends as far as Monterey, though situated eleven hundred leagues (by land) from his capital.

"Senor Fages, commandant of the forts of the two Californias, had already received orders to give us the same reception as to the ships of his nation, and he executed them with an air of graciousness and warmth of interest that deserve our sincerest gratitude. He did not confine himself to kind expressions, but sent on board oxen, milk and vegetables in great abundance.

"The desire to serve us threatened even to disturb the good understanding that reigned between the commandant and the two corvettes and the commandant of the fort, each being desirous to preëmpt the right of exclusively supplying our wants; and to compensate these attentions, and balance the account, we were obliged to insist on paying for them before they would accept our money. The vegetables, the milk, the fowls, all the labor of the garrison in assisting us to get wood and water, was furnished gratis, and the oxen, sheep and grain were charged at so moderate a price that it was evident they only presented the account because we had been so urgent in demanding it.

"Senor Fages added to generous manners the greatest politeness of behavior. His house was ours, and everyone under his command was at our disposal.

"The monks of the Mission of San Carlos, situated two leagues from Monterey, soon arrived at the presidio, and with the same politeness we had experienced from the officers of the fort and ships, invited us to dine with them, promising to make us acquainted with the minutiae of the institution and missions, the manner of life of the Indians, their arts, their newly-adopted manners, and, in general, everything that would excite the curiosity of travelers. We eagerly embraced the offers, and should not have failed to make an application to that effect had they not anticipated our solicitations. We agreed to go two days later. Senor Fages was desirous to accompany us, and undertook to procure us horses. After crossing a small plain covered with herds of cattle, and only furnished with a few trees that serve as a shelter to those animals from the rain or sultry heats, we ascended some hills, where we heard several bells announcing our arrival, of which the monks had been apprised by a horseman previously sent forward by the Governor.

"They received us like lords of the manor making their first entry on their estates. The President of the Missions, in his ceremonial habiliments, and with holy water in his hand, received us at the door of the church, which was illuminated as on the grandest festivals, and, conducting us to the steps of the high altar, began to chant a Te Deum for the success of our voyage.

"Before we entered the church, we had crossed a square, where the Indians of both sexes formed a line; but their countenances showed no sign of surprise at our arrival, and even left it doubtful whether we should become the subject of their conversation during the remainder of the day.

"The parish church is very neat, though covered with thatch. It is dedicated to St. Charles, and decorated with tolerable good paintings, copied from those of Italy. Among others is a picture of hell, where the artist seems to have borrowed the imagination of Callot. But it is indispensably necessary to strike the senses of these new converts in a lively manner. I am convinced such a representation never was more useful in any country, and that it would be impossible for the Protestant religion, which proscribes images, and almost all the ceremonies of the Gallican Church, to make any progress among this nation. I doubt whether the picture of paradise opposite produces on them so good an effect. The quietism portrayed and the soothing satisfaction of the elect who surround the throne of the Most High are ideas too sublime for the minds of uncultivated savages. But it is necessary to place the rewards, as well as the punishments, before them, while it was an indispensable duty not to admit of any deviation from the kind of pleasures held out to man by the Catholic religion.

"On coming out of the church, we passed the same ranks of Indians, who had not quitted their post during the Te Deum. The children alone had moved, forming groups near the house of the missionaries, which, with their several storehouses, are opposite to the church. On the right hand is the Indian village, consisting of about fifty huts, inhabited by seven hundred and forty persons of both sexes, including children, who altogether compose the Mission of San Carlos, or Monterey.

"These huts are the most miserable that exist among any nation. Their form is circular, and six feet diameter by four high. Some stakes about the size of the arm, being fixed in the ground and brought together in an arch on top, compose their frame, and eight or ten trusses of straw, badly arranged upon these stakes, protect the inhabitants more or less from the rain and wind. More than half this hut remains open in fine weather, and their only precaution is to keep two or three trusses of straw near each of the houses.

"This architecture, which is universal throughout the two Californias, the exhortations of the missionaries have never succeeded in changing. The Indians reply that they love the open air, and that it is convenient to set fire to their houses when they are too much annoyed by fleas, and then rebuild them in an hour or two. The independent Indians, who so frequently change their abode, have, like every nation of hunters, additional motives for this preference.

"The color of these Indians, which is that of negroes; the house of the monks, their storehouses, which are built of brick and plastered; the threshing floor on which they tread out the corn, the cattle, the horses—in short, everything we observed, presented the appearance of a plantation in San Domingo, or any other colony. The men and women are also assembled by the sound of a bell, and a monk leads them to work, to church and to all their employments. We declare with pain that the resemblance is so exact that we saw both men and women loaded with irons, while others had a log of wood on their legs; and even the noise of the lash might have assailed our ears, as that mode of punishment is equally admitted, though employed with little severity.

"The answers of the monks to our various questions made us perfectly acquainted with the regulations of this religious community, for such the administration established here must be called. They are the temporal, as well as the spiritual superiors, and all the produce of the earth is confided to their management. The day is divided into seven hours of work and two of prayer, but four or five on Sundays and feast days, which are wholly devoted to rest and religious worship. Corporal punishments are inflicted on the Indians of both sexes who neglect their pious exercises, and many faults which in Europe are wholly left to divine justice are here punished with irons or the log. In short, to complete the parallel with the religious communities, from the moment a neophyte is baptized, he seems to have taken an eternal vow. If he runs away and returns to his relations among the independent villages, he is summoned three times, and should he still refuse to come back, they apply to the authority of the Governor, who sends a party of soldiers to tear him from the bosom of his family; and deliver him to the Missions, where he is condemned to a certain number of lashes.

"Yet these people are so destitute of courage that they never oppose any resistance to the three or four soldiers who so glaringly violate the rights of nations in their persons. Thus is this custom, against which reason exclaims so loudly, continued merely because a number of theologians have chosen to decide that baptism shall not be administered to men of so much levity, unless the Government become in some measure their sponsors, and engage for their perseverance in Christianity.

"The predecessor of Senor Fages, Don Felipe de Neve, commandant of the inland provinces of Mexico, who died four years since, was a man of great humanity, and a kind of Christian philosopher. That worthy man protested against this custom, thinking the progress of the Christian faith would be more rapid, and the prayers of the Indians more agreeable to the Supreme Being, if they were voluntary. He wished for a less monastic constitution, more civil liberty for the Indians, and less despotism in the executive power of the presidios, the administration of which might sometimes be placed in barbarous or avaricious hands.

"He thought it might even be necessary to moderate their authority by erecting a magistracy which should be as it were the tribunal of the Indians, and might have sufficient authority to protect them from oppression. Though this just man had borne arms in the defense of his country from his infancy, yet he was free from the prejudices of his profession, knowing that a military government is subject to great inconvenience when it is not tempered by an immediate authority. He ought, however, to have perceived the difficulty of maintaining this balance of three powers at so great a distance from the Governor General of Mexico, since the missionaries, though so pious and so respectable, are already at open war with the Governor, who appeared to me to be a meritorious officer.

"We were desirous of being present at the distribution made after each meal; and as every day is alike with these monastic kind of men, by delineating the history of a day, the reader will know that of a year.

"The Indians, like the missionaries, rise with the sun, and then go to prayers and to Mass, which lasts an hour. During this time three great caldrons of barley meal are boiled in the middle of the square, the grain having been roasted before it is ground. This mess, which the Indians call *atóle,* and which they are very fond of, is neither seasoned with butter nor salt, and would be to us very insipid food.

"Each family sends for the allowance of all the inhabitants of their cottage, which they receive in a vessel of bark. There is no confusion or disorder in the distribution, and when the caldrons are empty, what cakes to the bottom is given to the children who say their catechism best.

"This repast continues three-quarters of an hour, after which they all go to work, some to plough with oxen, others to dig the garden, each according to the different labors requisite in the colony, and always under the superintendence of one or two monks.

"The women have little other employment than the conduct of household affairs, that of their children, and the roasting and grinding their grain. This operation is very long and tedious, because they have no other method than crushing it on a stone with a cylinder. M. de Langle, observing this operation, presented his mill to the missionaries; we could scarcely have rendered them a greater service, for now four women can do the work of one hundred, and even have time to spin the wool from their flocks, and manufacture some coarse stuffs. Hitherto the monks, more occupied with their celestial than temporal concerns, have neglected to introduce the most common arts. They are even so austere with regard to themselves as not to have one chamber with a fireplace, though the winter is sometimes severe; nor did the strictest anchorites ever lead a more edifying life.

"At noon the bells ring for dinner, when the Indians quit their work, and send for their messes to the same caldron as at breakfast time. This second broth, however, is thicker than the first, for besides the corn and maize, it contains peas and beans. The Indians call it *poussole*. They return to work from two o'clock till four or five, after which they go to evening prayers, which last near an hour, and are followed by another meal of *atóle*, similar to their breakfast. Thus these distributions suffice for the subsistence of the majority of the Indians, and this very economical soup might, perhaps, be advantageously adopted in Europe in years of scarcity, with the addition of some kind of seasoning. But all the arts of cookery practiced here consist in roasting the grain before it is reduced into flour.

"As the Indians have no earthen or metal vessels for this operation, they perform it in baskets of bark over small lighted coals, turning them with so much adroitness and rapidity as to make the grain swell and burst, without burning the baskets, though composed of very combustible materials. We may even venture to affirm that the best roasted coffee does not approach the equality of roasting produced by the Indians. It is distributed to them every morning for this purpose, and the smallest infidelity in their return is punished by the lash, to which, however, they rarely expose themselves. These punishments are ordered by Indian magistrates, called *caciques,* of whom each Mission has three, elected by the people from all those not disqualified by the missionaries. But to give a just idea of this magistracy, we shall observe that these *caciques*, like stewards of plantations, are mere passive beings, and blind executors of the will of their superiors, their principal functions being those of beadles and maintaining good order and an air of seriousness in the church.

"The women are never flogged in the public square, but in a secret place, and at a distance, in order, perhaps, to prevent their cries exciting too lively a compassion, and thereby stimulating the men to revolt, whereas the men are exposed before all their fellow-citizens, that their punishment may serve as an example. In general they ask forgiveness, upon which the executioner diminishes the force of his strokes, but the number is always irrevocably fixed.

"Their rewards consist in small individual distributions of grain, of which they make small cakes, baked under the brazier; and on feast days their mess is of beef, which many eat raw, especially the fat, which they esteem equally delicious with the finest butter or the most excellent cheese. They skin all animals with the greatest adroitness, and when they are fat, they croak with pleasure like a crow, devouring, at the same time, the parts they are most fond of, with their eyes.

"They are often suffered to hunt and fish for their own benefit, and at their return present the missionaries with some fish or game, proportioning the quantity to their precise wants, but increasing it if they know their superiors to have any additional guests. The women keep a few fowls round their huts, and give the eggs to their children. These fowls are the property of the Indians, as well as their clothes and other utensils, both domestic and for the chase. There is no example of their robbing one another, though they have no other door than a truss of straw laid across the entrance when all the family are absent.

"These manners will appear to some readers to belong to the patriarchal ages, who may not consider that in these huts they have no objects capable of tempting the cupidity of their neighbors, for, their subsistence being secure, they can have no other object of desire but to give birth to beings destined to be equally stupid as they themselves.

"The men have sacrificed more to Christianity than the women, for to them polygamy was allowed, and it was even the custom to marry all the sisters of a family. The women, therefore, have gained by it the exclusive enjoyment of their husband. But I confess that, notwithstanding the unanimous account given by the missionaries of this pretended polygamy, I never could conceive it possible among a nation of savages, for, the number of men and women being nearly equal, many of them must live in involuntary celibacy unless conjugal fidelity were less strictly observed than in the Missions, where the monks have made themselves the guardians of the women's virtue.

"An hour after supper they shut up all those whose husbands are absent, as well as all girls about nine years old, and place them under the care of matrons during the day. Even these precautions are insufficient, for we saw men wearing the log, and women in irons, for having escaped the vigilance of these female arguses, whose eyes are inadequate to watch them.

"The converted Indians have preserved all the ancient customs not forbidden by their new religion—the same huts, the same games, the same dresses. The richest wear a cloak of otter skin, which covers their loins and reaches below their knees. The least industrious only wear a piece of cloth furnished by the Mission to cover their nakedness, and a little cloak of rabbit skin, tied with a pack thread under the chin, which covers their shoulders and reaches to their loins, the rest of the body being naked, as well as the head; some, however, wear a straw hat extremely well matted.

"The women's dress consists of a cloak of stag's skin, badly tanned. Those of the Missions generally convert them into a little jacket with sleeves, which, with a small apron of rushes, and a petticoat of stag's skin, that covers their loins and reaches half down the legs, forms their whole attire. Young girls under nine years old have only a girdle, and the boys are totally naked.

"The hair of both men and women is cut four or five inches from the roots. The Indians of the *rancherias,* having no iron utensils, perform their operation with fire brands, and paint their bodies red, changing it to black when in mourning. The missionaries have proscribed the former, but have been obliged to tolerate the black, these people being so strongly attached to their friends as to shed tears when reminded even of those who have been long dead, and feeling offended if their names are inadvertently mentioned in their presence. But here family connections have less force than those of friendship, and children scarcely know their own father, deserting his hut as soon as they are able to provide for themselves. They retain, however, a more durable attachment to their mothers, who bring them up with the greatest tenderness, and only beat them when they show cowardice in their little battles with children of their own age.

"The old men of the *rancherias* who are no longer able to hunt, live at the joint expense of the whole village and are treated with general respect. Though the independent savages are very frequently at war, their fear of the Spaniards prevents their committing any outrages on the Missions, which is, perhaps, not the least of the causes of the augmentation of the Christian village. Their arms are the bow and arrow pointed with a flint very skillfully worked, their bows being made of wood and strung with the sinew of an ox, and are very superior to those of the inhabitants of Port des Francais.

"We were assured these Indians neither ate their prisoners nor their enemies killed in war, although when they have conquered and put to death some chiefs and very brave men in the field of battle, they eat some morsels of their bodies, not so much to demonstrate their hatred and vengeance as to do homage to their valor, and from a belief that such food would increase their courage. Like the Canadians, they take off the scalp of the conquered, and tear out their eyes, which they have the art of preserving from corruption, keeping them as the most precious trophies of victory. They are accustomed to burn their dead and deposit their ashes in a *morai*.

"Two games employ all their leisure time. One is called *takersia*, and consists in throwing or rolling a small circlet three inches in diameter, on an area ten *toises* square, clear from grass, and inclosed with *fascines*. Each party has a stick five feet long, of the size of an ordinary cane, on which they endeavor to catch the ring while in motion. If they succeed, they gain two points, but if they can only catch it at the end of its motion, they count one; and three points are the game. This play becomes a violent exercise, as the circlets or the sticks are in constant action.

"The other game, called *toussi*, is less fatiguing, and is played by four hands, two on a side. Each party in turn hides a piece of wood in one hand, while his partner endeavors by a thousand gestures to engage the attention of the adversaries. It has a singular effect to a spectator to observe them squatting opposite each other in perfect silence, watching each other's countenance and the minutest circumstance that may assist them in guessing which hand conceals the piece of wood. They gain or lose a point according to their guess, and those who win have the next turn to hide. Five points make the game, and the stake usually consists of some beads, or, among the independent Indians, the favors of their wives. These last have no knowledge of a God or a future state, except some of the Southern nations, who had a confused idea on the subject before the arrival of the missionaries. They placed their paradise in the middle of the sea, where the good enjoyed a coolness never to be felt among their burning sands, while they imagined a hell situated in the hollows of the mountains.

"The missionaries, convinced, either by their prejudices or their experiences, that the reason of these men is never matured, deem this a sufficient motive for treating them as children, and only admit a very small number to the communion. These individuals are the men of genius of their village, who, like Newton or Descartes, might have enlightened their countrymen and their age by teaching them that two and two make four, a calculation above the powers of a considerable number. The regulation of the Missions is not likely to emancipate them from the reign of ignorance, where everything is merely directed to obtaining rewards of a future life, and the most common arts, even that of a village surgeon of France, wholly unexplored. Children frequently perish in consequence of hernias which the smallest degree of skill might cure, and our surgeons were happy in relieving a few and teaching them the use of bandages in that disorder."

CHAPTER XII

The Military, the Pueblos and the Indians.

BOOK II
Chapter XII

The Military, the Pueblos and the Indians

NEXT to the Missions, the presidios occupied the most important place in the reduction of California Alta.

The history of the military efforts in the undertaking to "homestead California for Spain against the threatened foreign invasion" is closely interwoven with that of the religious endeavors, for it was the duty of the military establishment to protect the Missions. These two agencies of the State were interdependent. The Missions could not have survived without the protection of the military, and the latter became increasingly more dependent on the Missions for subsistence.

In accordance with the decree of the King of Spain, issued September 10th, 1772, the military and naval departments of both Californias were to be composed as follows:

Department of San Blas.

The cost of maintaining the dockyard department and the employees, including a commissary at $3,000 a year, soldiers, a chaplain and a sacristan, amounted to $29,869.

Marine Department.

One frigate, salaries of the officers, including the Captain's at $70 a month, wages of the men, etc.	$14,842
One packet boat, salaries of the officers, including the Captain's at $70 a month, wages of the men, etc.	19,196
	$34,038

Department of Lower California.

A Governor in command of both Californias, residing at Loreto, with a salary of $4,000 a year	$ 4,000
A lieutenant at $500 a year	500
A sergeant at $400 a year	400
Three corporals at $350 a year each	1,050
Thirty soldiers at $300 a year each	9,000
A commissary at $1,500 a year	1,500
	$16,450

For Alta California two presidios were provided:

Presidio of Monterey.

A captain, who was to be in command of the troops in Upper California, with residence at Monterey, acted as Vice-Governor, subordinate to the Governor of both Californias, in residence at Loreto.[1]

His salary was fixed at $3,000 a year........................	$ 3,000
A sergeant at $450 a year....................................	450
Two corporals at $400 a year each...........................	800
Twenty-two soldiers at $365 a year each.....................	8,030
Two carpenters to serve presidio and Missions at $300 each.....	600
Two blacksmiths for the presidio and Missions at $300..........	600
Four muleteers at $150 a year each..........................	600
A storekeeper, who kept account of the goods received and distributed them subject to the approval of the captain, at $1,000	1,000

$15,080

Presidio of San Diego.

A lieutenant commanding the presidio at $700 a year...........	$ 700
A sergeant at $450 a year....................................	450
Two corporals at $400 a year each...........................	800
Twenty-two soldiers at $365 each............................	8,030
Two carpenters to serve at presidio and Mission at $300 each....	600
Two blacksmiths for the same purpose at $300 each............	600
A storekeeper as at Monterey at $1,000 a year...............	1,000

$12,180

Each presidio had a number of Missions within its jurisdiction, for which it had to furnish a military guard *(escolta)* under command of a petty officer—generally a corporal. The military also exercised a semi-civil and criminal jurisdiction, and consequently there was continual friction between these soldiers and the padres.

Later new presidios were established at San Francisco and Santa Barbara, and the military branch was greatly increased.

The total annual cost of maintaining the military establishment in Upper California amounted to $38,385, including incidentals not tabulated above; but as payment was made in goods which were delivered at Monterey and San Diego at a discount of one hundred and fifty per cent, the expense to the royal treasury was only about $15,904.[2]

---

[1] Engelhardt, Missions and Missionaries of California, Vol. II, pp. 144, 145.
[2] Engelhardt, Missions and Missionaries in California, Vol. 11, p. 146.

Closely connected with the Mission idea was the system of the pueblos. The doctrine of the pueblo settlements was an old one:

It was the policy of Spain, adopted as early as the year 1551 by Emperor Charles V, and never departed from by him or by his successors, that the Indians should be induced and compelled to live together in villages, this being considered the only possible condition of their becoming civilized. The ordinances decreed for this purpose are exceedingly minute and well digested and are principally to be found in the *Leyes de las Indies,* Lib. V. Titulo III.

It was decreed that the Indians should be settled in villages, that churches should be established for them, that they should be governed by Indian *Alcaldes* and Indian *Regidores* (council men); that no Indian should remove from his own village to another, nor live outside of his own village; that no Spaniard, negro, mestizo or mulatto should live in an Indian pueblo.[3]

Here we have the principle of the pueblo *Missions* clearly defined. A community of Indians, vested with a title in lands which the missionaries in charge were to hold, in *loco parentis,* until the time when the natives should be considered capable of self-government without supervision, when the lands were to be granted to the natives in severalty and fee.

The pueblos of California were founded in three different ways, and are generally referred to in the following manner:

First: The pueblos of *Gente de Razon,* or whites, founded as purely secular establishments, with elaborate laws, fully covered in the "Plan of Pitic,"[4] besides being provided for in *Recopilacion* and various later Mexican *Reglamentos.* Los Angeles and San Jose, founded by Governor Felipe de Neve, are the best known of this type of pueblo; sometimes these pueblos were known as "villas," though the latter name was more especially applicable to frontier towns to which some special privileges were accorded. Branciforte, founded by Governor Borica, was the only "villa" founded in Alta California. In reality, there was little or no difference between pueblos and villas.

Gente de Razon, or "civilized people," included everyone except Indians, and in Mexico whole villages of mulattoes were listed as "white." When Los Angeles Mission was founded in 1781, forty-six persons assembled as *pobladores.* They were a motley crew, of all mixtures of blood,

---

[3] This last rule proved impractical and was constantly violated.

[4] Dwinnelle's Colonial History of San Francisco, Sec. 9, p. 7. N. B.: In 1780-1781 a plan had been tried to found a villa,—a cross between a fortress and a civil foundation, amongst the Indians on the Colorado, and in 1789 the same plan had been tried in Sonora, at Pitic, this time for the white people.

and had mated in all different ways; Spaniards with mulattoes, mulattoes with Indians, negroes with mulattoes, etc., all recognized by law to be *Gente de Razon*.

Second: The presidial pueblos, which originated in the settlement of the presidios and grew up under their shadows. San Francisco was a notable example.

Third: The Mission pueblos, composed of "neophytes," or Indians, under the temporary guardianship of the Franciscan Fathers, who at first appointed Indian officials known as *alcaldes, regidores,* etc. After the secularization in 1834, they were known as "Indian pueblos," or simply "pueblos," the terms being interchangeable. During part of the Mission period the neophytes were supposedly permitted to vote for their Indian officers, but the padres controlled the elections, which were in reality mere shams.

Of these, the Pueblo of the Mission of Santa Cruz was a very good illustration. This pueblo was known later as the "Pueblo de Figueroa," and still later, together with the Villa of Branciforte, was incorporated as the City of Santa Cruz.

The Spanish Government provided skilled artisans from Spain or Mexico, and paid their hire, for the purpose of aiding the settlers in the various pueblos. Master mechanics, carpenters, blacksmiths and stone masons are mentioned in Governor Neve's Rules and Regulations, and some of the Indians were trained by these men.

Governor Fages proposed to the Viceroy that artisans imprisoned in Mexico City and Guadalajara should be exiled to California to work at the presidios and to remain as pueblo settlers on the expiration of their sentence. This plan was carried out, for we read that in 1791 such a convict blacksmith taught the Indians in San Francisco.

From 1792 to 1795 about twenty manual training teachers were sent out to California, all skilled artisans. They were distributed amongst the presidios and Missions, some of them being itinerant instructors. In the years 1793 and 1794 the San Carlos Indians were instructed in brick making, brick laying, stone cutting, etc. Up till 1795 the padres had the services of these men, free of charge. After that the services had to be paid for, but at the presidio pueblos the instruction continued without cost.

Later twenty foundlings were sent out by the Government, ten girls and ten boys—mostly illegitimate children. We read in the reports that the girls came out surprisingly well, notwithstanding . . . their great fondness for cigars!

Any pueblo, of whatever origin or population, acquired as such the right to certain lands of which four square leagues was the accepted mea-

SISTERS OF CHARITY, MONSIGNOR FISHER AND THEIR CHARGES
ATTENDING A PICNIC AT VILLA FAIR VIEW, AT
SANTA CRUZ, CALIFORNIA

sure, for the laws had decreed from time immemorial that every fully organized pueblo, as such, was entitled to four square leagues of land.[5]

Comandante-general Pedro de Nava, of the frontier provinces, wrote to Governor Romeu of Alta California in 1797, confirming this doctrine of four leagues measurement, thereby emphasizing the rule laid down in *Recopilacion,* which in part declares: "the boundaries assigned to each pueblo must be four leagues of land, in a square or oblong body, according to the nature of the ground."[6]

The land was rarely granted formally by the Government at the founding, but the pueblo might at any time take steps to have the boundary fixed by a survey, which in reality amounted to a grant. This procedure was often long delayed in California, and sometimes omitted altogether. When once established, pueblo lots were sold or distributed by the municipal authorities instead of being granted by the Governor, as for instance in the case of private ranchos.

At first the Church had an equitable right to the actual Mission property, which with the years grew into a legal right and included the collection of houses, such as church buildings, priests' houses, cemeteries, vineyards and orchards in the immediate vicinity of the churches, and used for the support of the priests and for their personal purposes, including the livestock and other property in the possession of the priests, and useful in carrying on the establishments.[7] To the remainder of the four square leagues the priests had only a claim as guardians of the Indians, for the Indian and Mission pueblos were reserved to the Indian neophytes to provide them with common lands for grazing, water, etc.,[8] and eventually it was intended that they should obtain grants to such lands like other citizens.

That this theory was well established is shown by the following extract from the opinion of Judge Felch, of the California Board of Land Commissioners, in the case of "the Bishop of California's petition for the Churches, etc., at the Missions," which clearly and concisely expresses the theory of the missionary colonization:

"The Missions were intended from the beginning to be temporary in their character. It was contemplated that in ten years from their first foundation they should cease.

"It was supposed that within that period of time the Indians would be sufficiently instructed in Christianity and the arts of civilized life to assume the position and character of citizens; that these Mission settle-

---

[5] Dwinelle, Colonial History of San Francisco, Sec. 28, p. 22.

[6] Laws of the Indies, Law 6, title 5, book 4.

[7] See *Recopilacion de las Indies.*

[8] Ritchies Case, 17 Howard, U. S. S. C. Rep. pp. 540, 561.

ments would then become pueblos, and that the Mission churches would become parish churches, organized like the other establishments of an ecclesiastical character, in other portions of the nation where no Missions had ever existed. The whole missionary establishment was widely different from the ordinary ecclesiastical organization of the nation. In it the superintendence and charge was committed to priests who were devoted to the special work of Missions, and not to the ordinary clergy. The monks of the College of San Fernando Zacatecas, in whose charge they were, were to be succeeded by the clergy of the national church, the missionary field was to become a diocese, the President of the Missions to give place to a Bishop, the Mission churches to become curacies, and the faithful in the vicinity of each parish to become the parish worshippers."

It is obvious that the missionaries, if not actually opposing this with open hostility, did not and could not be expected to have any sympathy with it; and this attitude was partly the cause of the criticism of the Fathers which was already active prior to the establishment of the Santa Cruz Mission.

How did the Indians respond to these conditions?

Most writers agree that the California Indian could hardly be called a "desirable citizen," though some give us more favorable accounts, like Vizcaino (1602-1603),[9] Don Miguel Costanso (1770), Padres Crespi and Boscano.[10]

Englehardt classes him as "amongst the most stupid, brutish, lazy, filthy and improvident of the aborigines of America."

We have already seen what La Perouse's opinion of these Indians was.

Tuthill voices the impression of most of the early navigators, explorers and travelers, when he says that of all wretchedly debased and utterly brutal beings, the Indians of California had fallen farthest below the average Indian type. They were neither brave nor bold; neither generous nor spirited.[11]

Venegas claimed that the Lower California Indians were the most stupid and weak, in both body and mind, of all mortals, and goes into detail about their life and customs to prove this point. The settlers of Upper California, who had seen both types of Indians, thought the northern natives far inferior to the southern.

Some worshipped as their chief deity "Chinchinich" (for instance, those living near Capistrano), whom they personified in the form of a

---

[9] Letter of Vizcaino to the King of Spain, dated May 23, 1603.
[10] Fray Geronimo Boscano, Chinigchinich, An Historical Account.
[11] Tuthill, History of California, pp. 88-90.

coyote skin stuffed with the claws and teeth of other animals. They lived in "tule" huts, which, when they became unbearable on account of vermin, were burned to the ground and new ones built on the same spot, or at a little distance.

Their domestic relations were a matter of personal inclination; polygamy was a matter of course, and the women, as in most primitive races, were the gatherers of food and the builders of fires.

The food they ate was a conglomerate mixture of any animal or vegetable matter that was at hand and easily obtained. Rattlesnakes they did not eat, but a dead whale cast on the beach was counted a luxury. Their weapons of the chase being very primitive, bear or deer meat was difficult to obtain.

Of the dress of the Indians around San Francisco Bay, it is recorded that the women wore skirts of grass and capes of twisted squirrel skins, while the men, with a fine disregard of vanity, plastered themselves with mud in the chill of the morning, and as the day grew too warm for comfort, they disrobed by plunging into the water to wash off any superabundance of mud clothing that annoyed them.

To cap the climax of the difficulty of civilizing this people, each *rancheria*[12] or settlement of Indians had a different language.

Father Pedro Font, the diarist of de Anza's Second Expedition, described in some detail the Indians found on the shores of the Santa Barbara Channel. He estimated the population from ten to twenty thousand, divided in about thirty *rancherias*.

Fishing along the coast supported this large population. The Indians had no agriculture, living on fish, wild fruits, seeds and nuts.

These Indians were of good stature; the men going naked, the women using deer skin skirts and small capes. They were, like all savages, fond of ornaments, pierced their ears and noses; used for weapons good arrows and strong bows, and a dagger made of bone or of wood with a flint point. They had houses which Father Font described as round in form, like a divided orange, and spacious. The doors consisted of mats swinging inward. They had community playgrounds, cemeteries, and sweathouses, or *temescales*. These temescales were hot closed rooms, and, having copiously perspired, the Indians ran out and bathed in the ocean. This was their general cure for all ills.

---

[12] Some of these rancherias were entirely free from missionary influence, while others were *pueblos de visitas,* where the missionaries occasionally performed religious services. Sometimes there was a representative of the Padre—an Indian, known as the master of doctrine, but these last named rancherias retained their liberty, though they received some worldly benefits mostly in the form of supplies.

Amongst them were fine basket weavers and stone workers and experts in building and managing launches.

They were also skilful as fishermen and in seamanship, using large and small nets of fibre and fish-hooks made of shells. They appeared to be clever pickpockets. Several articles were stolen, from which fact Father Font deducted "this incident is proof of the inclination of every Indian to steal."[13]

These Indians had of course suffered from the impositions and outrages inflicted upon them by the soldiers, who had passed through this country prior to the advent of Lt. Colonel de Anza and Father Font in March, 1776. It appeared that the conduct of the soldiers was especially objectionable towards the Indian women. In fact, one of the gay lotharios, named Camacho, conducted himself in such a ruffian way and became so famous for his abuses committed amongst the dusky belles of the Channel that after his departure every Spanish soldier was called *camacho*. There are several ways of making a family name famous.

Father Font at no time seemed to have had a high opinion of the California Indians. He recorded that he found the aborigines of Contra Costa timid and very poor and speaking a most unpleasant language, eating a kind of grass which they called *morren*.

Left to their own devices, evolution seems to have accomplished little or nothing for these Indians. A most surprising similarity is seen in the notes of Frances Fletcher, the Chaplain of Drake's ship, the *Pelican,* later renamed, after the passage through the Straits of Magellan, the *Golden Hind,* and those written two hundred years later by the Chaplains and diarist accompanying the expeditions of Portola and de Anza. One record may almost be considered a transcript of the other.

Fletcher, who sailed with Drake from Plymouth on November 15th, 1577, returned to England on the 26th of September, 1580, after circumnavigating the globe.

His notes and those of "diverse followers" of Sir Francis were incorporated in the account of the famous voyage under direction of Drake's nephew and heir, and published in London in 1826 under the title, "The World Encompassed by Sir Francis Drake."

Drake, whose passage through the Straits took seventeen days, spent several months sailing north, preying upon Spanish ports and Spanish ships. He arrived early in March, 1579, at Cape San Francisco, just north of the equator, and on April 15th ran into the port of Guatuleo, Guatemala, for supplies.

---

[13] Bolton's Anza's California Expedition. Vol. I, p. 360.

He may have gone as far north as Vancouver, but this is uncertain; however, fog and cold turning him back, he records that on June 17th he arrived at a harbor, situate 38 degrees 30 minutes, where he remained from June 17th to July 23rd. This was probably the present Drake's Bay, and not the harbor of San Francisco, as was formerly believed, though it is still an open question.

Captain Fletcher gives us a vivid account of the natives who came to visit the English camp in 1579. He writes:

"Their men for the most part goe naked; the women take a kind of bulrushes, and kembing it after the manner of hemp, make themselues thereof a loose garment, which being knitte about their middles, hanges downe about their hippes, and so affordes to them a couering of that which nature teaches should be hidden; about their shoulders they weare also the skin of a deere, with the haire vpon it. . . ."

During the visit of the men to the camp, Captain Fletcher notes:

"In the meane time the women, as if they had been desperate, vsed vnnatural violence against themselues, crying and shrieking piteously, tearing their flesh with their nailes from their cheekes in a monstrous manner, the blood streaming downe along their brests, besides despoiling the vpper parts of their bodies of those single coucrings they formerly had, and holding their hands aboue their heads that they might not rescue their brests from harme, they would with furie cast themselues vpon the ground . . . dashed themselues in this manner on hard stone . . .; yea women great with child, some nine or ten times each, and others holding out till 15 or 16 times (till their strength failed them) exercised this cruelty against themselues: a thing most grieuous for vs to see. . . . This bloudie sacrifice (against our wils) being thus performed, our Generall, with his companie, in the presence of those strangers, fell to prayers . . .; neither were it the women alone which did this, but euen old men, roaring and crying out, were as violent as the women were."

The Chaplain then tells us:

"This one thing was obserued to bee generall amongst them all, that euery one had his face painted, some with white, some with blacke, and some with other colours, euery man also bringing in his hand one thing or other for a gift or present. . . ."

"They are a people of a tractable, free, and louing nature, without guile or treachery; their bowes and arrowes (their only weapons, and almost all their wealth) they vse very skillfully, but yet not to do any great harme with them, being by reason of their weakenesse more fit for children then for men, . . . Their houses are digged round within the earth, and haue from the vppermost brimmes of the circle clefts of wood set vp and joyned close together at the top, like our spires on the steeple of a Church; which being couered with earth, suffer no water to enter, and are very warme; the doore in the most part of them performes the office also of a chimney to let out the smoake: . . . Their beds are the hard ground, onely with rushes strewed vpon it, and lying round about the house, haue their fire in the middest, which by reason that the house is but low vaulted, round and close, giueth a maruelous reflexion to their bodies to heate the same."

George Wharton James, who wrote a number of books about the North American Indians—"In and Out of the Old Missions of California," "In and Around the Grand Canyon of the Colorado River in Arizona," "Indians in the Painted Desert," "Indian Basketry," etc.—does not agree with this. He states that all the old writers, as well as the padres, were mistaken in believing that these Indians were degraded and brutal.

Mr. James' words deserve respectful consideration. For twenty-five years he was acquainted and frequently associated with the Indians of Nevada, California and the Southwest. He was their friend in the best sense of the word, understanding their thoughts, their hopes and despair. If ever the "disappearing American" had a true friend, he was George Wharton James. Anyone who has had the privilege of knowing Mr. James personally,[14] perceiving his enthusiastic friendship for these people and his towering indignation at their treatment, will understand the fine spirit in which his *pronunciamentos* were written. Still his arguments as to the state of civilization of the California Indians at the advent of the Fathers are not very convincing. He points out that they were skilled in the making of pottery, basketry, canoes, stone axes, arrowheads, stone knives and the like. The Dayaks in Borneo, the famous head-hunters, are even more skilled, but they are savages; like their prototypes in the Island of Formosa, they have with few exceptions resisted all efforts of civilization, and are rather dangerous to come in contact with when aroused, as the Netherlanders and Japanese have had ample reason to find out.

The Mission Fathers did wonders with apparently hopeless material, for during their short period in California they had made the natives into masons, carpenters, plasterers, soap makers, tanners, shoe makers, blacksmiths, millers, bakers, cooks, brick makers, carders and cart makers, weavers, spinners, saddlers, ship hands, agriculturalists, herdsmen, vin-

---

[14] Mr. James spent several days and nights with the author at his country home at Santa Cruz, overlooking the old location of the Mission. His conversations were as interesting as his books; his knowledge of Indian lore profound.

tagers—in a word, they taught the Indians all the useful occupations known to civilization at that time.[15]

The physical evidences of this rude civilization may still be seen, for at several of the Missions massive stone churches were built, of an architecture at once simple and harmonious. The ruins of these Missions are today the finest in America—monuments to the Fathers who designed them and superintended their construction, and to the patient Indians who built them.

There is much food for serious thought in the painful difference between the fate of the Indians on the Atlantic Coast—the noble Redmen— and that of the degraded Diggers on the Pacific Coast. On the Atlantic Coast the Redmen were swindled, robbed of their patrimony, murdered and well nigh exterminated. The stern Puritans—praying and working hard—drove the Indians back and killed them whenever they thought necessary; the Spanish Mexicans, likewise praying, but more given to dancing and singing, watched their priests gather the Indians in large communities, feed them, baptize them, and teach them the useful trades of civilization. Verily, Spain wrote pages of honor in its Book of History in dealing with the natives, bigoted as the rule may have been; while most of the records of the other white men's dealings with the red brothers fill pages with scarlet infamy.

On one hand we have the record of Dr. Increase Mather and the Reverend Cotton Mather of Cambridge, the Reverend Mr. Parus of Salem Village, and other divines in the East;[16] on the other hand, Father Serra and his missionaries in the West—all followers of the Son of Man.

Further comment seems superfluous.

---

[15] Helen Hunt Jackson, a recognized authority on Indian affairs, states in a note to her book, "A Century of Dishonor"—"The Mission Indians, having been for the past century under the Catholic missions established on the California coast, are tolerably well advanced in agriculture, and compare favorably with the most highly civilized tribes of the east," which would tend to show that the Fathers succeeded in bringing the most backward of the Indian tribes to the level with the most highly civilized tribes.

[16] Cotton Mather, Keeper of the Puritan Conscience, by Ralph and Louise Boas.

CHAPTER XIII

Criticism of the Mission Fathers.

BOOK II

Chapter XIII

Criticism of the Mission Fathers

R EALIZING the danger of misrepresenting motives, independent historians take refuge in the over-cautious theory that a discussion of conditions stands on a much higher plane than a discourse on personalities.

But historic conditions are not acts of God, nor do they grow all by themselves out of the rocks or the heads of small men. They are the results of the ideas and ideals, or lack of ideals, of the leaders who succeed in influencing the classes and masses of their times. Without considering the mental processes of these men, it is well-nigh impossible to understand the great drama of the human race.

An endeavor to present the absorbingly interesting Mission Period in California, without paying due attention to the inner personalities of the leading *Dramatis Personae,* could only result in the presentation of a flat image, lacking a third dimension and being void of perspective.

It is a trait, ingrained in the human character, to make a shop-window display of virtues which the displayers are never called upon to supply; this especially applies to the virtues of our own ancestors, who may have woefully failed in practicing these virtues, even though they may have had abundant opportunities to do so. With equal facility we often deprive others of their just dues. This is most unjust when practiced by Nordics at the expense of the Mission Friars; still even slander is a form of flattery; no stories spring up about unimportant or weak men.

Those who condemn the Fathers are sometimes intentionally or unconsciously prejudiced against the Catholic Church and its works, while the defendants are prone to overdraw the favorable picture of the Friars, thus destroying much of the value of their advocacy.

The chief banner-bearer of the California Mission Fathers is the learned Father Engelhardt, of Santa Barbara. He bitterly denounces not only those who in any way criticise the padres, but has been unsparing in comment on the "idiotic," "cruel" and "stupid" attitude of the secular authorities. Captain (later Governor) Pedro Fages, Captain Fernando Rivera y Moncada, Governor Felipe de Neve, Commandant General de Croix, Captain Nicolas Soler, Governor Diego de Borica, Captain Juan Bautista de Anza and many others are one and all hoisted on the pillory by this zealous historian, their viewpoints being denounced with vigor. He condemns with equal force the viewpoint of Bancroft, Hittell, Dwinelle and others.

Everyone of the commanders and Governors so bitterly complained of were devout Catholics. Why then should they have taken a malicious pleasure in thwarting and hampering the efforts of the Fathers? It seems hard to believe that select Catholic laymen should be guilty of wanton acts against priests of their own faith; priests who on the march were recognized as belonging "among the gentry," and who ate at the commander's table. It is more logical to believe that each category of men served faithfully and conscientiously their immediate superiors, *i. e.,* the State and the Church, and that the conflict was not due to personal malice, but more to the fact that Church and State, whenever closely associated, always clash.

The system of subordinating the Church to the State had been in existence for two hundred and fifty or three hundred years—therefore, long prior to the Mission period. Had not the churchmen had sufficient time to adjust their minds to this condition, in so far as it is ever possible to adjust religious to secular ideas? Apparently not, for the churchmen charged with secular administrative duties were inclined to grasp for the temporalities, while the lay officers in retaliation interfered with the spiritual offices. One wonders if the situation was not partly due to the isolation, which was bound to bring on a condition known as "getting on one another's nerves."

The attitude of the Fathers towards the Indians differed from that of the military. These early commanders were generally men of breeding and education, of great courage and sound judgment, who had become hard-bitten, stern soldiers and administrators, and whose sympathies with the natives were often absent in individual cases, though generally broad toward the masses.

The profound sympathy of the Fathers, on the other hand, was especially noticeable in dealing with the single native, and often exacting and unrelaxing when they enforced general policies.

The Franciscan Fathers, raised in austerity and self-discipline, strongly believed in the maintenance of conditions once ordained; in other words, "in the system." As spiritual leaders and estate overseers, their attitude towards their dusky collective charges was uncompromising, and was somewhat analogous to the viewpoint of the white slave holders in our Southern States—kindly and indulgent to their bondspeople, but unflexible in the resolve to maintain and enforce the bondage system.

The military and civil servants, of high and low rank, were guilty of many private and often gross wrongs against the natives, but nevertheless sympathized with the Indians *en masse;* the same difference in attitude between our pro-slavery Southerners and anti-slavery Northerners. The Southern slaves individually received kinder and far more understanding treatment from their Southern masters than from the Northern men with whom they came in contact then or later; still the Northern people sacrificed their own lives to free them, while the Southerners spilled their blood to maintain them in forced bondage.

This strife, in evidence through the whole Mission period, was raging in a most unpleasant way in Alta California just about the time of the founding of the Mission Santa Cruz, when the Mission idea was in full flower.

Don Pedro Fages had been Governor from July 12th, 1782, to April 16th, 1791. He had been so conciliatory, especially in the beginning, that he was nicknamed the *frailero,* or panderer to friars. Still Fages desired to remain loyal to the secular government and had to carry out its policies. As a result he found favor with neither side, and even Father Palou treated Fages with scant courtesy, though the former knew Fages' difficult position. Fages had as an adjutant one Nicholas Soler, who, fired with ambition to fill the Governor's shoes, proved only too ready to report to the authorities in Mexico City any lapse of his chief in the enforcement of the *Patronato.*

A change of Governors did not improve the situation, for under Governor de Borica (1794-1800) an order was given that the election of the Indian *alcaldes* and *regidores* in the Mission pueblos should be resumed. Although de Borica stipulated that the Indians should be under a Father's supervision, except in case of serious crimes, when they were to be handled by the corporal of the Mission guard as representative of the secular authorities, still the order was much against the will of the padres. They could not fail to realize that in a public election a man of merit is seldom preferred over a nincompoop, and they knew this would undoubtedly be the case with Indians still in their political infancy.

Occasionally there were some good reasons for restraint of the religious by the secular authorities, for instance in 1795, when two hundred and eighty neophytes deserted for the Mission of San Francisco. Father Antonio Dantí was held responsible on account of too great severity. This was recognized by his successor, Father Jose Maria Fernandez, and Governor de Borica made an investigation. As a result he severely criticized the conditions and admonished Father President de Lasuen to see that reforms be introduced.

What kind of men were the padres? What was their education, their intelligence, and their moral qualifications? What was their general conduct?

Their defenders have painted them pure as angels, descending from the azure Castilian skies to brighten the lives of the unregenerate heathens of California, who, unfortunately, preferred laziness, ungodly dirtiness, and their own superstitions to labor, cleanliness and the Glad Tidings.

By their detractors, the padres have been accused of all the crimes under the sun, from being horse thieves to gay seducers and voluptuaries; and it was noised about that they kept harems populated with Indian women. The Fathers of the Mission of Santa Cruz also came in for their share of the blame.

Neither the accusation nor the defense is correct; the truth lies somewhere between these two extremes.

The vast majority of the Fathers were well educated, often graduates of famous universities, high-minded, self-sacrificing men. Many of them, likes Garces, Font, Serra, Palou, de Lasuen, etc., were eminent men, who would at any time be great ornaments to any church or to any profession. These great religious and moral leaders were simple, even austere, in their private lives.

That the Mission Fathers were bound to be more successful in handling the neophytes than the military officers was inevitable, for with the North American Indians the humbler amongst the settlers have always been more successful than the mighty.

Consequently, the missionaries, as far as their own viewpoint would allow, often stood between the natives and the Europeans, and shielded the former against rapacity—a rapacity which was sometimes cloaked in the garb of popular governmental righteousness. In such cases the Indians found their only refuge in the foresight and humanity of the padres.

That there were some black sheep amongst them, like Fathers Rubi and Gili (1793) and Antonio de la Concepcion (1797), who finally was declared insane,[1] is admitted.

These Spanish renegade priests would have been speedily deported by their ecclesiastical superiors were it not for the fact that the Vice-Royal

---

[1] Fr. Mariano Rubi and Fr. Bartolome Gili, were two friars who arrived early in 1788 from Spain. Both were dissolute men, the first one even contracting a loathsome disease. The religious authorities endeavored to get rid of them, as they were a disgrace to their Order, but the Spanish Government system prevented this without the consent of the secular authorities, and these men seemed to have influence with the authorities in Spain. Finally Fr. Gili was shipped off to the Philippines in 1793 and Fr. Rubi was disciplined some other way. (Fr. Pangua to Fr. Lasuen, April 29, 1795, Santa Barbara archives.)

Patronato, in the face of most absolute proof of lewdness and debaucheries, for some unknown reason, blocked the efforts to dismiss them.

In later years we meet some exceptions again, for instance when a priest was charged with violation of the secrecy and sanctity of the confession. (See Appendix No. 1.)

No matter in what particular field of endeavor a large number of men are placed, there will always be a few who are untrue to their vows and promises. Members of the Catholic or of any other clergy do not escape this natural law of averages.

We see the same phenomena in every walk of life. Each nation, from times immemorial, has discovered traitors amongst its commissioned army and navy officers, even in the hour of great danger—like Benedict Arnold. The Greeks, standing embattled under Leonidas in the rugged gorge of Thermopylae, had their traitor Ephiates, selling their lives and his soul to Xerxes. Judges who have solemnly sworn to uphold the Constitution and the laws of their country sometimes become grafters; sworn physicians now and then become malpractitioners and abortionists, while lawyers who have taken the oath of fidelity to their clients before the highest courts occasionally prove to be shysters. Is this a reason to traduce all high-minded and loyal men who wear their country's uniform, or who sit on the woolsack or practice other noble professions?

Many attacks on the integrity of the Fathers must be heavily discounted in view of racial dislikes or religious prejudices.

Intolerance has stained the history of Christianity with endless wars and brutalities, with a record of deplorable crusades, inquisitions, *auto-da-fes,* massacres, pogroms, and other horrors which the spirit of Jesus could not stop. This spirit of intolerance reared its ugly head when the story of the Missions in the West was to be written and the Mission Fathers did not escape its consequences.

Racial dislikes were always near the surface in early California. The Spaniards and their descendants were lazy "greasers" in the eyes of later arriving Nordics, while the "greasers" looked with scorn on the newcomers, referring to them as *gringos,* a corruption of the uncomplimentary Spanish *griego,* or sharper. In the eyes of the Nordic settlers, the Spanish Fathers were not exactly heroic figures.

The more specific charges against the Mission Fathers are that they failed to give the neophytes proper scholastic education, or do anything for their intellectual development; that they resorted to corporal punishment in order to maintain discipline; and that they enriched themselves at the expense of the natives, whom they held in actual slavery, with the result that when force was removed they relapsed into barbarism.

CHAPTER XIV

Criticism for Lack of Scholastic Instruction
and Infliction of Corporal Punishment
to Maintain Discipline.

BOOK II

Chapter XIV

*Criticism for Lack of Scholastic Instruction and Infliction of
Corporal Punishment to Maintain Discipline*

THERE were only two priests at each Mission; one to attend to the
temporalities, the other to attend to the spiritual welfare of the
neophytes; no more priests were allowed by the secular authorities,
except in a very few cases, when for special reasons there were three.

How could they spare much time to become school teachers—instructing Indians to write, read and make numbers? This would have come in
the course of events if matters had not moved too swiftly to allow the
Missions to arrive at a mature age. It is a fallacy that a savage race can
be civilized in one or two decades. Our own race had to bleed on a thousand battle fields, going through the dark and middle ages, before a semblance of order and humanity was established. Notwithstanding our
heritage from the great River Empires, from the Greek, Roman and
Moorish civilizations, superstition and ignorance were well-nigh universal
up to the time of the Renaissance, and only a few persons outside of the
clergy could read or write.

Even half a century ago, knowledge or secular teaching was not dif-
fused. It was not considered a disgrace if a man were unable to write his
name. Many were reared in all nations unable to read or write. Even
today there are a great many of our native Americans, of old Colonial
stock, who labor under this handicap. How much more excusable that
Indians, passing from a savage state to one of industry, lacked scholastic
attainments! We certainly did not do much better with our black population in the East and South.

Each age has its own political and scholastic maturity; it is wrong to
reproach those who lived before us for not having advanced to the point
where we are now.

Instead of criticizing the Fathers for what they failed to do, we should
admire them for the great deal they accomplished in the short time the
Missions were under their control. If we consider the condition of the
savages when the missionaries came, and the general inability of the North
American Indians of adapting themselves, a condition which even the
American Government with all its resources seems to be unable to over-

come, it looks rather like a miracle that a few of the Indians of the Mission did learn to read and write.

It may be claimed that all this is but the vulgar argument of the kettle against the pot and can lead to nothing, but this is begging the question. Obviously, the faults of the Spanish Mission Fathers in the West cannot be cleansed by washing them in the sins of the forefathers of their Eastern critics; nor is one shortcoming a justification for another; but it must be equally manifest that it behooves persons whose own ancestors are so open to criticism, to refrain from throwing stones at the Mission Fathers.

A like criticism has been made against the Roman Catholic Church in Mexico, and in the Latin Catholic countries of Europe, where illiteracy is far greater than in the northern Protestant countries. This may be due more to lack of opportunity or to climate or to the disinclination of the inhabitants than to negligence of the Church. Non-Catholics who have had an opportunity to watch the unselfish work of the Catholic orders in their institutions in the United States have profound respect for these men and women who devote their lives to teaching. In one such institution on the very spot where the Fathers of the Santa Cruz Mission used to teach their neophytes, little waifs, white, yellow, brown, black, or of mixed races, some of them plucked out of the poverty of large cities, are being raised, educated and encouraged to become self-respecting human beings and good citizens of the Republic.

In a great many Catholic schools and colleges all over the United States excellent education is given to all qualified applicants, immaterial of race, creed or financial condition; many Protestant and non-conformist parents believe that such Catholic institutions are unsurpassed in character building.

In judging the educational efforts of the Fathers on behalf of their Indian wards, one should not limit the meaning of education to the teaching of the three R's and various ologies. There is no greater fool than the educated fool—the product of the theory that book learning is the only thing. This rule, of course, applies particularly to the more primitive races—especially for them are the hands as potent educators as the eyes and ears, and often convey more valuable information to the brain. Common-sense, the mother of all wisdom, is often possessed by one poorly trained scholastically, but well trained along manual lines.

The Fathers had to teach the Indian people first of all how to live; how, by working, to deserve food, clothing and houses, and how, by industry, to produce that which they needed to lift themselves out of savagery, so that they might subsist in a more secure and civilized way than they had so far been accustomed to.

As in other matters, the Mission Fathers were not free agents in regard to education. They were servitors of a department of the Government, subject in their temporal policies to the criticism of the secular political agents, the Governors, presidio commanders, and even corporals of the Mission guard.

In teaching the neophytes, the Fathers often had to battle with the discouraging fact that the secular population, by precept or other means, tore down what they had built up. The Mission and Indian pueblo of San Diego was removed six miles up the valley; San Carlos Mission (Monterey) to Carmel Valley, away from the neighborhood of the presidios, on account of the lay people debauching the Indian women, and sometimes killing the native husbands who objected. Under such conditions, teaching savages to become civilized must have been a heart-breaking task, indeed.

That the Fathers flogged the Indians to enforce discipline, and to punish them for transgressions, is indisputable. Not only have travelers reported this, but we have the testimony of the Mission Fathers themselves.

In those times parents demanded reverence and obedience, even from their adult sons and daughters, and did not hesitate to administer a flogging with a rawhide in case of lack of respect. This rule of conduct was time-honored. It was the task of the padres to educate and correct the natives, just as it is the task of a natural parent to educate and correct his sons. It was a common thing for the padres to call the neophytes their children,[1] and under Isabella and Charles V the Indians were declared minors by law and for life. This law remained in full force until 1810.[2]

The Lima Council had determined that correction by words was not sufficient for the Indian. Even the liberal Governor de Borica pronounced that twenty-five lashes were moderate punishment. (See Appendix No. 1.)

No one less than Father Serra himself, in a letter to Governor de Neve, gave his opinion as follows:

"With regards to the correction of the Indians, though we introduced enough distinctions of *gobernadores, alcaldes* and *fiscals,* nevertheless, when it seemed to us anyone deserved it, he was given the punishment of the lash or of the stocks, according to the guilt. This practice resulted in having the work accomplished. In all the regions of the dominions which I have traversed, I have observed such officials subject to the order of the missionaries or parish priests. . . .

"The punishment of the lash which the spiritual Fathers of the Indians inflict upon the Indians as children seems as old as the conquest of these

---

[1] Blackmar, Spanish Institutions of the Southwest, p. 115.
[2] Palou, Noticias, Vol. I, p. 190.

dominions, and so general that it does not seem that even the saints departed from this manner of correction. . . .

"The *alcaldes* themselves are children mentally, and as such in charge of the Fathers. They are not less in need of education, correction and support. I do not know what law or reasons there could be to exempt them. In truth, when the illustrious Fernando Cortes allowed, or rather commanded, himself to be whipped by the Fathers, in the presence of the Indians, he did not wish to set an example for those who generally received the rod, but for all, for no matter how high stood the Indian chiefs, never could they reach the position of him whom they beheld so humiliated. For these and other reasons it has always appeared strange to me that your Honor should deem it a personal slight that here the lash is applied *under the direction of the assistant missionary* upon an Indian of this Mission, who has but recently become a Christian, just because he is an *alcalda*. . . .

"No doubt in the chastisements of which we speak *disorders and excesses have occurred* on the part of some of the Fathers; we are all liable to some of them; but that militates equally against the chastising those who are not alcaldes. . . ."

Father Serra mentions the Cortes episode as a shining example of wisdom and devotion. For this example he had to go back about two hundred and fifty years; evidently oblivious of the fact that looking back at antiquity may be instructive, but that going back to it is quite another thing.

The illustration strikes us today as not a very fortunate choice, for Cortes could hardly be accepted as a model of Christian virtue. Though historians, almost without dissent, proclaim him a military genius of the first magnitude, they do not hesitate to state at the same time that his reputation for treachery is almost unparalleled. His wife, Dona Catalina Juarez Marcaida, who accompanied him on his exploration, was conveniently and definitely disposed of, and Cortes replaced her with the lovely Marina, a reputed Indian princess, captured by the Aztecs from another tribe. She became his interpreter, mistress, adviser and philosopher in Indian affairs.

He had the Aztec Prince, Cuahutemoc, tortured to death in order to make him reveal the hiding place of the State treasures; and he ordered Alvarado's men to slay the assemblage of Aztecs, who had received him as an honored guest, and for whom he pretended friendship. (See Appendix No. 2.)

Most of the history in which Cortes figured is stained with blood. Both the beautiful Marina and a son of Cortes were subsequently tortured by the Inquisition. Those were some of the good old days we hear so much about.

Still Cortes was a great commander, and the idea of a man of his status asking for a public flogging at the hands of ecclesiastics "to give a lesson to the Indian chiefs, who never could reach the position of him whom they beheld so humiliated," is rather painful.

Father Serra believed that the impression made on the Indian chiefs was beneficial. It would be interesting to know what the chiefs really thought of that scene.

But brutality towards the Indians persisted long after Cortes' death. In December, 1763, only six years before the Franciscans entered California, occurred one of the first of the outbursts of mob fury, which have been since so common in American history, and which have nearly always been directed, here as elsewhere, against the weak and unprotected.

There were twenty harmless Conestoga Indians near Lancaster, Pennsylvania—men, women and children—living in amity with the peaceful Quakers and Moravians. Early one morning, a mounted band, known as the "Paxton boys," surrounded their village and set fire to it. Only six Indians were found at home; these were butchered.

The Lancaster magistrates collected the fourteen survivors. The "Paxton boys" returned, broke into the workhouse and slaughtered them —men, women and children—carefully removing the scalps, in order to collect the provincial bounty.

Religious circles were silent or openly commendatory. Benjamin Franklin, however, issued a blazing pamphlet of indignation. He wrote scathingly to the clergymen who tried to justify the deed as "an act of God," and the perpetrators as "blessed crusaders." He plead for more magnanimity towards the helpless Indians. He might as well have used an atomizer on gorillas.

The "Paxtons" turned the countryside into a hell and on their return were received by their own people as heroes.

Factions arose, and Franklin was alternately praised and cursed. Governor John Penn, grandson of the great William, in a panic, signed a proclamation raising the price of Indian scalps, including those of women.[3]

Puritanism displayed not only holiness but hardness; Quakers were hanged and witches were sent to the gibbets. The ferocious "righteousness" of some of those early praying settlers is appalling, and their treat-

---

[3] Philip Russel, Benjamin Franklin (1926), p. 197.

ment of the Indians, who had kept them from starving in the first hard years, was no less startling.[4]

The whites not seldom encouraged the Indians in acts of cruelty. Helen Hunt Jackson in her famous book, "A Century of Dishonor,"[5] states:

"In the wars between France and England and their colonies, their Indian allies were entitled to a premium for every scalp of an enemy. In the war preceding 1703 the Government of Massachusetts gave twelve pounds for every Indian scalp. In 1722 it was augmented to one hundred pounds—a sum sufficient to purchase a considerable extent of American land. On the 25th of February, 1745, an act was passed by the American Colonial Legislature entitled, 'An Act for giving a reward for scalps'— 'Sketches of the History, Manners and Customs of the North American Indians,' by James Buchanan, 1824.

"There was a constant rivalry between the Governments of Great Britain, France and the United States as to which of them should secure the services of the barbarians to scalp their white enemies, while each in turn was the loudest to denounce the shocking barbarities of such tribes as they failed to secure in their own service; and the civilized world, aghast at this horrid recital, ignores the fact that nearly every important massacre in the history of North America was organized and directed by agents of some one of these Governments."

Our dark-skinned brothers have received strange Christian treatment from their white relatives; in the stories of all early colonial enterprises cruelty and rapacity towards the natives is always chronicled. Horrifying brutality, both by the Governors and the governed, has been displayed.

In 1732 the British General, Jeffery Amherst, after whom the well-known college and village in Massachusetts are named, wrote:

"You will do well to try to inoculate the Indians by means of blankets in which smallpox patients have slept, as well as by every other method which can serve to extirpate this execrable race."[6]

In 1740 Governor General Valkenier and his successor Imhoff were both implicated in brutality against Chinese residents of the Island of Java, which ended in a massacre.[7]

To make apologies for such conditions is useless and only breeds hypocrisy, but they give us a key to the white man's mental state during the Mission period on the Pacific Coast.

---

[4] George Wharton James writes—"Our treatment of these Indians reads like a hideous nightmare. They were the helpless victims of white infamous wretches aided by the Government"—In and Out of the Old Missions, p. 293.

[5] p. 404 et seq.

[6] Hendrik van Loon, America, p. 42.

[7] Van Deventer, History of the Netherlands in Java, Vol. 2, p. 61 et seq.

Again, the tendency of the strong to suppress the weak seems to be inherent in human nature. Wherever a few white men have been placed in charge of many natives, standing much lower in the scale of civilization, the temptation arises to exercise autocratic power. This is partly based on the fallacious idea that the "heathen's" rights are limited, and partly on the powerful impulse of self-preservation.

Granting that all this brutality was prevalent in the world, how can we justify the fact that the Fathers—professed followers in the footsteps of the gentle Christ—countenanced cruelty in their own fold?

One may just as well ask, how could all the brutality, formerly participated in by judges, juries, the clergy, and the public at large, be justified?

Only recently we heard solemn discussions by humanitarian American jurists, regarding the advisability of reintroducing the lash, in order to curb our ever-rising wave of violent crimes, while not more than a score of years ago President Theodore Roosevelt advocated the re-establishment of the whipping post for wife beaters.

Flogging horrifies us today, though this punishment was administered in almost all armies and navies, including those of the United States, as well as the merchant marine, well into the last century.[a]

It was administered in the penitentiaries all over the Christian world, long after the Mission system disappeared. In the abominable prison camps in the Southern States of the Union, prisoners were farmed out for their labor and far more inhumanely treated than the California Indians. The system was continued until recently in several of the States, when the hue and cry of the press awoke the public conscience.

Even after the secularization of the Missions flogging seems to have been taken as a matter of course. We find in the old records of the Magistrate's office, when the famous William Blackburn was the Alcalde of Santa Cruz, that in a misdemeanor case the accused was found guilty and the Honorable Blackburn sentenced the culprit to a number of lashes on the bare back with the end of a riata "well put on." Again we note that on February 10th, 1848, Truman Truman was accused of robbing one Brock. He was tried by a jury and the verdict was that the prisoner should immediately receive twelve lashes on the bare back, well laid on, and that he be banished from the jurisdiction forever; in the event that he ever be found there again, he was to be hung by the neck until dead.

In the same book there is an entry, bearing date of July 19th, 1848, where the accused was convicted of perjury and punished by fifty lashes

---

[a] Dana, Two Years Before the Mast, 1834.

and banishment, death being the penalty if he returned. (Alcalde Book, Santa Cruz County Records.)

Compared with these reports, the story of the Missions of California before the gringos came, especially during the first half of their existence, is a story replete with high devotion and unselfish effort.

Whipping, as penance, was a commonplace occurrence of comparatively little moment. Daily, the Mission Fathers were reminded of their vows by self-inflicted scourging with the three knotted girdles which they wore. Serra was noted for his acts of contrition by whipping himself with a chain and beating his breast with a stone.

How would it have been possible for the Fathers, under all these circumstances, to have considered flogging inhuman or unnecessary?

Much of the criticism levied against the padres is rooted in religious prejudice, which can hardly be considered a sound predisposition for the critical examination of social conditions, and while invectives may relieve feelings, they carry scant conviction.

CHAPTER XV

Criticism for holding the Indians in Virtual
Bondage, while the Fathers lived in Luxury;
what they really accomplished.

BOOK II

Chapter XV

Criticism for Holding the Indians in Virtual Bondage While the Fathers Lived in Luxury; What They Really Accomplished

IT has been charged that the neophytes were kept in virtual bondage. This is true, especially in the later Mission period.

We recognize now, at least some of us do, that the keeping of slaves in any form is wrong. To endeavor to justify the system of forced labor, in vogue at the Missions, on the ground that the Indians were unruly and often vicious children is hardly to be reconciled with the fact that labor was required from them which could not have been performed by naughty children. When it came to labor, these people had to work full days like adults. When it came to transgressions, they were punished as children—with punishments "which had been in vogue in the old Mexican prisons." This was the theory.

Nevertheless, unless the Indians had in practice been properly treated they could never have been controlled by a few priests and soldiers, and Forbes, in his "History of California" (London, 1839) testifies that most of the Indians venerated and loved the Fathers, while de Mofras assures us that in 1834 over thirty thousand Indians were peaceably employed at the Missions under a few overseers. (See Appendix No. 1.)

Surgeon G. H. von Langsdorff, of the Russian ship *Juno,* has nothing but praise for the work of the Fathers, yet involuntarily he gives, at least to the modern mind, a somewhat too optimistic picture. He visited certain of the Missions in the year 1806, and tells enough details to establish the existence of practical villainage of the neophytes, to which, however, he seems to have no objections. He states:

"Disobedience is commonly punished with corporal correction.

"Monks go on horseback with one or more soldiers for runaways. Twelve hundred Indians work at San Francisco Mission."

That two or three monks, with four or five soldiers, could keep order, he attributed to the mildness and forebearance of the monks, and extreme simplicity of the poor natives, "who in stature, not less than in mind, are certainly of a very inferior race of human beings."

"When longing for freedom," he said, "they run away, but they can only go to their own tribes, as others are hostile, and they are therefore soon caught. When taken back to the Mission, they are bastionadoed, and

163

an iron rod a foot or a foot and a half long, one inch in diameter, is fastened to their feet."

Working for shelter and board, pursued, brought back, whipped and put in irons for deserting the Mission, this might look perfectly proper to a Russian gentleman of those times. What he saw was perhaps a cross between the rural conditions then existing on the land estates in Russia and the later state under the first Communistic rule.

The padres were intensely practical; they knew that the rule they gave brought beneficial results, and Father de Lasuen therefore did not hesitate to write to Governor de Borica in 1794 as follows:

"The neophytes are content with the benefits of Christianity, and of human society, also with the quality of subsistence and shelter they receive. Very frugally fed and simply clad, the neophytes labor in the fields, churches, dwellings, barns and shops, and in this manner uphold this conquest and prepare a further extension in due time."

True, the system was patriarchal and not modern even for those times, but generally speaking the Indians were at peace under this regime and made steady progress towards civilization.

Junipero Serra, his associates and their successors electrified the lazy and worthless Indians into more or less willing workers; they showed them by personal example how to work. They did not hesitate to tuck up their gowns and tread bare-footed in the pit with the Indians, to mix the mud which was to be sun-baked into bricks, or to do any other kind of manual labor. To them taking the life of an Indian was a horror.

The treatment of the natives must have varied with the different temperaments of the individual Fathers, and likewise with the period in which the Fathers lived. It seems that especially towards the last, when great wealth had come to the Missions, the relationship became less personal, more institutional, and therefore less kindly.

The conclusion may well be drawn that the Mission Fathers, under the laws and their instructions, and in accordance with the universally prevailing ideas, exercised a benevolent despotism, a despotism which was far milder and far more beneficial to the "heathen" than the kind generally exercised in the other parts of the world, under various regimes, but a despotism nevertheless.

Very likely this was the only method which could have been applied. Fifty years more of such despotism might have advanced the members of the Indian race to a condition resembling citizenship. Its removal and the granting of freedom brought these same Indians total destruction.

History has amply vindicated the judgment of the Mission Fathers.

Long after the neophytes had been emancipated on the Pacific Coast, hundreds of Protestant ministers in the Eastern and Southern States declared and proved from the gospel (at least to their own satisfaction) that it was ordained by God that slavery was an entirely proper institution.[1]

The bill abolishing the slave trade in the District of Columbia was only passed in 1850. That same year President Fillmore signed the infamous Fugitive Slave Act. Public opinion forced him to do so, for the South was incensed by the forcing of "free California" as a non-slavery State into the Union, and a rejection of the act would probably have brought on immediate secession by the South. Yet it took a civil war of four years before the American slaves were finally freed.[2]

California never suffered from the baneful results of interstate slave trade, which disgraced large parts of the Union—selling a man and his wife and children to different masters, who lived hundreds of miles apart, when there was no hope of their meeting again, was legalized cruelty, which finds few parallels in history[3] and none in California.

Even the most virulent critics of the Mission Fathers never claimed that such conditions existed under their administration, for the Fathers were stern in their efforts to keep the individual families together.

By many it is maintained that the Fathers lived in great luxury and abundance, while others as firmly believe that they courted poverty and hard living.

The Friars all belonged to the Franciscan Brotherhood, one of the great mendicant orders of the Church. By their vows of poverty, as well as by the regulations of their order, they were not allowed to acquire, accumulate, or own any property for their own uses, but there was no moral or legal impediment for the order to acquire and hold property for the Church, or for charitable, missionary or other kindred purposes.

During the early explorations, and during the founding of the Missions, the Friars sustained with devotion and fortitude a great many hardships, like all pioneers who went West. Incredible hardships were the lot of those who crossed the plains and mountains to come to the promised land—California, Oregon and Washington. The history of the treks of

---

[1] The Episcopal Bishop of Louisiana, Leonardas Polk, who afterwards became prominent in the Civil War, owned 400 slaves and trained them in religion. (Elsom, History of the U. S. Vol. 3, p. 210.

[2] The Emancipation proclamation for the liberation of slaves was issued by President Lincoln on January 1st, 1863, as a war measure.

[3] Elson, History of the United States, Vol. III, p. 213.

the Fathers towards the Unknown fortunately does not contain such horrible stories of sufferings—even cannibalism—as were recorded in other treks, especially that of the famous Donner party. Still few of their critics would care to follow their example.

With the development and increasing wealth of the Missions, the living conditions of the padres ameliorated. This was fortunate, for they were getting older and needed more of the comforts of life, and if ever any persons deserved the rewards of their labor, the padres did.

California, like any other semi-tropical country, offers eventual rich rewards to energetic settlers, but it gives its aborigines less natural food than either a country situate in the tropical zone or in a colder climate.

In the tropics, nature is lavish to its children, offering fruits—cocoanuts, bananas, breadfruit, and so forth—in abundance; the forests of the mountains and valleys contain any number of fibre-producing plants— palms and bamboos—providing the little clothing necessary and material for homes.

In the medium cold countries, small game is generally abundant the year around and the forests produce nuts, berries, mushrooms, etc.; when there is a reasonable rainfall in the spring, summer and fall, the soil, if structurally adaptable, readily responds to the slight efforts of man, and there is always some natural pasturage. The Indians in the Eastern and Northwestern part of the United States, as far as the Rockies, had besides their maize and tobacco patches, good pasture for the herds of buffalo and other large game, off which they lived.

In a semi-tropical country it is different. California, in the springtime, with her myriads of brilliant wild flowers, looks like a veritable paradise, but this picture is of short duration, for soon the dry season sets in, and unless the land is copiously irrigated and thoroughly cultivated, it is, in most places, more of a desert than a garden of Eden. Large game, always difficult to capture with primitive weapons, retreats to more favorable and isolated locations; the scant native grain dries up, and little or nothing is left for the natural sustenance of man, except acorns, a few other nuts stored in the fall, some seeds from native grasses, small game, venison, and on the coast some fish. This was the kind of country the Mission Fathers found and had to battle with. Even today lovely California is essentially a man-made country, and must forever remain so.

The California Indians were a product of this primeval condition, and it is small wonder that the vast majority of writers, including most of the padres, described them as "almost naked and half-starved, degraded and brutal, living in filthy little hovels of tule, cruel, simple and lazy."

There were no horses, mules or domesticated cattle, hogs, goats, sheep or fowl, not even cats and dogs in the country; there were no farm implements nor irrigation ditches, no bridges, roads, houses, temples or other even semi-substantial buildings, but when the Missions were finally secularized, the Mission property included large herds of domestic animals, valuable buildings, cultivated fields, orchards, vineyards, etc. In other words, civilization had arrived.

How was all this property acquired and created?

Developing ranch and farm property from virgin soil under primitive conditions in a semi-arid country to such a high state of cultivation can only be accomplished by the application of great intelligence and the expenditure of a tremendous amount of physical labor.

In the eighties and nineties of the last century (1880-1900) there were several such barren stretches still in existence in California. By that time work stock was abundant and some power machinery was in use. Scrapers, ditchers, excavators, stump-pullers, breaking and gang plows were put to work; a very army of laborers—mostly hardy, cheap labor from Europe was employed; yet it took a prodigious effort to reclaim an estate from the plains.

The Mission Fathers opened up the country to civilization and became perforce great plantation executives besides spiritual leaders; they accomplished their appalling task with the crudest tools, and the poorest human material to draw from; it was humanly impossible for them to have done this except with a horde of workers.

How well these men succeeded! From 1769, when the first Mission was founded in Upper California, until 1834, when the Missions there were finally secularized, the land lying along the coast had been turned from an uncultivated wilderness into a productive agricultural and stock-raising country.

The Missions of Alta California had, in 1832, over 420,000 cattle, 60,000 horses and mules, 320,000 sheep, goats and hogs, and raised over 340,000 bushels of wheat, corn and beans, 90 per cent of which was wheat. The native population had advanced both intellectually and physically.

After secularization all this was squandered and destroyed, and with it perished most of the Indian race.

Over-enthusiastic admirers are apt to claim that the Fathers personally taught the aborigines all the arts and crafts of the white man's civilization, and that the Missions were erected by these wild people, under sole instruction of their spiritual leaders. Verily, the Mission Fathers do not need any spurious laurels for their crowns.

There were only two priests, and occasionally three, at each Mission. Only one was engaged with the practical work. As time went on, buildings were erected, gardens with palms and fountains were established, orchards and vineyards planted and cultivated, grain was grown, harvested and milled; cattle raised, wool carded and spun, hides tanned, clothing manufactured, shoes and sandals made, wine and olive oil pressed, wood carved, silver and other church ornaments produced, etc. To believe that any one Father could be an expert in all these trades is making too large a draft on a person's credulity.

Right from the beginning artisans were sent out by the Spanish Government to each of the presidios, and the services of these men were "lent" to the missionaries. Likewise, the Government encouraged the immigration of colonists, who were skilled mechanics, to the mission-pueblos and presidios.

It is sufficient honor for the padres that they were able to co-ordinate and direct these different and varied agencies, and that very often under the most difficult circumstances.

The California Indians came under the sway of three foreign dominations: Spanish, Mexican and American. The last one, bringing so-called individual liberty to the Indian, is by far the worst.

During all the Spanish occupation of California by the missionaries and military, no Indian was ever driven from his land. Under American rule, the poor devils have been exiled and expelled from the lands of their ancestors to worthless hill and desert lands, there left to degenerate and die.

Under Spanish rule, the right of the Indian to the land was inalienable; he was protected at any cost; under American rule he was left plundered and despoiled.

And after the padres had gone and the neophytes had been liberated from their "evil" masters, they and their descendants were sold to pay their "legal" fines, once each week, for seven days' work. This took place in the open market at Los Angeles, where a pompous town marshal, as a limb of the law officiated, and was vindicated by Amercian courts and American justice.[4]

---

[4] George Wharton James, In and Out of Old Missions, p. 300.

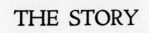

THE STORY

BOOK III

CHAPTER XVI

The Founding of the Mission
Santa Cruz

BOOK III
Chapter XVI

The Founding of the Mission Santa Cruz

DURING the comparatively short period of twenty years since the establishment of the first Mission at San Diego in 1769 much had happened and a great deal had been accomplished.

California had known five Governors: Gaspar de Portola, who left July 9th, 1770; Matias de Armona, resigned November 9th, 1770; Felipe Barri, resigned March 4th, 1775; Felipe de Neve, retired July 12th, 1782, and Pedro Fages, retired April 16th, 1791.

It had known two *comandantes-militair* or Vice-Governors: Pedro Fages, 1770-1774; Fernando Rivera y Moncada, 1774-1777.

The first two Governors had their official residence at Loreto, and so had de Neve, until February, 1777, when Monterey had become the capital of the Californias and his residence was moved there. At the same time the *comandante-militar* became Vice-Governor of Lower California.

The sacerdotal authorities had established eleven Missions:

San Diego de Alcala (near the present city of San Diego), San Carlos Borromeo (near Monterey), San Antonio de Padua (near Jolon), San Gabriel Arcangel (near Los Angeles), San Luis Obispo de Tolosa (near city of same name), San Francisco de Asis (in San Francisco), San Juan Capistrano (near Santa Ana), Santa Clara de Asis (in the town of Santa Clara), San Buenaventura (in Ventura), Santa Barbara (in Santa Barbara), and La Purisima Concepcion (25 miles from Santa Ynez).

The secular authorities had done their part in erecting four presidios or military posts; the first established at San Jose, November 29th, 1777, with sixty-six persons, including fourteen families, nine of soldiers from Monterey and five from de Anza's expedition, Lieutenant Moraga representing the Governor; the second Los Angeles, named Pueblo Nuestra Senora, Reina de Los Angeles (Our Lady, Queen of the Angels), founded in 1781, with eleven families, consisting of forty-six persons, of which only two were of pure white blood.

In both cases the lands were divided in house lots, planting plots or fields (550 feet square), commons and income-producing lots for public use, respectively called *solares, suertes, ejidos* and *propios.* Each settler was given one *solar,* two dry and two irrigated *suertes,* two horses, a saddle with bridle, a gun and other arms.[1]

---

[1] Richman, California Under Spain and Mexico, p. 126.

The population of Alta California in 1790 consisted of 970 Spaniards, or those declared to be "white," and 7,353 neophytes, besides an unknown number of Gentiles and savages.

While the population of the Indian pueblos at the Missions had steadily increased, the mortality was great. The statistics show that from 1769 to 1797, 21,653 baptisms took place and 10,437 deaths occurred.

Under Governor de Borica, a few years later, mortality tables were prepared, covering the averages of the yearly periods between 1792 and 1796, which showed that the lowest yearly rate was at San Diego, being 6.25 per cent; the highest at San Francisco, 15.75 per cent; while Santa Clara listed 12.62 per cent, and Santa Cruz 11.75 per cent. Governor de Borica ascribed this appalling death rate to lack of freedom of a nomadic race, insufficient food—grain not being raised in sufficient quantities and beef being generally prohibited to the Indians except on feast days—to filth of body, and to crowding the girls and women, for morality's sake, in so-called *monjas* or nunneries, where, according to de Borica, "the stench was unbearable."[2]

While there had been a great many mutations among the civil officers during these twenty momentous years, California had only known two *Padres-presidente*—Junipero Serra, who died in 1784, and Fermin Francisco de Lasuen, who served until his death on June 26th, 1803,[3] Father Palou functioning as Acting President for some time.   (See Appendix 1.)

Of the Franciscan padres, some returned to Mexico or Spain; others died a peaceful death in Alta California;[4] a few had broken down under the strain, while others had found martyrdom at the hands of the Indians.

For six years after the expiration of Serra's right, in 1784, no confirmation had taken place in California. True, on March 13, 1787, this right was bestowed by the Father Prefect of the Apostolic College of Mexico, under authority of a decree of convocation issued at Rome in 1785, on Father President de Lasuen, in case of his death on Father Pablo Mugartegui, and in default of both on Father Pedro Benito Cambon. The document, on account of various delays, did not reach Monterey until March, 1790. Governor Fages was at the same time directed by Jacobo

---

[2] Resumen y Notas de los Estados de Missiones, July 8, 1897, M. A. Arch. Genl. Prov. Int. 216.

[3] Father de Lasuen is generally recognized as one of the very great men sent to Alta California by the Franciscan Order. Even de la Perouse, who was far from being in sympathy with the mission system, writes of him: "His sweetness of temper, his benevolence, and his love for the Indians are beyond expression."

[4] These supernumerary missionaries were without compensation, and the Fathers President were classified amongst them! They lived, therefore, upon the alms of their Franciscan Brethren, whom they were supervising.

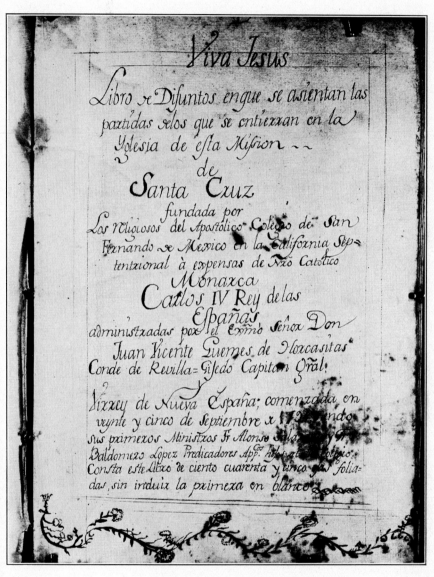

Viva Jesus

Libro de Difuntos en que se asientan las partidas delos que se entierran en la Yglesia de esta Mission

de

Santa Cruz

fundada por Los Religiosos del Apostólico Colegio de San Fernando de Mexico en la California Septentrional à expensas de Nro Catolico

Monarca

Carlos IV Rey de las Españas administradas por el Exmo Señor Don Juan Vicente Guemes de Horcasitas Conde de Revilla=Gigedo Capitan Gral.

Virrey de Nueva España; comenzada en veynte y cinco de Septiembre de 17__ siendo sus primeros Ministros Fr Alonso Sala[...] y Baldomero Lopez Predicadores App[...] [...] Consta este Libro de ciento cuarenta y cinco [...] foliadas, sin incluir la primera en blanco.

TITLE PAGE FROM OLD RECORD OF DEATHS
AT MISSION SANTA CRUZ
Courtesy of the Rev. Father McGrath, of Santa Cruz, California.

Ugarte y Loyola, the *comandante-general* of the Internal Provinces of the West (by that time carved out of the old *Provincias Internas*), to throw no obstacles in the way of its execution.

The Padre *Presidente* lost no time in saving and securing souls from perdition, and in the following years he confirmed more than ten thousand persons, mostly Indians, of course.

Father de Lasuen had been President only a few years, when on September 22nd, 1789, Fra. Matias de Noriega (who had labored for six years at the Alta California Missions, and was now guardian ad interim of the San Fernando College) wrote to the Viceroy advising the establishment of two new Missions.

So far the founding of other Missions had been repeatedly and often vehemently insisted upon by the Fathers President before being approved. This time no such difficulties were encountered, for now impetus was given by the lay authorities to the provisions contained in the de Neve *reglamento,* providing for a second, interior chain of Missions, to be located equi-distant between the existing ones.

The Viceroy, Conde de Revilla Gigedo, after consultation with Guardian de Noriega and after reading the latter's report, "de Condiciones de Missiones,"[*] gave the following opinion on October 31st, 1789:

"Agreeing to the proposition which your Reverence makes in your report of September 22nd last, I have resolved that two Missions should be established in Nueva California, one in the valley called Soledad, close to the Rio Monterey, between the Mission of San Antonio and that of San Carlos, and the other between the Missions of San Carlos and Santa Clara, about twenty-five leagues distant from the former, at the spot called Santa Cruz.

"In order that this resolution, so beneficial to the Gentiles, may be carried out as quickly as possible, I beg and charge your Reverence to name four 'religious' who shall found and serve these Missions. They should leave the capital in time so as not to lose the first opportunity of a ship that makes the voyage to Monterey. For that purpose on this day I issue orders to the ministers of the royal treasury of the capitol, and direct them to deliver to the *sindico* of your apostolic college $2,000 for the necessary goods, and the traveling expenses for four religious to the port of San Blas, to whose commissary I give similar orders for their embarcation, and for the subsistence which they are to receive during the voyage. I hope that your Reverence will inform me of the results, and that on your part you will procure the discovery of suitable localities between San Diego and San Juan Capistrano, San Gabriel and San Buenaventura, in order to fill

---

[*] Santa Barb. Arch. M. S. VI, 280-2 B. C.

up those gaps with other intermediate Missions and that you will communicate whatever else is useful and feasible."[6]

The news of the resolve to found the Mission of Santa Cruz in honor of the Holy Cross, and Soledad, in honor of Our Lady of Solitude, reached Monterey on August 2nd, 1790, by the same ship that brought the four new missionaries appointed by the President of the San Fernando College.

The intelligence that one of the Missions was to be located at a place which had several times been indicated as ideal for such a purpose was received with great satisfaction by the Mission authorities.

As we have seen, Father Crespi, the conscientious chronicler of Portola's expedition in 1769, had made entries in his diary regarding the crossing of the San Lorenzo River and the Santa Cruz Creek, not far from the sea. He noticed with pleasure "the good pasture and the variety of herbs, and the rose bushes of Castile," that the sky was clear, that there was no fog and that the company was so delighted that they remained sixteen days near the Bay.

To understand his delight, one should realize that the middle of October is, as a rule, the end of a long dry season in California, and irrigation, except in the immediate vicinity of the Missions, being practically non-existent at that time, such favorable conditions could only exist in a very few places between San Diego and San Francisco. Santa Cruz was one of these favored exceptions.

Father Palou had written even more enthusiastically about the location:

"After crossing the creek of Santa Cruz, we forded the river San Lorenzo, which is rather large and deep, the water reaching to the stirrups. The banks were covered with sycamore, cottonwood and willow trees, and near the crossing, close to the hills, there are many *palo Colorado* (redwood trees). The place is fit not only for a town, but for a city, without wanting any of the things necessary. With good land, water, pasture, wood and timber just within reach, and in great abundance, and close to Monterey Bay. The town could be put a quarter league distant from the sea with all the said conveniences."

In the forested coast regions of semi-tropical countries, the foothills are generally heavily wooded on the north and east sides, but rather denuded, except for shrubs, on their southern and western slopes, while the canyons between offer no end of delight in a great variety of vegetation, such as huckleberry bushes, maiden-hair ferns, wild flowers, etc.

---

[6] Santa Barb. Arch. Revilla, Gigedo to F. Matias, Noriega, Oct. 31, 1789.

For a residential location in such regions, one needs sunshine, for the difference in temperature between the shade and the sun is more marked than in more northern or tropical countries.

Knowing these climatological conditions, the Fathers selected for the building site of the Mission of Santa Cruz a level spot, exposed to the unobstructed rays of the sun, and only a stone's throw from the flowering canyons, the rushing river and the wooded slopes.

It would have been hard to find a more delightful place. It had all the advantages of the other coast Missions and many more; its climate had no equal except possibly that of Santa Barbara, but it far surpassed the latter in natural benefits.

Father de Lasuen took a personal interest and pride in the selection and approval of the site. He wrote:

"I found in the site the most excellent fitness which had been reported to me. I found, besides, a stream of water, very near, copious and very important. On August 28th, 1791, the day of Saint Augustine, I said Mass, and raised a cross on the spot where the establishment is to be. Many Gentiles came, old and young, of both sexes, and showed that they would gladly enlist under the Sacred Standard, thanks be to God!"[7]

One can understand that they thanked God many times, for the life of the padres was made up of hardships, isolation, privation and long years of fatiguing labor in an untamed country.

What a joy Santa Cruz must have promised. One can see them standing on the hill, looking down upon the San Lorenzo River, lined with a great variety of deciduous trees, flowing through the small, lovely valley towards the west, or gazing towards the deep blue Bay of Monterey, on the opposite side of which the San Carlos Mission and presidio were situated, and admiring the glorious sunsets over the Pacific Ocean. Then again they may have walked up the rock-strewn canyon of the upper San Lorenzo, its slopes covered with towering evergreens, and its audible waters boiling and tumbling in their steep descent over high boulders. They must have found it good, indeed.

Those who know Santa Cruz can relive their pleasure, for the general physical aspects of the country are the same today—still untouched by the desecrating hand of civilized man. Soft purple shades still cover the mountains, and Loma Prieta is a landmark as it was then; gentle fogs still gather over the Bay and slowly rise, chased away by a brilliant sun, which leaves the waters blue and sparkling. Warm sands invite one and great trees offer shade.

---

[7] George Wharton James, In and Out of the Old Missions, p. 34.

Besides scenic beauty and a salubrious climate, the Fathers found that abundant forests were close at hand, containing redwoods *(Sequoia Sempervirens)*, readily split and sawed. (See Appendix 2.) The nearby hills contained lime rock and the so easily worked chalk rock; building material did not have to be brought, as in many cases, from long distances, and this added much to their comfort and convenience.

We cannot but hope that they knew and loved the small grove of Sequoia Sempervirens now owned as a public park by the County of Santa Cruz (see Appendix 3), and situate only six miles up the gorge of the San Lorenzo River from the Mission site. We wonder whether they ever penetrated the mountains to the water divide, several miles higher up, and walked there among the towering trees of a similar group, now embraced within the limits of a public recreation ground, known as the California State Redwood Park in the Big Basin. (See Appendix 4.)

Beside their great height and immense girth, these trees are peculiar in that they grow in little groups amongst their smaller sister redwoods— small only in comparison with the giants.

Like their cousins, the *Sequoias Gigantea* (see Appendix 5), the only other Sequoias known, which grow in a few separated groves amongst the pines in the Sierra Nevada mountains of California, they are the oldest living things in the world—in fact, it is claimed that many of the latter were old when Christ walked upon the earth. How such trees must have inspired the beauty-loving Fathers of Spain, who often mentioned the *palo alto* and the *palo colorado* with admiration!

The Indians worshipped the trees in the Santa Cruz grove—a reverence understandable to those who have stood beneath these awe-inspiring trees and looked up toward the first branches, often one hundred and fifty feet above the ground, and then to their far-off tops, seemingly so near the sky. Even today, anyone whose soul and mind are at all attuned to the wonders of nature walks slowly among these forest giants, feeling that he is in a sacred cathedral, the pillars of which might well support the canopies of Heaven. He senses the succession of centuries, and leaves the place with a feeling of the greatness of the directing spirit of the universe and of his own infinite smallness. (See Appendix 6.)

We know that the Fathers were greeted with the beauty and aroma of flowering shrubs—of mountain lilac and wild azalea, of manzanita and madrone, covered with white flowers in spring and red berries in winter, and also by Toyon berries growing so profusely in the Santa Cruz mountains—the real Christmas berries of California. (See Appendix 7.)

"FATHER TREE," SANTA CRUZ BIG TREE GROVE

"ANIMAL TREE," SANTA CRUZ BIG TREE GROVE

Beside the lovely San Lorenzo Valley,[8] the Pajaro Valley[9] was within easy distance (twelve miles), a short natural pass through the hills connecting the two. Though this valley was too far removed from the Mission to make agriculture feasible, still it must have been a delight, for it was covered knee-high with natural vegetation, through which the deer and bear roamed at will, and it offered rich promise for the future—a promise which has been completely fulfilled. Today it is one of the most productive garden spots in the world. (See Appendix 8.)

How they must have reveled in that climate!

Monterey is often foggy—the wife of Governor Fages, the aristocratic and colorful Dona Eulalia, is known to have complained bitterly of the climate, as she complained of many other things, including her husband's peculiarities; San Francisco was windy in the summertime, while San Luis Obispo de Tolosa, the San Gabriel Mission and others were bathed in a shimmering heat during that season. Here in this new Eden they were to escape all these drawbacks!

No wonder Padres Isidro Alonzo Salazar and Baldomero Lopez, detailed by the *Presidente* as the first missionaries, considered themselves fortunate indeed. With all the joyous enthusiasm of religious zeal, they looked forward to their task at the lovely Mission of the Holy Cross, so favorably situated at the northern end of the great indentation—Monterey Bay—only twenty-five miles in a direct line from San Carlos, and thirty miles southwest of the Santa Clara Mission.

---

[8] The San Lorenzo River and Valley were named in memory of the Holy Saint Lawrence, on whose birthday the river was crossed by Portola.

[9] The valley was called Bolso del Pajaro, Bolso meaning "pocket" therefore small valley surrounded by hills, and Pajaro of course meant bird. (See Crespi's Diary Oct. 8, 1769.)

CHAPTER XVII

The Mission Dedicated

BOOK III
Chapter XVII
The Mission Dedicated

THE four new Fathers who came to Alta California from Mexico, Antonio Danti, Jose de Miguel, Mariano Rubi and Esteban Tapis, brought with them to Monterey all the necessary effects with the exception of the church utensils. We find in Santa Cruz Libres de Mission, M. S. 3, B. C., that the *sindico* Fr. Geronimo de Samelayo sent from Mexico provisions and tools for Santa Cruz to the value of $1,020 on April 1st, 1790.

On August 3rd, 1790, Father de Lasuen announced the arrival of the padres to Governor Fages, and declared that all was ready for the expedition but the sacred vessels.[1]

It was not until January 20th, 1791, that the Viceroy wrote a positive assurance that the sacred utensils would be sent, together with an order to proceed at once, borrowing the needed articles from the other establishments, and that he would give orders the same day to hasten the goods for Monterey.[2]

This letter reached California in the early part of July, 1791, and on July 15th Father de Lasuen wrote the Viceroy agreeing to the orders therein.

Then on July 22nd, 1791, the President issued a circular to the padres at the different Missions making known the Viceroy's orders and asking each padre to mark on the margin the articles he was able to lend.

The next step in the founding of Santa Cruz is best told by Fr. de Lasuen himself, in the letter he wrote to Governor Romeu, on September 29th, 1791, reporting his activities:

"In view of the superior order of His Excellency, I at once named the missionaries. I asked and obtained from the commander of the presidio the necessary aid for exploring anew the region of Soledad, and there was chosen a site having some advantages over the two previously considered.

"I applied to the Missions for vestments and vessels, and as soon as the commander of the *Aranjazu* furnished the *sirvientes* allowed for the new establishments I proceeded to Santa Clara, in order to examine anew, in person, the site of Santa Cruz.

---

[1] Lasuen to Fages, Aug. 3, 1790, Arch. Arzobispado M. S. 1, 10 B. C.
[2] Gigedo to Lasuen, Jan. 20, 1791, S. B. Arch. B. C.

"I crossed the *sierra* (the Santa Cruz Mountains) by a new and rough way, and I found in the site the same excellent fitness that had been reported to me. I found, besides, a stream of water, very near, copious and important.

"On the day of San Augustin, August 28th, I said Mass, and a cross was raised in the spot where the establishment is to be. Many Gentiles came, large and small of both sexes, and showed that they would gladly enlist under that sacred standard, thank God! I returned to Santa Clara by another way, rougher but shorter and more direct.

"I had the Indians improve the road, and was perfectly successful, because for this, as for everything else, the commandant of San Francisco, Don Hermengildo Sal, has furnished with the greatest activity and promptness all the aid I have asked for.

"I ordered some little huts made and I suppose that by this time the missionaries are there.

"I found here in Monterey the *corvettes* of the Spanish expedition, and the commander's pleasure obliged me to await their departure.

"I endeavored to induce them to transport the Santa Cruz supplies by water, but it could not be accomplished. Day before yesterday, however, some were sent there by land, and with them a man from the schooner which came from Nootka, under Don Juan Carrasco.

"The plan is to see if there is any shelter for a vessel on the coast near Santa Cruz, and then to transport what is left.

"Tomorrow a report is expected. This means is sought because we lack animals.

"Today eleven Indians have departed from here with tools to construct a shelter at Soledad, for the padres are making preparations, and my departure thither will be, by the favor of God, the day after San Francis, October 8th, at the latest."[3]

Thus, on August 28th, 1791, two years after the first plans were formed and the first letters written, Father de Lasuen planted the cross at the place known now as Santa Cruz. With him were Corporal Luis Peralta and five soldiers from the San Francisco presidio.

This same Peralta, upon his return to San Francisco a few days later, pronounced the spot one of the very best for a new establishment in the entire province.[4]

---

[3] Lasuen, carta al Sr. Gobernador Romeu, Sobre fundacion de Missiones, 29 de Septembre, 1791, M. S. B. C.

[4] Hittell I, p. 462, cites here Cal. Arch. M. S. II, 544, and Cal. Arch. St. Pap. VII, 42.

OLD HAND-MADE LEATHER COVER OF RECORD OF BAPTISMS
AT MISSION SANTA CRUZ

161

Casam.to y Velac.on a th à Segismundo con Segismunda bautizados par
Segismundo con   tidas 695, y 701: para q.e conste lo firmo.
Segismunda.

                                    Fr. Baldomero Lopez

162.
Casam.to de   En 22 dias al mes de Marzo de 1796 en la Iglesia de
Marcial con   esta Mision de Santa Cruz haviendo precedido las diligencias
Theodomira   debidas, y leida las tres canonicas monociones en otros tantos dias
                 festivos, sin q.e hubiese resultado impedimento alguno, case in
                 facie Ecc.a alos siguientes = Primeram.te a Marcial Soltero con
                 Theodomira Viuda contenidos en el libro de Bautismos par
                 tida 584, y 393.

163   th. a Fran.co Xavier Viudo con Maria Trinidad Viuda
Fran.co Xavier con
Maria Trinidad. bautizados partidas 361, y 218.

164   th. a Jose Ignacio Viudo con Monitora Soltera bauti-
Jose Ygn.o con
Monitora.   zados partidas 672, y 152

165   th. à Antolin Jose Viudo con Margarita
Antolin Jose   Corona Soltera contenidos en el libro de Bautism.
con   partidas 708, y 522. fueron testigos el M.ro Santiago
Margarita   Ruiz, y el M.ro Ramon y otros: para q.e conste
Corona   la firmo.   Fr. Baldomero Lopez

PAGE FROM RECORD OF BAPTISMS AT MISSION SANTA CRUZ,
SHOWING SIGNATURE OF FATHER BALDOMERO LOPEZ

Ensign Hermengildo Sal was the acting commandant of the troops at the Presidio of San Francisco in 1791. Although Monterey was much nearer, Santa Cruz was to resort under the San Francisco Presidio.

On September 17th, 1791, Ensign Sal wrote to Governor Romeu, making excuses for having sent, at Father de Lasuen's request a mule train to the new Mission,[5] without having awaited the arrival of the Governor, nor having received his orders.

It is evident that Sal was in full sympathy with Father de Lasuen, and the latter, in his letter to the Governor, referred to his assistance with appreciation.

Sal seems to have been an enthusiastic church member and a thoroughly capable officer, for his instructions to the Corporal of the Mission Guard are most explicit and to the point.[6] He ordered constant watchfulness, kindness to the Gentiles, harmony with the padres, and a strict performance of all religious duties and military details.

On September 22nd, 1791, Sal started, in accordance with the request of Father de Lasuen and under orders from Governor Romeu, from San Francisco. He was guided by Corporal Peralta, and accompanied by two soldiers, arriving in Santa Clara in the afternoon. On the following day he reached the site of the new Mission, having been joined at Santa Clara by Fathers Isidro Alonzo Salazar and Baldomero López, the first two missionaries to function at this Mission. Like all the others, Sal found the place ideal for the purpose for which it had been selected.

He reported to Governor Romeu that the grounds for cultivation were rather small, but he noted the presence of water and limestone. He found that there was but one objection to the spot selected for the new Mission, and that lay in the fact that Santa Cruz was off the main road from Santa Clara to Monterey, and that in times of flood it might be difficult to maintain communication, but he declared that throughout the whole length of the country from San Diego to San Francisco, there was no other place so well supplied with natural advantages for a Mission.

Father de Lasuen was not present at the dedication of the Mission, for, after having consulted with Ensign Sal at Santa Clara, he proceeded to Monterey to attend to other pressing duties.

On September 24th, the Christian Indians, brought from Santa Clara, were set to cutting lumber, and to building a rude hut for the shelter of the Friars, while the Fathers busied themselves finding a place fit for sowing twenty-five *fanegas* of wheat.

---

[5] State Papers, Sac. M. S. VII, 18-20.
[6] Instruccion al Cabo Luis Peralta al cargo de la Escolta de la Mission de Santa Cruz, 1791, M. S. B. C.

Their search was rewarded by the discovery of a fine plain, capable of being irrigated from a small stream, that had been named by the explorers of 1769—Arroyo de San Pedro Regaldo. The Mission site was about five hundred yards from the San Lorenzo River, and within one mile of the mountains.

That day Chief Sugert came in with a few followers who promised to become the first Indian neophytes of this tribe, Sal agreeing to be godfather or sponsor.

On Sunday, the 25th day of September, 1791, Fathers Salazar and López were ready to celebrate the formal ceremonies of the founding of the Mission.[7]

The previous day some of the contributions from the neighboring Missions had arrived. Santa Clara gave thirty cows, five yoke of oxen, fourteen bulls, twenty steers, and twenty-two horses. "Two pairs of the oxen," the record runs, "were very bad." They also contributed twenty-six *fanegas* of grain and twenty-six loaves of bread.

The San Carlos Mission gave seven mules and eight horses.[8]

From San Francisco came five yoke of oxen, seventy sheep and two bushels of barley, but it is quaintly noted that "of those five yoke of oxen, we had to kill a pair, so bad were they, and of the seven mules received from Carmel (San Carlos) one was so gentle (!) that he died three days after.[9]

In addition the guard furnished the padres with $42.50 worth of provisions, which was to be repaid.

The missionaries accordingly robed themselves, the soldiers burnished up their accoutrements, and loaded their muskets for the salute, and the Indians gathered around.

The Indians were first warned against the noise of exploding gunpowder. They appeared under Sugert, their *capitanego* or principal man. He had been invited to attend and came with his wife and two daughters. The two young women, Lucenza and Clara, were already Christians and had well disposed the neighborhood Indians towards the newcomers. They all witnessed the entire ceremony, including the Mass, the act of taking possession, the salute, the music and singing. (See Appendix 1.)

---

[7] St. Pap. Sec. M. S. II, 137.

[8] Willey Historical Sketch.

[9] Copied from the Mission records in Vallejo, Dc. Hist. Cal. M. S. XXVIII, 102-3, B. C.
There is some confusion in the records of just what each Mission sent. For instance, some records disclose that San Francisco sent hogs and Santa Clara cattle. (Bancroft Vol. I, p. 495, note 28.) Other records (for instance, Salazar, Condicion actual de Cal. 1796) give different reports and figures.

Ensign Sal, as he reported, took possession of the site in the name of His Majesty, the King of Spain, "in such words as my moderate talent dictated," and at the conclusion of his speech the guns were fired.

Five more salutes were given while the padres said Mass and chanted the Te Deum. The Gentiles looked on with great interest and favor, readily promising to assist in building up the Mission.[10]

On the same day Sal prepared a formal certificate, which he, the missionaries, Corporal Peralta and one citizen, Salvador Higuera, signed, stating that upon that date at eight o'clock in the morning, in the presence of the witnesses mentioned and in the name of the most Holy Trinity, he had taken possession of the place for His Catholic Majesty, King Charles IV.[11]

Sal's report of his proceedings at Santa Cruz on this occasion, in the form of the *Diario* quoted briefly above, constitutes with its accompanying document the most minute account, perhaps, of the founding of a Mission which has been preserved.[12]

Next day the Padres López and Salazar wrote their official report to the Governor. Among other things, they assured him that the site was fine and the prospect flattering.[13]

The Mission was ready at last to settle down to the serious business of caring for the souls and bodies of the Gentiles. The Mission pueblo had been born.

After Sal returned to his headquarters in San Francisco, he sent Corporal Peralta a series of minute instructions to be enforced in governing his men and the Mission settlement:

(1)   Excess rations were not to be allowed; exact amounts of maize, beans, tallow, cigars, soap and chocolate were to be given weekly to each of the soldiers and the six servants of the Mission.

(2)   The Indians were not to be permitted to taste beef, for fear of the evil consequences which might result.

(3)   The soldiers were to obey written and oral orders of the missionaries.

(4)   An armed sentinel with musket and sword was to be maintained day and night.

(5)   Indians must not associate with the guards.

---

[10] Sal, Diario de Recondicemiento de la Mission de Santa Cruz, 1791, M. S., B. C.
[11] Cal. Arch. SP II, 813.
[12] Hittell, Vol. I, p. 463.
[13] "Lopez and Salazar, Conta de los Padres de S. Cruz, al Gobernado," Sept. 25, 1791. M. S., B. C.

(6)   Indians were not to be permitted in the Mission unless disarmed, and the strictest precautions were to be maintained against surprises or uprisings.

(7)   Horses and cattle were to be under constant observation; if they strayed, they must be sought for, and if stolen, the thief was to be informed of the magnitude of his crime and punished with fifteen stripes; in case of repetition of theft, or the killing of an animal, word was to be sent to the presidio.

(8)   Two horses were to be kept ready saddled by day and four by night, picketed near at hand, to meet emergencies.

(9)   The Indians' autumn grass fires were to be carefully watched, to prevent damage.

(10)   If one of the missionaries left the Mission on foot, he was to be accompanied by a soldier armed with a musket.

(11)   If he left mounted, he was to be asked his destination and must be accompanied by two or three armed soldiers, according to the distance.

(12)   Soldiers were not to be permitted to gamble among themselves or with anyone else.

(13)   Soldiers were to have no communications with the Indian men, and especially not with the women, on pain of severe punishment.

(14)   Prayers were to be attended regularly.

(15)   The last week of each month a report on the condition of affairs was to be sent to San Francisco via Santa Clara.

(16)   On account of the lateness of the season and the approach of the winter rains, the Indians were to be invited to help construct the buildings needed for immediate use, and be paid for their labors in blankets and maize.[14]

Corporal Peralta was, like his immediate superior, an enthusiast, and followed his instructions strictly.

It was considered best not to begin building a church and the more substantial Mission buildings until they had all the Indians together and had taught them at least the rudiments of building and other arts of civilization. The conversions, owing no doubt in great part to the intermediary of Lucenza and Clara, were rapid.

In a short time several buildings were up, including a church. But it was soon found that the new establishment was too near the river[15] and had to be rebuilt on higher land.

---

[14] State Papers, Sacramento Series MS., Vol. II, pp. 142-149.
[15] Cal. Arch. P. R. II, 562.

TITLE PAGE FROM OLD RECORD OF BAPTISMS
AT MISSION SANTA CRUZ

Courtesy of the Rev. Father McGrath, at Santa Cruz, California.

The first Santa Cruz Mission had been built of split timbers or palisades as a temporary structure in which the Fathers conducted services, baptized and married the Indian neophytes, but now a more substantial building was needed.

On October 9th, 1791, at the Mission de Exultacion de Santa Cruz, the first baptism was celebrated. The little neophyte was sponsored by Corporal Luis Peralta of the *escolta*. The first marriage recorded was on November 6th, 1791, between Josefa and Hermengildo.

The first year must have been one of considerable hardship. Father Adam, the Catholic priest in charge of the Church at Santa Cruz in 1867, wrote:

"From old documents standing in this Mission record, we find that scarcely had the Fathers arrived here, when they applied themselves to call around the Mission the waning tribes of Indians and began immediately to instruct them through an interpreter in the mystery of Christianity. To that effect they brought with them some other Indians already baptized and instructed to facilitate their work.

"From a very old leaf of paper half blotted out by age, and written a few months after arrival, we find the following items:

" 'Information of the state of this Mission of Santa Cruz, founded on the 25th day of September of this year (1791) and written down on the 31st of December, 1791.

" 'Baptizing. We baptized in this year eighty-seven persons, nineteen of them adults, the other sixty-eight under age.

" 'Marriages. We celebrated six marriages, all of Indians.

" 'Dead. Died on this Mission, a child baptized in the Mission of Santa Clara, his parents are Gentiles, and a grown person.

" 'The Indians at present in this Mission are eighty-nine, three of them from the Mission of Santa Clara, who were incorporated in this Mission.

" 'Horned cattle. 130 heads of cattle, counting what the Mission of Santa Clara and that of our Father St. Francis gave to us.

" 'Sheep, 146; horses, 23; mules, 5.

" 'Crops. We sowed, the following year, twelve bushels of wheat, and one and a half bushels of horse beans, or vetches.

" 'We have built a house 26 varas or ells long, by six wide, with the rooms necessary for the Padre and offices.

" 'The church is twenty-one varas or ells long, and six wide, with a vestry four varas wide by six long. All these buildings formed of palisades.

" 'We have enclosed the place for cattle, sheep and horses. We have brought the water to the Mission, and we have fenced the orchard. The tools used at this Mission belong to other Missions, and we shall return them, when we receive those which the King is going to send.

" 'We brought with us four candle-sticks of brass, a painting of our Lady of Sorrow, and an image of our Father St. Francis.

" 'This is copy of the original sent on the 31st Dec., 1791.

Fr. Baldomero Lopez.' '"

* Elliot's History of Santa Cruz, p 6

CHAPTER XVIII

The First Ten Years (1790-1800)
Foreign Visitors.

BOOK III

Chapter XVIII

The First Ten Years—1790-1800
Foreign Visitors

THOUGH the Government was liberal with orders for the management of the Missions, the Pious Fund was too dainty a plum to be cut into freely, even by the rightful owners. Actual aid from the authorities was forthcoming sparingly. Nevertheless, the Fathers proceeded with courage to perform their various tasks.

The neophytes had increased in 1792 to two hundred and twenty-four, but there were often "Indian scares." The fears of the white people were largely based on rumors, occasioned either by the flight of a neophyte, who failed to become enamored of Christianity and steady labor, or by the theft of live stock. Cattle also disappeared from other causes, *i. e.,* bears were so plentiful that once the soldiers of the guard were ordered to hunt them for target practice. These bears were a real danger to the pioneers and to the Indians and continued to be a menace for a long time; even when the country was more settled and the use of guns universal, they still attacked live stock and human beings. (See Appendix No. 1.)

In the midst of rejoicing in February, 1793, occasioned by the success of nine neophytes in securing nine pagans for Christianity, the disquieting news was brought that the mountain Indians were making arrows,[1] which was taken as an indication that an uprising was to be expected. In December of the same year a soldier and a corporal were wounded, the road to Monterey was threatened, and two parties were sent from the San Francisco presidio to punish the natives.

On February 27th, 1793, the cornerstone of the new church was laid on higher land. This was a tremendous undertaking, without modern facilities and with nothing but hand labor of a very crude sort. But they set about it. They made adobe bricks, and the solid adobe walls, when finished, measured five feet in thickness. They cut down the trees on the mountain slopes. They hewed out the timbers, and by some means got them to the spot.

It took a little more than a year to build the church. It was one hundred and twelve and a half feet long, twenty-nine feet wide, and twenty-five and a half feet high. The front was of masonry, the foundation walls up

---

[1] St. Pat. Sac. M. S. VI, 70-71.

to three feet were of stone, and the balance of adobe. It was ready to be dedicated to its holy use on the 10th of May, 1794.

The dedication was a great occasion. Father Tomaz Pena came from Santa Clara, *Alferez* (sub-lieutenant or ensign) Hermengildo Sal, commanding officer of the Presidio of San Francisco, came down together with several priests. Sal, as godfather of the church, received the keys. A full account of the ceremony and of the building, signed by Fathers Pena of Santa Clara, Gila and Sanchez, the two ministers of the Mission, and *Alferez* Sal, besides Francisco Gomez, Joseph Maria López, Ignacio Chumazero and Jose Antonio Sanchez, can be found in Sta. Cruz. Lib. de Mission M. S. 38-40.

All the ceremonies of the Roman Catholic ritual were performed, the neophytes, servants and troops attending. The next day a Mass was celebrated in the new edifice.

Life at the Mission began in earnest. Flour mill stones were ordered made for Santa Cruz at San Carlos, and a house for the mill was built, while a granary of two stories and a house for looms had been finished. That year they harvested one thousand two hundred bushels of wheat, six hundred bushels of corn, sixty bushels of beans, and a half bushel of lentils.

In January, 1795, Sgt. Amador, from the presidio, was sent to capture some Indians who were making trouble on the Rio Pajaro.

In the same year the last two sides of the square of the Mission building were completed, and in February, 1796, Sgt. Amador was sent a second time to investigate a rumor that the Indians would rise and kill the padres, and on March 7th Padre Sanchez once more asked for aid, stating that the Indians were threatening.

However disturbed in mind the padres were, they carried on, for the loom building, with two looms, was operating, while in the autumn of 1796 the flour mill was grinding corn, but became badly damaged in the following December rains.

The elements seemed hostile, for during the rainy season of 1797 the church building was badly damaged by the rains.[2]

In April of that year some relief was gained when Corporal Mesa, of the guard, gathered ninety of the fugitive Indians and returned them to the fold.[3]

---

[2] Fernandez, Carta del Padre Monstro sobre de la condicion de Santa Cruz, 1798, M. S., B. C.
[3] Prov. St. Pap. M. S. XII, B. C. 101.

MISSION SANTA CRUZ
As it probably appeared between the years 1794-1799.
From a painting by Oriana Day, in the de Young Memorial Museum,
Golden Gate Park, San Francisco, California.

At the beginning of 1798 Father Fernandez wrote that everything was in a bad way; that 189 neophytes had deserted, leaving only 30 to 40 to do all the work; that the land was overflowed and only half of the planting done; that the live stock were dying; that a dead whale on the beach was attracting an unusual number of wolves and bears, and that the establishment of the Villa de Branciforte added to the general despondency.

About this time an effort was evidently made to classify the lands under the Santa Cruz Mission, for we find an official register dated August 1st, 1798, of Engineer Cordoba. Herein he states that Santa Cruz has 3,434,600 square varas of irrigable lands, of which 1,120,000 are *sin abir*. The pastures are 1.5 x 1, or 9 leagues, with 7 permanent streams.[4]

The next January (1799) more tribulations visited the long-suffering missionaries, for the church, the water-mill for grinding corn and the other structures in the neighborhood were wrecked by a violent storm. A great deal of heart-breaking work of rebuilding had to be performed for the second time.

We, who at the present time know the extremely mild climate of that locality, wonder at the consecutive destructions of the Santa Cruz buildings. Frame houses constructed in this Mission zone eighty to a hundred years ago are as sound today as at the time of their erection. Within the memory of living man no buildings constructed of lumber, reinforced concrete, hollow tile, or so-called plaster construction, have ever been destroyed by the elements in Santa Cruz or in the neighborhood, if well constructed.

The mode of construction of the Santa Cruz church, like that of most other churches of the time, being of adobe, roofed with tiles, and connected with the numerous adjuncts, such as priests' house, barracks, warehouse and shops, proved therefore to be inadaptable to the locality, though parts of the reconstructed church of 1799 remained in evidence as late as 1885.

All these drawbacks proved small in comparison with the annoyances which the Fathers experienced later from the adjoining Villa Branciforte.

The Mission of Santa Cruz, notwithstanding the unanimously enthusiastic predictions of Father de Lasuen, Corporal Peralta, Ensign Sal and the first missionaries, Fathers Salazar and López, never became one of the major units in the Mission system of Alta California.

Five years after its foundation, there were 523 neophytes attached to the Mission, the greatest number in its whole history. After that year the number of Indians who accepted Christianity in the Santa Cruz Mission declined steadily. By 1800 there had been all told 949 persons baptized, 272 couples married, and 477 persons buried.

---

[4] Prov. Rec. M. S. VI, 99 B. C.

When we take in consideration that the Mission of San Gabriel Arcangel had 1,701 neophythes in 1817, that San Diego de Alcalda had 1,829 neophytes in 1824, and San Luis Rey had 2,869 in the year 1826, and furthermore that Santa Cruz had fewer conversions than any of the other Missions, it becomes apparent that this Mission did not respond to the great expectations of its founders, although they were seemingly justified on account of the extraordinary favorable climatic and scenic conditions. (See Appendix 2.)

It is one of the ironies of fate that this unfavorable result was directly due to its so apparently favorable site.

Ensign Sal had reported that one of the drawbacks was the small area of fertile land immediately available. He was an experienced man, and knew the fundamental principle that "feeding" the Indians was the most effective means of conversion and subjection.

The lands in the Bolsa de Pajaro were extremely rich, but they were too far away to allow a proper protection of the crops against predatory Indians or wild animals, and were therefore not usable for the agricultural operations of the padres at Santa Cruz.

True, right at the foot of Mission Hill was the fertile valley of the Delta of the San Lorenzo River, but this did not comprise more than a few hundred acres of bottom land. The country between this valley and that of the Pajaro River consisted of table land of rather light quality, needing more intense cultivation than the Mission Indians could give with the means at hand.

Most of the Costanoan Indians, in the vicinity of the Santa Cruz Mission, if they had been inclined to become Christianized, had had the opportunity for twenty years prior to join the establishment of the neighboring San Carlos Mission in the Carmel Valley, near Monterey. Those who had not taken this advantage were, in all probability, no more inclined to join the newer Mission.

The nearness of the mountains, with an abundance of game, like quail, deer, cotton-tails, squirrels, etc., had made hunting comparatively easy for the Indians of that vicinity, and the multitude of fish in the Bay of Monterey offered other means of subsistence.[5] Even at present Santa Cruz County is famous for its fishing and hunting opportunities. Perhaps the

---

[5] Mr. C. L. Anderson in a chapter devoted to the fishes in Monterey Bay, from data chiefly composed from papers of Prof. David Star Jordon, published by the U. S. Commissions of Fish and Fisheries, stated in 1892 (Harrison, History of Santa Cruz County) "in this list of the food fishes of Monterey Bay and streams entering therein, we have indicated about 150 species. The list may be considerably enlarged."

MISSION SANTA CRUZ, DEDICATED AFTER 1799

Several times repaired before completely destroyed.

From an old newspaper print, and also the subject of an etching of Henry Chapman Ford in the Academy of Sciences, Golden Gate Park, San Francisco, California.

old motto, *Montani-semper-liberari*[6] (Mountaineers will forever be free men), applied more or less to the Costanoan Indians of the mountain rancherias, and the principles of Christianity, with its single marriages, regular work hours, its punishments with lash and stocks, appealed little to free children of the mountain forests.

While the general Mission period (1770-1820) is sometimes referred to as "peaceful and pastoral," the Santa Cruz padres had plenty of pastoral experience, but the peacefulness was often absent. Indeed, for them the closing years of the century were a period of turmoil and difficulty.

Already by the first of November, 1794, the padres complained that the soldiers sent to assist them as laborers knew nothing of their work and should be sent back to the presidio.

However, by the next year the Mission showed progress and its value as a producer, for it sent to the presidios $2,000 worth of supplies.

The missionary founders, Fathers Salazar and López, served here, the former to July, 1795, and the latter to July, 1796, when they left the country to find retirement at their College.

Both had come to California in 1791 and served only at Santa Cruz; both were often exasperated by the difficulties encountered, and therefore short-tempered and quarrelsome; they were reproved by their superiors. Father López was ill—a victim of hypochondria. After his return to Mexico his health must have been restored, for on August 8th, 1818, he was elected the Guardian of San Fernando College, a signal honor.

They were succeeded by Fathers Manuel Fernandez and Jose de la Cruz Espi, who, however, did not remain long, for in May, 1797, Father Espi was already replaced by Father Francisco Gonzales, and in October, 1798, Father Domingo Carranza succeeded Father Fernandez.

These several replacements and changes cannot have added to the success of the Mission or to the comforts of the Fathers themselves.

Father Fernandez had served, prior to coming to Santa Cruz, at Santa Clara. He is reported as being a bad manager of the neophytes, harsh and violent, and several times exhausted the patience of his President, Father de Lasuen. There are, however, no complaints on file against this monastic while he was serving in Santa Cruz, and in 1798 he obtained license to retire on account of ill health.

Although the live stock and grain yields were steadily increasing during the decade 1790-1800—large stock from 202 to 2,354 head; small

---

[6] This phrase is used as the motto of the Coat of Arms of many states and communities, for instance, of the State of West Virginia in America, and the village of Zelbio, near Como in the Alps of Italy.

stock from 174 to 2,083 head;[7] agricultural products from 650 bushels to 4,300—still the Fathers were despondent.

Another blow had also fallen, for by Governor de Borica's orders, the annual election of Mission pueblo alcaldes, which was required by the regulations, but which had been neglected here as elsewhere, was again instituted.[8]

It is obvious that the padres at Santa Cruz, as those at the other Missions, were honestly convinced that the neophytes had not yet reached a condition which enabled them to enjoy any reasonable degree of citizenship. The Santa Cruz neophytes, having been gathered around the Mission for only a few years, must have been of all Indians the least prepared to exercise the franchise or toy with the paraphernalia of modern local government.

It is obvious, nevertheless, that the secular authorities, represented by the Governor, were determined to bestow certain rights of citizenship— including a qualified form of local self government—on the neophytes as soon as possible, the opinion of the missionaries notwithstanding.

The secular authorities believed that under the guidance and management of the padres alone, undisturbed by any accelerating process from the outside, the neophytes would remain practical serfs of the Church.

The difference of opinion was of long standing. As early as June 30, 1771, the Guardian of the College of San Fernando (Father Verger) wrote with regard to the Missions of Alta California, that they never had been, were not, and never would be complete pueblos.

Differences of opinion continued to arise in various forms during the whole Mission period.

The padres felt compelled to use the hobble, the stocks, the shackles and the lash to stimulate the natives in religious observances and in the performance of duty, which caused Governor Pedro Fages to complain of this punishment. He made protest in 1785, 1788 and 1791.[9]

It is rather curious to observe that both the secular and the sacerdotal authorities sometimes cheerfully and courteously and sometimes bitterly reproached one another and made accusations of abusing the Indians.

---

[7] As the cattle herd of the Mission increased the Fathers were compelled to request permission of the Commander of the Monterey Presidio to use the pastorage along a small creek in the Valley of the Pajaro, which had the curious name of Salsipuedes. This name was derived from the Spanish expression *Sal-si-puedes,* meaning Get-out-if-you-can, which in more polite language would be expressed by *Salga si usted pueda.* However, politeness was not intended at that time for it was the expression used by some Californians, who saw a hated Gringo, in attempting to cross a stream, struggle for his life in the quicksand.

[8] Bancroft, Cal. Vol. I, p. 497.

[9] B. C. Prov. Rec. Vol. III, pp. 51, 67; Prov. St. Pap. Vol. X, p. 167.

On September 27th, 1793, the Guardian of San Fernando reported to Viceroy de Gigedo that the Alta California Missions were in no condition to be secularized. "These new Christians," said the Guardian, "like tender plants not yet well rooted, easily wither, reverting to their old Gentile liberty and indolent savage life."[10]

The Guardian seemed to have been able to convince the Viceroy to a considerable extent, for on December 27th of the same year, he wrote to the Government at Madrid: "I am not well satisfied with the Missions that have been secularized (in Sierra Gorda), nor will I take this step unless success is assured. Curates can do no more than Friars."

Twenty-five years later, on August 3rd, 1796, Governor de Borico wrote to Pedro de Alberni in regard to the neophytes at Monterey that "at the rate they were then moving, not in ten centuries would they be out of tutelage."[11]

The old quarrels were more or less crystallized by the actions of Father Antonio de la Concepcion Horra, who on July 25th, 1797, when the foundations were laid for Mission San Miguel, was appointed with Fr. Buenaventura Sitjar, resident missionary. The following month Fr. de Lasuen had to write to Governor de Borica that manifestly Fr. Horra was insane and acted like a mad-man, showing signs of violent fury. After consulting with two surgeons at Monterey the Governor pronounced the Friar insane.

Upon his arrival at the College of San Fernando, Father Horra secretly addressed a long memorial to the Viceroy, in which he complained about the treatment he had received, and further accused the other Friars of cruelty to the Indians and of general mismanagement of the Missions.

The Viceroy in turn presented the charges to Governor de Borica with instructions to investigate, and de Borica ordered the four presidio commanders to procure information on fifteen questions which had been raised in Father Horra's report.

De Borica transmitted the reply of Commandant Felipe de Goycoechea, of the Santa Barbara Mission, to the Viceroy, with the notation that the answers of the Commandants of the other three presidios corresponded in substance.

As far as can be ascertained, *Fr. Presidente* de Lasuen called upon the Fathers of the Mission Purisima and Santa Barbara to comment on Commander Goycoechea's answers.

On October 30th, 1800, Fathers Estévan Tápis and Juan Cortés, of Santa Barbara, refuted the charges on twelve closely written folio pages,

---

[10] M. A. Arch. Genl. Prov. Int. 51.
[11] B. C., Prov. St. Pap. Mil. (Benecia), Vol. XXIV, pp. 7-8.

while the Father of Purisima crowded his observations on a little more than three folio pages.[12]

The nearly eighty-year-old *Fr. Presidente* de Lasuen devoted seven months to preparing a comprehensive exposé of the whole subject, of which document Bancroft speaks very highly.

Father de Lasuen acknowledged that in the nature of things there must be certain defects, but otherwise defended the Missions eloquently. He compared the task of making adobes and tiles at the Missions with similar tasks required of the Indians at the presidios, and pointed out that the Indians from the Missions fared much better than those who had to work for the very military commanders who manifested such compassion for the Mission neophytes.

In the end, as in all similar quarrels, neither party was convinced, although Viceroy Iturrigary wrote to Governor de Arrillaga, who had succeeded de Borica meanwhile, that the representations of Father Horra were quite unfounded and that the favorable opinions, to which the Friars were entitled, should not be diminished by these charges. He winds up by exhorting both sides—that is, the missionaries and the commandants of the presidios—to work in harmony. The whole question was, therefore, left exactly where it was at the beginning.

What was the condition of the neophytes attached to the Santa Cruz Mission, when they were considered by the secular authorities to be fit to elect their own local officers?

The missionaries at least were quite discouraged about them. Some of the Indians appeared to be more willing to worship at the shrine of dusky Venuses or Aphrodites than at that of Christian duty, for in 1799 Fathers Gonsalez and Carranza, of Santa Cruz, reported to Governor de Borica that besides the fear of death during periods of epidemics and the disinclination to work, "the motive with most of those who run away is the ungovernable passion for other women. Those at this Mission cannot entirely gratify their lust, because of the vigilance of the missionaries. Hence they run away in order to give full sway to their carnal desires."[13]

To those who know primitive people, this sounds quite plausible.

These gay Lotharios remained thorns in the side of the Fathers, until finally in exasperation they sent one or two back to the military authorities—for instance, one Andres—with a supplication that "Your Honor deign to relieve us from this molestation."[14]

---

[12] Engelhardt, Missions and Missionaries of California, Vol. II, p. 568.
[13] Archb. Arch. No. 126.
[14] Engelhardt, Missions and Missionaries in California, Vol. II, p. 526.

From independent evidence we cannot come to any conclusion, for most of the foreign observers did not visit this Mission.

The best known amongst these chroniclers, Jean Francois Galoup de la Perouse, was referred to in a previous chapter. He sailed from this coast to the Indies in 1786, and from there sent his journals to France, but never returned again to this coast, for his ships were wrecked and he and all aboard were lost in 1787, four years before the establishment of the Santa Cruz Mission.

The next distinguished visitor who left valuable information as to the Mission period was Captain George Vancouver, commanding the British sloop *Discovery*.[15] Together with the *Chatham* he crossed from the Sandwich Islands, sailing on March 18th, 1792, and passed Cape Mendocino on April 19th, making explorations northward. He reached Nootka, Vancouver Island, on August 28th, where he found the Spanish brig *Activa*, under command of Captain Salvador Menédez Valdés, and flying the pennant of Don Juan Francisco de la Bodega y Cuadra, commandant of the marine establishment of San Blas and California. The latter was to act as Spanish Commissioner, while Captain Vancouver was to act as the English Commissioner, to discuss and determine certain differences still pending in a dispute between England and Spain, and known as the Nootka matter. Official correspondence and *pourparlers* did not bring about a settlement. By the terms of a treaty signed in 1790 Spain was to restore all the lands of which England "had been dispossessed." The Spanish Commissioner maintained that England had been dispossessed of none, suggesting that a boundary line be established between British and Spanish possessions in the Strait of Juan de Fuca, in which case Spain would relinquish Nootka. The British Commissioner not conceding the point, it was agreed that the question be presented to their respective governments.

On the 22nd of September Bodega left, and on October 13th the English ships departed.

On November 14th the *Discovery* entered the harbor of San Francisco at dusk, the first vessel other than Spanish to enter the harbor. Next day, Lieutenant Don Hermengildo Sal, in command of the presidio, made his official call. Monterey[16] was notified of the arrival, and Sal was instructed to furnish such supplies as might be needed and to accept no pay, but to charge everything to the Boundary Commission.

---

[15] The *Discovery* carried 20 guns and 100 men, while the *Chatham*, its consort, carried 20 guns and 45 men, and was under command of Lt. William R. Broughton. On April 29th, they spoke to the *Columbia*, commanded by Captain Robert Gray of Boston, near Cape Mendocino.

[16] De la Bodega y Cuadra was at Monterey at that time.

Not only were the officers entertained at the presidio and Mission, but Don Sal gave them the freedom of the country, permitting a two-day journey on horseback down the San Francisco peninsula to Mission Santa Clara. Governor de Arrillaga, adverse to allowing any foreigner to penetrate the interior, reproved Don Sal for this indiscretion, and the latter acknowledged himself in the wrong, but added that nothing short of the removal of the horses would have prevented the journey.

The Spanish military authorities fully understood the danger of these so-called friendly excursions into the interior. The country was far removed from Mexico and was poorly armed to give resistance; the garrisons at the four presidios and the escoltes at the Missions formed a negligible military force. Moreover, the wealth created at the Missions made California Alta an inviting country for a foe to enter, for such an invading force would find abundant supplies and easy subsistence.

On November 26th, the *Discovery,* accompanied by the *Chatham,* joined another British ship, the *Daedalus,*[11] in the port of Monterey. The two first-named boats remained fifty days, repairing and loading. Astronomical observations were made and there was opportunity for research of many kinds, but entertainments interfering with investigations were constantly planned for the visitors.

On January 15th, 1793, the *Discovery* and *Chatham* set sail for the Sandwich Islands.

The order from the Viceroy to be on guard against English ships, and especially to prevent the weakness of the Spanish establishments from becoming known to the foreigners, was enforced on Vancouver's return to San Francisco in the spring of 1793, and he was informed that no individual could come ashore except himself and one officer, who might pass to the presidio. Provoked at this rebuff and cool reception, he set sail for Monterey, where he received the same treatment, and departed on November 5th without taking on the wood, water or supplies prepared for him.

Vancouver continued on down the coast, and while given no greater privileges than at San Francisco and Monterey, he received more consideration at Santa Barbara and San Diego, where he was furnished with fresh supplies. Cordial relations between the English Commander and *Padre Presidente* de Lasuen were strengthened by the gift from Vancouver to de Lasuen of a fine barrel organ for the Mission San Carlos, where, during his former visit, he had been so kindly treated.

On December 9th, Vancouver once more left the North American coast to cross the Pacific, but returned from the Sandwich Islands and

---

[11] This ship remained at Monterey until December when she sailed with a load of cattle for New South Wales.

reached Nootka in September, 1794, after receiving word that in June a royal order, dated March 23rd, 1793, had been received granting shelter to English vessels in Spanish ports. General Jose Manuel de Alava, who had succeeded Bodega y Cuadra as commissioner, was already there. Both being without instructions, they sailed on the 15th of October for Monterey, but no official communication awaited either commissioner.

From information contained in despatches which de Alava received on the 11th of November, Vancouver learned that "no further altercation would take place," that the Nootka matter had been adjusted in an amicable way, special commissioners for disoccupation had been appointed, and he had been relieved.

An agreement for the mutual abandonment of Nootka was signed at Madrid on January 11th, 1794, by Spain and England.

An *entente cordial* was established with the Governor, Don Diego de Borica, and after completing reports and charts and having copies prepared to send to England via San Blas, Vancouver started on his return voyage to England, which he reached October 20th, 1795.

Shortly after his return to England he began the preparation of his "Voyage of Discovery," but he died on May 10th, 1798, before the task was finished. However, the work was completed by his brother, and published in London in 1801, but Santa Cruz is not mentioned, which showed that it still remained rather isolated even at that late date.

The next foreign observer was Dr. George Heinrich von Langsdorff, surgeon on the Russian vessel *Juno,* bearing the Imperial Chamberlain von Rezanov. The *Juno* arrived in the Bay of San Francisco on April 8th, 1806.

Von Langsdorff, besides being a trained physician, was a natural scientist. He studied the Missions thoroughly, not only on the Bay, but also at San Jose and Santa Clara. Afterwards he published his observations in a book, "Voyage and Travels" (London, 1813; the second volume deals with California).

None of these men visited the Santa Cruz Mission, but it is safe to assume that their observations applied to those Missions which they did not visit as well as to those they did, always making due allowances for the different temperaments of the Fathers in charge, and length of their establishment.

These foreign observers showed considerable difference in their opinions as to the "system" under which the padres ruled their wards.

There is the difference of time to consider. The report of De la Perouse was written in the year 1786, that of Vancouver in 1793, and the one of von Langsdorff in 1806. There was a period of twenty years between the first and last one.

In these two decades Governor de Borica had made his appearance in California; he infused a totally different spirit into the whole social structure of this province, influencing the treatment of the Indians. There is also the respective mental attitudes of the observers to be weighed.

De la Perouse was imbued with the liberal ideas which had become a fetish in the French Kingdom. Voltaire, Rousseau, Corneille and others, preaching modern social doctrines, created a certain contempt for doctrinaire religion. The Rights of Man was a thought permeating the French air, and few Frenchmen escaped this influence. Many of them had crossed the Atlantic to join the Americans in their fight for political freedom. De la Perouse might therefore have been inclined to look with a none too friendly eye upon ecclesiastical endeavors.

Vancouver, on the other hand, belonged to a democratic-aristocratic nation which had succeeded for centuries in blending the Rights of the King and Nobles with those of the Commoners, and it was natural therefore that he would take a middle ground.

The third one, von Langsdorff, was partly subordinate and partly boon companion of Baron Nicolai Petrovich de Rezánov, first Russian Ambassador to Japan, circumnavigator of the globe, Chamberlain at the Court and Privy Counselor, chief partner in the great Golikov-Shelikov Fur Company of Russia and America. For many decades after this period Russian gentlemen considered it quite proper to inflict severe corporal punishment on their serfs, and conditions condemned by De la Perouse were considered natural by von Langsdorff.

In whatever details the chroniclers differ, they all agreed that the Fathers in general conducted themselves with prudence and kindness and showed individually a paternal attitude to the natives. They are likewise agreed as to the character and stage of development of the Indian neophytes, wherever they met them.

Von Langsdorff describes them as "rough, uncivilized men . . . who in stature, no less than in mind, are certainly of a very inferior race of human beings;" observing further, "I believe them wholly incapable of forming among themselves any regular and combined plan for their emancipation."[18]

Vancouver described the huts "as the most miserable of human habitations, infested with every kind of nastiness and filth."

Verily, these Indians must have been sorry material from which to make citizens. It is small wonder that the Mission Fathers at Santa

---

[18] Hittell, History of California, Vol. I, p. 472.

Cruz received with alarm the news that the neophytes were to hold elections. One sometimes wonders if the Spanish system was not at fault by being too inflexible; by laying down a course of conduct to be observed in all places of the Indies, without realizing the enormous difference of adaptability to new conditions which the Indians of the various nations and tribes exhibited.

CHAPTER XIX

De Borica and Indian Elections

BOOK III
Chapter XIX

De Borica and Indian Elections

LIEUTENANT Colonel Don Diego de Borica, a native of Victoria, the Basque Province of Spain, who had received his appointment of *Gobernador Proprietario* from the King at Madrid in June, 1793, arrived in Monterey the following year.

To him the appointment was somewhat in the nature of an exile, for de Borica was a man of excellent education, a literatus of no small attainments, of aristocratic birth and high ideals—in other words, a scholar and a gentleman who loved bright and intelligent companions. He, his wife, Dona Maria Magdalena de Urquides, an heiress of great wealth, and his daughter, Dona Josefita, were close companions and friends, and the three formed a small intimate and cultured circle. His family group was a pleasing contrast with that of Governor Fages, who had resigned a few years before (1791), and who had a brilliant but erratic wife; she had called the Governor's residence at Monterey "an adobe hovel," had flirted with the other officers "to make her husband jealous," and had never curbed the bitter tongue in her handsome mantilla-draped head. With her there could be no peace in the Governor's family—even though she had dutifully borne many children, as the women of her race and time were wont to do.

Governor de Romeu,[1] who succeeded Fages, suffered from insomnia and tuberculosis, and died shortly after his arrival. Things remained in *status quo* under Don Jose de Arillaga, who served as *Gobernador interino* until the arrival of the real Governor.

De Borica, besides being a scholar, was also an active and energetic soldier and administrator, who demanded obedience to his orders, and infused energy in those under his command. With his rule of almost six years a new period of progress and advancement opened.

So-called "liberal" ideas, at that time so popular in Catholic France, under the influence of the encyclopaedists and philosophers, were foreign to the padres, absorbed as they were in administering their large and ever-growing estates, and in the education of the Indians in the Catholic religion. Religious had no sympathy for profane knowledge, and in Mexico even the reading of "Fénélon's Télémaque" brought excommunication to the layman.

---

[1] Don José Antonio de Romeu.

The commandants and other officers at the presidios[2] were more of a practical than an intellectual turn of mind; their free time was not taken up with scholastic studies, but with flirtations, bull and bear fights, cock fights, and similar pleasures, while the Government settlers at the pueblo were an inferior lot of people, who, failing to develop the true pioneering spirit, sank lower and lower in the social scale, some degenerating into complete failures.

De Borica towered above these conditions. There were no schools for the white children except those kept by the padres, who were already overburdened with other duties, so he established secular schools, appointing the best available teachers. He at once strengthened the fortifications along the coast, creating additional protection against foreign invasions, and sternly insisted upon the reform of the pueblo administrations,[3] making it clear to the alcaldes that dire punishments would follow unless there was a marked increase in agricultural and other useful pursuits of the settlers and a decrease in gambling, drinking and brawls.

To the consternation of the *gente de razon,* who belonged originally to the military officers' families, and who had either returned to California after their first repatriation or otherwise had remained in the new country after the term of their service had expired, he ordered that their sons should be educated in the mechanical arts. The parents protested; it was against all their traditions. De Borica pointed out to them that nothing could be expected from the degenerate colonists which were being sent out, and the boys of intelligence must work at more practical studies.

Such was the new Governor's character and viewpoint, and the Fathers at Santa Cruz knew that when de Borica gave the order for the election of Indian officers at the Mission pueblo, they had to obey.[4]

The sacerdotal authorities had already received a decided proof that this Governor was the master in his province, not only in name but in fact.

Complaints had been made about the mistreatment of neophytes at the Missions, either for refusing obedience, overstepping the rules, or for desertions. The Governor investigated the charges, and if they proved true, was most determined in suppressing them with a heavy hand.

The attention of Governor de Borica had been called to the San Francisco situation by Fr. Jose Maria Fernandez, a supernumerary at that

---

[2] The presidios in Alta California were the centers of social life.

[3] There were four centers of Spanish influence:—the Presidios, the Missions, the Pueblos and later the Ranchos.

[4] Governor de Borica's order was based on Governor Philip de Neve's *reglamento,* sanctioned by the King on October 24, 1781 (therefore ten years before Santa Cruz was founded) which contained a new provision that every year the neophytes at each Mission pueblo should elect from their own number two *alcaldes* and two *regidores,* or councilmen, in order to accustom them to self-government.

Mission, who had arrived by sea on July 18th, 1796. Not long after his arrival he quarreled with the other missionaries. It is said that a blow on the head, received previously and accidentally, had made him erratic, and apparently not expecting relief from his immediate superior, President de Lasuen, he wrote directly to the Governor, bringing very grave charges of cruelty against his fellow-religious.[5]

De Borica was thoroughly aroused by the conditions prevailing there, and the treatment the Indians received at the hands of Fathers Landaeta and Danti. On September 22nd he wrote to the Father President:

"Setting aside the considerations and forbearance which until now have been of no avail in correcting excesses committed against the poor and deplorable Indians of Mission San Francisco, I shall know how to take rigorous measures to relieve them with regard to treatment, work and warm meals. There have occurred two hundred and three deaths in 1795, and about two hundred Indians have run away. This is a blot which will scandalize the secular as well as the monastic authorities. For God's sake, I beg Your Paternity to reform this entirely, so that at once and forever these wretched people may be placed in a condition in which they may live pleasantly. This is a subject which deprives me of sleep, and it is this that makes me speak. Would it not be a shame if two countrymen should be compelled to quarrel to the scandal of the province? . . ."[6]

Fr. de Lasuen, as always, was conciliatory and answered the Governor that he would see that the causes of the complaints disappeared, and the Governor wrote a handsome and gallant reply. He did not, however, release his vigilance.

Ever since the establishment of the Missions four dangers had harassed the minds of the padres. There was the standing threat of complete secularization (disestablishment) of their beloved institutions. There was the threat that the Mission work in Alta California might be taken away from the Franciscan Order and turned over to their rivals, the Dominicans, who operated in Lower California. These two major dangers did not seem to be eminent or pressing in 1796, but the padres were brought face to face with two minor dangers—the proposed advancement of the Indian settlement surrounding the Mission proper into official Mission pueblos; and the establishment of entirely secular pueblos or villas in the near proximity of the Missions. Governor de Borica was determined to change the existing state, partly sacerdotal and partly secular,

---

[5] Fr. Fernandez to Borica, Sept. 12, 1796, Gov. Borica to Fr. Fernandez, Sept. 15, 1796. Cal. Arch. Prov. Rec. IV, 153, etc., Prov. St. Pap. XV, 57-67.

[6] De Borica te Fr. de Lasuen, September 22, 1797, Cal. Arch. Prov. Rec. IV, 639-640, Englehardt, Cal. Missions and Missionaries of California, Vol. II, pp. 519-20.

into an exclusively secular state, in which the Missions would be gradually relegated to less and less important positions.

The election of native civil officers in the Mission pueblos was a decided step in that direction and the Fathers were fully aware of this.

The orders of de Borica were, of course, no novelty or innovation born in his active brain. He was simply carrying out the ancient and well-established colonial policy of Emperor Charles V, who had given the order that the Indians of new Spain should dwell together in communities and should be governed by Indian *alcaldes* and *regidores,* elected by the natives.

So far the padres had always been able to maintain that this applied to the secular pueblos and not to the Mission pueblos. Of course, the Mission Fathers had used Indians to maintain order for some time and had given each of them as emblems of authority a baton and a coat, which did service as some kind of uniform. There were also Indian magistrates, called *caciques*. Each Mission had three elected from a select number of Indians chosen by the Fathers. They were therefore the executors of the will of their superiors, maintained good order in the Missions and in the churches, and quite often ordered punishments for transgressions.

It was, however, a different matter for the Indians to elect independent officials, for this would seriously threaten the authority of the padres.

The opposition of the missionaries to all these elections was historic. Already on March 29th, 1779, Fr. Serra wrote to Fr. de Lasuen in regard to de Neve's insistence on the election of Indian *alcaldes* as follows:

"Well, what I have thought out is that what the *caballero* demands should be executed, but in such a way that it cannot cause the least commotion among the natives, nor in the government which your Reverence has established. Let Francisco, with the same baton and coat which he has, be the first *alcalde*. It is nothing more than a change in name. With regard to the *regidores,* who as such carry no staff, let the one be of the Mission and the other of any *rancheria,* whether he is a chief or not, though it will be more expedient that he be a chief, and thus the things will remain without creating wonderment.'"

It will therefore be seen that Fr. Serra, while advising compliance with the letter of the law, endeavored to evade the spirit as much as possible, thereby preventing what he believed to be the evil consequences of actual acquiescence.

This advice seemed to have been followed at most of the Missions, for the Fathers never considered the Indian officers of the Mission pueblos

---

[7] Engelhardt, Missions and Missionaries in California, Vol. II, p. 361.

very seriously. In fact, all through the Mission period they maintained that these men, as well as the other neophytes, were subject to the church discipline, including corporal punishment, and proceeded accordingly, and in truth they had good justification, for many of the native officials promptly abused the power obtained by their election. For instance, the *alcalde* at San Luis Obispo trafficked in women for the benefit of the soldiers. Many of them were thieves or tyrannized over their people, and one of the *alcaldes,* as soon as elected, seized another Indian's wife and fled with her.

Governor de Borica's order could, however, not be ignored entirely, but Fr. de Lasuen proved to be a good pupil of Fr. Serra, for on November 2nd, 1797, he instructed those under him, including of course the Santa Cruz Fathers, to this effect:

"Let the election be held at a convenient hour, because His Honor so directs, but only in the manner in which it is possible to have it in Missions for which there is no law to determine it. In these Missions we are preparing the neophytes for the fulfillment of the laws; but the being governed by such laws should be left for the time when they cease to be Missions, and when they shall be declared pueblos or *doctrinas* by the King, our Lord. Then we must leave them. Meanwhile, the said election may be held in a preparatory and instructive manner, but by no means after the formality of the law which is quoted, because said law does not speak of Missions. Your Reverences may tell the Governor in the report which you send that you have obeyed him."[8]

From this it must be apparent that the Fathers did not in any way consider the Indian settlements which grew up in the shadows of the Missions, and were often called Mission pueblos, as real pueblos, and that as soon as they were real pueblos, the Fathers were ready to leave.

There was, of course, a good deal to be said for this view of the missionaries, for a regular pueblo manifested itself in various ways, besides having a proprietary existence. It had a political jurisdiction embracing all the legal voters within a certain territory which was much more than the four square leagues. It had also a judicial jurisdiction which extended far beyond the four square leagues, and it had a qualified right in adjoining lands[9] which were generally called *dehesas* or great pasture lands, and were separated from the land proper of the pueblos by the *ejidos,* or vacant suburbs.

---

[8] Engelhardt, Missions and Missionaries of California, Vol. II, p. 367.
[9] Dwinelle, Sect. 9.

The "Laws of the Indies" divided the pueblo lands into a number of classes, which we have mentioned previously—*terminos, propios, tierras communes, suertes, sitos, tierras de labor, pastores,* and *ejidos.*

Sandy and other wastes were rejected by the Spanish law from the computed measurement, though they were still included within the boundaries of the pueblo. The measurement might be made in the direction of the sea, lakes or other wastes, but if these were the *ejidos,* they were likewise excepted from the computation.[10]

[10] Ordenanza de Tierras, Aquas, pp. 181-187, Edition 1855.

CHAPTER XX

The Mission's Neighbor, — The Villa Branciforte.

BOOK III
Chapter XX

The Mission's Neighbor—The Villa de Branciforte

THE history of the Mission Santa Cruz is inextricably interwoven with that of the Villa Branciforte, the only civil or military establishment founded in Alta California after Felipe de Neve left the province.

As we have seen, the Fathers, by exercising consummate skill, managed to comply in appearance with the orders of the secular authorities in regard to the Mission pueblos, while in reality they blocked them, yet they were unable to prevent the founding of several purely secular pueblos and a villa. They managed to control the election of two *alcaldes* and two *regidores* at each Mission, held on the eve of New Year's day or the day thereafter, but this control did not extend to these other establishments, representing the civil colonization activities of the Government, separate from the presidios or Missions.

The new villas were to be something more ambitious than mere pueblos; it was hoped that they would become something akin to the Cities Palatine, and they were to receive special favors and privileges, while each citizen, called a *poblador,* was to be equipped with arms and two horses, ready at short notice to march against an enemy.

To understand the wish of Miguel de la Grua Talamanca Marques de Branciforte, who in 1794 had succeeded Juan Vicente Guemes Pacheco de Padilla conde de Revilla Gigedo as Viceroy in Mexico City, to establish additional pueblos and villas in Alta California, one should take into consideration the local as well as the political, international conditions prevailing at that time.

Prior to the advent of Governor de Borica, Alta California had been practically without defenses. Fortifications were expensive, only few *gente de razon* had settled in the pueblos, and it had occurred to the Viceroy that the promotion of colonization might add a great deal to the security of the Province. De Borica was in entire accord with de Branciforte's ideas. As an invasion by France was feared, and a war with England was expected (in 1796 Spain did declare war on England), the Viceroy welcomed a report from the Royal Tribunal of Accounts, dated November 18th, 1795, suggesting as a remedy the founding of a villa.

This report, prepared by Beltran on November 17th and approved by the Tribunal on the 18th, went into a good many details. It provided that "this establishment as a coast defense should be put on a military basis, securely fortified, and settled with soldiers as *pobladores*. The site must be selected and the lands divided according to existing pueblo regulations and the Laws of the Indies. Each officer and soldier is to have a house-lot, and between those of the officers, lots are to be assigned to the chieftains of *rancherias* who may be induced to live with the Spaniards, thus assuring the loyalty of their subjects. Live stock and implements may be furnished by the Government as hitherto. Instead of an *habilitado* there is to be a town-treasurer; and Alberni may command, acting as lieutenant-colonel. As the time of the infantry soldiers expires they are not to be re-enlisted, but new recruits obtained from New Spain will create an immigration without the heavy cost of bringing in settlers as such."

It was recommended as a most important measure for the welfare and protection of the Spanish possessions in California that the Governor, with the aid of Engineer de Cordoba and others, proceed to select a site and found the first villa, to be called Branciforte in honor of the Viceroy.

Prior to this (1789) a villa had been established at Pitic, in Sonora, Mexico. It was organized as a presidio under a *comandante*, subject to the *Audiencia* of the district, but was to be transformed as rapidly as possible into an armed pueblo, ruled by two *alcaldes* and six *regidores* and a *sindico*.[1]

Each villa was entitled to four leagues of land, to be distributed in the name of the King; after there were thirty families, *alcaldes, regidores* and an *ayuntamiento* (town council) were to be chosen.

Don Alberto de Cordoba, an able military officer with the rank of *ingeniero estra-ordinario*, was sent by de Branciforte to California. He received his orders in November, 1795, "to proceed to the Port of San Francisco and locate the villa so as to give it connection with a battery and make it defensive of the coast—a sally-post against disembarkations; the engineer availing himself of the rules of fortification wherein he is well versed."

He arrived in the beginning of 1796 and at once reported to Governor de Borica. They became friends at sight, co-operating and supporting one another in a most refreshing way, especially in those times of constant bickering, incriminations and recriminations.

Prior to this Lieutenant-Colonel Pedro de Alberni and Sergeant Jose Roca had appeared on the scene, with seventy-two Catalonian volunteers and eighteen artillerymen, to assist in the repulsion of the French, in the event of an attack, which fortunately never took place, France having need of all her forces in Europe. These troops were distributed over the prov-

[1] See Plan of Pitic, B. C. Miss. and Col., Vol. 1, p. 343, translated by J. W. Dwinelle, in The Colonial History of San Francisco.

MISSION SAN FRANCISCO DE ASIS (DOLORES)

ince, twenty-five Catalans going to San Francisco, where de Alberni became the *comandante*.

Even before de Cordoba's arrival, de Borica had instructed the different presidio commanders to report on suitable sites for pueblos, and Sergeant Amador had explored the coast region from San Francisco to Santa Cruz with this in view.

In order to make some personal explorations of the suggested sites, Governor de Borica requested de Alberni and de Cordoba to meet him at Santa Cruz on May 28th, 1796, with an escort of six men. Explorations were made and an interesting correspondence ensued between the Governor and de Cordoba. On June 16th, 1796, the Governor wrote the following letter to de Cordoba from Monterey:

"At the Mission of Santa Clara I delivered you a certified copy of the official order of the 19th of December of last year (1795) sent me by His Excellency, Viceroy and Marquis de Branciforte, together with the report made by the General Auditor of Accounts, and to which he refers, mentioning that for want of time the second company of Volunteers of Catalins have not been provided with the articles solicited for them; also that they are destined to perform miliary service in this province, and indicates they will be compensated for such services, because there is to be established a new place in which they will be permitted to reside when they are discharged.

"In order to inform His Excellency of what follows, that he may decide as appears proper to him, and with full knowledge, I wish you would inform me at length of your views and ideas which were formed and had in my company when we were making reconnoissance of the lands of the Mission of Santa Cruz and vicinity, from the Pajaro River to Santa Clara, and also in company with Lieutenant-Colonel Pedro de Alberni when exploring the place called Alameda (opposite side of the bay from Mission San Jose) and vicinity, and the Presidio of San Francisco and Mission of the same name. In the report you will make, state whether or not the lands in the vicinity of the aforesaid presidio or Mission are proper upon which to form a settlement of Spaniards, and give the qualities of such lands. Also state the same concerning the land near Santa Cruz, and whether, in your opinion, there will be caused any damage or hurt to the Indians should there be established on the side of the river nearest to Monterey a town inhabited by people of reason (other than Indians), and what advantages may arise from making such a settlement. You will state the same concerning the place called Alameda, and other places that you may know of. Also, state what precise and indispensable aid should be given, in your opinion, to the settlers, distinguishing them from the volunteer soldiers who have served their enlistment, or the pensioned soldiers who may arrive, considering the former as settlers who expect to be permanent residents. You will report upon these and other matters referred to in the official order, expressing yourself clearly, using your knowledge and intelligence. May our Savior protect you many years.

DIEGO DE BORICA,
Military Commander of California.

To Alberto de Cordoba,
Monterey, June 16, 1796."

To this letter de Cordoba replied from the Presidio of San Francisco on July 2nd, 1796, in these words:

"In answer to the official communication of your Honor, dated the 16th of last month, requesting me to report my views as to the best and most appropriate place in which to form a new settlement and town, and concerning which I made an inspection with your Honor of the lands contiguous to the Mission of Santa Cruz, and with Senor Pedro de Alberni, also inspected the place called Alameda, and the lands of the Presidio and Mission of San Francisco, I should say that the only place that presents advantages sufficient for the desired end is that which is situated on the side of the river of the Mission of Santa Cruz next to Monterey. Good land is found there, some of which is susceptible of irrigation and some moist enough to grow crops, and other portions are pasture lands, for large and increasing herds of cattle of all kinds; also having all the necessities, such as timber, stone, limestone, clay, to make adobe bricks and tiles for the construction of edifices, and plenty of water for all uses; also with the advantage of being near the sea, which affords an abundance of different kinds of fish, and a means of transportation, at little cost, of the fruits and grain that may be raised by the settlers, who will be permanent residents. It is my opinion and belief the Indians will not suffer any damage or drawback by reason of founding a new settlement, because at the Mission there will be left to them good and large tracts of land, which they can use for cultivation, and upon which their animals can pasture.

"The place called 'Alameda' has not the necessary advantages for the intended enterprise. Indeed, although its lands are good and not mountainous, it is without sufficient water for irrigation, domestic and mechanical purposes; neither is there to be found in its vicinity timber, firewood, nor stone, and by reason of these wants it does not appear to me to be a suitable place upon which to found the new settlement.

"At the place called 'Presidio of San Francisco' and Mission of the same name, and its environs, there are not to be found agricultural lands for a distance of seven or eight leagues, not even sufficient to compose a very small farm, because the lands are thin and arid, and covered with hills of loose sand; running water is exceedingly scarce, and nothing grows there, excepting some bushes and shrubs; even if the lands should prove to be fit to farm, it appears to me that it would be difficult to do so, because of the fierce and incessant winds that one meets with there; this is the reason that the Mission has been obliged to select a place about six leagues distant near Mussel Point, where they found some land fit for cultivation, upon which they could grow enough to maintain the Indians with, there being but a very small quantity of land good enough for cultivation anywhere in the vicinity of the said Mission. Therefore, when it is intended to put in practice the project of founding a new settlement, it should be done at the place before mentioned, adjoining the Mission of Santa Cruz, which is distant thirty leagues (ninety miles) from the Presidio of San Francisco and twenty-five[2] leagues from Monterey. Whenever the superior authorities conclude to execute the project of founding a settlement of Spanish people, it should be understood, in order that it progress favorably and with rapidity, that the houses are to be built at the charge of the royal treasury, and that there be given to the settlers all the agricultural implements necessary for their use, and all kinds of live stock, to the end that immediately upon taking possession of their tracts of land they can apply themselves to cultivation, so that they may be enabled soon to harvest enough for their support. Indeed, if they should be obliged to build their homes and barns, in which to preserve their crops when harvested, they will require one year, perhaps two, to do it in, because of the scarcity which exists in this country of mechanics or builders, and they would be prevented from cultivating their land until the third year, which delay would retard their progress, and still more so if the facilities are not extended for the sale of their fruits and grains. The soldiers belonging to the volunteer corps, and who have served out their enlistment, and also those of the regulars who are discharged with a pension, believe themselves entitled to greater and other aid than that which may be furnished to the settlers, because of the service rendered by them during the years while serving His Majesty honorably, bearing his arms.

"With respect to the Indians of the country, they have neither captains nor chiefs,[3] and live where best they can, seeking herbs and wild fruits upon which they subsist, so it is not practicable to bring into the settlement their captains, and in such a way be assured of the fealty of the tribes. The only mode to civilize them is to locate a certain number at the various Missions or near towns, and set them to work, so that in time,

---

[2] 25 leagues or 75 miles must have been calculated along a very roundabout way, for on the present highway around the Bay the distance is hardly 50 miles.

[3] This is only partially correct.

learning from the Spaniards, they may be able to govern and maintain themselves.

"The advantage of the new establishment is that it can be self-supporting, by supplying and having a market at Monterey and San Francisco for its products, thus augmenting the cultivation of its lands, and increasing its population, provided means of transportation are furnished; the inhabitants will then apply themselves with energy and zeal to better themselves, so that their descendants may prosper. Thus I report as requested by prior command of the 18th ult.

"May God protect you many years.

ALBERTO DE CORDOBA, C. E.

To His Honor, Diego de Borica, Governor of California,
Presidio of San Francisco, July 2nd, 1796."

Lieutenant-Colonel de Alberni's report was dated July 1st, but inasmuch as it is nearly identical with that of de Cordoba, it is not necessary to quote it *in extenso.*[4]

On August 4th, 1796, the Governor transmitted these reports, with his enthusiastic approval, to the Viceroy, declaring that Santa Cruz was the best site between Cape San Lucas and San Francisco, and giving some additional particulars about the anchorage. He recommended "that an adobe house be built for each settler, so that the state of things prevailing in San Jose and Los Angeles, where the settlers still lived in tule huts, being unable to build better dwellings without neglecting their fields, may be prevented; the houses to cost not over two hundred dollars each." On September 23rd another communication of the Governor to the Viceroy contained suggestions of similar purport, and asked for four classes of settlers: "first, robust country people from cold or temperate climes; second, carpenters, smiths, stone-cutters and masons; third, tailors, tanners, shoe-makers and tile-makers; and fourth, shipwrights, and a few sailors, to take advantage of the abundance of whales." Having received this report and also the opinion of the legal adviser of the royal treasury, the Viceroy on January 25th, 1797, in accordance with that opinion, ordered the Governor to proceed immediately with the foundation. He had already sent a list of eight men who had volunteered at Guadalajara as settlers.[5]

It took an enthusiast like the Governor to have such faith in the establishment of a new villa, for the condition at the pueblos of San Jose and Los Angeles were far from encouraging. Father Alonso Salazar wrote to the Viceroy in 1796:

---

[4] The text of de Alberni's report may be found in Addenda No. IX, p. 18 of Dwinelle's Colonial History of San Francisco (1863).

[5] Bancroft, History of California, Vol. I, p. 567-8.

"The two towns founded twenty years ago have made no advancement. The people are a set of idlers. For them the Indian is errand-boy, vaquero, and digger of ditches—in short, general factotum. Confident that the Gentiles are working, the settlers pass the day singing. The young men wander on horseback through the *rancherias* soliciting the women to immorality."[6]

And the same month Fray Jose Señán[7] declared:

"In Alta California the pueblos hardly deserve the name, so formless and embryonic is their state. The cause is scant relish for work on the part of the settlers. One is more likely to find in their hands a deck of cards than the spade or the plow. For them the Gentile sows, ploughs, reaps and gathers the harvest. Debased, moreover, by the bad example of his white associates, the Gentile continues in the darkness of heathenism, when from distant *rancherias* many are won to the fold of the Holy Church."[8]

Upon their return to Mexico from the Missions, both Fathers, when the Viceroy demanded their opinion, also pointed out that various troubles would surely arise if pueblos were established in the immediate neighborhood of the Missions, and suggested that two sites were available midway between San Francisco and Santa Cruz, very suitable for a colony, "as there is sufficient land with water and no Indians to suffer damage." They also suggest that a resident priest should be appointed.

Subsequently, Fr. de Lasuen (May 1st, 1797) informed his College of the plan, and on August 30th a protest was sent to the Viceroy against the founding of a white settlement so near a Mission. The document was signed by all the directors, but came too late.

In the document, it was stated that the site chosen for the Villa of Branciforte was too near the Mission, that it was on the pasture ground of the natives, that trouble would surely result, and that the Mission laws entitled each Mission to at least a league of land in each direction. To this the Viceroy replied that the Mission had more land and raised more grain than they needed, that the neophytes were dying, that there were no more pagans to convert, and there was not a better site between Santa Cruz and San Francisco for the Villa of Branciforte.[9]

---

[6] B. C. Arch. Sta. Barb. Vol. II, p. 73.

[7] Señán later became Father-President (1812).

[8] M. A., Museo, Dosc, Rel. a las Mis. de Califs, Uto ii; B. C. Arch. Sta. Barb. Vol. II, p. 42.

[9] Bancroft, History of California, Vol. I. p. 572.

On January 25th, 1797, the Viceroy approved the establishment of the Villa of Branciforte on the east side of the San Lorenzo River, directly opposite the Mission of Santa Cruz. The anchorage there had been described by de Borica as good, well protected from northwesterly winds, and he had said that vessels could lay there with safety during the summer months and easily find shelter during the six winter months at Monterey.

The order and approval of the Viceroy read:

"The Attorney General of His Majesty having informed himself of the late report and other proceedings concerning the founding of a village called de Branciforte, and on the 29th of December last, among other matters, advised me as follows:

"Your Excellency, the necessary and effective orders concerning the sending of families of proper status have been given. There is solely wanting the action of the military inspector, to whom was sent your communication, ordering their transportation to San Blas, there to take ship for California, so that the first lot of them who arrive can proceed to their destination at the new settlement. In the meantime, the rest of them will be sent (to San Blas).

"For quite a long time now, there have been sent your Excellency mechanics of all trades, and advises from His Honor, the same Governor, have been received, that these are making good progress. In fact, they now know how to weave, to make saddles, also shoes and other manufactures; some of the natives (Indians) of that far-off peninsula (California) have taken instructions from them; these Indians have been made use of, making it unnecessary to solicit the assistance of others. Whenever mechanics have been employed on account of the royal treasury, the tools that have been considered very necessary have been sent, not for the personal use of anyone, but for the use of all in common.

"In reference to the plan of the new town, the only defect thought of by the office of the Attorney General is that there is no designated lot for the public offices and the town hall. According to statute 8, title 7, book 4, these buildings should be near to the chapel and hospital, as provided in statute 2, title 4, book 1, in order that in time of necessity they can mutually protect one another. All other matters are found to agree with the instructions as contained in said statutes referred to as title 7, book 4, and although these cannot be entirely complied with in all their parts, they will be in the future, as time progresses.

"With these remarks and those expressed by the board of directors, in its communication of November 18th, of the past year, this office approves the establishing of the new villa, with the glorious name of Branciforte, at the site or place as proposed by His Honor the Governor of California, he acting as decided upon with Lieutenant-Colonel Pedro de Alberni and Civil Engineer Alberto de Cordoba, who considered it to be the proper place.

"May God protect your Honor many years.

BRANCIFORTE,
Viceroy of Mexico.

To the Governor of California.
Mexico, January 25, 1797.

A true copy,
May 9, 1797.
DIEGO DE BORICA,
Governor of California."[10]

The Governor gave notice that he would found the Villa of Branciforte in person, and thereupon issued orders to de Cordoba to lay it out on a scale commensurate with the instructions, so as to include a church, government buildings, hospitals, and comfortable houses for the colonists, and also to make specifications and estimates. . . . He enclosed a copy of a set of regulations as per the Plan of Pitic and directed de Cordoba to proceed in all respects in compliance with its provisions, except where specially otherwise ordered.[11]

In April, in further compliance with the Viceroy's orders, de Borica sent information to Santa Barbara and San Jose to the effect that the villa was to be established. He asked that recruits be secured locally from the surrounding country. Fr. de Lasuen also co-operated by asking the missionaries to help recruit settlers. Few, however, seem to have been forthcoming.

The Villa was laid out on high, level land in what is now East Santa Cruz; a bridge was built over the river connecting the Mission and the Villa, and both a water-mill and a lime kiln were constructed.[12]

On May 12th, 1797, nine colonists with their families, in all seventeen persons, recruited in Guadalajara from the vagabond and undesirable classes, arrived in a pitiful condition at Monterey on the little ship *Concepcion,* which had sailed from San Blas. Their health was poor and they were destitute in body and soul,[13] while some of them were diseased before they started. Among them were five bachelors (although married people

---

[10] Harrison, The History of Santa Cruz County, pp. 41-44.
[11] Hittell, History of California, Vol. I, p. 578.
[12] Id. Vol. I, p. 588 from California Archives, Provincial Records.
[13] Hittell, History of California, Vol. I, p. 581.

had been requested), two were farmers, two tailors, one carpenter, one miner, one merchant, one engraver, and one unclassified. They were mostly Spaniards.

They arrived at the new site under the direction of Corporal Gabriel Moraga, who had the reputation of being an excellent soldier, and who became famous as an Indian fighter. He was at that time about thirty-five years old, had been *comisionado* at the Pueblo of San Jose, and was selected for his military and civil abilities. He was to act as *comisionado* and was authorized to erect temporary shelters for the men; he was also instructed to put the colonists to work and watch over their morals.

On July 24th, 1797, the Villa was formally founded by the Governor, while by August the superintendent of the formal foundation had all surveying accomplished, part of an irrigation canal dug, and temporary houses partially erected.[14]

Each colonist was to be aided with from $20 to $25 and to receive annually $116 for two years from the Government, and $66 for the next three years.[15]

Upon arrival they were put to work to erect redwood huts with thatched roofs to replace the temporary shelters built by Moraga and the few soldiers under him. They had been promised, without cost, homes of adobe and tile built at the expense of the Spanish Crown, but instead found themselves compelled to help in the erection of shelters which looked crude even to them. None too eagerly they commenced planting crops.

Meanwhile, word was received that orders had been issued for the collection of nineteen more undesirables, to be gathered at Guanajuato and sent via San Blas.[16] Evidently the authorities had an abiding faith in the cleansing effect that the salubrious climate would have on the morals of the new *pobladores!*

The Governor's wishes were not always carried out, for he had written the Viceroy that a better class of settlers should be sent out, including young women who could become wives of the unmarried men of the settlement, as only three of the nine colonists were married. In his specifications the Governor demanded that each girl should be healthy and strong, and besides have in her possession "a serge petticoat, two woolen shirts, a pair of stockings, and a pair of strong shoes." In other words, the far-

---

[14] Id, p. 578. "Each colonist was to have an adobe house, roofed with tiles, built for him at the expense of the King, besides being maintained for a year out of the public treasury and furnishing on easy conditions of payment, two horses, two mares, two cows, two sheep, two goats, a yoke of oxen, a musket, a plow, and other agricultural implements." (See Early History of the Santa Cruz Region, Narcissa L. Parish, pp. 43-44.)

[15] Bancroft, History of California, Vol. I, p. 570, 571.

[16] Hittell, History of California, Vol. I, p. 582.

sighted Governor realized that success in building up a solid community is not based on the fanfare of military trumpets, but on healthy, growing families. He said that while it might be possible to supply wives from the Indian women at the Mission, this was not probable, for they were disinclined to leave their relatives, and the missionaries demanded from the men good moral character. "This," he added wisely, "was hardly to be expected from vagrants."

History does not record that any consignment of girls, up to specifications, ever arrived at Monterey, though the Mexican authorities availed themselves of the opportunity of shipping a score of foundlings from an orphanage who, after becoming of marriageable age, found husbands, and turned out very well.

The instructions from the Governor for governing the settlers touched every detail of their daily life.

"The townsmen must be made to live in peace and harmony." There was to be no gambling or drunkenness. "Neglect of public work must be punished." Mass was to be attended on holidays, and prayers and the rosary said at the close of each day's labors. There was to be no intercourse with the Mission Indians or the Gentiles. "The most friendly relations must be maintained with the Friars of Santa Cruz. The greatest precautions must be taken to insure proper care of the colonists' clothing, implements and other property, and to prevent sales, which were to be void." All labor before the arrival of de Cordoba was to be directed towards the building of shelter for the men and animals, and progress was to be reported monthly to the Governor.[17]

As was to be expected, the gentlemen from Guadalajara found little pleasure in domesticity. The Pueblo of San Jose, older and larger, was comparatively near at hand and offered so many attractions that it became necessary to order that no resident of Branciforte might go there without permission, and then he must return on a specified day. Failure was punishable by confinement in the stocks.[18] Still the threat was not sufficient to curb the desire for diversions, for a year after their arrival in Branciforte, two of the Guadalajuarans, Fermin Cordero and Jose Arceo, left without permission. Corporal Moraga, having reported them to Governor de Borica, received orders that if they were caught they were to be compelled to do their work in irons. By 1800 pleasure trips were entirely forbidden.

Poor Moraga's duties embraced more than seeing that the men built their homes, tilled their fields and stayed in Branciforte. (See Appendix

[17] Bancroft, History of California, Vol. I, p. 568.
[18] In one case the day set for the return of the party was exceeded and a penalty of eight days in the stocks was specified.

No. 1.) In December, 1797, he received from *Comandante* Sal in San Francisco for each settler six varas of *jerga* (six lengths of coarse linen, about one yard each), to be used for covers for their straw beds. The following October he was ordered by de Borica to inspect the wardrobes of the settlers' wives and report what each needed!

Unfortunately for everyone concerned, the enthusiastic official backing from Mexico City did not last very long. On August 12th, 1797, de Cordoba arrived in person. After a careful survey, he furnished the Governor with an estimate of expenses amounting to $23,405, a prodigious amount for those times. The budget was forwarded to the Viceroy, but already on October 24th the funds at hand were exhausted and de Cordoba returned to the presidio. (See Appendix 2.)

Having put the settlers to work in accordance with his instructions, Moraga reported in January, 1799, that the progress of affairs was satisfactory. In September the settlers were joined by others, bringing the number up to forty, including six *invalidos* and one discharged soldier. The names of these *invalidos* are given as: Marcelino Bravo, Marcos Briones, Marcos Villela, Jose Antonio Rodriquez, Juan Jose Peralta and Joaquin Castro.

The crops were good that fall, in fact better than the previous year, and the Governor felt hopeful that the foundation would be a success. Still it was necessary for Moraga to give the colonists permission to use the provisions of the pensioned soldiers,[19] and inasmuch as a prejudice had grown up against the place, few people desired to settle there.

Complaints having reached the Governor, he wrote Moraga saying that he believed that the Guadalajuarans planted only wheat and "do not sow or plant any other kind of grain or vegetables, because of their want of experience and energy. It is very necessary that you should in a prudential manner teach them how to labor, and rid themselves of their natural sloth. You are therefore authorized to punish those who fraudulently make excuses not to work, or who do not apply themselves to their labor. I count upon you to make honest and energetic men of them. . . . Ask for whatever you need in the way of seed for the use of the colonists."[20]

Moraga once more tried to carry out his superior's wishes, but did not seem to meet with much success, for the missionaries across the river were unanimous in their opinion that the settlers were a lazy, good-for-nothing lot, with evil interest towards the young women and girls at the Mission.

---

[19] Santa Cruz, A Peep into the Past, p. 23, a series of articles published by Williams, an old resident, in the Santa Cruz Item, 1876-1877.
[20] Santa Cruz, A Peep into the Past, pp. 7-9.

In December of 1799, Ignacio Vallejo was chosen as Moraga's successor. It was hoped that he would be able to get the settlers to work. The Government paid the $116 promised to each settler for the first two years; in addition, during the spring of 1798, each settler had received three milk cows.

In January, 1800, the *comisionado* of San Jose was required to make a contract with Branciforte agreeing to furnish corn and beans at the expense of the Mexican Government. However, that year the settlers were able to produce about 1,100 bushels of wheat, maize and beans. Their cattle amounted to approximately 500 head.[21] This quick increase in the number of their live stock may explain, to some extent, the suspicion in which they were held by most of their neighbors.

In 1800 the Mexican Government appropriated $540 for Branciforte, but this amount did not pay the debt of the past year to the national treasury. The prospects were not very bright for the little community and many concerned had come to the conclusion that the founding of the Villa Branciforte was a mistake. The only grandeur was in its name. One writer decided that "the settlers are a scandal to their country by their immorality. They detest their exile, and render no service."

Before very long the Viceroy fully realized the cost of the establishment, and that, in spite of its excellent backing at the start, it had not become more than a poor settlement, and was a constant thorn in the side of the padres.[22]

Though forced to give up its original elaborate plans, the Government did not altogether abandon the little settlement to its fate.

On June 3rd, 1801, the Viceroy informed Jose Joaquin de Arrillaga, who had become Governor *Interno* in 1800 on the departure of de Borica, that he had ordered tools and supplies to be purchased for Branciforte, and had provided for the remission of two-thirds of the $15,000 debt, the settlers to pay the balance from their savings.

In 1802 the Governor decided that an attempt should be made to establish civil government. Jose Vincente Mojica, one of the original colonists (1797), was elected *alcalde;* Fermin Cordero and Tomas Prado were elected *regidores;* and a *juez de paz* (justice of the peace) was appointed.

In 1803 Commandant Jose de la Guerra y Noriega, in a letter to the Governor, gave his idea of the settlers at Branciforte: "They are not so bad as other convicts sent to California; still, to take a charitable view of the matter, their absence for a couple of centuries at a distance of a million

---

[21] Bancroft, History of California, Vol. I, p. 571.
[22] James, In and Out of the Old Missions, p. 211.

leagues would prove most beneficial to the province and redound to the service of God and the King."

The trouble was not all over morals. Land squabbles followed. In 1805 Commandant Felipe de Goychoechea informed the Viceroy that Branciforte did not have the advantages of other pueblos, as the Mission had seized all the best land.[23]

The civic government did not last long, for it lapsed in 1805, when Felipe Hernandez was *alcalde;* thereafter and until 1822 the only authority was vested in a series of *comisionados.* The first two, Corporal Gabriel Moraga and Sergeant Ignacio Vallejo, had been picked from the active military service to be sent to Branciforte, but after Vallejo the *comisionado* was a home town selection.

In 1805 Jose Antonio Rodriquez was named. He had been a soldier since 1793 and had come to Branciforte as an *invalido* in 1797. Succeeding him came Juan Joseph Peralta, and Marcos Briones, both *invalidos;* Luz Garcia, Joaquin Buelna and Manuel Rodriquez.

Hittel says that in 1806 the Governor wrote that of the first settlers only five remained who had the status of *pobladores,* the balance having either enlisted or died. There were seven houses made of palisades and mud, badly roofed with tule, which were inhabited, and seven which were unoccupied.[24]

In 1807 the trouble between the Villa of Branciforte and the Mission about land took definite form, and was followed by a series of rather bitter bickerings.

The missionaries always looked upon the Villa's existence as an outrage upon the rights of the neophytes, and affirmed that the lands of the Villa from which fields might be assigned to *vecinos,* veterans and invalids, extended only to the Rancho de Bravo (situate from Branciforte to the Rio de Soquel), but that from that point to the Rancho de Aptos, and especially in the place called Corralitos, the lands unquestionably belonged to the Mission pueblo, upon which the Villa had no legitimate claims whatsoever. The Branciforteans were of a different opinion, and acted accordingly.[25]

For a long period there was little progress in the Villa. By 1815 the population had dropped again to forty. In that year, the new Governor, Lieutenant-Colonel Don Pablo Vicente de Sola, who was a Basque, as his

---

[23] Bancroft, History of California, Vol. II, p. 155-156. From Goycoechea, Medios para el formentodo California M. S.

[24] Hittell, History of California, Vol. I, p. 615, Cal. Archives Provincial Records, IX, 237.

[25] Bancroft, History of California, Vol. II, p. 156-7.

two predecessors, de Borica and de Arrillaga, arrived at Monterey, on August 30th, on the *Paz y Religión,* from San Blas.

In 1816 de Sola issued a series of instructions to the *comisionado* (corporal in charge of the Villa). The burden of his orders were that harmony and good morals should be maintained; he warned against adultery, gambling and drunkenness; he prohibited intercourse of any kind between citizens and Indians; no person might settle in the Villa or leave it without the Governor's permission; the settlers were to work hard and reports as to crops, etc., must be sent to the Governor. It was the same old story and all the warnings were disregarded. (See Appendix 3.)

In 1817 the Rancho Salsipuedes was provisionally ceded to the Mission by the Villa of Branciforte, provided that it be given up at any time upon six months' notice.[26]

In 1822, when the population had reached one hundred and twenty-two, the succession of *alcaldes* was resumed, with Jose Joaquin Buelna, followed by Serafin Pinto, Jose Boronda, Francisco Rodriquez, Joaquin Castro and others, changing yearly. While their choice of *alcalde* was indicated by the residents of Branciforte, he was actually an appointee of San Jose, for since the population was too small to entitle it to an *ayuntamiento,* Branciforte was placed under the civil jurisdiction of the northern pueblo. Both San Jose and Branciforte were transferred from Monterey to the original presidio jurisdiction of San Francisco, but in 1828 Branciforte was retransferred, together with the Ranchos of San Isidro and Las Animas, both as to civil and military jurisdiction, to Monterey, and that status lasted until the American occupation.

By 1830 the population had increased to one hundred and fifty-three, with thirty-four citizens, which included four "foreigners." Two of these were William and Samuel Buckle, young English sailors, who worked in the redwoods. Another was Julian Wilson, an American trapper, who had married Josefa Aribto and settled here. The fourth was Jose Bolcof, a Russian from Kamchatka, who was naturalized as a Mexican in 1833 and became *alcalde* of Branciforte the following year.

De Mofras gives a picture of Branciforte in 1840:

"This little village has today three hundred white inhabitants, most of them North Americans, married to women, descendants of the Spanish colonists. Some of them are occupied in commerce and agriculture, but the largest number are woodsmen or work in the saw-mills. These Americans have the reputation of being very turbulent; they assisted Alvarado to capture the Government, and later, after being made prisoners by his order, returned triumphant to California, ready to engage in any adventure.

---

[26] Bancroft, History of California, Vol. II, p. 389.

"One can travel on horseback to the Village of Branciforte and Monte Rey in eight or ten hours, and by sea in two or three hours. Immediately and by the first signal given by James[27] Graham, the chief of the Revolution, whose farm is situated close to the Villa, he is in a position to call around him about one hundred riflemen, American hunters, armed with long-sight guns; and it is a fact that any day that they would wish to, they could as easily capture Monte Rey as their countrymen could capture the pueblo of Los Angeles.

"One mile to the east of Villa Branciforte is situated the Mission of Santa Cruz. These two establishments are splendidly located one mile from the beach; they face the south and enjoy the full view of the whole Bay of Monte Rey. The houses are spread on an enormous grass field, shaded by groups of pine, and seven creeks rush down from the Santa Cruz mountains, drive the mechanical saw-mills and irrigate and fertilize the agricultural plots as well as the pasture."[28]

---

[27] This evidently was a mistake. His name was Isaac and not James.

[28] Exploration du Territoire de L'Oregon des Californies, 1840-1842, p. 409, Vol. 2. (Published at Paris, 1844, by order of the French King) by M. Eugene Duflot Count de Mofras.

BOOK IV

CHAPTER XXI

Santa Cruz Mission in the First Decade
of the Nineteenth Century and
De Rezanov's Visit.

BOOK IV

Chapter XXI

Santa Cruz Mission in the First Decade of the Nineteenth Century,
and de Rezanov's Visit to California

SOME writers declare that the first decade of the nineteenth century may be designated as the golden age of the California Missions.[1] It is hard to subscribe to this theory.

True, during the years 1800-1810 the Missions enjoyed an unusual amount of worldly prosperity. There were more neophytes at the Missions during this decade than at almost any other time,[2] but spiritually the Mission movement had lost a great many of its high ideals. As long as the Fathers had had to meet dangers, hardships and difficulties, they were full of zeal for the evangelization of the neophytes, and were sustained and inspired by the example of the first founders of the Missions in Alta California, but as wealth grew, ideals had often to give way to practical considerations, for the Fathers became more and more overseers and administrators of large landed properties, on which enforced labor was the source producing the desired wealth.

Between the years 1770 and 1795, when the Franciscan Fathers, fresh from San Fernando College, were the leading spirits in the movement, the Star of Bethlehem stood high in the western skies; after that date its brilliancy was occasionally obscured.

All historians are agreed that the Indians worked under forced labor conditions; once a Christian always a Christian, and the Indian had no right, when once baptized, to return to his savage, idle state in his own rancheria.

Probably this system was the only feasible one to follow. These Indians stood low in the scale of humanity. They could not cope with modern conditions. When afterwards liberated, they speedily fell a prey to predatory whites, and would have been destroyed much earlier if it had not been for the system of the Fathers. Granting this, still the fact remains that the Fathers operated by means of indentured labor, which, for a pittance, produced the wealth of the country.

It seems, therefore, better to conclude that the golden age was in the first twenty-five years after Serra's arrival in San Diego, although the

---

[1] Father Engelhardt, in Vol. 2, p. 619, uses these words, but by mistake calls it the first decade of the eighteenth century.

[2] See Appendix 2, Chapter XVIII.

following thirty years was admittedly a period of great industrialization and creation of wealth.

At the Santa Cruz Mission, the Fathers, notwithstanding all the annoyances met on account of the proximity of the new Villa, carried on the Mission activities with unabated energy. They directed the industry of the Indians, whom they clothed and fed, and eventually, through the increase of herds and by means of trade with the outside world, collected some wealth.

By 1800 the live stock had increased to 2,354, while the planting had yielded 4,300 bushels that year.

They received from Tepic and Mexican ports the goods they needed, in return for which they sold breadstuffs, hemp, cordage, hides and tallow. When more mariners came to California ports the trade increased, notwithstanding the difficulties the authorities threw in its way. The presidios also made increasing demands, against pay, for the products of the Mission.

Governor de Borica had resigned on March 8th, 1800, and had been succeeded by Don Jose Joaquin de Arrillaga as *Gobernador Militar y Politico* of the Californias.

The decree making Alta California a separate province, dated August 29th, 1804, reached the Governor on November 16th. He remained Governor of the northern province until July 24th, 1814, while Don Felipe de Goycoechea became Governor of Baja California in 1806.

The new Governor was decidedly *persona grata* with the sacerdotal authorities, as he refrained from interfering in any way with spiritual matters, and, though he never lost his independence of thought and action, he was always willing to assist them in all temporal affairs.

California, in the beginning of the nineteenth century, not only sustained a loss in the departure of its progressive Governor, but likewise in the death of the venerable Father President de Lasuen, beloved by everyone and affectionately known as Father Fermin. He died on July 26th, 1803, at the Mission of San Carlos.

He was succeeded by Father Estévan Tapis, of Santa Barbara, who assumed office at once, thereto authorized by a decree made in Mexico City on January 26th, 1798, to provide for such an emergency.

The Mission of Santa Cruz, being near an anchorage on the seashore, was adversely affected by a decree of King Charles V of Spain, who notified the American Government that vessels caught smuggling on the California coast would be confiscated. The Spanish authorities were disturbed by the realization that American influence was beginning to be felt in the West. In 1806 Governor de Arrillaga complained that the Amer-

MISSION SANTA CRUZ SANCTUARY, 1868 (Day after the Earthquake)
From drawing by Mrs. Julia Matthieu.
Courtesy of the Pioneer Society of California at San Francisco.

MISSION SANTA CRUZ—SANCTUARY
(after part restoration—from old photograph)

icans already possessed New Orleans and that New Mexico, and even Santa Fe, were beginning to use American goods. He was apprehensive:

"Having personally witnessed in our own waters the enterprise of this Republic, I do not wonder at their success. They flourish in trade and know its value. And who at present does not, except ourselves, who pay for our neglect with our purses? . . . The American States sometimes send out ten or fifteen regular robbers, who, on account of our small force, are able to disturb our peace and corrupt our honesty."[3]

In 1806 Governor Felipe de Goycoechea urged that the naval station at San Blas be transferred to the peninsula better to check the American designs.

De Goycoechea was certainly no friend of Santa Cruz, for the previous year he had recommended that inasmuch as all the Gentiles had been converted, the neophytes of the Santa Cruz Mission might be divided between Santa Clara and San Juan, and the Friars be employed in new fields.[4] His judgment was wrong, for the conversion of many Gentiles followed in the next years. Notwithstanding desertions and the great death rate, their number increased. The number of baptisms was 668; 1810 showed the largest number of baptisms—131. The deaths during this period were 593; the largest number being 101 in 1806, and the smallest 34 in 1803.[5]

The large stock decreased from 2,355 to 1,753; in 1810 there were 953 horses.

The small stock showed an increase of from 2,083 to 3,098; the crops in 1800 had been 4,310 bushels; in 1810 there were 2,730 bushels, while the highest and lowest mark had been reached in 1806 with 4,850 bushels, and in 1802 with 1,120 bushels, making an average yearly yield of 2,150 bushels.

De Goycoechea's recommendation was the first official hint that secularization of the Mission was by no means far off, though nothing came of this at that time, and the work went on.

A great many mutations took place among the missionaries at Santa Cruz, as well as elsewhere, during the first decade of the century.

In 1805 Father Francisco Gonzales obtained leave to retire, and was succeeded by Father Andres Quintana. Father Domingo Carranza was succeeded in August, 1808, by Father Antonio Rodriquez, and the two

---

[3] Richman, California Under Spain and Mexico, p. 202.

[4] Goycoechea, Medios para el Fomento, de Cal., 1805, MS. 16. An important official in the Alta California administration was the *habilitado general* located in Mexico City, who was elected by the commissioned officers of the four presidios in Alta California. Goycoechea, who was the commander at Santa Barbara, was unanimously elected and retained the office until he became Governor of Lower California.

[5] Bancroft, History of California, Vol. II, p. 154.

who served as supernumeraries were Father Jose Antonio in 1806-7, and Father Francisco Xavier in 1808.

The Santa Cruz missionaries were also concerned with two official documents—one the Governor's report in 1804, in which he stated as a result of his experience that the Indians were not cruelly treated. The second was a *Letras Patente* of Jose Gasol, Guardian of the College, of 1806, in which he gave strict orders that no more than twenty-five blows (recognized by all as a better way of correction than filling the prisons with petty offenders) should be given at any one time; no women flogged by men or in public; and that five or six hours in winter, or six or seven in summer, should be the limit of a day's work. That the authorities had become aware and sensitive to the criticism of the outside world as to physical punishment is evident from the same *Letras Patentes,* in which a warning was given not to inflict punishments before visitors, or mention them.[6]

All the missionaries had likewise been instructed not to indulge in luxury, and were warned not to employ female servants, but to depend entirely on men or boys.[7]

During this decade the local Friars were little bothered by private land grants. The only one which might have caused trouble was to Mariano Castro, who in 1803, while in Mexico City, had obtained a Vice Royal license to occupy "la Brea," near Mission San Juan Baptista. The Friars there did not wish to have interference with their cattle, and Castro did not succeed in establishing himself, so then he asked in 1807 for the rancho Salsipuedes, near the present town of Watsonville, in Santa Cruz County. The records do not show that anything came of his request, but to the contrary, the Mission cattle had increased to such an extent that soon the missionaries applied to the Commandant at Monterey for permission to occupy the rancho themselves.

In a few years more than fifty houses had been erected for the Indians; very large protreros had been enclosed, and even as far as New Years Point, they had houses for the servants and Indians to watch the cattle.

---

[6] "The missionaries shall never chastise in the presence of strangers or persons who do not belong to the community save in an extraordinary case; nor shall they communicate to such persons the punishment that has been meted out to an Indian."— Engelhardt, Missions and Missionaries of California, Vol. II, p. 648.
What is more surprising to the layman is that the missionaries were also warned not to give any information whatsoever to the Archbishop.

[7] Bancroft's Collection Patentes, 1806, Sec. 1.

The known population of California had increased by the year 1810 to 2,052 *gente de razon* (many of mixed race), 39 Friars, and 18,780 Indians, or a total of 20,871.

Since the founding of the Missions twenty Friars had returned to their college, mostly on account of ill health; ten had died in California proper. and twenty-eight new missionaries had arrived from Mexico.

While a great many Gentiles had been baptized, the death rate was enormous, comprising seventy-two per cent of baptisms, and forty-five per cent of the original population (including baptisms) ; seven hundred neo-phytes had deserted, which does not seem extreme, taking in consideration the total neophyte population.

In 1806 an event had occurred which might have had the far-reaching consequence of placing present California permanently under the Russian flag, and replacing the golden Roman cross, now surmounting the spire of the Catholic Church at Santa Cruz by the emblem of the Orthodox Greek Catholic Church.

This was the arrival of the Russian ship *Juno* in the harbor of San Francisco on April 4th, 1806, and thereby hangs a tale which may just as well be told here.

For centuries the huge Russian Empire had been trying to acquire harbors on year-around open seas. Archangel, in the north, was ice-blocked the greater part of the year ; the harbors of the Baltic Sea were frozen part of the time ; the Russian ships, in case of war, could readily be blocked in the narrows between Denmark and Sweden. Odessa and the other ports of the Black Sea were open, but could be cut off by the forts dominating the Dardanelles, and further west by the Straits of Gibraltar, while her harbors on the Siberian coast, facing the north Pacific, were frozen for long periods.

The huge Russian bear was stretching his strong paws towards the south, along the western coast of the American continent. The Russian-American Fur Company, while gathering the profits of an extensive trade, in the beginning of the nineteenth century fulfilled the same semi-political role that the Oost Indische Companies had filled for the Hollanders in Indoasia, and the Chartered East Indian Company and other similar organizations for the English in the Far East.

The fur company's ships went as far south as Chile to obtain the grain necessary for the subsistence of its hardy Siberian and Aleutian fur hunters and settlers at Kadiak, Behrings Bay, and along the northern Pacific coast, and it occurred to the managers that these supplies might be obtained much nearer to the scene of the operations by trading with the California Missions. It likewise occurred to them that under the conditions existing on the Pacific coast the flag of old Castile might eventually be replaced by that of the Moscovite Empire, for in the history of the world, political alliances had already often been changed via the trade route. Had this been accomplished, it is not impossible that Russia would never have parted with Alaska; that through conquest against Spain and through negotiations with England, she might have consolidated her holdings, and that the western boundary of the United States of America today would not be the Pacific Ocean, but the Rockies and Sierra Nevadas.

The *Juno* sailed through the Golden Gate, and anchored in the most magnificent harbor of the world in defiance of the Regulations and in defiance of a challenge from the fort, but as another Russian expedition under Captain von Krusenstern, was expected, the *Juno* was mistaken for one of these vessels, and therefore passed the San Joaquin battery without being fired upon.

Baron Nikolai Petrovich de Rezanov, a middle-aged man of distinguished and commanding appearance, one of the ten barons of Russia, Privy Counselor, Chamberlain to the Czar, and Knight of St. Anne, was in command. A powerful factor in the Russian-American Company, and formerly Ambassador of Russia to the Court of Japan, de Rezanov had become, on the death of his father-in-law, the head of the company, and was now a widower, his wife having died the previous year. With him served Dr. George Heinrich von Langsdorff, a surgeon, distinguished scientist, and also a Knight of St. Anne, several officers, one a Lieutenant Davydov, and a few scientists.

De Rezanov had gone to the company's headquarters at New Archangel, in Unalaska, in July, 1805. Two supply ships had failed to arrive, and his people were starving. He therefore purchased the *Juno* from J. de Wolf, an American slave dealer of Bristol, Rhode Island. It was a copper-bottomed fast sailer with a cargo of Yankee notions on board.

De Rezanov sailed for California, his immediate object being to obtain supplies, and his second, though more far-reaching object, was to ascertain the possibility of establishing the Russian interests more strongly and permanently on this coast.

Courtesies were exchanged on his arrival, and the commander and officers were invited to dine at the Presidio of San Francisco, where *Alferez* Luis Arguello, in the absence of his father, received them.

News of the arrival was at once sent to the Governor in Monterey, who was disinclined to allow any trading, as this was illegal, and besides, he became suspicious of the ultimate aims of his unwelcome visitors. The Russian understood the situation, and stretched the truth a little by sending a message stating that he had been intrusted by the Czar with command of all his American possessions, and in this capacity had resolved to visit the Governor of New California to consult him with regard to mutual interests. He furthermore explained that contrary winds had driven him to San Francisco, but that he would soon pay his respects to Monterey.

The Governor did not favor any trips inland, for Spain barred land visitors as well as ships from California, and replied that he expected soon to come to San Francisco, where de Rezanov should await his arrival.

Doña Maria de la Concepcion Marcela Arguello was the daughter of the Commandant in San Francisco, Don Jose Dario Arguello, and his wife, Doña Maria Moraga. De Rezanov fell in love with her, or at least pretended to be, but at the same time he also wanted to do some trading.

To his distress, the Governor, who had come meanwhile to San Francisco, remained silent on this subject, even after the exchange of many courtesies; the padres, on the other hand, by whom he had been invited to dine at the Mission, "showed a very noticeable desire to trade."

Writing home to his Minister in Moscow, de Rezanov gave a rather amusing explanation, in which he mixed diplomacy, trade and affairs of the heart.

The Chamberlain received the immediate benefit of a betrothal, for on May 21st, the *Juno,* laden with flour, peas, beans and maize, and with de Rezanov on board, sailed for Sitka, amid the farewell thunders of the battery of San Joaquin. He had promised to obtain the consent of the King of Spain and the Pope in Rome for their marriage, and to return as soon as possible.[8]

In September, 1806, he crossed to Kamtchatka, whence the same month he set forth overland for St. Petersburg. Ill on starting, he was attacked by fever, met a fall from his horse, and on March 1st, 1807, died at Krasnoyarsk.

Had the Chamberlain not met an untimely death he would have returned to California Alta, and it is possible that this resourceful and powerful man might have eventually succeeded in adding this province to the Russian Empire,[9] taking in consideration the weak defenses and defective internal organization.

---

[8] See Langsdorff, Voyages and Travels, etc., London, 1813, Vol. II, p. 153.

[9] The fear of Russian domination did not cease with the Spanish rule in Mexico. Jose Antonio de Andrade, the military and political Governor of Guadalajara, wrote to Iturbide, the President of the Regency (instituted by the latter in February, 1821) in October, 1821 that the military forces in Alta California had been neglected for several years, and he feared that Spain would now cede the Californias to Russia, which was already firmly intrenched on the Coast.

CHAPTER XXII

The Santa Cruz Mission, 1810-1820, Bouchard's Invasion

BOOK IV

Chapter XXII

The Santa Cruz Mission From 1810 to 1820, and Bouchard's Invasion

THIS decade was full of alarms and difficulties for the Santa Cruz Mission authorities.

In November, 1812, at the College of San Fernando, Fray Vicente Francisco de Sarría was elected *comisario-prefecto,* and Fray José Francisco de Paula Señán, *presidente,* to succeed Father Estevan Tapis, who had petitioned to be relieved of office.

The Father-president was directly responsible to the Guardian of the College of San Fernando, while the *comisario-prefecto,* elected for the first time on July 13th, 1812, had charge of all business matters and was the direct representative of the Franciscan *comisario-general* of the Indies, residing in Madrid. Both worked in perfect harmony.

In 1813 the Cortés of Spain passed a decree to the effect that all Missions in America that had been in existence for ten years were to be given up at once to the Bishop "without excuse or pretext whatsoever and in accordance with the law."

This was the first determined move to secularize the Missions. The decree declared that all such Missions should be converted into ordinary parishes or curacies, and placed spiritually in the hands of the secular clergy. (A full translation of the decree is to be found in Dwinelle,[1] "Colonial History of the City of San Francisco," page 20, Addenda, No. XI.) Although no definite steps were taken to fulfill this decree, it was the foreshadowing of the decree of the Mexican Government in 1833, actually accomplishing the secularization.

At the Santa Cruz Mission in 1810 a large house with two wings had been built for the widows and girls, and local matters seemed to have proceeded fairly peacefully until 1812, when on October 12th, Father Andres Quintana, one of the missionaries who had succeeded Father Gonzales in 1805, was found dead in his bed. Although the Friar had been for some time in poor health and unable to dress himself unaided, the suddenness of his death aroused suspicion among the authorities, but when an

---

[1] John W. Dwinelle, Counselor and Advocate, filed a brief in the District Court of the United States for the Northern District of California, in the case of the City of San Francisco vs. United States of America. Mr. Dwinelle was the attorney for the plaintiff who claimed four leagues of land, including the present city site. The brief was first printed in 1863.

inquest was held, it was determined that the padre had died a natural death. (See Appendix No. 1.)

What really happened was this: For proper precaution the Fathers were not allowed to travel far from the Mission, or go out at night *without* the escort of a soldier or two. Neglect proved fatal in this instance.

Late one night the Father was called down to the orchard, where an Indian was said to be dying. In order not to disturb the soldiers in their sleep, he went alone with the Indian caller. On his return, after visiting the sick person, some ambushed Indians got hold of the priest and ordered him to prepare for death, since he would not see his native place any more. All his entreaties were of no avail. He was hung from a tree, just where the track of the Felton Railroad passes now, not many yards from the tunnel.[2]

They brought his body home and put it in his bed, covering it as if he were asleep. This was possible, for his associate priest was away that night in Monterey, and Father Quintana was alone. His attendant, trying to call him at the usual hour in the morning, found the body. He was buried as if he had died a natural death, but his friends had suspicions, and took measures to ascertain the truth.

After two years a new investigation was held, and it was ascertained that Father Quintana had been overpowered and brutally murdered by strangulation, and multilated in an unnameable fashion.

A surgeon came from Monterey to examine the body, bringing an order from the commanding officers at Monterey to the surviving missionary, to allow the disinterment of the remains. The autopsy disclosed the truth, but who had done it was a secret which was kept for years before discovered.

An Indian *Majordomo* went from the Mission on business to New Year's Point. He understood the language of the Indians living there, but this was unsuspected. While his dinner was being prepared, he overheard some of them saying: "This fellow is from the Mission Santa Cruz, don't you remember how we killed Father Quintana there, many years ago?"

"Yes, we remember it well, but it never was found out."

"Well, let us kill this fellow, too, before he gets away."

The *Majordomo* pretended to be asleep while this talk was going on, but heard and understood it all. Rousing himself leisurely, he told the Indians not to hurry about dinner, that he did not feel very well, and wanted to go to the beach and take a bath. He went towards the sea, but got quickly out of sight among the rocks, found a horse that he could

---

[2] See *Libro de Entierros de la Mission de Santa Cruz.*

Viva Jesus.

Libro de matrimonios, en que se asientan las partidas de los, que se casan en esta Misión de Santa Cruz.

Fundada

Por

Los Religiosos del Apostolico Colegio de San Fernando de Mexico en la California Septentrional,

à Expensas

de

Nrō Catolico Monarca Carlos IV, Rey delas Españas, subministradas por el Exmo Señor Don Juan Vicente Guemez de Horcasitas, Conde de Revilla Gisedo Virrey, y Capitan Grāl de Nueva España.

Fundada en veynte y cinco de Sept.re de 1794: Siendo sus primeros Ministros: Fr Alonso Salazar y Fr Baldomero Lopez, Predicadores Apostolicos, del dho Colegio.

Costa este Libro de ciento noventa y ocho ojas buenas, numeradas exceptuando la primera en blanca.

TITLE PAGE FROM OLD RECORD OF MARRIAGES
AT MISSION SANTA CRUZ

mount, and escaped. He made his way over the mountains to Mission Santa Clara, and there told his story, revealing the long-kept secret.

Information was at once sent to headquarters at Monterey and the guilty parties were taken into custody. The culprit neophytes, numbering nine or ten, were tried for the crime; the case was sent to Mexico for final sentence, and in the spring of 1816 the sentence came back.

Five were condemned to receive two hundred lashes each, and to work in chains from two to ten years. Two others had died in prison, and one of the five, Lino, supposed to have been the leader, died in 1817 at Santa Barbara, where the convicts had been sent to serve their time. Galindo states that only one survived the punishment.

As to the charge of excessive cruelty made against the murdered Friar, especially the use of an iron strap to punish for fornication and theft, it was testified that he had two neophytes almost beaten to death, and had invented new instruments of torture. Pablo Vicente de Sola, who had become Governor on August 30th, 1815, declared, however, after a thorough investigation, that he could find no substantiating evidence.[3]

An inventory taken in 1814 shows that at this time the lands of the Mission were estimated to be eleven leagues along the coast, and three leagues inland from the shore. There were known to be 2,900 head of cattle belonging to the Mission at New Year's Point, so that eleven leagues places the southern limit not far from Aptos.[4] In that year the sowing was 45 bushels of wheat, 7 bushels of barley, 6 bushels of horse beans, 1 bushel of corn, 1 bushel of beans, 1 bushel of peas, while the harvest was: wheat, 500 bushels; barley, 200; horse beans, 200, and corn, 189 bushels; and there were 3,300 cattle, 600 horses, 25 mules and 46 hogs.

No wonder the Mission was famous for its fertility and productiveness, though this could hardly account for the tales which arose of "great wealth."

The treasure was estimated at over $30,000. For example, there is cited: a gold chalice valued at $280; another at $608; priest's vestment, still preserved, $800, and two capes at $1,200. (See Appendix No. 2.)

In twenty-three years there had been 1,794 baptisms, 565 marriages, and 1,242 deaths. The death rate had been very high, an average of 54 dying yearly out of an average population of 388, or nearly one in every seven.

[3] Sola to Viceroy Feliz M. Calleja, June 2, 1816. Sta. Barb. Arch.
[4] Willey, History of Santa Cruz County, p. 14.

1800 of 7,000. There were twenty Mission establishments. Live stock (cattle, horses, mules and sheep) had reached 349,882 head, a gain of 162,882 in twenty years; and 113,625 bushels of products (wheat, barley, corn, beans and peas) were harvested, or an annual gain of 57,625.

The Mission had lost heavily in population during the first half of the decade, but gained after 1816, some new rancheria apparently having been discovered.[5]

In 1817 the crops at Santa Cruz were destroyed almost completely by *chahuistle,* a sort of rust.[6]

In the same year Wilcox, in the *Traveller,* visited the Mission, which was then recognized as a regular port of entry.

The statistics for this decade of the Mission of Santa Cruz are as follows:

Decrease in population, 506-461; baptisms, 393; largest number, 112 in 1820; smallest, 8 in 1813; deaths, 399; largest number, 51 in 1813; smallest, 33 in 1817; large stock increase, 1,753 to 3,492; horses, etc., 953 to 492; sheep, 3,098 to 5,700; crops in 1810 were 2,734 bushels; in 1820, 4,300 bushels; highest number being 8,400 in 1818, and the lowest, 826 in 1817.

As to the Province at large, in 1818 Governor de Sola reported to the Viceroy that there were 20,238 neophytes in California (besides approximately 3,200 *gente de razon*), of whom 700 were soldiers, or a gain since

As if the secularization menace and the excitement caused by the murder of Father Quintana were not enough, the Mission Fathers had to face still more serious trouble in 1818, when a privateer arrived in the Bay of Monterey.

To understand this "privateer" scare, one has to go back again for a few years.

The Californias were, so far as foreign trade was concerned, closed territory. Except in cases of distress or official business, Spain did not allow foreign ships to enter the harbors to ply their trade. This policy of *mare clausum* was rigorously enforced as far as the means at hand made it possible, but theory is one thing and necessity is quite different.

The flag of Spain, while theoretically covering the whole Northwest, waved, in fact, only over a small strip of land along the coast, from the southern end of California Antiqua to the Bay of San Francisco. There Spain had planted the advance posts of her authority and civilization, and from there she regulated her entire foreign trade.

---

[5] Bancroft, History of California, Vol. II, p. 390.
[6] Idem.

For several years predatory fur gathering, fur trading and smuggling flourished along the whole coast. "Yankee" captains, some under contract with the Russian-American Fur Company, which had established itself north of San Francisco Bay, slaughtered fur animals and exported the skins to Russia and China, and also indulged in smuggling. Though these activities were prohibited by the laws, the poachers and smugglers were, nevertheless, welcomed by the padres and inhabitants in general, for very often the most necessary supplies, which had to come by vessel from San Blas or Lima, were cut off by privateering vessels in the service of insurgent Spanish colonies in the south.

The Russians soon became important factors in the situation, for whatever the Russian attitude might have been towards her own serfs, it was decidedly friendly to the Californian Indians around Bodega Bay, where Ivan Aleksandrovich Kuskov had firmly established himself.

They considered the territory north of San Francisco Bay as New Albion, where the writ of the Spanish authority did not run, and acted accordingly.

In 1812 about one hundred Russians (twenty-five being mechanics), with eight Aleut Indians, who in their bidarkas were famous hunters and fishermen, established themselves firmly and built a substantial fort, calling it Ross, or Fort Ross (taken from the root of the word Rossiia, in English Russia).

They became more popular with the "savage" Indians around the Bay of San Francisco than the Spaniards, for the latter brought the Gospel and hard work, while the former made no effort to force their religion on the Indians, but placated them with small presents and other friendly acts, while the Aleuts often fraternized with them.

The Russians had two practical aims in view—fur gathering and trade with the Spaniards, particularly in Mission products.

Lieutenant Gabriel Moraga, the son of the founder of San Francisco, was sent to investigate and reported to the Governor of Monterey in September.

He recognized that this trading was prohibited by the Spanish law, but pointed out that transports sometimes failed to arrive, and the Governor, who was tender for the care of his soldiers, being known amongst them as "Papa Arrillaga," having received a report from the Commander of the San Francisco Presidio "that the soldiers were destitute of almost everything," shut his eyes and soon a cargo valued at $14,000 arrived in boats from Bodega Bay. Breadstuffs and other necessities for Fort Ross were exchanged.

"Bootlegging" in supplies now began to flourish in earnest; while both parties officially and solemnly declared or acknowledged that the trade was illegal, a traffic outside the law and against the treaty existing between Spain and Russia arose, in which everybody participated energetically and joyfully, the Russian cargoes often being placed under the protection of the Spanish commandantes!

When Governor de Arrillaga died at Soledad on July 24th, 1814, Captain Jose Darin Arguello became Governor *interino,* and he was succeeded by Lieutenant-Colonel Vicente de Sola.

The new Governor, being somewhat strange to the situation, endeavored to put a stop to the illegal trafficking, and resolved to do more than indulge in ineffective protests, for a good many foreign ships continued to arrive on the Pacific Coast—the *Albatross* under Captain Winship, the *Il'men* under Captain John Eliot de Castro, the *Suvorov,* the *Chirikov,* the *Columbia* under Captain Jennings, etc., all bound on illegal trade or fur poaching or both.

In January, 1816, the *Albatross,* under Captain Winship, and the *Lydia,* under Captain Henri Gyzelaar, a Hollander, lay off the coast at El Refugio, both eager to do business with the de Ortegas, who were the go-betweens for the Mission Fathers in their export transactions. To the astonishment of everybody, the ships were suddenly seized, by order of the Governor. However, after a while they were released—very likely the Governor had a powerful public opinion against him—and in August of the next year he decidedly fell from grace himself, when the good ship *Colonel* came to this coast with a tempting cargo of merchandise to be exchanged principally for flour, hides, tallow and other Mission products. The need being pressing, he discarded the orders of the Viceroy and obtained supplies from the Missions, the Santa Cruz padres willingly doing their part, and receiving in exchange seven thousand dollars worth of much-needed goods.

The Governor then proved himself to be a true *caballero,* for instead of trimming, he wrote to the Viceroy, frankly acknowledging his guilty actions and giving his reasons.

In this case the produce of the Missions, especially their herds, once more saved Alta California from total want; in fact, from that time on the Missions "carried the Province."

Quite another type of ship dropped anchor in the San Francisco Bay on October 2nd, 1816. The *Rurik*[1] flew the Imperial Russian flag, and was

---

[1] Visit of the *Rurik* to San Francisco in 1816 by August C. Mahr, Stanford University Press.

under the command of Lieutenant Otto von Kotzebue, its aim being science and exploration. The ship was made officially welcome, many festivities were arranged, including the inevitable bear and bull fight. (See Appendix No. 3.)

The Spaniards, who on one hand desired to continue the illegal trade between the missionaries and presidios and the Russians, but on the other hand desired equally to get rid of Fort Ross, endeavored to use the good offices of Kotzebue to curb the activities of Kuskov, but nothing came of this effort. One of the scientists on board the *Rurik,* Dr. Adelbert von Chamisso, acted as interpreter at the conferences. He wrote subsequently of his visit, remarking: "Only a smuggling trade, which the new Governor tried to suppress, furnishes this province with the most indispensable articles."

After the departure of the *Rurik* both legal and illegal trade continued unabated. (See Appendix No. 4.)

In October, 1816, the supply ship *San Carlos* had arrived, but the stores were damaged. The following year two Lima ships arrived, the *Hermosa Mexicana* and *San Antonio,* both "legal" traders, and the *Cazadora,* from Panama, which was "illegal." The *Cazadora* had no trouble in obtaining a full cargo and sailing away.

In the meantime the Hollander, Henri Gyzelaar, reappeared on the scene, this time as commander of the American brig *Clarion,* dropping anchor at Santa Barbara on October 6th, 1818. It was he who brought the first warning of the approach of two ships, quite different from what the Californians were used to, for they flew the flag of an insurgent sister colony—Buenos Aires.

Buenos Aires had declared her independence in 1816, and in a time-honored manner endeavored to assist the other Spanish colonies who desired to follow her example in a struggle for independence, by issuing letters of marque to vessels, which were then recognized under the laws of nations as privateers, allowed to prey on the commerce of the enemy, without being classed as pirates.

History often repeats itself, for Prince William, the Silent, had encouraged the same tactics two hundred and fifty years previously, during the struggle of the Netherlands, also against Spain. His "privateers" became the terror of Spanish commerce and were known far and wide as "Sea Beggars."

The Buenos Aires privateers, often called "Baltimore ships," were outfitted in the United States, like the ships of the American Revolution, which the British called "Boston ships," and despite their "letters of marque" were looked upon by the Spanish authorities as pirates. They soon appeared in the Southern Pacific waters, preventing the supply ships from Lima from reaching Alta California, and created in that far-away province a serious situation.

After Commander Gyzelaar had informed the Commandant at Santa Barbara, Don Jose de la Guerra y Noriega, of the possible advent of privateering ships, the latter sent word to the Governor, and warnings were dispatched in every direction. Governor de Sola gave orders which went into the smallest details to the presidios and Missions, regulating the use of gun-powder, cartridges, provisions, couriers, guards, etc.

The Governor felt that the interior was the only safe place, out of reach of the privateers, or pirates, as he called them. He therefore ordered the missionaries in every jurisdiction near the coast to forward all articles of value, such as sacred vessels and church ornaments, to interior points. From the San Francisco district, under which Santa Cruz resorted, these articles had to be sent to the Pueblo San Jose. Likewise, stores of provisions for the four presidios had to be gathered at interior points. Women and children must be ready to retire at the first warning. All live stock, except horses fit for use, must be driven inland as far as possible, whenever pirates were descried. Pensioners, settlers and *rancheros* must repair to their respective presidios, and hold themselves in readiness to obey the commandant's orders. Two-thirds of all available gun-powder, except thirty or forty charges for each cannon, must be removed to the interior, and *spikes must be prepared for the guns in case of abandonment* (from which it will be seen that the enthusiastic Governor did not forget the rule that sometimes discretion is the better part of valor).

Immediately on sight of a vessel, a flying company must be sent out to reconnoitre all points, and to see that each man had five hundred cartridges. Sentinel parties of one soldier and two Indians must be stationed at convenient points, and two mounted couriers must be posted each twenty-five miles. Neophyte archers, previously organized, must be sent to the presidios. Mission guards must be replaced temporarily with invalids; settlers and retired soldiers must be made to understand in the Governor's name that the safety of their families and of the province depended largely on them. In case of actual hostility, prisoners might be liberated to fight for the country.

Governor de Sola, in the last instance, proved to be a trusting soul, but anyhow he provided that in case he fell on the field of honor, Don José de la Guerra was to be recognized as the Acting Governor. The latter did not want to be outdone by his chief, so he wrote in answer: "Under the protection of the God of battles, I believe I can destroy all such villains as may have the rashness to set foot upon this soil."[8] The first opera bouffe struggle, to be followed by many others, had begun.

The missionaries were notified of the impending danger, and entreated to obey the orders of the commandants.

As no pirates appeared, the excitement wore off, and the Governor, provoked that all his efforts were apparently in vain, wrote a rather insulting letter to Don José de la Guerra at Santa Barbara, chiding him for listening to unfounded rumors!

Padre Olbés, in charge of the Santa Cruz Mission, did not, however, relax his vigilance, for late in October he wrote that all was astir in the Mission and Villa, and added that he expected in case of invasion that the pirates would only harm the Spaniards and Friars, letting the Brancifortians get off free, adding: "They do not wish to fight, but to join the insurrectors."

On November 20th, two vessels were seen to make for the port of Monterey. The larger one, the *Argentina,* or *La Gentila,* was commanded by Captain Hippolyte Bouchard, a French sea rover, and the smaller one, the *Santa Rosa,* or *La Libertad,* was under Peter Corney, an Englishman, known as Lieutenant Pedro Conde. Corney kept an excellent ship's journal,[9] from which many details of the raid were afterwards ascertained. The first vessel carried forty-four guns and two hundred and sixty men, the second eighteen guns and one hundred men. Most of the officers were Americans, the crews consisting of Americans, Spanish-Americans, Spanish-Portuguese, Malays, Negroes, Filipinos, etc.

It would take the genius of Cervantes to describe the actions of the "Don Quixotes" and "Sancho Panzas" and others involved in the comic opera then enacted, and to bring back to life the bombastic talk of the different actors of this vaudeville war.

At eleven o'clock at night on November 20th, the smaller of the vessels, the *Santa Rosa,* generally known as *fragata chica,* came in port, and anchored near shore. The usual formal questions were shouted through the trumpet, and the answers came back in English that nobody understood! The commander was ordered to send a boat ashore to bring the ship's papers, which it was believed he promised to do next day; but instead of living up to this promise, the guns on board ship opened fire on the shore battery at dawn.

The Spanish guns, eight in number, not all of which were serviceable, returned the fire, and the Governor reported afterwards to the Viceroy

[8] Bancroft, History of California, Vol. II, p. 224.
[9] Early Northern Pacific Voyages—Peter Corney. Thos. G. Thrum, publisher, Honolulu (1896).

that "the two artillerymen with their *alferez* (ensign) kept up a constant and effective fire, doing much damage to the frigate, aided by the soldiers of the presidial company, *who bore themselves at the battery with an unspeakable serenity, despite the balls that were falling round them."*

At any rate, the *Santa Rosa* lowered her flag, and the commander was ordered sent ashore.

The reply was that the officer had gone to the other ship, and in fact had taken almost all the men with him, in six boats. Suspecting a ruse, the Governor ordered Corporal Jose de Jesus Vallejo, in charge of the shore battery, to continue firing, but this did not suit Manuel Gomez, who was in charge of the main defenses, for contrary to the Governor's orders, he ordered Vallejo to cease firing. Vallejo then became suspicious of Gomez's loyalty to Spain and was inclined to disregard his orders, whereupon Gomez informed his inferior that unless his orders were obeyed that the guns of the fort would be turned on the battery. When Vallejo remained obdurate, this order was actually given, but now in turn the gunners of Gomez refused absolutely to execute it, and he himself had no way to enforce it.

For some reason or other, Governor de Sola thereupon seems to have given the order to cease firing, and peace was restored to the Spanish military family.

The Governor finally demanded that if the captain were no longer on board, a responsible person should be produced, and Joseph Chapman, an American and second mate, was sent ashore. This "responsible person" was thereupon promptly cast into durance vile—the usually filthy Spanish jail.

There has been much speculation why the *fragata chica* exposed herself to the shore battery. The most plausible guess is that Bouchard was in possession of a diagram, furnished very likely by Manuel Gomez to his nephew, Luciano Gomez, an *insurrecto,* who was a lieutenant on Bouchard's ship, and that the diagram unfortunately had been drawn prior to the placing of the new battery by Governor de Sola.

However, the *Argentina*—the *fragata negra*—was now seen approaching under full sail, and Bouchard anchored just out of the range of the guns. A boat was lowered and sent ashore under a flag of truce, with a formal demand on the Governor that he surrender the whole province. Governor de Sola at once arose to the occasion and informed Bouchard that he looked with due scorn upon all that the communication contained; that the great Monarch whom he served had confided to him the province, to defend and keep under his rule; and added that if he (Bouchard) should use force as threatened, "I with mine shall make him know the honor and firmness with which I shall repel him, and while there is a man alive in the province he cannot succeed in his plan of taking possession, since all its inhabitants are faithful servants of the King, and will shed the last drop of blood in his service!"

Notwithstanding the Governor's lofty language, events did not bear out his brave intentions. In the morning nine boat-loads of men, with four small cannon, put off from the *negra* and headed for Point Potreros, while the ship itself, having placed the fort within range of its guns, opened fire. The gallant Governor, realizing that it was Bouchard's nefarious intention to place him and his noble defenders between two fires, sent *Alferez* Estrada, with a small force, to prevent if possible their landing, but the enemy moved forward with a band playing and carrying a red flag, whereupon the Spaniards spiked their guns, and the Governor retreated with all his men and what supplies they could carry towards the Rancho del Rey, near the Salinas River, apparently forgetting all about the "responsible person" still in jail.

It is hard to say whether it was the martial music of the band or the fierce waving of the red flag that put them to flight, but anyhow the Royal Presidio of Monterey was left to the tender mercies of the contemptible pirates.

Though the Spaniards were joined the next day, while camping on the Salinas, by reinforcements from San Francisco and San Jose, the *caballeros* did not deem it safe to attempt offensive measures.

Meanwhile the foe lost no time, but feasted on cattle which they had killed, looted the presidio and the fort, set fire to them, but did not harm the Mission at San Carlos, in fact they never visited it.

Corney, who gave a detailed account, stated that the dead were buried, the wounded cared for; vessels were repaired and the town was sacked. It was well stocked with provisions and goods of every description, which were sent on board the *Argentina*. The Sandwich Islanders (Hawaiians), who were quite naked when they arrived in Monterey, were soon dressed in the best Spanish fashion, and all the sailors were searching the houses for money, and breaking and ruining everything.

On the first of December, according to Corney, both the *Argentina* and the *Santa Rosa* moved down the coast, their only prisoner being a drunken settler, named Molina, who in a maudlin way had wandered into the middle of things.

The serious damage in the presidio was confined to the northern side and to three houses of the southern block, in all of which the roof beams were burned, allowing the tiles to fall. The wooden esplanade was likewise fired, and so was the artillerymen's house at the battery. Two cannon were left in a serviceable state. Bouchard seems to have had a sense of humor! The houses of the Governor and commandant were among those partially destroyed, and those officers lost about $5,000 worth of private property.

The scattered families gradually came back as the houses were repaired, and by April, 1819, Monterey resumed its old-time aspect.

Bouchard now sailed to Santa Barbara and anchored off El Refugio.

Before the actual landing, letters were exchanged between Bouchard and the *comandante,* in one of which Don Jose de la Guerra stated: "If your men are very anxious to fight, I can assure you that mine are desperate to meet them." Bouchard, who was a Frenchman, undoubtedly answered with another *gasconade,* and if the fate of California could have been decided by words and not by guns, there is small doubt but that the old proud flag of Castille would never have been lowered.

The privateers had heard about the wealth and possessions of the de Ortegas, who were agents between the padres and the smugglers in their illicit and highly necessary dealings, and were eager to collect their treasures. Unfortunately for them, they found all the buildings deserted, and the valuables removed, so after first liberally indulging in the brandy and wines they found in the cellars, they burned everything and proceeded on their way, not without losing three men as prisoners, for while they were searching for the treasures of the de Ortegas, Sergeant Carlos Antonio Carrillo, with thirty men, arrived on the scene, and from ambush had lassoed three of the bold, bad pirates, who very likely were still under the influence of "high spirits."

Bouchard seems to have had a tender heart, with which all French commanders are credited when it comes to the care of their men, so he sent a boat ashore with a flag of truce, asking for the exchange of prisoners, and promising to cease hostilities and leave the coast if this request was granted.

Don Jose replied that the prisoners were all alive, but that he had to submit the matter to Governor de Sola and would dispatch a courier to him. His men were few, but he marched the meager forces round and round a small hill, so as to impress the pirates with their limitlessness. One wonders what effect this manoeuvre had on the experienced and cynical naval commander.

Governor de Sola agreed to the exchange, and when de la Guerra made this known to Bouchard he learned for the first time that Bouchard had only one prisoner, and when the exchange was finally accomplished, the commandant was furthermore dumbfounded that that one, described as "a valuable prisoner of war," was the disreputable Molina from Monterey. Indignation, of course, had to be vented on someone, so immediately after his landing, the unfortunate Molina was given, by the reception committee of his own countrymen, one hundred lashes on his bare back and six years in the chain gang!

The climax of the whole matter was that Don Jose de la Guerra was severely blamed by the Governor for not doing certain things with his small force that the Governor with a much larger force had never been able to accomplish or dared to undertake.

After this the ships sailed south. They dropped anchor at San Juan Capistrano, where *Alferez* Santiago Arguello was awaiting them. The occupants of the Mission had already been sent inland, and Bouchard demanded "an immediate supply of provisions," with the promise that if they were forthcoming he would "spare their town." This was an excellent opportunity to indulge in more strutting and another flowery speech, so the message came back that they might land if they pleased and would be given "an immediate supply of powder and shot."

Corney was ordered ashore to "bring Bouchard a sample of the powder and shot," and one hundred and forty men, well armed and equipped with two fieldpieces, landed. Of course, they met with little resistance, and finding the town well stocked with everything but money, they pillaged, set fire to buildings and destroyed much wine and spirits. This destruction, however, was not confined to pouring the spirits out, but a good deal must have been poured into the throats of the invaders, because many got extremely drunk, and the next day Bouchard, who was something of a disciplinarian, had to punish twenty of his own men.

From there the vessels sailed further south, arriving in Valpariso on July 9th, 1819, where Peter Corney left the ship.

In Alta California the year 1818-19 was afterwards called *"el año de los insurgentes."*

It may well be asked why Bouchard went to all this trouble. Very likely he was ordered by his principals at Buenos Aires to assist any *insurrectos* he might find in the other colonies, and ascertaining that California was not sympathetic to his cause, but to the contrary desired to remain loyal to Spain, he resolved to strike a blow at Spain by attacking and damaging its distant loyal colony.

When the ships were at Monterey, the news was spread by couriers to Santa Cruz, and the plans so carefully made after Captain Gyzelaar's warning were put in operation at the Mission. The excitement of the invasion ran high, though there is no evidence that the pirates even intended to visit this Mission.

On November 21st, by advice of *Ex-prefecto* Sarria, Governor de Sola ordered Father Olbés to abandon Santa Cruz Mission and at once proceed with his neophytes to the Santa Clara Mission.

We must remember that Santa Cruz is only about twenty-five miles across the bay from Monterey, and that very likely the Fathers could see both the ships and the flash of their cannon, and also hear the thunder of the guns. This all naturally must have added to their anxiety.

Father Olbés loyally complied with the order, and departed with his flock. Governor de Sola was inclined a day or two later to have the Mission burned, to keep the grain and other property from falling into the foe's hands, but instead of this, he contented himself with sending word to *Comisionado* Joaquin Buelna of Branciforte, to go to the Mission, telling him that as soon as his orders had been carried out and the Mission was abandoned by the padres and neophytes, to remove all he could of the property. Buelna went with a party to execute the order on the 24th and set to work with gusto. Afterwards it was claimed that they were quickened in their movements by the approach of some of Bouchard's boats, which, however, could not land on account of the surf. There is no evidence that this was a fact, and it is safer to assume that the *villanos,* knowing that the missionaries entertained such a low opinion of them, received the Governor's order with rejoicing and availed themselves of the opportunity to take revenge on their enemies across the river. The excuse of the approach of Bouchard's boats looks doubly ridiculous if one reflects that the privateer commander had only two ships, that his boats were fully occupied, and that he held San Carlos Mission (a much richer and larger one) in the hollow of his hand, but never even took the trouble to visit it, though it was only a few miles away. Why then should he send sail or rowboats to a smaller and poorer Mission twenty-five miles distant? No wonder the Mission Fathers took little stock in a defense so obviously spurious.

Padre Olbés, who had left with his neophytes and a few soldiers of the guard for Santa Clara the previous day, sent Joaquin Castro, the *majordomo* and a number of Indians back to Santa Cruz to save some of the Mission goods. Castro was surprised to find Buelna at work, but when he heard of the Governor's order, he readily joined his force to that of the *comisionado*. One or two casks of wine and brandy could not be carried away, and after consultation it was considered best to spill the contents, not improbably into the throats of those present. The work proceeded with a will, but naturally the goods were not saved with the systematic care which would have been desired by the Friars. Doors were broken, curtains were torn, vestments were soiled, images were defaced, and in the confusion many articles were appropriated by the settlers as well as the Indians. Of the Mission effects a part was buried or otherwise concealed; others were listed in an inventory and taken to the Villa, while some were taken to Santa Clara by Castro and his Indians.

On the way, Castro was obliged to leave unwatched for a short time a trunk which was owned by the Father; it was broken open, and the two guilty *pobladores,* afterwards imprisoned at San Francisco, were detected by means of certain pairs of the padre's stockings, which one of them had given to a young lady at the pueblo of San Jose, who was famous for her dancing and her easy smiles.

No wonder the Father complained to the Governor in rather forcible language, and charged theft, wanton destruction and desecration of the church and holy images, and furthermore declared that the establishment must be abandoned, for he "would not go back to submit longer to the inhuman outrages of the people of Branciforte," but after some time, the good Father, calming his wrath, returned to his post, and the Mission continued to exist.

The next year the long-suffering padre complained to Arguello that all but three neophytes had fled, because they had been told at the Villa that the soldiers were coming to take them all prisoners, and that his troubles with his Villa neighbors were well-nigh unceasing.

CHAPTER XXIII

The Results of Spain's Half Century in Alta California.

BOOK IV

Chapter XXIII

The Results of Spain's Half Century in Alta California

IN 1770 Alta California ceased being only a name and had begun to emerge from its state of mystery; now for fifty years it had been under the active rule of the Spanish Government. Soon it was to change its allegiance and become part of the Mexican Republic.

Before considering what happened during the quarter century when it was sheltered under the Mexican flag, let us see what Spain had accomplished during the half century of endeavor; what stamp she had left on the original inhabitants of the province, and what results she obtained in the last thirty years of the cycle in the district of Santa Cruz.

Presidios at San Diego, Santa Barbara, Monterey and San Francisco had been established. At each, troops were stationed, directly under the authority of the military commandant, who dominated his district as a kind of deputy or vice-governor. The presidios consisted of a square, about one hundred yards on each side, surrounded by a ditch, generally twelve feet wide, enclosed by adobe or brick walls, from four to twelve feet high and three feet thick, and pierced by two gates, within which were the residence of the commandant, the presidio church, the houses of some colonists, warehouses, lodging for some of the troops, etc. The armament consisted of eight bronze cannon—eight, twelve and sixteen pounders. In addition, at or near each presidio, in accordance with the topography of the surrounding lands, was a so-called castillo, or fort, which in reality was an open battery, generally dominating the water-approach. These fortifications were about the same as those erected by Spain throughout its colonies.

The presidios and the *castillos* in this province were rather modest military establishments. They may have been proof against the Indian attacks, but of little account against an attack of foreign warships.

Forbes (see Appendix No. 1) tells us that the few troops were almost invariably, except for the officers, of inferior quality. The best were those recruited on the Indian border of Sonora, a kind of militia, who had accompanied de Anza and other commanders, and who were called *companias de cueras,* from their wearing a *cuirass* of leather or hides. The better kind of *cueras,* which made both men and horses invulnerable to the arrows of the Indians (many of which were poisoned) was made of seven-ply leather taken from the hides of the antelope, known as *cureo de gamuza*

This armor was only worn in the field, and in battle a double-visored helmet and leather buckler were added. All troops were mounted, and the horses likewise covered with leather armor. The artillery was furnished by the Marine establishment.

Two hundred and fifty soldiers were supposed to be stationed at each presidio, but this number was hardly ever maintained. Except in the very beginning, the men were badly clothed, badly paid, undisciplined, often looked like ragamuffins, and were of little value, except for retaking the neophyte Indians who had escaped from the Missions. Later the soldiers sent to California were the refuse of the Mexican army, often deserters, mutineers or men guilty of other crimes.

If there is any doubt as to the worthlessness of the so-called forts, from a genuine military standpoint, one has only to consider the invasion of Bouchard, described in a previous chapter, where a handful of privateers—mostly free lances gathered from all over the world—were able to impose unchecked their will all along the coast.

Spain had also been unfortunate with her civil foundations.

Only three civil establishments, separate from the Missions and the presidios, had been founded during these fifty years; the pueblos at Los Angeles and San Jose and the Villa de Branciforte.

The Spanish Government labored under peculiar difficulties, for notwithstanding the great colonial empire that it had created, the nation as such was not then, nor is it today, a colonizing nation in the sense of an immigrating people. The best element, especially in the middle classes, had no desire to leave their peninsula. Representatives of the upper classes went as civil or military officers, or in some other official or semi-official capacity; the lower classes, often the extremely poor classes, produced the soldiery and necessary subordinates and menials; only once in a while did some truly volunteer-privates, from Catalonia especially, enter the service. The solid middle class stayed at home.

The principal pueblo was the Pueblo de Nuestra Senora de Los Angeles (see Appendix No. 2), situate about eight miles from the Mission of San Gabriel, and about twenty miles from San Pedro, the roadstead on the Pacific. The pueblo had been at various times described as a cesspool of iniquity, a pesthole, a very fragment of Hades, or a paradise on earth—the land of *dolce far niente* for the whites—all in accordance with the moral viewpoints of the observers.

For a long time it was considered by many to be the logical place for the capital of the State, for Spain invariably preferred to locate the centra of its power in inland cities, free from the attacks of invading ships. Later, under Mexican rule, this was the case for some time.

In northern California, the Pueblo de San Jose de Galvez, situated about three miles from the Mission of Santa Clara, lay in a fertile country, and according to the chroniclers, its civic and moral qualifications were somewhat, though not much, higher than those of Los Angeles. (See Appendix No. 3.)

The Villa de Branciforte has already been fully described.

How had the Spanish Government discharged such other civic duties as are usually attended to by civilized nations? What had it done to develop commerce, navigation, harbors, mining, roads, education, etc., in Alta California?

The answer is little, compared with its splendid efforts in other colonies more centrally located.

Domestic trade was insignificant: the three civil settlements were small and unimportant, and each Mission, except for foreign goods, was practically self-sufficient.

Foreign commerce was prohibited. Trade among the different Spanish colonies was discouraged, hampered by exorbitant taxes, known as *alcalaba,* and endless obstructive regulations. Occasional trade with foreign ships was almost exclusively a smugglers' business, abetted by the inhabitants, especially the padres, who were often at their wits' end for goods which could not be manufactured domestically. Only after the revolution of 1821 were North American and foreign traders welcomed by the Mexican authorities.

Exclusive of small launches, there were throughout the full extent of the Spanish Americas but thirty vessels engaged in legitimate trade. Of harbor improvements there were consequently but few in this far-off province.

Notwithstanding that Alta California had an abundance of precious metals, and Spain needed them, mining was practically unknown. Manufacturing, such as spinning, weaving, melting tallow, shoemaking, blacksmithing, combing of wool, curing hides for leather, saddle making, metal works, etc., was confined almost entirely to the Mission establishments.

Of road-building there had been little. The Camino Real was in fact only a well-traveled path for horse and ox-cart travel (see Appendix No. 4); there were no permanent bridges or culverts. Even the streets of the older settlements, such as Monterey and Santa Barbara, were in the winter time little more than so many mud-holes.

Secular schools were unknown.

For agriculture Spain had done a good deal. Through the missionary efforts magnificent agricultural estates had been carved out of the wilderness, and cultivation went hand in hand with its allied industry—animal husbandry.

The grains cultivated were maize or Indian corn, wheat, barley and beans *(frijoles)*.

Of course, old-fashioned methods were used; the plows, drawn by two oxen, had only one handle, and no mold-board to turn over the furrow. Consequently the soil could only be broken by several successive crossings and recrossings. The harrow was unknown—a brush or a heavy long piece of wood being used for covering barley or wheat; maize was covered by hand.

Harvesting was also done by hand. In Southern California irrigation was used for raising grain, but in Northern California, for instance Santa Cruz, this was unnecessary. (See Appendix No. 5.)

The mills for grinding flour were of primitive construction, even for those times.

Potatoes were raised to some extent and a few vegetables; cabbage, greens, etc., not being popular. The vine throve in California to an extraordinary degree, and good wine and brandy were manufactured, while olive oil was pressed and preserved with care. Other fruits like figs, pomegranates, oranges, apples and pears were cultivated.

As to animal husbandry, this was almost entirely confined to the raising of horses, exclusively for horseback riding (being seldom used before vehicles or in farm work), and other domestic animals, used for their wool, meat, fat and hides. Dairying was not practiced; milk, cream, butter and cheese were, if not entirely lacking, always of very poor quality, and ships preferred to go to Fort Ross to obtain these supplies from the Russians.

It is curious to note that this is a custom still prevailing on many cattle ranches in the Southwest, where it is difficult to obtain a glass of milk, though thousands of cattle are kept. (See Appendix No. 6.)

A peculiar custom which attracted the attention of all foreign observers was the postponement of the operation of castration of male calves until the animals were three or four years old, with the result that in each herd there were too many bulls, and a continual roaring, goading and fighting. A great part of the beef consumed was of bulls, which of course had a strong and unpleasant flavor, but which seemed to be liked by some of the Spanish people. The cattle being seldom penned up (or "folded," as our British cousins say), were naturally wild and hard for the vaqueros to handle with the lasso in the approved cowboy fashion.

The men—the Indians used as herdsmen, the mestizos and the whites then in the province—were excellent horsemen; the saddles were well fitted to the exercise; the horses were thoroughly trained and were masterfully managed.

Mutton was little used, the sheep being kept especially for their wool; while swine—of a Chinese breed—were very popular, chiefly for their lard, of which much was used in Mexican cooking, especially *frijoles*.

In the 1810-1830 decades a fat ox brought on the average an equivalent of $5.00, a cow the same, a saddle horse $10.00, a breeding mare $5.00, a sheep $2.00, and a mule $10.00, the value of a hog being measured by the estimated amount of lard.

In addition to the missionary agricultural operations, the Government had endeavored in various ways to stimulate the rather lazy "white" population of the pueblos to exert themselves along useful lines, by distributing to each *poblador* pieces of land fit for cultivation *(solares y suertas de tierras)*.[1] The results, however, were rather negligible.

Actual beneficial immigration to develop the country was lacking. Pueblos were established, but the character of the *pobladores* was generally less than doubtful. These pueblos could not alienate any of their lands, and the rest along the explored coast was occupied, or at least claimed, by the Missions.

The whole of these lands were under the temporal and spiritual dominion of the missionaries. No one could possess land except by a grant approved by the missionaries, who were much averse to make any grants. The Governor could not interfere, even if he so desired, with the internal business affairs of the Missions; besides the Religious claimed, and very properly so, that the location of the white men near any of the Missions would be detrimental to the good conduct and welfare of the neophytes.

Consequently, under Spanish rule, real, vital immigration was impossible, and only after the revolution, and especially after the Congress of the United Mexican States had passed a decree on August 18th, 1824, inviting colonization, was the country properly opened up.[2]

And how had all this affected the natives of Alta California?

Whatever the position of the missionaries was, as instruments of State in the subjection and colonization of California, their own principal aim was the conversion of the Indians to Christianity, and their training, if possible, in some sort of civilized life.

The Catholic Church was particularly well fitted for this enterprise; far better than any of the Protestant denominations. In the Philippine Islands, the Catholic Church made a definite and lasting impression on the

[1] Regulations of de Neve, Section 2d, Cal. Archives, Vol. I, Missions and Colonization.
[2] Halleck's Report, Ex. Doc. No. 17, House of Rep., 1824, pp. 134-139.

Filipinos; the Protestant missionaries in the Netherlands East Indies and in British India have seldom entered, to any extent, in the consciousness of the natives. To most savages, the Catholic service is fascinating. The ceremony of the Mass, accompanied by music,[3] and the display of beautiful objects appeals to them. Its doctrines are positive; when once accepted in good faith, they bring contentment; while Protestantism is often austere, if not gloomy, inviting reflection and introspection; demanding reasoning, which the natives cannot understand or follow; often enforcing prohibitions which to the free children of nature seem undesirable. The chief diversion among savages everywhere has been music and dancing. The Catholic missionaries were indulgent to these pleasures; by some of the Protestant denominations, dancing, at least, was frowned upon.

Fortunately, most California natives were malleable in the hands of the few white invaders. What the story would have been if California had been populated by war-like tribes, such as the Delawares, Sioux, Apaches or the Yumas, is another question. With the weak forces at hand, many Christian martyrs would have met an untimely end, the system would have been overwhelmed, and the whites driven into the Pacific.

Various descriptions of the "Digger Indians" have come to us.

To those accustomed to the proud, war-like Indians of the plains and mountains to the East, all with a considerable civilization of their own, these California Coast Indians looked a primitive and wild lot. They are generally described by the travelers as short, squat-muscled, with small black eyes, coarse, straight hair, and flat, expressionless, stupid faces. Most of them were totally naked, except for scraps of fur or rushes; several were tattooed.

It is dangerous to generalize too much about them, for there were several varieties. Dr. John Marsh found the Bolgones on the arroyo when he bought a rancho in the San Joaquin Valley near Mount Diablo in 1837. They had been there from times immemorial. They were as hairy as Esau, with beards that would do honor to a Turk, and their eyes had a Chinese formation, showing that at some distant time there had been a shipwrecked Mongolian marines.[4] They were a degraded type of Red Men, and made him homesick for the Sioux. There were thirty in the tribe—wild and savage—and they bore an evil reputation.[5]

[3] The church services were made as attractive as possible; the music consisted by no means of sacred hymns only, but lively waltzes and other dancing tunes were executed by the musicians and choirs.

[4] Smith and Elliott, History of Contra Costa County, p. 7.

[5] John Marsh, Pioneer, by Dr. Geo. D. Lyman, p. 220.

Even the visitors at the Missions are not in entire accord. Dr. Rollin, the surgeon of de la Perouse, gives their average height at five feet two or three inches; Dr. von Langsdorff, of the de Rezanov expedition, observes that none of the men seemed over five feet high, while Captain Beechey[6] says: "The stature of the Indians we saw in the Mission was by no means diminutive."

Almost all foreign observers who came to Alta California during the Spanish regime, like de la Perouse, Langsdorff, Vancouver, etc., were confined in their descriptions of California Indians either to the Mission varieties (for the Spanish Government discouraged visits inland), or otherwise to those seen in special parties; while the travelers who came during the Mexican period, like Beechey (see Appendix No. 7) had more opportunity to meet the real "wild Indians," though by that time many had become sophisticated by proximity to the white men; they had not, however, lost their native cunning, for the first three tell us of watching Indian deer hunters, de la Perouse describing the stalking of deer, and Beechey stating that they could even imitate the voice of the deer, thereby enticing the animals within reach of their arrows.

As all their reports are so similar, it seems obvious that these foreign observers were "personally conducted" by the padres or by the secular authorities, and saw exactly what they were wanted to see.

Those whose investigations were unhampered, like Fremont (see Appendix No. 8) seemed to be no more enthusiastic than Father Venegas, Father Palou or Father Garces and other early Spanish chroniclers.

On his second expedition (1844), when he returned via the Sierra, entering them near where the San Joaquin River emerges into the plains, Fremont wrote that he met many Indians who were dark-skinned, but handsome and intelligent, living principally on acorns and roots of the tule, and of course on the flesh of stolen horses, for the Indians of the Sierra made frequent descents upon the settlements west of the Coast Range, which they kept constantly swept of horses.[7] He informs us that the Indians living in the mountains only came to the plains to rob and murder, and made no other use of horses than to eat them.[8]

Horse stealing was by no means confined to the mountain Indians, for in the low foothills near the Merced River, Fremont and his party saw horse bones dragged about by wild animals—wolves and bears—and trails

---

[6] Capt. Frederick William Beechey visited California in 1826, and subsequently wrote his "Narrative of a Voyage to the Pacific," published in two volumes in London in 1831.

[7] Memoirs of My Life by Fremont, pp. 359-360.

[8] Idem., p. 373.

freshly traveled by large bands of horses coming from the valley, which convinced them that they were in a horse-thieving country.

Father Senan, who was succeeded in 1815 by Fra. Matiano Payeras, stated in his biennial report for 1817-1818:

"The Tulare Indians are inconstant. Today they come, tomorrow they are gone, not on foot as they came, but on horseback. With such guests, no horse is safe in the northern valley. And the worst of it is, that having crossed the Tulare Valley and the mountains that surround it, they kill the horses and eat them. The Government has not been neglectful in pursuing such deadly enemies, but little has been effected, because great lagoons surrounded by green tules furnish them shelter from our horsemen."[9]

Evidently the Gentile Indians had learned to ride horseback, and like their red brethren across the Rockies, were good equestrians. So many horses were stolen from the Missions that the Father President in July, 1819, wrote to his padres:

"The Governor of this province, Don Pablo Vicente de Sola, advises me that he has been informed from the south of the scandalous abuse at certain Missions (San Fernando and San Gabriel) of neophyte equestrianism. Neophytes take with brazenness, and in broad daylight, horses even though tied. They load them with women in the public roads. I am reminded by the Governor of the many royal *cédulas* forbidding Indians to ride, and that even your reverence cannot give them permission to own or use a horse, if Law 33 of Book VI, Title I, of the *Recopilación* is observed. . . . In the Tulares (I am told by the Governor) both Christians and Gentiles make their journeys on horseback. Even the women are learning to ride. Fairs are held at which horses stolen from the Missions are put up for sale."[10]

Surprise is often expressed that the California Indians could exist for weeks on a diet of acorns only, much as the Indians in Mexico and adjoining territories existed on maize or Indian corn. Oaks were to these Indians what the breadfruit trees are to the Polynesians. They were in fact the principal staff of life of all the northern wild Indians, many tribes storing these nutritious nuts in cribs or bins of wicker work. Large trees belonging to the family of white oaks produce large acorns, called by Dr. Torrey, of the Second Fremont Expedition, *Quercus longiglanda*. They somewhat resemble Indian chestnuts in taste, and many a white traveler found them palatable and made a meal of them.

[9] B. C. Arch. Sta. Barb., Vol. XII, p. 101.
[10] B. C. Arch. Sta. Barb., Vol. VI, p. 102.

Were the wild children of the coast, the plains, the mountains or the forests really benefited by the fifty-year rule the Spanish had imposed on them? We may just as well ask, were any wild aborigines ever benefited by the advent of white men?

In all cases they are foreordained to destruction. Such has been the case with the wild aborigines of Australia, South America, India, etc. Either they are killed outright, or they are eventually lost in the race of their conquerors.

The California Indian was no exception to the rule. What his fate would have been eventually under continued Spanish rule is difficult to say. Very likely he would have continued in servitude for a long time, and then slowly have been absorbed in the ever-growing wave of immigration. What happened under Mexican rule is only a continuation of the processes inaugurated by their Spanish kinsmen; what happened under American rule was tragic.

It must have been apparent before 1820 that the Indians were well-nigh hopeless material from which to make civilized Christians. The devoted Franciscan Fathers had by then been at their task for sixty years, and as far as mental and moral progress of the neophytes was concerned, history gives us, with few exceptions, little evidence.

One marvels at the undaunted courage and hope with which the Mission Fathers stayed with their labor.

Whatever the general submissive state of the aborigines of California might have been during the first twenty-five years, after the advent of the Fathers—with their greater physical stature and church pomp, with their high learning and energy, backed by the military authorities—the Indians had ceased to believe that they had been visited by supermen descended from Heaven. To those not born under the shadow of a Mission, the Fathers had become task masters and persons to be avoided, lest liberty be lost.

Many of the military commanders, like de Arrillaga, de Sola, etc., had staunchly defended the Religious against charges of cruelty and misuse of power, while other officials, like de Neve, Fages, Goycoechea, etc. (see Appendix No. 9), had disagreed with the Fathers as to the treatment of the Indians.

Even some of the missionaries, for instance Fathers Fernandez and Concepcion, found fault with the system, and, although their complaints were in a few instances directed by erratic minds, still this sort of criticism from within was beneficial—but a far more serious condition arose when the Indians began to show increasing disrespect and unrest, and a desire to flee from the Missions, while those who remained displayed marked dissatisfaction.

In 1801, at the Mission San Miguel, Padres Baltasar Carnicier, Andriano Martinez and Francisco Pujol were seized with a terrible illness, the latter dying.[11] An epidemic spread, the cause of which was unknown.

In the same year, at the Santa Barbara Mission, a woman wizard *(shaman)* declared that Chupu had appeared, assuring her that the Gentiles and Christians would perish of the epidemic, if they did not offer Chupu alms, and did not bathe their heads with a certain water. The news of her revelation flew throughout the huts of the Mission at midnight, and nearly all of the neophytes, including the *alcalde,* went to the woman's house to offer beads and seeds, and to witness renunciations by the Christians. Though the tale was spread to the Channel *rancherias* and far into the coast mountains, the missionaries remained ignorant of it, for Chupu had said that whoever should tell the padres would die immediately. But after three days a neophyte woman, casting aside fear, related the whole story.

No doubt if the frenzied *shaman* had added to her tale the injunction that in order to make the epidemic cease, it would be necessary to kill the padres, the two soldiers of the guard, the alcaldes and others, as much credit would have been given to this as to the first part of her account.[12]

In 1805 President Tapis wrote to Governor de Arrillaga that forty neophytes from San Gabriel had fled toward the Colorado; from Santa Barbara, two hundred; that at all the Missions there were mal-content neophytes ready to fight, and he counseled that the evils could only be corrected and prevented by an increase of troops and repeated expeditions.[13]

The advice seems to have been followed, for in 1806, Ensign Gabriel Moraga and other commanders ranged the Tulare region, across the Coast Range from Tejon Pass almost to San Francisco, in search of fugitive neophytes. In 1810, Moraga, who had quite a reputation as an Indian fighter, fought a pitched battle with Indians on the east side of San Francisco Bay, and succeeded in killing more than one hundred of the enemy and capturing twenty women and children.

At San Diego a neophyte cook endeavored to poison Father Jose Pedro Panto. Nazorio, the accused, did not deny the act, but declared that on December 15th he had received a great many lashings, all for minor offenses. The prosecutor himself, in summing up, stated that in two days

---

[11] B. C., Prov. St. Pap., Vol. XVIII, pp. 200, 202.
[12] California Under Spain and Mexico, Richman, p. 464, B. C. Arch. Sta. Barb., Vol. VI, p. 32.
[13] B. C. Arch. Sta. Barb., Vol. XII, p. 75.

the Indian had received more than two hundred lashes, and this without serious cause. His sentence was therefore only eight months' detention at the San Diego Presidio.[14] Father Panto was fortunately an exception, for the Mission rule was generally benign and kindly.

As we saw in a previous chapter, the murder of Padre Andreas Quintana by Indians occurred at Santa Cruz in 1812.

One of the difficulties was the numerous changes which took place in some of the Missions among the padres. Where the same ecclesiastic remained and was beloved, no trouble occurred. At the Mission San Luis Rey, Father Antonio Peyri had charge from 1799 to 1832. Everything went smoothly. He began by building a small cabin, asked for a few cattle and neophytes, and after thirty-four years the population amounted to 3,000 Indians, the domestic animals numbered 55,000, and there were raised annually 13,000 bushels of produce. When he finally left, the cries and lamentations of his parishioners followed him.

Father President Senan had little use for these Indians in their free state, for he wrote that the *rancherias* east of the Tulare lake, where about 4,000 were collected, were "a republic of hell and a diabolical union of apostates." Rather strong language for a churchman, but then some of the missionaries were discouraged, if not disgusted. It is no wonder that the College of San Fernando formally petitioned Viceroy Apodaca to cede part of the Missions to another college. The desired permission was obtained, but before it could be acted upon, Payeras, who had become Prefect in 1819, opposed the cession with success.

One of the real causes for this unrest was the frightful mortality amongst the neophytes.

It is natural that the majority of later writers seek a cause in the defects of the management of the Fathers, but on second reflection this accusation does not seem logical.

California is a country as large as France. At the present time it has a population close to six million prosperous people, and qualified economists assure us that it could easily support forty million in comfort.

In accordance with the best estimates, there were only 40,000 Indians scattered throughout this large territory when, in 1770, the Franciscan Fathers appeared on the scene. Prior to this no Spaniards or other intruders had disturbed the sylvan peace of the native race on this coast. Taking in consideration the mild climatic conditions, the fecundity of the soil, the ocean teeming with fish, and other favorable elements, it would have been natural if a large Indian population had been found, like the

[14] B. C. Prov. St. Pap. Benecia, Vol. XLIX, p. 4.

Aztecs in Mexico or the Incas in Peru, especially as they were protected from the war-like tribes to the east and north by the high range of mountains, the desert to the south, and with but a few exceptions there were no wild aimals preying on human beings, or poisonous reptiles indigenous to the country. Yet all that was found was a scattered population, living in wretchedness, far beyond that which was found among other Indian tribes on the North American Continent.

As great a mortality must have existed among these native races prior to the advent of the Fathers as afterwards, notwithstanding the statement of foreign travelers that in spite of their filth they were a very healthy people.

Wise Mother Nature established the usual balance, for while California holds out golden fruits to those who are industrious, and is a loving mother to her energetic children, it likewise offers very little subsistence to those who are too lazy to work the soil or uncover the natural resources.

These Indians did not want to work to better their condition. They were happy in their benighted state; they did not care to build houses of the timber and rocks of the country that would shelter them against the winter rains or the occasional blasts of the storms. Their vermin-infested hovels were dear to them, and under such conditions the many offspring, naturally the result of their promiscuous living and the fecundity of their women, were doomed to an early death.

Mother Nature, therefore, through pestilence and other means, must have kept the number of Indians down, holding a balance between the available subsistence and population.

Obviously, Nature works in circles to accomplish its ends; it struggles for a long time against the efforts of men to disturb its balance. When the Indian population increased, the food supply did not, for this could only have been accomplished by mankind's determined effort. There was, therefore, less food for each individual; they consequently weakened and their resistance power was lowered; disease took hold, and the population was reduced to numbers for which the food supply was sufficient.

One may wonder if the Mission Fathers did not enormously increase the food supply, and if so, why the population did not increase?

The Fathers certainly did increase the supply, but there was simultaneously introduced through the soldiers and worthless settlers those curses which always seem to accompany the introduction of Christianity—that is, strong drink and loathsome blood diseases—which caused a death rate of fifty per cent of the baptisms in 1800, seventy-two per cent in 1810, and eighty-six per cent in 1830.

No matter how much the Fathers tried to prevent it, syphilis was brought by these men to the Indian women, whom they often took by force, though many of course were willing enough, their own habits being promiscuous. Other diseases followed in the wake of the red scourge brought by the white man, which annulled all the efforts of the ecclesiastics to ameliorate the health of their wards.

Diseases caused by fungus, insects, microbes, germs, etc., are far more virulent in a new field than in an old one. Nature has not had time to establish a balance by building up resistance power, or even to make many of the species immune through natural inoculation; neither have they natural enemies, parasites having not as yet been developed. Any government which understands its modern duties, therefore, takes various strenuous quarantine measures at its borders, against the introduction of new diseases of men, beasts or plants.

The natives of California, naturally filthy, furnished excellent new breeding grounds for the white men's plagues; and the white men's disease germs destroyed far more of them than the white men's bullets, and certainly far more than the missionaries could save.

The Fathers could not change such conditions, partly because the disease germs were carried by their fellow conquerors, and partly for mental reasons.

Anyone who has traveled in the Far East will subscribe to the saying of Europeans of long experience—"once a native always a native." Servants in Java who have been taken from their native villages *(kampongs)*, and trained for years by the Hollanders in sanitation and hygienic methods, and who appear to have reconciled themselves to all the new conditions, with few exceptions, revert to their former condition of blissful filth, as soon as they have left the European settlement and have returned to the place from whence they came.

Cholera may sweep a Far-East possession; the natives may die by the thousands, but very few if any white people, or natives living with them, will be stricken by the disease. Despite all warnings, their servants will violate orders, go for visits to their native villages, and die in consequence.

The Fathers were fully alert to the dangers of the pestilences which threatened their own existence. With heroic and sublime confidence and self-sacrifice they visited the sick and eased the death of their neophytes. In fact, Father Quintana, of Santa Cruz, was an example of this unselfish work. Yet he was murdered.

If the Fathers were at fault at all, their mistake was of the head and not of the heart. Their zeal seems to have blinded them to the fact that it takes a long, long time to change the mental processes of a race, either by gentle or strenuous efforts, and that different races have different mentalities and unalterable points of view.

Notwithstanding endless disappointments, the Fathers carried on, sustained in their conviction that the perishing of the bodies of the heathen was of less consequence than the saving of their souls from condemnation to everlasting torture in the hereafter.

Paradoxically with the great death rate, the longevity of some of the Indians was astounding.

Dana, in his "Two Years Before the Mast," spoke of one old man at the Mission of San Diego, whom he supposed to be the oldest man he had ever seen, and he wondered that a person could exhibit such marks of age and still retain life:

"This superannuated specimen was sitting in the sun, leaning against the side of a hut; his legs and arms were not larger round than those of a boy of five years; his skin was withered and shriveled like burnt leather; and he was so feeble that, when his visitors approached, he slowly raised his hands to his face, and, taking hold of his eyelids with his fingers, lifted them up to look at the strangers, and then, being apparently satisfied, let them drop again. Inquiries as to his age evoked no answer from the other Indians except, *Quien sabe*—who knows? Nearly every Mission contained one or more of these old patriarchs who had outlived their families; and it was no uncommon thing for a rancheria to have ancient members, who had to be wrapped in thick furs to preserve their animal warmth, and to be nursed and fed like infants to keep up nutrition."

CHAPTER XXIV

Testimony of an Indian Eye Witness
and Others

BOOK IV

Chapter XXIV

Testimony of an Indian Eye-Witness and Others

THE Fathers at Santa Cruz had, of course, no better success with their Indian wards than their brethren elsewhere. Everywhere they had an almost impossible task allotted to them. They were expected to accomplish within a few score years that which was bound to take centuries.

There were no records of any kind when Governor Portola and Father Serra entered Upper California. Generally a successful invader could steer his course by the light furnished from the records of the development of the native race.

When Cortes invaded Mexico in the year 1519, he found, besides the evidences of the Aztec civilization, the remains of an equally interesting Maya period; and when Pizarro marched into Peru the well-organized system of government of the Incas was found, with an irrigation system, public treasury buildings, houses, temples, etc. But in California there was absolutely nothing of the kind.

Hittell tells us: "There were no government, laws or customs aggregating these Indians of the Californias into political organizations; there were no nations or even large tribes as on the Atlantic Coast; there were nowhere kings or chiefs exercising any authority beyond their immediate neighborhood."[1]

They had no writing, letters, hieroglyphics, pictures, or characters of any description from which information could be obtained, and their superstitions were as vague as they were varied. Some small tribes had sorcerers, who exercised great power. Those Indians who lived in a rancheria had a counsel called the *puplem,* and their chief God was represented by an object of reverence or fetish, consisting of the skin of a wild animal, stuffed with feathers, talons, horns, etc., and presented with the hide inside. This was kept in a rude building constructed of bark, boughs, twigs, etc., and called a *vanquech,* which was also a sanctuary for criminals.

True, Father Gerónimo Boscana, who was a missionary of San Juan Capistrano, and who died there a very old man in 1831, left a manuscript in which he endeavored to explain what he called the religious observances of the Indians, and that of their God, *Chinigchinic.* This manuscript was

---

[1] In the Santa Cruz vicinity, at the establishment of Branciforte, even such local chiefs were lacking, though one chief was mentioned when the Mission was founded.

279

published in English by Alfred Robinson in New York, in 1846. The good Fathers, however, were men who endeavored to find in the notions of every wild tribe of Indians a resemblance of the faith they brought and adored, and it seems that in most cases the wish dominated the thought.

Unfortunately, no specific records have been kept covering the habits, beliefs and actions of the original settlers around the Mission of Santa Cruz.

Father J. Adam, the Pastor of the Catholic Church, wrote in 1870 to Messrs. Wallace W. Elliott & Company, publishers of the "Illustrated History of Santa Cruz" (a curious volume dedicated to the dead past and made possible for publication by appealing to the vanity of the living by copiously producing pictures and laudatory biographies), as follows:

"I regret that amongst the old papers I cannot find any account of the condition of the Indians of this place at the arrival of the first missionaries, nor anything concerning their language; but from historical facts in general on the Indians of California, *we may guess more or less the condition of the ones under our charge."*

Prior to this he wrote:

"Please find enclosed here the record of the burial of the old Indian, as it is kept in the Second Book of Death of this Parish, No. 2,699: On the 12th of March, 1875, I gave (ecclesiastical) Christian burial to the remains of Justiniano Roxas, an Indian of this Mission, who reached to the advanced and wonderful age of 123 years, having been baptised in this Mission in the year 1792, and being then a man of about forty years of age, as appears from part No. 609 of the first Book of Baptism, of this Parish. He received the sacrament, and was buried near the cross in the new cemetery. He died on the 10th of March, 1875.

Yours truly,

J. Adam, Pastor."

In Santa Cruz, in 1890, there was found an eye-witness of the conditions existing at the Mission during the last years prior to the secularization. His name was Lorenzo Venancio, and he was interviewed by Mr. E. L. Williams.

This old Indian was baptized in the Mission of Santa Cruz in 1819, was educated by the priests and sang in the choir. Mr. Williams declared that he possessed extraordinary intelligence for an Indian, could read and write the Spanish language, and was comparatively well educated.[2]

The conditions which this neophyte described were about the same as those described by travelers of a somewhat earlier period.

---

[2] Harrison, History of Santa Cruz County, 1890, p. 45.

Mr. Williams translated the interview as follows:

"I was born at the Mission of Santa Cruz, on Monday, the tenth day of August, 1819, and given the name of Lorenzo by Padre Ramon Olbez. Three days afterward I was baptized at the baptismal font. My father's name was Venancio. My mother's name was Maria; my brother's name was Jacinto. I was with the reverend Fathers of the Mission of Santa Cruz until I was grown up, and then I went to Monterey, and was employed by General Figueroa, and was taught to play the clarinet by Sergeant Rafael Estrada. There were other military officers there named Eugenio Montenegro, captain of infantry; Augustin Zamarano, captain of cavalry, and Lieutenant-Colonel Nicolas Guiterrez. The barracks and officers' quarters were where now is the church at Monterey. Afterwards I lived at the Mission of Carmelo for one year, during the time of Padre Rafael Moreno, who was a missionary. I conversed at that time with Indians of that Mission about the death of Padre Junipero Serra. They told me that they were at his funeral, and for three nights the corpse was watched, and afterwards he was interred, as some of them thought, at San Antonio Mission. Others insist the corpse was embalmed and sent to New Spain (Mexico). When Figueroa died, his corpse was embalmed and taken to Mexico.

"Afterwards I came to the Mission of Santa Cruz, and was instructed how to read and write in Spanish by Padre Antonio Real. I was the sacristan, and sang and played in the choir. There were about twenty of us that composed the choir, of which I am the only one living.

"The land cultivated in those days was all of the tract between the hill at the end of Pacific Avenue and the hill where the public school now is.[3] There were eight hundred and thirty-six who received rations as I read from the roll. The list was kept by Padre Jose Jimeno, and one day, he being out, I counted the names. They all slept in houses where now is the Sisters' School.[4] All the space about there was covered with dormitories. Some of them were engaged in weaving blankets, others were carpenters, others blacksmiths, tanners, and many worked in the field, cultivating and harvesting. The women prepared the wool for the weavers, did much of the sewing of clothes, and also at times worked in the field. The tanyard was near to the adobe house owned by Mrs. Boston, formerly belonging to Rafael Castro, who was the grantee under the Mexican Government of the Rancho Aptos, now owned by Mr. C. Spreckles.

---

[3] This land is now partly occupied by the local gas works of the Coast Counties Gas & Electric Co.

[4] This is the school and orphanage which is at the present time conducted by the Sisters of Charity.

"The names of the Fathers whom I remember were, first, Francisco Moreno, following him, Luis Altaguada, Juan Moreno, Antonio Jimeno, Jose Jimero, and lastly, Antonio Real. These were missionaries belonging to the Santa Cruz Mission. There was a tribe of Indians living up the coast called Jaraum. The Indian children were brought to the Mission, and afterwards came the grown ones. They were all Christianized by being baptized. Another tribe called Esuans also lived up the coast, and another tribe living farther up the coast was called Joali; another tribe living at Soquel, had for their captain Balthazar, a name given by the Fathers. These different tribes fought with each other with bows and arrows. Those of Soquel had for their boundary what is now known as Arana Gulch. Soquel is an Indian proper name, so also is Zayante, and are not translatable. The names of the Indian tribes were given them from the lands they occupied. Santa Cruz was called Aulinta in the Indian tongue. I will give you in their language some words: One, *hinumen;* two, *uthiu;* three, *caphau;* four, *catwaz;* five, *nissor;* six, *sacen;* seven, *tupucy;* eight, *nizatis;* nine, *nuku;* ten, *iwes* (beyond this there are no numbers, but in counting, twenty, for instance, is called *uthiuiwes,* meaning two tens) ; *mancharas,* woman; *ketchkema,* boy; *ciui,* girl; *atchsema,* wife; *hounsen,* husband; *maco,* knife; *chipay,* ax; *hatis,* arrows; *temo,* bow; *liti,* come here; *hai,* sick; *ena,* dead; *esu,* hand; *coro,* feet; *uri,* head; *hein,* eyes; *ochi,* ear; *uss,* nose; *hais,* beard; *summup,* eyebrow; *siit,* teeth; *tur,* nails of the hand.

"I have always lived in Santa Cruz, except a time in Monterey, and San Jose, three years, and at the presidio, San Francisco, four years. I was employed at the latter place by Jesus Noe, who was *alcalde*. This was in 1846 and 1847. I worked about his house and milked the cows and did the chores. When Fremont came, I was made a soldier, and served in the presidio with other Indians at San Francisco. Afterwards I returned to Santa Cruz. There were too many people in San Francisco for me. At the presidio, Francisco Sanchez was our captain. One day there came a man-of-war vessel, flying the Mexican flag. We were in doubt about her nationality, because she also had the American flag flying lower down the rigging in the stern. Soon the vessel came to an anchor, fired their guns, lowered their boats, hoisted the American flag on top, and we knew then it was an American war vessel. What could we do? There were fourteen Indians of us, without arms, shoes or much clothing. The crew then commenced to ascend the hill of the presidio. Our officers were Francisco Haro, Francis Guerrero, and Jesus Noe. They were obliged to put down their arms and surrender. We said one to the other, 'Now we shall be killed.' We were made to stand to one side, and then we were laughed at, not having hats, shoes nor arms. They told us not to be afraid, we should have clothing and plenty to eat, and soon we had a grand feast. We got drunk, and then we were very brave. The next day came three more vessels, and thus was San Francisco taken by the Americans.

"The Indians at the Mission were very severely treated by the padres, often punished by fifty lashes on the bare back. They were governed somewhat in the military style, having sergeants, corporals, and overseers, who were Indians, and they reported to the padres any disobedience or infraction of the rules, and then came the lash without mercy, the women the same as the men. The lash was made of rawhide. I was never punished except a few slaps for forgetfulness. I was always busy in the padres' house, doing the work of a house servant. Sometimes the padres would leave a *real* (silver coin, one-eighth of a dollar) in some corner, or under the bed, to see if I would take it. I was never tempted in that way, but often others were, and then punished. It was the custom of one of the padres to go about at night disguised, and he would come upon his Indian officers playing cards by the fire. One would say during the game, 'I play this card,' another some other card. He would approach nearer and say, 'I play this card,' showing his hands in the light of the blaze of the fire, when the others would discover by his white hands that he was not one of them.

"The Indians at the Mission of Santa Cruz, after prayers in the morning at church, received their orders as to their labors at the church door; then they went to breakfast, and had their meal altogether of boiled barley, which was served out to them from two large caldrons by means of a copper ladle. This full was the ration to each in a *cora* (a small kind of basket), from which they ate with a shell or the fingers. Some had small gourds into which they received their rations. Boiled barley was all they had in the mornings. The labors were in the fields mostly. All of the land where Santa Cruz is was cultivated, also the meadow near Kron's tanyard. At eleven o'clock A. M. the bell was rung to call them together—the same bell that was on the church a few years ago. The dinner consisted of a mixture of cooked horse beans and peas. At the end of an hour the bell was rung again, and all went to work until about sunset, when each received his rations of boiled corn. Such of the Indians as had families were given meat also. A beef was killed every eight days.

"The land cultivated was all fenced with posts driven in the ground, and tied with hazel bark, and a ditch outside. They worked in plowing time from one hundred to one hundred and thirty oxen. The surplus products were sold to vessels that came to buy. The Russian vessels carried away the wheat and barley, Spanish vessels taking beans, corn, dried peas, and dried horse beans. English vessels carried away hides and tallow.

"The Indians were dressed with pantaloons of coarse wool, and a blanket over the shoulders. The women wore a skirt of the same material and also a blanket. We had no shoes or hats. If any of us entered the church with a dirty blanket, he was punished with fifty lashes, men and women alike. We were always trembling with fear of the lash. The padres nominated an *alcalde* and assistant for each of the different bands, of which there were about thirty. These tribes nearest to the Mission, such as up the coast a way, and as far south as Aptos, could understand each other, but those from a few miles farther off did not. Those at Gilroy were in their own language called *Paxen;* San Juan, *Uiuji;* Pajaro, *Noot-sum;* Aptos, *Aptos;* Soquel, *Soquel;* up the coast *Tili* and *Ulsicsi;* at Red Bank Dairy, up the coast, *Posorou;* on the San Vicente Creek, *Sorsecsi;* near the old limekilns of Williams' Landing, *Coyulici.*

"To capture the wild Indian, first were taken the children, and then the parents followed. The padres would erect a hut, and light the candles to say Mass, and the Indians, attracted by the light, thinking they were stars, would approach, and soon be taken. These would bring in others, such as their relatives. My father's tribe was Jlli, and he belonged to the tribe that lived up the coast. They lived upon shell fish, which they took from the sea coast, and carried them to the hills, where were their rancherias. The remains of the shells are there now, and can be seen in numerous places. They made their huts of branches of trees, which they cut down by firing and then using sharp stones. They also had acorns to eat, which they ground in stone mortars called *urwan.* The pestle was called *packshan.* To cook the acorn after being ground, the mass was put into large baskets, which were made water-tight, being woven with grass roots of a kind very long and tough. Into these were put hot stones, which caused the water to boil, and so the meal was cooked. Their meat was deer, killed by the bow and arrow; also rabbits, rats, elk and antelope.

"There were many bears in those days; they used to come and sit on their haunches on the hill where now is the water reservoir and residence of J. H. Logan (see Appendix No. 1), watching for a chance to kill one of the calves of the Mission. The Indians killed bears with bows and arrows and clubs. The wine the padres had to drink was brought from the Mission of San Gabriel on mules, being a journey of nearly one month. There were no vineyards about Santa Cruz. Afterwards a vineyard was planted in San Jose. My father planted and cultivated the orchard of apple and pear trees at Santa Cruz, known as the Mission orchard. The trees were brought to the Mission very small, in barrels, so that the roots were kept damp. My father told me that they had brought them from New Spain."[5]

The statement of this witness that "the Indians at the Mission were very severely treated by the padres, often punished by fifty lashes on the bare back," also, "that then came the lash without mercy, the women the same as the men," and, "we were always trembling with fear of the lash," must be accepted with many grains of salt.

In the first place, the Mission was secularized in 1834, when Lorenzo Venancio, who was born in 1819, was still a youth. He therefore spoke of the experiences he had when the human mind is in the most romantic and exaggerating mood. In the second place, he qualifies these statements by saying, "I was never punished except a few slaps for forgetfulness." In the third place, all petty criminals at those times were punished everywhere by a whipping; and finally, we have the book of a Protestant Englishman, Mr. Alexander Forbes, published in London in 1830. He was far from enamored of the Mission system; in fact, gives a caustic criticism of the whole institution, but adds: "Notwithstanding this dark picture of the general mode of life of the converted Indians, it must not be imagined that it is one of much real hardship, or that it is generally thought so by the parties themselves. On the contrary, it accords too well with the native indolence of their character and total defect of all independent spirit. It is true that the system tends most powerfully to keep up and to aggravate the natural defects in their character, and to frustrate all prospect of true civilization and all rational improvement. Still, it cannot be said that they are discontented. If they lead the life of groveling animals, they have, at least, their negative happiness. If they are cribbed like the stalled ox, they are fed like him, and they have hardly more care or fear for the future than he has."[6] (See Appendix No. 2.)

Captain F. W. Beechey, R. N. of the *Blossom,* who came to the Pacific Coast in 1826-7, spoke of the kindness of the Fathers. He visited a good many Missions and made extensive trips inland, which was permitted under the Mexican regime.

He was a rather stern critic and did not hesitate to report "we had, however, occasionally some difficulty in maintaining our good temper in consequence of the unpleasant remarks which the difference of our religion brought from the padres, who were very bigoted men, and invariably introduced the subject. At other times they were very conversible, and some

---

[5] Harrison, The History of Santa Cruz County, pp. 45-48.
[6] Alexander Forbes, California, p. 221-222.

of them were ingenious and clever men; but they had been so long excluded from the civilized world that their ideas and their policies, like the maps pinned against the walls, bore date of 1772, as near as I could read it for fly spots."

Still he declares "the worthy and benevolent priests of the Mission devote almost the whole of their time to the duties of the establishment, and have a fatherly regard for those placed under them who are obedient and diligent; and too much praise cannot be bestowed upon them. . . ."

Perhaps he puts his finger on the whole "lashing" question in these words: ". . . severe corporal punishment, inflicted in the same manner as is practised in our (English) schools, but with a whip instead of a rod, is sure to ensue if they are discovered (in serious misdeeds). Though there may be occasional acts of tyranny, yet the general character of the padres is kind and benevolent, and in some of the Missions the converts are so much attached to them that I have heard them declare they would go with them, if they were obliged to quit the country."

It would seem that even the best of missionaries were unable to change permanently the nature of the California Indians to any great extent.

Padre Antonio Peyri had charge of the Mission San Luis Rey de Francia, situated between the Missions San Capistrano and San Diego, founded in 1798, the site being selected on account of the many docile Indians in the neighborhood. Alexander Forbes describes him as the beau ideal of a Friar of the olden times, with his jolly figure, bald head, white locks and gray Franciscan habit. He was much beloved by his Indians.

Alfred Robinson, known in early California as Don Alfredo Robinson, who visited this Mission in 1829, declares that it had a population of about three thousand Indians, that many were carpenters, masons, coopers, saddlers, shoemakers, weavers, etc. In the interior of the square (formed by the buildings) might be seen the various trades at work, presenting a scene not dissimilar to some of the working departments of our State prisons.

He says: "The conditions of these Indians is miserable indeed, and it is not to be wondered that many attempt to escape from the severity of the discipline at the Missions."

Yet Mr. Robinson declares that the old gentleman, "Reverend Father Peyri, was held in universal respect, not only as a man of great mental energy and capacity, and being dearly beloved by his people for the extreme benevolence of his disposition."

Mr. Robinson had unusually good opportunity to know California. Born in Boston in 1806, he came in the ship Brookline as a clerk to California when twenty-eight years old. He was in the employ of Bryant,

Sturgis & Company, of Boston. He married in 1836 Maria de la Guerra Carillo, a California beauty, fifteen years old. Except for some trips East, he remained in California until his death (San Francisco, October, 1895), and was an important figure in California business life.

He visited most of the Missions, and his comments are always interesting. For instance, he describes Padre Francisco Gonzales Ibarra, who presided over the Mission San Fernando Rey—one of the first that Robinson saw—as "a short, thick, ugly-looking old man, whose looks did not belie his character. His meanness and unpopularity had gained for him the nickname of Cochine or hog."

Later he came to the Mission of Santa Clara, where he found a great contrast:

"The Friar's knowledge of the world and his super education give him a station far above the unenlightened state of the laity, and place him in a sphere to do incalculable good or disseminate evil. Fortunately for the country, the original founders of Christianity in California were truly pious, excellent men, and their successors generally have endeavored to sustain their honorable character." Evidently young Mr. Robinson had learned that Father Ibarra was a great exception.

After riding over to Mission San Jose, he found Padre Narciso Duran and states: "He is a venerable old man, generous, kind and benevolent; the natives not only revered him, as their spiritual father and friend, but seemed almost to adore him. He was universally beloved, and the neighboring village bore testimony to his charitable heart, while many a transient traveler blessed him, and thanked God that such a man existed among them."

But were the Fathers not mistaken when they considered all this discipline necessary?

Captain Beechey returned to the Pacific Coast from his trip to China and Behring's Strait, and in October, 1827, he writes in his diary:

"In my former visit to this country I remarked that the padres were much mortified at being desired to liberate from the Missions all the Indians who bore good characters, and who were acquainted with the act of tilling the ground. In consequence of their remonstrances the Governor modified the order, and consented to make the experiment upon a few only at first, and desired that a certain number might be settled in the proposed manner. After a few months' trial, much to his surprise, he found that these people, who had always been accustomed to the care and discipline of schoolboys, finding themselves their own masters, indulged freely in all those excesses which it had been the endeavor of their tutors to repress, and that many, having gambled away their clothes, implements, and even their land, were compelled to beg or plunder in order to support life. They at length became so obnoxious to the peaceable inhabitants that the padres were requested to take some of them back to the Missions, while others who had been guilty of misdemeanors were loaded with shackles and put to hard work, and when we arrived were employed transporting enormous stones to the beach to improve the landing place."

BOOK V

CHAPTER XXV

The Years 1820-1830; the Mexican
Revolt.

BOOK V

Chapter XXV

The Years 1820-1830; The Mexican Revolt

THE half century of Spain's dominion in Alta California was drawing to a close. Soon the old flag of Castile would be lowered, and the new flag of Mexico would float over the presidios of the province, thereby inaugurating almost a quarter of a century of Mexican rule, which was to give a totally new direction to the march of events.

To understand how this was brought about we must go back a few years.

On March 18th, 1808, King Carlos IV, of Spain, abdicated in favor of his young son, the Prince of the Asturias, who was proclaimed King as Fernando VII. It took almost a year before this news reached California, and not until March 5th, 1809, was the new King announced and homage paid to him. At the several presidios a salute of fifteen guns was fired at sunrise, noon and sunset, and at the Missions and pueblos special Masses were celebrated. Governor de Arrillaga swore allegiance to the King at the Church of San Carlos on August 10th, and obedience to the *Junta Superior Gubernativa* of Mexico, which was to rule during the minority of the King.

Soon thereafter Spain was invaded by Napoleon, who forced his brother, Joseph Bonaparte, on the throne. A state of unrest ensued both in the mother country and in the colonies.

In Mexico Viceroy Iturrigaray was forcibly deposed on September 16th, 1808. He was succeeded by Pedro Garibay, and the latter by the Archbishop of Mexico, who acted until the arrival of the new royal appointee, Francisco Xavier de Venégas.

On December 8th, 1810, a rebellion broke out in Mexico under leadership of Father Miguel Hidalgo y Costilla, Curate at Dolores, Guanajuato, and of Captain Ignacio Allende (see Appendix No. 1). Many of the creoles (men of pure Spanish blood but native of Mexico) and of the mestizos (generally illegitimate descendants of Spanish fathers and Indian mothers) hated the haughty *gachupines* (wearers of spurs), the ruling dons, born in Spain and showing no less greed than the Spanish officials. They and a large number of Indians joined the rebel leaders. After considerable early success, they were defeated in a pitched battle. A traitor, Ignacio Elizondo, turned over the principal rebels to the Government, who tried them, found them guilty and executed them at Chihuahua. They were shot in the back as traitors, after Hidalgo had first been degraded from his priesthood according to the Roman ceremonial; and the heads of four of them—Hidalgo, Allende, Aldama and Jiménez—were exposed in iron cages at the four corners of the Alhóndiga de Granadits[1] at Guanajuato as a warning to others. (July 31st, 1811.)

The warning did not seem to have been effective, however, for the next year another rebellion broke out, this time under the leadership of Father José Maria Morelos y Pavon, a mestizo, and one of Hidalgo's pupils. Patriot Morelos y Pavon suffered the same fate as Hidalgo y Costilla. He was condemned as a "heretic, an abettor of heretics, and a disturber of the ecclesiastical hierarchy, a profaner of the holy sacraments, a traitor to God and to the King and to the Pope." He was shot on December 22nd, 1815. Some of his adherents, urged by Guerrero, kept up the fight until 1817.

The blood of martyrs always waters the plant of liberty, and before long another revolutionary leader arose, who advocated independence from Spain. These successive rebellions affected the Missions in California, for the roads became dangerous to travel, supplies were cut off, the pay of the soldiers was stopped, and the missionaries themselves failed to receive their stipends. Under such conditions it is no wonder that there was no sympathy in California for the revolutionists, and Alta California remained loyal.

In Spain, Fernando VII had been restored to the throne in 1814. He proved to be a real Bourbon, who, according to Napoleon, never forgot, nor ever learned anything. He repudiated the liberal Spanish Constitution of 1812, and in 1820 a military uprising took place restoring it. This Constitution was proclaimed in Mexico in May of the same year by the Viceroy, Juan Ruiz de Apodaca, Conde del Venadito, who was nicknamed the "Unfortunate." In 1813 the Cortes of Spain had passed a law, generally known as the *Bando de la Reforma* (Edict of the Reforms), which was directly aimed against the missionaries, and in favor of secularization. The King procrastinated in approving the Law, but finally, said to be in fear of his life, affixed his signature on October 23rd, 1820, and it was then promulgated.

Trouble now broke out anew *outre mer,* this time under the leadership of the ill-fated Agustin de Iturbide, a mestizo, though called a creole, and a retired colonel of the Spanish army. He joined forces with Vicente Guerrero.

---

[1] Public granary.

On February 24th, 1821, from Iguala, Iturbide published his manifesto, afterwards famous as "the Plan of Iguala," proposing an independent limited monarchy in New Spain under a Bourbon Prince, which would secure equal rights for all, and guarantee religious freedom. The Viceroy de Apodaca[2] declared the revolutionary leader an outlaw, but the latter took possession of the capital on February 27th, and the Viceroy was forced to resign in July, 1821, after a junta had declared Mexico a free and independent nation with General Iturbide at its head, which junta would act as a regency "until the new Prince could arrive."

A new Viceroy was appointed by Spain, Don Juan O'Donojú, but he was never allowed to proceed to the capital. He remained at Vera Cruz until given permission by Iturbide to advance as far as the town of Cordoba, where on August 24th he was obliged to sign the treaty of Cordoba surrendering Mexico.[3] He was the sixty-second and last Viceroy of New Spain.

News traveled slowly, for in California so little seems to have been known of all these events that on October 8th, 1821, the day of the death of the last Viceroy, Governor de Sola swore to observe the re-established Spanish Constitution of 1812, and on October 22nd, Father-president Payéras did the same, while in the beginning of the following year, Governor Pablo Vicente de Sola was still ignorant of the new developments, for he wrote to his colleague, Arguello, of Baja California, on January 10th, 1822, that he had received from Mexico "such documents as are printed in a country of dreamers, since independence is a dream. Day by day their presses will turn out absurdities by the thousand; but you and I, aware that the immortal, incomparable Spanish nation has many and great resources with which to make herself respected, must look with contempt on such absurd views." Amongst these "documents" he no doubt included Iturbide's manifesto, the Plan of Iguala, of February of the preceding year.

By March, 1822, the "Royal" Governor was better informed and he called a *Junta* at Monterey of presidio commanders, some other military officers, the Comisario Profecto, and the Father President of the Missions. They met on April 9th, and on April 11th the oath of independence and allegiance to the Mexican Empire was taken. The troops took the oath in the public plaza, religious services followed, and Alta California ceased to be a dependency of Spain. Similar oaths had been taken at the presidios of Santa Barbara on April 13th; San Francisco, April 14th, and San

---

[2] Juan Ruiz de Apodaca Conde del Venadito.
[3] The name "New Spain" was abandoned and "Mexico" took its place.

Diego on April 20th. De Sola had become, as a holdover, the first Mexican Governor of Alta California.

Wonder is sometimes expressed that all these political events affected Alta California so little, aside from material inconvenience of the failure of supplies to arrive. Still this is easily understood.

As a matter of necessity, California had become largely self-dependent and self-sufficient. The transports which formerly came each year from Mexico with supplies and money had become rarer and rarer. The Missions had not only become the backbone, but the blood and life of the Province. It was the Missions which had the grain, tallow, hides, meat, etc., which the foreign ships wanted, and it was the Missions which kept the presidios in provisions and many other supplies. True, they were paid for the latter with orders on the national treasury, but the presidio commanders, as well as the missionaries, knew that in such troubled times drafts would not be paid; and they were therefore accepted by the missionaries with tongues in their cheeks. An independent local viewpoint as to the illegal but very desirable trading with foreign ships was fast developing.

The College of San Fernando, to which the Fathers in California looked for guidance, now received a taste of what was to be expected under Mexican rule. In a circular, one month after the declaration of independence, Fr. Jose Gasol wrote from San Fernando that he had been elected Guardian on July 28th, and pictured the situation as follows:

"From La Gaceta and other papers forwarded to Your Reverences you will learn the new plan of government to which we must submit. I therefore do not stop to write concerning the decrees of the new government. What I enjoin upon you is that in everything and in every event you proceed with prudence and strive for union, peace and tranquility, and that you permit the infliction of wrong rather than break the bond of charity. I am not unaware, dear Fathers, of the need of missionaries in your Missions, nor that some of you wish to retire to the College; but I must describe to you the deplorable condition in which the College finds itself. Today we are not more than nineteen priests in the house. In less than three months, since the celebration of the last chapter, six priests and three lays brothers have severed their connection with the College. Most of them were from Spain. God knows those who may yet ask to leave, and whether it shall be possible to procure others from Spain, supposing that the independence of Mexico is realized.

"Under these circumstances, my dear Fathers and Brothers, Your Reverences will comprehend how impossible it is for me to console you by sending new laborers for the vineyard of the Lord in California. No other course is open to me, my dear Fathers, than to call upon the Lord of the

Vineyard (and no more upon our Catholic monarch, as Most Rev. Fr. Truxillo said in his letter), and to exhort all Your Reverences to remain in the same Rule, and to warn you that whithersoever you may go, when you leave your forced exile, you will not improve your lot. If you want to retire and come to the College, do not believe you will find it the quiet and silent retreat which it was when you departed from here. Since the 27th of last month it has been transformed into a barracks for the cavalry, whence you can infer how we are mortified by day and by night with the noise of the soldiery, the horses, dogs and trumpets. So it is at present; what it will be later on we do not know. If you desire to return to Spain it will be nothing less than leaving the smoke in order to leap into the flame.

"I shall in no way exaggerate, if I assure Your Reverences that the whole object of that government is to put an end to the religious state and to make it despicable before the world. The decrees of suppression of the converts, the prohibition of bestowing the habit, secularization, depriving the religious of their prelates general and provincial, extermination of all monks and Jesuits, and lastly, depriving the secular and regular clergy of their immunities, plainly manifest this, and yet we are only at the beginning. We may foretell what will be the end; and we need not hesitate to affirm that those religious who go back to Spain will find themselves the laughing stock and the objects of mockery and scorn; for so Fr. Garijo told us when he returned to the College three months ago, after he had observed during his six years' stay in Spain the impiety, the contempt and the ridicule with which the religious are covered, and how infidel free-thinking has infected the lower classes.

"You may therefore believe, my dear Fathers, that the most desirable corner at present is the one you enjoy in those remote regions, for which we entertain a holy envy against you. If my advice counts for anything, stay where conditions are nothing like those that afflict us, though there are some things that provoke resentment. They will always be more tolerable and reconcilable with the interior and exterior peace which your least Brother, who loves you in Jesus Christ, wishes you along with every consolation."[4]

On May 19th, 1822, after a military upheaval, Iturbide had been elected, and on July 21st he was crowned Emperor of Mexico, as Don Augustin I. His reign was short, for as early as on March 19th, 1823, he was compelled to abdicate. The following month the Mexican Congress vested the executive power in three generals, Nicolas Bravo, Guadalupe

Victoria and Pedro Celestino Negrete. The ex-Emperor was ordered to leave the country, which he did, but committed the folly to return in secret, was captured, sentenced and shot on July 19th, 1824, five days after landing.

The Franciscans, being mostly Spanish in blood and royalists in sympathy, viewed with little enthusiasm the fall of Iturbide's empire, and the beginning of native republican rule.

It was therefore considered advisable by the Mexican authorities to send an agent to California to probe the real spirit of the padres, to encourage independence, and to raise the new national flag. The Rev. Augustine Fernandez de San Vicente, Canon at the Cathedral of Durango, was selected to be the new Commissioner.

The instructions to the jovial and kindly Father de San Vicente were to go to Loreto, as well as to Monterey, with dispatches to the Governor and pastoral letters for the padres, and not to depart unil he had ascertained the general feeling as to Mexican independence. In addition, he had to inform himself as to the economic conditions existing in the colonies, as far as Alta California was concerned; he was to ascertain if Americans had already established themselves, arriving via the Columbia route, and if Russia was maintaining a strong post at Bodega. The genial priest, who had become an Imperial Commissioner, after Iturbide was raised to Emperor, reached Monterey on September 26th.

It was a wise choice, for he proved himself a liberal, energetic man who acted with great prudence and discretion. He visited and investigated all the Missions, including that of Santa Cruz; urged popular education, the arming of neophytes in case of invasion, the organization of a *deputacion* (legislature), the liberalization of the treatment of the Indians; relaxing their bonds and declaring them in possession of citizenship, allowing them, when competent, to live away from the Missions, and abolishing the correction by lash on the bare back. He also visited Fort Ross, where he was kindly and hospitably received by Captain Carlos Schmidt. He finally returned to Mexico with Governor de Sola on the *San Carlos*. He had accomplished much, had smoothed over many difficulties and left only a few enemies and many friends.

Under the provisional regulations of the Mexican regency the Californias were entitled to a delegate in the forthcoming federal congress. Five electors were chosen to designate him. No ecclesiastics or soldiers were allowed to vote. From San Francisco district, to which Santa Cruz Mission belonged, Francisco Castro, of Branciforte, was elected. These electors met at Monterey on May 21st, 1822, and chose Governor de Sola

DON LUIS ANTONIO ARGÜELLO
Governor of California
1822-1825
Courtesy of Mr. George H. Barron, Antiquarian de Young Memorial Museum,
Golden Gate Park, San Francisco, California.
(Mrs. Barron was the granddaugher of Don Argüello.)

as Congressional delegate, while Captain Luis Arguello was elected as substitute.

On November 9th the same electors met again at Monterey, and having been informed that they could vote for themselves, six representatives were elected, who comprised the first legislature of Upper California, with Francisco de Haro as secretary. They also appointed as Governor, Captain Luis Arguello, *comandante* of the San Francisco presidio, who thereupon took up his headquarters at Monterey.

Governor de Sola sailed from Monterey November 22nd, on the *San Carlos;* when in Mexico he served on the *Junta de Fomento de Californias,* a body to aid the Mexican President in California affairs. His first salary—he was supposed to get $4,000 a year from his district—was mostly obtained by assessing the long-suffering Missions, for prior to his sailing he obtained from Father President Payeras $3,000, partly in cash and partly in drafts, the Santa Cruz Mission contributing $300.

On January 17th, 1824, Arguello had called together at Monterey a *diputacion* of military and civil officers and a system of government had been devised and adopted and immediately promulgated. By this plan a *junta general* was called into existence, in which the prelates of the Missions participated.

Almost immediately afterwards the new government was faced by a serious general Indian revolt, which began on February 22nd, 1824, but which was speedily crushed.

Due to the class of immigrants previously sent to the pueblos, no less than to the bad character of the San Blas troops which were sent now and then into California Alta, lawlessness had increased to such an extent in 1824 that the kind-hearted and liberal-minded Governor Arguello was forced to issue a sanguinary proclamation against robbers and burglars. Every person guilty of burglary or house-breaking, or of stealing property of the value of two hundred *reals* or more, should suffer death. Those found guilty of murder were to be put to death and their bodies quartered. For small thefts, the punishments ran to ten years and six public floggings. The Governor, however, was merciful when it came to executing these sentences, only one man, Pomponimo, an Indian, was found guilty of murder and executed by shooting in San Francisco, in February, 1824.

On October 4th, 1824—the fourth year of the Mexican independence, the third year of liberty, and the second year of federation—the new republican Constitution was promulgated. Upper and Lower California ceased to be royal or imperial provinces and became republican territories.

On Sunday, March 26th, 1825, the new Constitution was sworn in by the Diputacion at Monterey.

On May 21st, 1825, the Governor made an extensive report to the central Mexican authorities. He spoke of the poor condition of the Indians, of the splendid physical characteristics of the country, and of the destitution of the soldiers—the royal and afterwards republican *memorias* for support (usually from 80,000 to 100,000 dollars yearly) not having arrived for several years.

He had previously stated that inasmuch as the ports were legally closed to foreign ships, the Government had no income except from the miserable tithes of the poor pueblos of Los Angeles, San Jose and Branciforte, and as the Missions did not pay any taxes, he was compelled to depend almost entirely on the missionaries for the maintenance of the military establishment. Fortunately, within two months the Mexican warship *Morelos* arrived at Monterey with money and supplies for the troops.

Under Governor Luis Arguello commercial prohibition from sheer necessity had to be abolished. A contract had been entered into with McCulloch, Hartnell & Company. This English firm agreed to take, for three years, at a stipulated price, all the hides and tallow of the province. Another contract had been entered into with the Russian American Company for hunting otters on shares. This latter contract was renewed in 1825 for five years by Jose Maria Herrera, a newly appointed fiscal agent of California, independent of the Governor. Herrera had arrived in July, 1825, with a company of eighteen Mexican convicts. Soon all kinds of trouble arose, which culminated in 1829 in a revolt of unpaid soldiers, under Joaquin Solis, one of the ex-convicts and ex-soldiers. But the rebels seem to have run away from their foes and the revolt was the usual bloodless farce, for which Alta California was to become famous.

With an interim of one year, in which Jose Minon was appointed Governor, but declined, Jose Maria de Echeandia took office in November, 1825, and served out the decade (until January 21st, 1831).

De Echeandia was the third Mexican Governor of Alta California, and likewise Governor of Baja California. He received on February 1st, 1825, the title of *Comandante-General* of the Californias from Victoria, the President of the Mexican Republic, and was directed to proceed at once to his jurisdiction.

By that time the Mexican Republic was fairly well established and de Echeandia received ample instructions as to the Republic's policies. He was to pay particular attention to the public lands, ascertain the names and character of the Indians; thoroughly examine the affairs of the Missions; investigate the relations between the missionaries, neophytes and Gentiles;

discover their respective attitudes towards the new Government and make proposals for the amelioration of the condition of both neophyte and Gentile Indians. The new political chief seems to have had little ambition for this field of his endeavors, for though he proceeded at once, he wrote from Tepic that he wished to resign and return to his place as Lieutenant Colonel of Engineers. However, his request was refused; he proceeded to Loreto and marched overland to San Diego, reaching there in October, 1825.

As Governor of both the Californias, he temporarily fixed his headquarters at San Diego, from which place he could easily reach either territory.

He at once wrote to Father Narciso Duran of San Jose, who had become *Presidente* of the Missions of Alta California, demanding that he take oath to the Federal Constitution. In April, 1826, he made the same demand on Fathers Sanchez, Zalvidea, Peyri and Martin, representing the four southern Missions in California.

The following month the Federal Congress abolished titles of nobility, coats-of-arms and everything calculated to recall to memory the old dependence on Spain, and this was followed by a decree in 1827 that no person of Spanish birth should exercise any public employment as long as Spain refused to acknowledge the Republic. The next year the first expulsion decree was promulgated against all Spaniards, except those who had married Mexican wives.

De Echeandia discharged his duties under most difficult circumstances.

Through all these changes and alarms the Missions had prospered and had grown into wealthy estates, administered by the padres, who besides being preachers, had developed into great farm managers, merchants and rulers of the Indian population.

Live stock, grain, orchards and vineyards throve abundantly and the Missions had erected larger and handsomer buildings of brick and stone; irrigation ditches had been constructed, and the padres furnished great quantities of supplies to the presidios, making the Government debtor.

With this prosperity of the Missions and corresponding backwardness of all other activities, dissatisfaction, if not jealousy, manifested itself amongst the officials in Mexico and the settlers of Alta California.

The anti-Church party, which grew steadily in power, asserted that the priests had gone too far, that in Christianizing the Indian they had practically enslaved him by exchanging hard labor for spiritual teaching, scanty board and keep. They claimed that the system had become feudal, the priests the lords and the Indians serfs; that the provincial government had become destitute while the Missions had become wealthy land-holding institutions, the missionaries usurping the power from the civil authorities.

There was of course some truth in this. The padres could never have accomplished their work without being inspired zealots. A similar charge was afterwards made against the Protestant missionaries in Hawaii. It was said that when they arrived the natives had the land and the missionaries the Gospel; that after due time the natives had the Gospel and the missionaries the land. Their descendants still have it.

It did not take the Governor long to realize that the difficulties connected with the secularization of the Missions, with which he had been instructed to proceed, were very great. All manufacturing in the province—soap making, tanning, flour milling, weaving—were carried on by the neophytes, and this was also true of the cattle raising, so that the whole economic structure was bound to collapse in case this was suddenly changed.

De Echeandia knew, however, that no matter what the consequences might be, the knell of the Mission system had been sounded, for the Mexican Government claimed that the spirit of republicanism was not favorable to further existence of a system of land monopoly by the Missions.

Realizing that notwithstanding all difficulties, it was imperative that something be done, he announced by proclamation on July 25th, 1826, that those Indians who desired to leave the Mission might do so, provided they had been Christians from childhood, or for fifteen years; were married, or at least not minors, and had some means of gaining a livelihood. The Indians must apply to the *comandante* at the presidio, who, after obtaining from the padre a report, was to issue a written permit entitling the neophyte and his family to go where they chose, their names being erased from the Mission register. Few were in a position to take advantage of it, and those who did soon came in contact with cultures of a "superior" race, who proceeded to devour them and their substance.

During this decade many foreigners came to Alta California, attracted by stories about the Mission wealth, furs to be procured, etc. This was made legally possible by the Decree of August, 1824, heretofore mentioned. (See Addenda No. 2, pages 23 and 24, of Dwinelle.) (Appendix No. 2.)

Among these foreigners was William Thompson, an Englishman, born in London, where his father was a sailmaker. He landed in the port of Santa Cruz about 1822, and while there unexpectedly met his brother, Samuel, who had come in another ship, and for whom he had been searching for a long time. Thereafter they remained together on this coast. Samuel remained single, but William was married, and in 1838 he was granted by Governor Alvarado the Carbonero Rancho, east of the San Lorenzo River and a few miles north of the Mission establishment. Subsequently he lived in a house on Mission hill, on ground now occupied by the Sisters' school.

Captain Juan B. R. Cooper came in 1823, obtaining permission to hunt otters.

In 1824 David Spence came from Scotland with the view of establishing a packing house for a Lima firm.

Eight years later, Thomas O. Larkin, a flour manufacturer, came from Boston; afterwards as United States Consul at Monterey, he did much to bring California into the American Union.

The following year Isaac Graham came to Santa Cruz, and established the first lumber mill about three miles from the Mission site.

Chase and Saunders, in "The California Padres and Their Missions," tell us of one John Mulligan, an Irishman, who was stranded in California from some ship about the year 1822, and was unable to get away. He was a roistering blade and great drinker, but as he was a practical weaver, the padres got him to teach his trade to the neophytes at the different Missions. He became very friendly with Father Taboada, of the Santa Cruz Mission, and the authors assure us that besides instructing the neophytes in their trade, he taught the Father English of a certain kind, and thereafter the Father innocently used the most outrageous profanity when he endeavored to speak the language of Albion. We leave the truth of this tale to the authors.

CHAPTER XXVI

1820-1830 Continued;
Santa Cruz Becomes a Port
of Entry

BOOK V

Chapter XXVI

1820-1830 Continued; Santa Cruz Becomes a Port of Entry

THE demands of the civil and military authorities on the Missions for contributions, supplies and support seem to have been incessant and exacting during this decade, but they were well-nigh inevitable, for the expenses of the newly-organized territory had to be met. Little could be expected from the central government, and there were but few other resources, such as customs, etc., from which any revenue could be derived.

Father Engelhardt says that in writing to Fr. Payeras on December 10th, 1821, "Fr. Jose complained bitterly about the demands of the Governor. The chief reason appears to have been that the soldiers . . . were inconsiderate and not content with the necessaries of life, and often coupled their demands with threats. No matter how much the Fathers exerted themselves, the ungrateful troops would always grumble. At the beginning of the same year Fr. Viadér had set forth the straitened circumstances of Santa Clara Mission—'we have been unable to give Sergeant Pico more than $25 of the $150 allotted by the Fr. Prefecto.' Even in the preceding year Fathers Catalá and Viadér jointly had to remonstrate with Governor (de) Sola . . . 'This year the providing of clothes for our neophytes was delayed until last month, owing to the fact that we had to supply the troops so much, and not less the wretched colonists. . . . If now, besides supplying 300 blankets and 300 yards of serge to the troops alone, not counting the very many pieces of both kinds of goods furnished the needy people of the adjoining town of San Jose, we must produce forty more for the infantry, we shall have to overwork the unfortunate neophytes whose lot is to go naked.

" 'In addition to what has been said, this Mission of Santa Clara has provided the troops with 300 pairs of shoes, 40 saddles, more than 200 soft tanned calf skins, and many other articles which require time and labor, not to speak of all the corn and beans which are raised and the fat which can be collected. Of the three products mentioned we use no part for the Indians. Besides this, the raising and transporting of all the garvanzos, peas and other things is a most heavy and almost insurmountable burden for these unhappy Christians. . . .'

"The commanders of the presidio sometimes made additional demands without consulting the Governor. For instance, Jose Maria Estudillo, of San Diego, on June 15th, 1821, wanted Mission San Juan Capistrano to furnish 500 *fanegas*[1] of corn and 120 *fanegas* of beans; Mission San Luis Rey was to provide 652 *fanegas* of corn and 200 *fanegas* of beans; poor San Diego Mission was directed to forward 200 *fanegas* of corn and 44 *fanegas* of beans. . . .

"Another Father who seemed to be at his wits' end by reason of orders for supplies, for which he received nothing but drafts, on which he could realize nothing to clothe his neophytes, was Fr. Luis Gil y Taboada, of Mission Santa Cruz. In a letter to Fr. Payeras he says: 'There is little wool on hand, and the Indians suffer very much from cold. The cattle have no young. Last year the Mission furnished fourteen saddles, as you directed. This year it gave $51 worth of beans and 207 *arróbas*[2] of fat. I have given seventy pairs of shoes; there were no more. Now, on bended knees I beg Your Reverence through the Blood of Jesus Christ and for the sake of the Blessed Virgin Mary to grant me permission to retire to the College. There is nothing new save that my leg begins to trouble me, but not so as to prevent me from celebrating holy Mass. The year has proved one of the worst. For days we have been praying for rain. For the last fifteen days they have been irrigating the soil to be able to plow it, but to little purpose.' "[3]

From these and similar letters it is only too evident that while the secular authorities were criticizing the missionaries for their presumed insistence on indentured labor of the Indians, they themselves were not slow to profit by the result of such labor, even over the protests of the Fathers that their charges were badly clothed and overworked.

When we examine the attitude of the Church toward the revolution, we find that the missionaries made no difficulty in swearing fidelity to the imperial independence in 1822; but on the other hand, when the Republic was established, most of them refused allegiance and many perished in this resistance.

It would be passing strange if it had been different.

Many of the Mission Fathers were getting old and fatigued; they desired to retire. They had labored for a great many years in the vineyards of the Lord and in the garden of the King. As men they were naturally loyal to their native country, and as ecclesiastics they had discharged all their sacerdotal duties, as they had seen them. As faithful servants of the King, they had created from sheer wilderness magnificent emblems of his authority.

---

[1] A grain measure equal to about 1.60 bushel.
[2] A measure of weight, equivalent to about 25 pounds.
[3] Engelhardt, Misisons and Missionaries of California, Vol. II, p. 125-129.

True, the rules under the *jus patronato* had often been irksome; they had at times endeavored to emasculate their orders by observing them in appearance and evading them in fact; they had often grumbled about the restraints of the secular authorities; they had many times been indignant about the criticism they received, but they knew that their worldly position and strength, and even the right to carry on, were embedded in the alliance between the Church and the State, and that after all their exalted position was due to the strong arm of the State.

They realized that these conditions were to be reversed under a Republican Government; that the new politicians, present, or carpet-bag fashion soon to be expected, were lean and hungry, anxious to get their fangs into the Mission prey.

They knew that what was now happening on the political stage under their very eyes was but a prologue to the drama of the long-threatened secularization of their Missions, which would inevitably mean the destruction of the Missions and of the whole Mission establishment.

Such destruction was inherent to the whole situation, for these large landed estates, situate in a semi-arid country, were operated under irrigation and cultivation. The land on which a fruit-bearing orchard in the West is today located may well be worth from $1,500 to $2,000 an acre, but let the orchard be neglected for two years and no cultivation, irrigation, fertilizing, pruning or spraying take place, it speedily deteriorates in value, and will not sell for more than ten per cent of its former legitimate worth, for values can only be created and maintained through continuous and sustained efforts.

The Missions did not even have the salvage of the value of the ground to look forward to; they had no title to the land, but only a leasehold, which could be terminated at will by the Government.

The cattle, live stock and other personal property represented great worth. They were very valuable assets to the operation of the Mission plants, and would have been so until the very last, if they could have been kept intact until disposed of in an orderly way. Unfortunately, this did not happen.

The Fathers were well aware that, with the systematic progressive plundering, the theory would be invoked that the Indian neophytes were the original owners of the soil, and that the time had arrived to distribute all the assets to the children of California. But very gullible, indeed, would they have been if they had not realized that the Indians and their property were bound to become the prey of unscrupulous white men, both in and out of the Government service, as soon as their wards were free from control.

How could the Fathers have been sympathetically inclined to the new scheme of things? New liberty spelled destruction to all their work, the nullification of all their hopes, the undoing of all their spiritual efforts, and a troubled, precarious old age, with hopes of a retreat to rest and meditation at the College of San Fernando destroyed.

In their administration, continuous mutations took place. In 1823 Prefect Payéras and former Presidente Señán died. Both were men of unusual attainments. Father Vincente Sarría, also of great ability, succeeded as prefect and *presidente*. Two years later he resigned, and Father Narciso Durán became *presidente*. He in turn was followed after two years by Jose Sánchez.

Early in 1825 both Sarría and Durán refused to take the oath of fidelity to the Mexican Government and the former was placed under constructive arrest.

Father Ripoll, whose sense of Spanish loyalty had been so outraged by the raid of Bouchard, had with a fellow priest, Luis Martínez, donned armor, joined the military, and refused to swear allegiance to Mexico. He escaped with Father Jose Altimira, the founder of San Francisco Solano, on an American brig, lying in the port of Santa Barbara, and sailed for Spain. Father Martínez was exiled.

Even as late as 1829 fourteen padres of Alta California persisted in refusing to take the oath of allegiance.

And how did the Santa Cruz Mission fare during all these troubles?

Padre Ramon Olbés had retired to his College in 1821, just in the nick of time. Born at Ateca, in Spain, on February 8th, 1786, he had joined the order of Zaragoza, and arrived at San Fernando College on June 10th, 1810. He reached California in 1812, served at Santa Inés, at Santa Barbara and San Luis Rey; he was stationed at Santa Cruz from June, 1818, to November, 1821. Though Padre Olbés was a man of much ability and energy, and highly regarded, ill health seems to have made him touchy and nervous, and he continually quarreled with his neighbors of Branciforte. He was charged with preaching a seditious sermon, and Asísara, an ex-neophyte, charged him with extreme severity towards the natives, though at other times he showed great generosity. License to retire was finally given him on account of ill health. Bancroft states that he was the only Friar who retired legitimately during this period.

His successor, Padre Taboada, served until 1830.

During the last four years of the decade, three newcomers, Fathers Antonio Real, Jose Joaquin Jimeno and Juan Moreno, were at the Santa Cruz Mission.

The revolution had been hovering over Alta California for a long time, but had not reached Santa Cruz in 1822, for in that year the regular Mission report was sent to the Spanish Viceroy.

The Mission lands were therein described as extending three miles north to south, and seven to nine leagues east to west. Only three miles were useful. The crops more than sufficed for the neophytes, leaving a surplus for the presidio. There were no lands fit for the further extension of agriculture. The grasshoppers and insects were troublesome.

At Santa Cruz, as at the other Missions, an Indian *Ayuntamiento* or council was formed in 1823, in accordance with Article 314 of the Constitution and by order of the Governor.

Alcaldes, aldermen, an attorney and secretary were elected. The Governor, approving the election, ordered that the *alcaldes* proceed in civil and governmental affairs with the cognizance of the Reverend Father Minister, and in criminal matters in conjunction with the *comandante* or the chief of the troops.[4]

It was in this year also that the suppression of the Mission of Santa Cruz was proposed by the new legislature.

The indication is that the *diputacion* voted in favor of the suppression on account of the Mission's claim for the Rancho Salsipuedes. Very likely this effort was instigated by the old enemies of the Mission, the Brancifortians. April 18th, 1823, brought a recommendation from Altimira to the new Prefect, Fr. Señán, asking the suppression of the Santa Cruz Mission. Fr. Sarría opposed the measure very strongly, and as in 1813 nothing further was done in the direction of secularization for a time.[5]

A report dated December 31st, 1824, states that the rainfall was greater than for twenty-four years. Much damage was done to the gardens and buildings, including the church, which was threatened with ruin, as there were no laborers there to repair the damage.[6]

The fugitive neophytes in 1825 numbered thirty-one.

In the meantime a considerable trade had been developed by the missionaries. Hides, tallow, wheat, etc., left the port of Santa Cruz, while general merchandise and supplies were brought in.

The ships of McCoullough-Hartnell and Company stopped regularly at the port, though Fr. Luis Gil complained quite often to the company that the dealings were not satisfactory.[7]

---

[4] Archivo del Arzobispado de San Francisco MS., Vol. IV, Pt. 2, p. 5.
[5] St. Barbara Arch. XII, 361-2, B. C.
[6] St. Cruz Arch. MS., 12-13, B. C.
[7] Hartnell Letter Book, Bancroft Library, MS., p. 87.

In 1825 the padre was ordered to abstain from all dealings with vessels on the coast. It was the habit of whalers and other coasting vessels to land there that they might supply themselves with the excellent vegetables which were to be found nowhere else in the vicinity in such profusion. (See Appendix No. 1.)

The missionary answered that he would obey, but had supposed his Mission was included in the port of Monterey, and therefore open. Some ships continued to stop and trade, for instance the Russian brig *Baikal,* which secured consent from the Governor. (See Appendix No. 2.)

In 1827 Santa Cruz was named as a port of entry in an order promulgated by the President and Congress of the Republic of Mexico permitting foreign vessels to touch at Santa Cruz, San Luis Obispo, Refugio and San Juan Capistrano.

Taking advantage of this order, the *Heros,* under Captain Duhaut-Cilly (see Appendix No. 3), dropped anchor and landed at Santa Cruz during this year. His description, principally of the natural features of the place, is very interesting and therefore we reproduce it here: ". . . All our business at San Francisco was ended, and we were quite well satisfied with the transactions we had carried out there. It was agreed with the padres that we should return in June to receive the value of the goods they had bought from us. We had now to continue the same operations with the other Missions; but Santa Cruz, situated between San Francisco Bay and Monterey, was one of those where foreigners were not admitted. But by a happy circumstance, I received permission to go there. The President of that establishment had informed me that he had quite a large quantity of grain to furnish to the commandant of Monterey, who had no way of sending to fetch it by water. I wrote him that if he would permit me to anchor, on our way past Santa Cruz, I would carry it to him. Necessity pleaded my cause, and it was decided I should load on the grain. . . .

"The 7th, we set sail (1827), and left the harbor with the help of the ebb; then a nice northwest breeze greeted us, and we went swiftly along the coast and only a little distance from it.

"There are eighteen leagues from the entrance to San Francisco Bay to the roadstead at Santa Cruz, and the way is south-southeast, without turns and dangers. All day we had the spy-glasses in our hands to examine the coast, whose aspect the swift progress of the ship altered every minute. In general it is very high in the interior, and everywhere covered with forests of fir trees; it then grows lower by a gentle slope toward the shore; but before reaching it, it rises again to form a long rise of hills, whence it descends finally to the sea, now bathing the foot of vertical rocky cliffs, now gliding in sheets of foam over sandy or pebbly beaches. Beautiful verdure clothed the plains and the hills, where we constantly saw immense herds of cows, sheep, and horses. Those belonging to Santa Cruz meet those, less numerous, of San Francisco; so that this long trip of eighteen leagues is but one continual pasture.

"The morning of the 8th, after some hours of calm, we anchored in eight fathoms, in Santa Cruz roads.[8]

"I went immediately to the Mission with Padre Ramon Abila, and I was cordially received by Fray Luis Taboada, its President. I informed him I was ready to receive the grain order from his Indian *majordomos* and to get the carts ready to carry it to the shore, where it would be taken on board. During this proceeding I trafficked with Fray Luis and the people in the vicinity. That was the real end of my stop, the freight of the grain being merely the pretext.

"At every Mission I visited I made a new friend. Hardly was I arrived at one than there grew up, between the missionary and myself, a trust, manifested at first by complaints against the Government which had taken the place of the royal authority. This barrier overcome, I was made acquainted with all the harassments that this want of harmony necessarily produced. I was then told about the persons with whom I was to trade, to the minutest particular; it was in this way, above all, that I learned of the degree of solvency of each one: proofs which were of the utmost use to me, and which I have never been sorry to have listened to: thus, during the whole course of my operations in California, I had only eight hundred piastres of bad credit.

"Nearly all of these religious were men of distinguished merit and great discretion: the counsels they gave me came from no motive of hatred, and they had no other aim than to serve me, like a friend, like a brother; they knew well I would not make bad use of it, and that I received it from them only as business information. This was the result of the happiness they found in treating with a captain of their communion. Never would they have approached a like subject with an American or an Englishman. Their fine souls and their tolerance made them, truly, hospitable to all; but from simple duties of courtesy to complete indulgence of confidence, there was a world.

"No situation is prettier than that of this Mission. From the shore the ground rises so regularly by steps that they might be said to be the symmetrical terraces of a fortification. I know not even if the grassy covering of an artificial work could ever equal the beauty of green sward clothing them like the carpet of green velvet spread out over the steps of a throne.

---

[8] Survey of the anchorage: The mission buildings north 22° west. Point Año Nuevo south 45° west.

The buildings are placed upon the third sward fronting the sea, and backed against a thick forest of large fir trees, which lend a new brilliance to the whiteness of their walls.

"To the right of the settlement, the natural steps supporting the mass of earth are abruptly broken by a deep valley, at the bottom of which flows quietly a river of clear water, bordered with trees, whose dense foliage protects its ripples from the burning heat of the sun. . . .

"The mooring-ground[9] being protected only from the north, we were compelled, on the 9th, to set sail in great haste, at the approach of a storm from the south which threatened us. We had again to congratulate ourselves, at this time, for the energy and good will of our crew. Indeed, when the danger was seen, all our boats were on the beach, loading on grain and hides. I ordered a gun fired at once to recall them, and Dr. Botta as well, he being gone to the village to visit a sick man; the loading was taken aboard; the boats hoisted up; the two anchors raised; and in less than a half-hour we were under sail, at the moment the wind blew violently into the bay.

"However good be a crew, they would not display this valuable activity were they not roused by the energy of skillful officers. The coolness and talent shown by M. Tréhouart, my mate and friend, on these occasions established order and commanded promptness.

"The storm was not, however, of long duration, and the wind quickly returned to the northwest; but none the less we kept on our way to Monterey, only seven leagues from Santa Cruz, and we anchored there at ten in the evening.

"The next day, at sunrise, I saluted the place with seven guns, which were returned by one sole shot. I went immediately after to see the commandant, Don Miguel Gonzalez, captain of artillery; and before any other business, I begged him to explain why the salute had not been returned in full. He opened a book, where he showed me that only a warship could claim to have the salute repeated shot for shot.

"I made a call also upon the deputy of the customs, Don José María Herrera, one of the administrators with whom I was to have constant relations, not only during my stop at Monterey, but also for the entire time I should be in California. He was, as it were, administrator of all the accounts and finances of the province.

"He told me the Mexican laws were observed in California, and that I must, strictly speaking, unload all my freight; but that, seeing the few

---

[9] This beach as an anchoring place was especially recommended by Cordoba, Engineer extraordinary, in a report filed with Governor Borica in 1796. (Calif. Arch. P. S. P. XXI, 642.)

resources of this single port for selling an entire cargo, I might unload only what I believed I could sell, and take back afterward, without paying duty, what should remain at my departure; adding that I might follow this method at all the other ports under his jurisdiction. . . ."

The *Heros* was only one of the many vessels that touched at Santa Cruz.

During 1826-1830, in addition to commercial imposts, a secular tithe on all Mission products was levied. The method of collection was to exact from each Mission the largest possible amount of supplies for the *escoltas,* and presidial garrisons, and at the end of each year to give credit on account for the excess of amounts thus furnished over taxes. There is no evidence that any part of this balance was paid in any instance.

It was but a step from the collection of these exorbitant taxes to the final despoliation of the Missions. Mexico had passed Colonization Laws in 1824, and General Rules and Regulations for the Colonization of the Territories of the Republic on November 21st, 1828. By these regulations the Governor was empowered to make grants of all lands not in private ownership, nor belonging to any corporation or pueblo.[10]

De Echeandia's plan was formulated in 1828, and adopted by the territorial *diputacion* in July, 1830. The plan was founded on a previous decree of the Spanish Cortez, and was intended to carry it into practical operation.[11] Article 15 of this plan provided that the new pueblos (former Mission-pueblos) had either to keep their old name or the Mission name, or the settlers could propose another name of laudable origin. The new pueblo availed itself of this provision and was afterwards called "Figueroa," after the *popular* Governor of that name.[12]

De Echeandia[13] merely followed the popular idea when he formulated his plan for the secularization of the Missions of Upper California. This was the second great move to this end, the first being the decree of the Spanish Cortez in 1813.

For two reasons de Echeandia's plan was not a success. The missionaries proved to have too much power over the neophytes to be antagonized by the Government, and when de Echeandia retired and was succeeded by

---

[10] Dwinelle, Colonial History of San Francisco, p. 41 and Addenda No. XIV, p. 25.

[11] Article 26 of Echeandia's "Secularization Decree" (Jan. 6, 1831), provided that "at Santa Cruz only *commissaries* and *majordomos* shall be chosen, the administration at present remaining with the Fathers."

[12] The governor was popular with a large class of men who expected to and did profit by his ill-advised handling of the Missions.

[13] Echeandia, *"plan para convertuen pueblos de los Missiones,"* 1829-1830, M. S. B. C.

Manuel Victoria, a clerical and reactionary official, the latter put a stop
to it.

The population declined rapidly at Santa Cruz Mission during this
decade,[14] as elsewhere, though in live stock the Mission about held its own,
and agriculture actually increased.

There was no *comisionado* in Branciforte in 1819. In 1822, the Villa
not having sufficient population of its own to have an *ayuntamiento,* was
attached to the civil jurisdiction of San Jose. Serafin Pinto became *alcalde*
in 1822, in 1826 Jose Joaquin Buelna, in 1827 Serafin Pinto again, in 1828
Comito Boronda, and in 1830 Francisco Rodriquez.

In 1826 it was transferred to the jurisdiction of Monterey, with the
ranchos of San Isidro and Las Animas.

The Villa doubled its population in this decade, from 75 to 150 in
1830. In that year the Villa had 2,500 head of cattle.

The health conditions seem to have been somewhat better here than
across the river, for Padre Gil wrote that the Indians were all impregnated
with venereal diseases, so that the slightest change of temperature prostrated them, and from sixty to eighty were sick at the same time.

It is regrettable to those who are true admirers of the work of the
Franciscan Fathers in Alta California, and endeavor to judge with minds
free of religious, racial or national prejudices, that these missionaries did
not withdraw from the field at the close of this decade, but waited until
they were actually forced to do so. Did they close their eyes to the actual
conditions and the inevitable consequences? Did they not sense that the
theory of the rights of man, including neophytes and Gentiles, was in the
air, coupled with endless charges as to the so-called sins of the Friars?
Apparently not, for instead of adopting a conciliatory attitude, a good part
of the decade between 1820 and 1830 was taken up with strife and bickerings between the Fathers and the lay authorities; between the missionaries
and the military; between the Fathers and the neophytes, and finally between the Fathers and the secular church authorities.

Though it was but natural that they lacked sympathy for the new
republican form of government, yet that form of government was the
expression of the will of the vast majority of the Mexican people in their
urge for political freedom. Other Spanish-speaking colonies on the American continent had revolted ere this, acquiring their freedom. The Fathers
had had sufficient time to readjust their viewpoint to the new trend of
things political, but, facing an accomplished fact after 1822, they remained
militant and irreconcilable to the new government and flag. Other Span-

---

[14] The Mission Indians understood by "freedom," no work, no punishments, liberty to
do exactly as they pleased, and unending support of never failing Mission supplies.

iards, who by training and birth, family relations and ideals had little sympathy with the new movement, discharged their duties to the old regime as long as possible; but then resolutely faced the inevitable and changed their allegiance, not only in name but in spirit.

The Fathers, who remained loyal to the irretrievably lost cause of Spain, were considered by the majority of their fellow Californians as enemies of liberty and traitors to the country in which they resided. That religious should have the same feelings as lay patriots and nationals is only natural; that the Fathers during the struggle for independence should be in favor of the land of their birth—in fact, stand pat, as the Tories did during the North American struggle for Independence—was likewise natural; it is more difficult to understand why they remained irreconciled to the government that sheltered them, especially after Spain had conceded defeat and recognized the independence of Mexico.

Duhaut-Cilly writes of his visit to Mission San Carlos (in 1827) as follows:

"Mission San Carlos is built upon a little bay, open to the southwest, and offering neither shelter nor anchorage. It is poor and almost depopulated of Indians. Padre Ramon Abila (the sudden bad weather having prevented him from re-embarking at Santa Cruz) had arrived by land. I found here also Padre Altimira, a young missionary, and Padre de Sarría, Prefect and head of all the Franciscans of California, a man of distinguished merit and great virtue.[15]

"At this time he was in utter disgrace among the Mexicans, for having refused to take the oath to the Constitution, and prevented his subordinates from consenting to it: he was also, in a manner, held as prisoner and kept in sight at San Carlos. The agents of the Mexican Government considering him, therefore, as the main obstacle to the submission of all the other missionaries, would have liked to send him back to Mexico. Commandant Gonzalez had already sought to sound my intentions, to learn if, on returning to Mazatlan, I would consent to take him; but I made that officer understand that, however disposed I was to do anything agreeable to his Government, I would never make myself the instrument for any act of violence toward whomever it might be; and that I would not take the padre *prefecto* aboard unless he himself asked me to do so. This good missionary had feared I might comply with the commandant's designs; and he showed me the liveliest gratitude when I disclosed to him my sentiments in this regard."

---

[15] Vicente Francisco de Sarria, born 1767, near Bilbao; came to California, 1809, at San Carlos, 1809-29, and at Soledad 1829-35; *comisario prefecto,* 1813-19, and 1823-30, president also, 1823-25; died 1835, and buried in the church at Mission San Antonio.

Public opinion in Mexico had turned permanently against forced Indian labor; unless the padres were willing to modify their views, their beloved institutions, the work of their hands and hearts, were bound to be swept to destruction by the ever-mounting flood of liberal ideas.

Their intentions were of the best, their aims were pure, and their conscience justified this course; many were martyrs of their loyalty to their Indian charges, but they did not seem to realize that a new period had arrived; that strangers of American, English and Russian blood were constantly filtering into the territory, marrying women of Spanish descent, and bringing with them new ideas, liberalizing the thoughts of the people; their only hope to save these Indians was by falling in step, guiding but not damming the stream. Perhaps they contemplated this, but considered it hopeless.

It is painful to read of the Mission Indian uprisings against the padre's rule, which they were taught by unscrupulous demagogues[16] to consider unjust, and consequently to resent bitterly; to read about the revolts along the Santa Barbara Channel, where Father Francisco Xavier Uria, at Santa Inez Mission, in February, 1824, shot (no doubt in self-defense) three Indians with his own hand,[17] and where the military, though their sympathy was divided, were compelled to kill sixteen more Indians in order to save the situation (March 16th, 1824, at Purissima); or to read about Ylario Garcia, *majordomo* of the Mission of San Diego, who was tried and convicted in 1830 of flogging a number of Indians so cruelly that one of them died.[18]

A report, dated May 5th, 1833, submitted by Mariano Guadalupe Vallejo, an ensign at Monterey (sent by Governor Figueroa to investigate certain charges made against the administration of Father Mercado at San Rafael Mission) is distressing indeed. In it Vallejo states:

". . . the Indians on the northern side of the bay were astonished at his coming among them in a friendly spirit and had received him as a great captain. For years past, as a rule, violence and injustice had been exercised towards them, to the shame of the Mission system and the scandal of religion. Under the circumstances, it was not surprising that they banded together and maintained a hostile attitude. Nothing else was to have been expected as a necessary consequence of the bad faith, the ill treatment and the sanguinary cruelty they had experienced from the missionaries, who had all the time been professing to be pursuing the method and following

---

[16] It was these same demagogues who robbed the Indians without mercy after the influence of the Fathers had been destroyed.

[17] Father Engelhardt denies this (Vol. III, p. 196), though other historians state these facts. Hittell, Vol. II, p. 60.

[18] Cal. Archives, D. S. P. III, 310.

the example of Jesus Christ! *'Que monstruosidades*—what monstrous pretensions!' 'It would not be difficult,' he continued, 'to relate particular instances of inhumanity which would petrify the most savage breast with horror; but he would reserve the sad recital for some other and more fitting opportunity in the future.'"[19]

Vallejo was a "liberal," and somewhat of a politician; still he was undoubtedly able and sincere, and afterwards proved himself to be an outstanding patriot.

It is likewise distressing to read about that preposterous episode at San Luis Obispo, where about the same time a quarrel took place between the corporal of the guard, Miguel Avila, and Father Luis Antonio Martinez—a fine priest but a man of violent temper. A disgraceful scene was enacted before the Indians, the padre trying to excommunicate the corporal, and the corporal tearing the book out of his hands. What thoughts must have passed through the minds of the neophytes!

Foreign books and papers were declared taboo; even the waltz was placed under the ban by the padre at Monterey, punishment by excommunication being threatened for those who indulged. The young people disregarded this threat at Monterey, as well as elsewhere.

One equally regrets to hear ecclesiastics justify the use of the lash as against the Governor who decided to abolish it. Perhaps the padres were more practical and right in the long run, but what an unfortunate position for ecclesiastics to place themselves in, and that in a country seething with modern ideas!

In 1832 Governor Figueroa notified Father Garcia Diego, the *Comisario* of the Zacatecan Friars, that whipping was forbidden by law. This priest was more in tune with the times, for he stated in referring to Vallejo's charges:

"The *alcaldes* of the Mission, seeing the just aversion which I have for whipping, and that when I came I commenced to abolish it, told me several times that if transgressions were not chastised as before, the Mission would be ruined. I replied that I had not come to change anything, and that they must perform their duty. In consequence of this, they, as well as the *majordomo,* inflicted a few lashes, but only a few times, because I always prevented it by means of the reasons which I gave to convince them. My mind, my ideas, my feelings are altogether opposed to this practice, which I shall never approve."[20]

---

[19] Cal. Archives, D. S. P. IX, 131.
[20] Archb. Arch. No. 2146.

Father Garcia Diego issued at once a long circular in which he forbade the Friars in his jurisdiction to use the lash in punishing the neophytes.

A Church historian, while acknowledging that the Father Prefect of the Zacatecan Friars took a high moral ground, asserts that he must have consulted theories rather than experience and the advice of those who had been in the ministry for a generation, and quotes with approval the answer of Father Jose Gutierrez, of San Francisco Solano, to the Governor's dispatch of May 13th, 1833, in which this ecclesiastic points out that he believes that whipping is the proper punishment for the "Indians that stay away from holy Mass, and do not come to be instructed in their Christian duties, and do not attend to their work, though there is so much to do. They run away to the mountains and stay there fifteen, nineteen and more days without letting me know. If we do away with flogging, with what punishment does your honor wish these transgressions to be chastised?"

There may be a good explanation for Father Guiterrez's attitude, but it is difficult for a layman to understand that a minister of the Gospel of the gentle Christ seems to approve of the application of the lash because the Indians declined to attend the holy Mass,[21] or were tired of working for a pittance in order to create wealth and support for the civil and military authorities and the missionary institutions.

Very likely the padres were right in claiming that corporal punishment of some kind was necessary to enforce obedience, but it seems doubtful judgment for religious to have advocated physical discipline for lack of obedience, when many of them had chosen the position of rebel against the established form of government of the country in which they lived, and that at a time when the province was seething with modern ideas!

---

[21] Attendance at church was compulsory in all Missions. The Indian *alcaldes* at the Missions searched the Indian huts for slackers, who, if found, were driven by rod and whip into the church. The men were placed generally on the left and the women on the right. Zealous officials were stationed in the passage ways with long sharp-pointed prods, to enforce silence and attention.

CHAPTER XXVII

The Situation During the Years 1830-1840;
Preparations for Secularization.

BOOK V

Chapter XXVII

The Situation During the Years 1830-1840; Preparations for Secularization

DURING this decade (1830-1840), California was in travail. The years were filled with tribulation, domestic quarrels, political dissensions, internecine battles and general turmoil. The difficulties were both of a secular and sacerdotal nature.

The secular troubles were partly due to a continual change of Governors, with their incompetence, their favorites, their inordinate vanity, and partly to quarrels and dissensions of their followers, resulting in a series of comic opera "wars" with grandiose gestures, proclamations and struttings, where much gun-powder and oratory were wasted, but little blood was spilled. (See Appendix No. 1.)

The sacerdotal troubles were due to the irreconcilable mental attitude to many of the missionaries, their inability to adapt themselves to the new conditions, and to the arrogance of the lay authorities towards them, causing much feeling of resentment.

In the fifty-four years of the Spanish-Mexican regime (1767 to 1821), California had known twelve Governors; one, de Arrillaga, acting twice. During the twenty-six years of the purely Mexican rule, or rather misrule, seventeen Governors and commandantes were appointed; four acted twice, and nine functioned in the last eleven years (1836-1847), the last three being mere figure-heads.

Whatever their faults, the Spanish-Mexican Governors, upholders of the best Spanish-Mexican traditions, were far superior to their Republican Mexican successors. The former were men of dignity and prestige; of strong personality, with great traditions supporting them; with long careers in the public service, mostly in Mexico, as preparation for their positions. They were supporters of Spanish ideals, as modified by Mexican conditions and aspirations, while the latter were mostly political opportunists.

José María de Echeandia, the second Mexican Governor, was succeeded in January, 1831, by Lieutenant Colonel Manuel Victoria, who arrived at Monterey on January 29th. He was half Indian, a friend of the clergy and opposed to secularization. He stopped its progress during his rule, and was supported by Carlos Carillo, Alta California member of the Mexican Congress. He endeavored to proceed without the representatives of the people, and undid much that de Echeandia had accomplished. His rule was short, for after considerable commotion and some little bloodshed he was driven away.

De Echeandia again took charge, and remained in office until January 14th, 1833, when there commenced a bewildering succession of Governors, until the advent of Juan Bautista Alvarado, who assumed office on December 7th, 1836.

In these three years eight Governors occupied the chair: Pio Pico, Agustin Zamorano, José Figueroa, José Castro, Nicolas Gutierrez, Mariano Chico, Gutierrez (again), and José Castro (second time).

Few of their tenures were free from conspiracy and revolts. Sometimes the revolts originated at Los Angeles (against Figueroa), sometimes at Monterey (against Chico); sometimes they were organized by the southern part of the province against the northern, and vice versa; sometimes by one practical patriot against the other. All prominent *caballeros* took part in the political cockpit; each proclaimed lofty patriotic sentiments, and tried to seize for himself, his family and his henchmen the power and the emoluments going therewith; their bombastic talk was only the sauce that went with the usual blue-plate political dinner, but the substance on the plate was the rich food, consisting of the wealth of the to-be-secularized Missions and the Government lands. If one were *persona grata* with the Governor, that meant that much land and cattle (the local standard of wealth) could be obtained. There were different ways to accomplish this; for instance, one Governor "loaned" Mission cattle to private land owners, upon condition that a like number be returned some time later. Generally the latter part of the bargain was conveniently overlooked.

The comical part of all the wars, rebellions, revolts and military demonstrations was the "Chinese paper and silk umbrella phase."

The Alvarados, Vallejos, Arguellos, Pachecos, Estudillos, Picos, Castros, de la Guerras, Carillos, Peñas, Estradas, de la Cuestas, Osios, Gonzalez, Requenas, Del Valles, Martinez, Peraltas, Bandinis, Avilas, etc., most of them owners of enormous ranchos, were all so closely allied by blood or marriage ties, and had so many interests, difficult to defend and easy to damage, that they shrank from seriously hurting one another.

Great lamentations were heard in the land, when on December 5th, 1831, José María Avila, *ex-alcalde* of Los Angeles, meeting a grandiose charge of Captain Rumualdo Pacheco[1] on Governor Victoria, shot the former through the heart. Victoria fled, and Avila, carried away by his

---

[1] Captain Rumualdo Pacheco was the father of Governor Pacheco—the only "native" Governor after the American conquest. He was born at Santa Barbara.

first exploit, made the mistake of pursuing the Governor, but was killed in the melee.

In 1833 Brigadier-General Jose de Figueroa, a Mexican by birth, but half Aztec Indian, a leader with a strong, heavy hand, courageous and quite an orator, took charge as Governor. He proved liberal in policy and a good friend of the foreign residents. He needed plenty of wisdom, for the sacerdotal troubles had multiplied.

Since 1810 demands had been continuously made on the padres for the support of the State authorities; but such demands made by Spaniards of the royalist regime, who fully recognized the dignity of priesthood, were very much less irksome than those of the Mexican Governors, with their personal pride and desire to make use of their office for personal gain.

The ancient College of San Fernando was on the verge of collapse, having been deserted by Guardian Jose Gasol in 1824. In 1828 it was under the direction of a *Vicario de casa,* and only inhabited by three priests, two invalid Spaniards and a few servants.

It is therefore no wonder that the College in such a state of disorganization ceded to another College of Franciscans—Nuestra Senora de Guadalupe de Zacatecas—the Missions in the northern part of California, and at the direction of the Mexican Government, ten of these Friars, called Guadalupanos or Zacatecanos, sailed on July 17th, 1832, from San Blas to accompany the newly-appointed Governor Jose Figueroa to Monterey. The new Fathers were all natives of Mexico. They had considerable trouble in reaching California Alta, for Figueroa's troops revolted while the ship was at Loreto, stole most of the treasure chest, and returned to San Blas. Finally, however, with the Governor and about thirty soldiers, they arrived at their destination on January 14th, 1833.

These Friars, under the supervision of a prelate known as Prefect Francisco Garcia Diego, who resided at Santa Clara, were assigned to the seven Missions from San Carlos northward, therefore including the Santa Cruz Mission, to which Father Antonio Surez del Real was delegated.

From that time on the Missions in Alta California had two prelates supervising them—the Father President of the Fernandinos, who had charge of the southern Missions, and the Father Prefect of the Zacatecanos, who had charge of the northern Missions. They seem to have co-operated in a friendly spirit.

Bancroft declares that as a class the Zacatecanos were by no means the equal, morally or intellectually, of their predecessors, and this is proven by their later actions.

The most serious complaint against them was brought about by Padre Mercado in the notorious San Rafael Mission case. The Friar apparently was of a quarrelsome nature. He had trouble with Corporal Ignacio Pacheco of the *escolta*. He used intemperate and insulting language both to Pacheco and his soldiers, calling them a pack of thieves, and in turn was charged with falsehood.

Troubles arose between the Father and some strange Indians, and the former sent out his *majordomo,* Molina, with thirty-seven armed neophytes, who surprised the Gentile Indians, killed twenty-one, wounded many more, and captured twenty women and children. Father Mercado reported this on the 25th of November, 1833, to Governor Figueroa, who sent Vallejo to investigate. The Governor referred the case to Prefect Garcia Diego, who called Father Mercado for trial, and suspended him from his ministry. Eventually the padre was restored to his Mission.

While sojourning at the Mexican capital, Figueroa had received minute instructions, which included the re-establishment of tranquillity, the question of secularization, a report about the country and about enfranchisement of the neophytes, the division of the lands among them, observation of the Russians and the Americans, etc. Moreover, he was required to report on the movements of Fathers Sarría and Duran, both being suspected of disloyalty towards the new Government.

Figueroa proceeded to make the investigations, and came to the conclusion that, while he favored general secularization, the change must come very gradually, as otherwise it would be ruinous. (See Appendix No. 2.) He reported both to the Mexican Government and to President Duran, and Father Francisco Garcia Diego, the Prefect. While neither of them approved, he did suggest the partial secularization of eight Missions, including Santa Cruz.[2]

Figueroa favored this plan, but apparently he acted too slowly, for even before his report was received, the Mexican Congress, on August 17th, 1833, issued a decree ordering the long-deferred disestablishment.

It was decreed that the Governor should proceed to secularize the Missions of both the Californias; that each Mission should constitute a parish to be served by a curate or secular priest with an annual salary of $2,000 to $2,500,[3] and no fees for marriages, baptisms, or any other nature, except that fees might be charged for processions, but only according to a list approved both by the Bishops and the Government; that the Mission churches with their ornaments should serve as parish churches, and each have $500 annually for the maintenance of public worship; that the Government should cause to be laid out for each parish a grave yard *(campo santo);* that of the Mission buildings, the most suitable with tract of

[2] Bancroft, History of California, Vol. III, p. 335.
[3] Hittell, History of California, Vol. II, p. 182, Halleck's Report, App. 13.

ground not exceeding two hundred varas square in extent should be appropriated for the residence of the curate, and others for the town house, primary schools and other public purposes. The establishment of a Vicarship, with jurisdiction over the two Californias, was ordered; $3,000 appropriated as an endowment for this office, and the Vicar was required to fulfill his duties without charging fees.

Further orders for the government under the new system and provision for salaries and expenses of the curates, diocesan and missionaries who moved about, completed the decree, this bringing them within the general operation of the secular laws, and especially a number of departmental laws, such as the Colonization Law of 1824 and the Regulations Act of 1828.[4] Finally, it provided that all expenses should be paid out of the Pious Fund.

Before this was carried out, the Mexican Congress issued a new decree on April 16th, 1834, ordering that all the Missions in the Republic be secularized and converted into curacies, and that the limits of these curacies should be designated by the Governors of the respective States.

As soon as the decrees reached California, Governor Figueroa and the *diputación* immediately went to work, and at the session of July 31st, 1834, adopted the plan by which the secularization of the Missions of Alta California was to be carried into effect.[5]

This plan, called the *Prevenciónes de Emancipación provisionales de Indios reducidos,* had rules which did not differ materially from the plan of de Echeandia.

The missionaries were exonerated from the administration of temporalities and were to confine themselves to the functions of the spiritual ministry until parishes could be established and curates appointed by the Government and the Diocesan. The territorial government was to administer the properties and distribute them among the neophytes, according to a system of distribution which the supreme government would be asked to approve.

Each head of a family or male person over twenty was entitled to receive from the common lands of the Missions a cultivable lot not more than four hundred varas, nor less than one hundred varas square. Each was to have the right of sufficient pasture for his cattle on common lands to be assigned to each pueblo.

Municipal lands should be set aside when convenient, while one-half of the cattle belonging to the Missions, according to the latest reports of

---

[4] Ex. Doc. of the N. E., XVII, 138, U. S. Printed Miss. Exhibit.
[5] Hittell, History of California, Vol. II, 185-186.

the missionaries, and one-half of the farming implements and seed grains, were to be distributed in a proportionable and equitable manner at the discretion of the Governor, among the individuals entitled to fields for cultivation.

The church of each Mission was to remain as such, and with its library, sacred vestments, ornaments, vessels and furniture was to continue under the control of the missionary padre, who was to choose a residence from among the buildings, which suited him best for his own habitation, and that of his servants and attendants; and he was to be furnished with the necessary furniture and implements.

The remainder of the lands and other property of each Mission was to be placed in charge of a *majordomo* or other officer named by the Governor, and was to be held by him subject to the disposal of the supreme Federal government. Out of the proceeds of such property the substances of the Mission padres, the expenses and pay of the *majordomo* and other employees, and the expenses of the religious worship, police and public works were to be paid.

It was further provided that no one should be able to sell or encumber his land or property, and in case an owner died without heirs, his lands were to revert to the State.

The plan further provided that the new Mission pueblos should be organized according to law; that the political chief should make regulations for the establishment of *ayuntamientos,* which were to have control of municipal affairs, and that the administration of justice should remain subject to the jurisdiction of the courts of first instance. Until further order, the emancipated Indians were to be required to perform in common the labors indispensably necessary for the cultivation of the fields, gardens and vineyards still held undivided, and also such personal services as might be necessary to assist the curates. To carry out these provisions the political chief, *jefe politico,* in casu the Governor, was authorized to name commissioners and give them such instructions as he might deem necessary; and meanwhile the missionaries were prohibited from slaughtering cattle, except such as might be necessary for the subsistence of the neophytes.[6]

The plan thus adopted by the *diputacion* was issued by Figueroa on August 9th, 1834; and he added to it a series of rules and regulations for carrying it into effect. He directed that the commissioners or stewards, immediately upon appointment, should go to their respective Missions, present their credentials to the missionaries, and proceed to make out

[6] Cal. Archives, L. R. II, 19-22.

OLD ADOBE HOUSES, WHICH TRADITION SAYS WERE USED AS
GUARDHOUSE OF SOLDIERS AT MISSION SANTA CRUZ

complete inventories of all the properties, specifying churches, houses, shops, structures, furniture, utensils, implements, fruit trees, shrubs, vines, vegetables, stock of all kinds, and also fine property of every description. These inventories were to be kept from the knowledge of the missionaries. The Indians were to be informed that the Missions were changed into pueblos; that they themselves were thenceforth to be under the government of the missionaries in spiritual matters only, and that the land and property to be assigned to each one was to belong to himself and to be maintained and controlled by himself, without depending on any other person. The distribution of lands was to take place immediately under the supervision of the commissioner, the missionary and a *majordomo,* who was to be nominated by the commissioner and approved by the Government; and at the same time the necessary implements of labor and seeds were to be distributed. It was further directed that the missionaries should immediately cease to act as such, and that the neophyte children, both male and female, whom "they kept locked up like lambs in a fold," should be delivered over to their fathers, who were to be instructed in their duties and obligations as parents. A settlement of more than twenty-five families at a distance from a Mission was to be entitled to form a separate pueblo and have lands and property like the others; but, if the settlement was smaller, it should form a suburb and be attached to the nearest pueblo. And for the purpose of organizing the new pueblos as soon as possible, the commissioners were to report a census of each community in order to designate the number of municipal offices and cause elections to be held to fill them.[7]

If the Missions as such ceased to exist theoretically and as a matter of law on the passage of the secularization law of August 17th, 1833, they may be said to have ceased to exist as a matter of fact on the promulgation of the foregoing plan and regulations of August 9th, 1834. Figueroa immediately named commissioners, who in accordance with the plan and instructions proceeded to the various Missions and began carrying out the new system. Inventories were drawn up, and partial distributions of land and property made. The Indians were to all intents and purposes regarded as emancipated, the missionaries as superseded, and the Missions as in effect transformed into Indian pueblos.

Several members of the territorial legislature, or the *diputacion,* now managed to obtain appointments to the commissionerships. Pio Pico, for instance, became *comisionado* of Mission San Luis Rey; Carlos A. Carillo secured San Buenaventura; Jose Tiburcio Castro obtained possession of Mission San Juan Bautista; Juan Bandini received Mission San Gabriel;

---

[7] Cal. Archives, M. & C. II, p. 363.

Mariano Guadalupe Vallejo assumed direction at Mission San Francisco Solano.

Most of the commissioners and other officials, whose duty it became to administer the properties of the Missions, and especially their great numbers of cattle, horses, sheep and other animals, thought of little else than enriching themselves. It cannot be said that the spoliation was immediate; but it was certainly very rapid. A few years sufficed to strip the establishments of everything of value and leave the Indians, who were in contemplation of law the beneficiaries of secularization, a shivering crowd of naked and so-to-speak homeless wanderers upon the face of the earth.[8]

The priests had no longer any power except in their religious character, and the great possessions of the Missions were given over to harpies of the civil power, who usually ended in a few years by making fortunes and leaving their stewardships worse than they found them.

On November 3rd the *diputacion* passed regulations dividing the territory into curacies, making two classes of them. Santa Cruz with San Juan Bautista[9] were declared curacies of the second class, being conjoined, the curate to receive a salary of one thousand dollars. Until further order, the missionaries were to act as curates, each to receive in addition to his salary $500 for expenses of public worship. Prefect Father Francisco Garcia Diego was to reside at Monterey; his salary was to be $3,000.

At once complications arose. According to Article 16 of the Plan, the Indians should be obliged to join in the cultivation of vineyards, gardens and fields which, for the present, remained unapportioned. This was a qualified emancipation, of which the Indians were suspicious; no wonder that out of one hundred and sixty Indian families at San Diego, to whom this kind of emancipation was offered by the lay officers, only ten could be induced to accept this very much qualified boon of freedom.

Father Duran, of the Fernandinos, did all in his power to soften the blow to the Mission priests under him. He sent a long circular to the Fathers, urging them to have patience and to comply with the conditions of the law. It is no wonder that they felt a deep sense of wrong, for as Father Duran expressed it: "We can never consent to be servile dependents to the gentlemen who have come to enjoy the fruits of our labor and hardships, and who have come to direct and manage certain advantages, the creating of which has caused them no trouble, but on the contrary, whose principal and perhaps entire business is to exclusively enjoy as well the fruit of our personal labor as the value of the voluntary donation which we have made of our stipends in favor of the Indian communities."

---

[8] Hittell, History of California, Vol. II, pp. 206-207.
[9] Later charged to Santa Cruz and Branciforte.

At this time, of the twenty-seven missionaries still laboring in the field of Alta California, seventeen were Fernandinos and ten Zacatecanos. Most of them, especially the former, had become old and infirm. It would also appear that the Fernandinos were less reconciled to the change in their conditions than the Zacatecanos, for the Father Guardian of the Zacateca College, while forwarding a copy of the Mexican secularization law of August 17th, 1833, congratulated Fr. Garcia Diego and his nine companions with the change, and directed them to comply with the regulations, and on arrival of the secular priests to retire to their College.

Shortly before the secularization up to 1832, 87,787 natives had been baptized, or as one religious writer expresses it: "The Friars had brought the truths of the Gospel and the means of salvation to nearly 86,000 natives, of whom about 63,789 by death had already gone beyond the reach of perversion, leaving still about 24,634 neophytes, of which 16,951 were under the spiritual care of the twenty-seven surviving missionaries."[10]

Six thousand eight hundred and twenty-two were either fugitives or dead and unreported. The Mexican census of 1831 gave the number of inhabitants of the entire Mexican Republic as 6,382,264, estimating that of Alta California at 27,000, and that of Baja California at 15,000. In all these calculations the Gentile or wild Indians were an unknown factor.

It seems probable, taking the most reliable accounts as a basis, that the Indian population of the two Californias (both neophytes and Gentiles) never exceeded 60,000 or 70,000 in the conquered area, and that in what is now the State of California as a whole, there may have been as many as 130,000.[11]

All these calculations are, of course, partly based on guess work, politely known as "estimation," but it seems a reasonable deduction that the Indian population between 1770 and 1830 had remained about the same in the conquered area;[12] after the secularization the decrease was rapid.[13]

Duflot de Mofras recorded that in 1834, when a disease broke out resembling cholera, 12,000 Indians died in the Tulare Country, and that in 1836, on the appearance of a contagious fever, nearly 8,000 died in the

---

[10] See Engelhardt Missions, Vol. III, p. 653.

[11] In 1881, Helen Hunt Jackson said that there were only 300,000 Indians in all the United States.

[12] The conquered or occupied area was only a part of the present State. Its boundaries were uncertain and changing, but considerably less than one-half of the present State was actually occupied by the white men prior to 1834.

[13] Dr. C. Hart Merriam, in an essay which is quoted by Dr. A. L. Kroeber, comes to the conclusion that the number of converted Indians, 1834, of the total number of 130,000, were about 25,000. To justify this he mentions the enormous mortality which had taken place at some of the Missions.

Sacramento Valley; but at the same time he estimated that this fearful mortality was due in great part to syphilitic predisposition. The same author stated that in 1842 the neophyte population was only 4,450, or about one-seventh of what it had been in 1834.

In 1842 the Indians of Alta California were estimated by Wilkes to be 8,000 or 9,000, and by Robinson 10,000.

CHAPTER XXVIII

The Situation During the Years 1830-1840
Continued; Secularization of the Santa
Cruz Mission and the Land Titles.

BOOK V

Chapter XXVIII

*The Situation During the Years 1830-1840, Continued; Secularization
of the Santa Cruz Mission and the Land Titles*

IN 1830 the Santa Cruz Mission was prosperous. The official reports
for that year showed the following figures: cattle, 3,600; horses, 400;
mules, 25; sheep, 5,211.

When the secularization began the Pueblo Mission was in the initial
stage of civil government, for in January, 1831, Father Jose Joaquin
Jimeno reported the election of a neophyte *alcalde* and *regidores,* as approved by the Governor.

The padre continued in charge until 1833, when he was transferred
to Santa Inez and succeeded by Padre Antonio Suarez del Real, one of the
new Zacatecan Friars, who remained throughout the secularization period
and the decade.

Prior to 1833 no grants of adjoining land in the Santa Cruz region
had bothered the padres—very likely the troubles with the Brancifortians
were sufficient. But in this year the first grants in Santa Cruz County were
made: San Andreas Rancho to Joaquin Castro; Aptos Ranchos to Rafael
Castro; Soquel Rancho[1] to Martina Castro; Calabazas Rancho[2] to Felipe
Henandez.[3]

On August 22nd, 1834, Ignacio del Valle took charge under the
orders of Governor Figueroa. Del Valle gave the former Mission Pueblo
the name of Pueblo de Figueroa, and likewise gave Spanish surnames to
all the neophytes.

On September 15th, 1834, Padre del Real, having given up the Mission, asked the Governor for a house, grain and other supplies for himself
and the horses, wine for worship, Indian assistants for the care of the
church, a division of the goods in store, and an assurance that the *comision-*

---

[1] Soquel is an Indian name, the meaning of which is unknown.

[2] *Calabazas*—means calabash, or water gourd, which grew wild there.

[3] The Mexican authorities had begun to use California as a penal colony in 1824.
Eighteen arrived in 1825, including Solis, mentioned in Chapter XXV. In 1826
over a hundred had been sent and in 1830 eighty came in one ship load. In 1831
Jose Maria Padres, with the assistance of Jose Maria Hyar, engineered another
colonization project and 120 colonists of the better class arrived in July, 1834, in
two ships. Governor Figueroa made a number of land grants to individual settlers
and by his order the town of Sonoma was founded by Vallejo. Soon thereafter
Figueroa died. He was a progressive governor—one of the best California had
under Mexican rule.

ado would not prejudice the Indians against the padre.[4]

On October 24th, the Governor ordered that Del Valle settle the Mission accounts at once, and arrange for the delivery of thirteen blankets for the troops at Santa Cruz.[5] No longer could the *escolta* depend upon the long-suffering Mission for supplies as before.

On October 31st, Figueroa wrote his approval of the appointment of Juan Gonzalez as *majordomo* at a salary of $40, exclusive of rations.[6]

In November the padre insisted upon having ten rooms and the granary for a stable, but the Governor decided that he might have only the rooms actually needed, and that the granary could not be spared; on the 17th of the same month Del Valle reported that he had selected a room for the *ayuntamiento* (Town Council of the Pueblo), one for the secretary, and one for a school.[7]

In 1834,[8] when the property was secularized, there were standing around the plaza twenty buildings within the square of the Mission and fifteen outside of it. The largest of these buildings was in length sixty varas, in breadth fourteen varas (a vara being about three feet), and was valued at $3,500. The various buildings contained workshops and manufactories, in which were produced nearly every article of mechanism necessary to the country. The work was mostly performed by skilled Indians under the supervision of the priests.

There was a vast amount of paraphernalia in the sacristies, consisting of tabernacles, crucifixes, statues, musical instruments, images, chalices, vestments, vessels and jewelry, valued at $7,500. Only a few of these articles remained in the church.[9] Fortunately, some of these valuable articles have been recovered and are now (1933) at the restored Mission church.

From the founding of the Mission in 1791 until the secularization of 1834, the total statistics were:

Baptisms, 2,466, of which 1,277 were Indian adults, 939 Indian children, 6 adults *de razon,* and 244 white children. The annual average of baptisms was 50.

Marriages, 847, of which 63 were of white couples.

Deaths, 2,025; 1,359 Indian adults, 574 Indian children, 45 adults *de razon,* and 47 white children. Annual average of deaths was 44, making an average rate of 10.93 per cent of the population.

---

[4] Sta. Cruz Rec. M. S. 23, B. C.

[5] Sta. Cruz Rec. M. S. 18, B. C.

[6] Sta. Cruz Rec. M. S. 12, B. C.

[7] St. Pap. Miss. M. S. IX 70-69 B. C.

[8] In 1834 administrators were appointed for 10 of the missions; in 1835 six more, and in 1836 five for the remaining missions.

[9] Hayes Mission Book I, 130 B. C.

The largest population was 644, in 1798. The males were always in excess of the females.

The largest number of cattle was 3,700, in 1828; horses, 900, in 1828; mules, 92, in 1805; sheep, 8,300, in 1826; swine, 150, in 1818; of all kinds of animals, 12,502, in 1827.

The total product of wheat was 69,900 bushels; yield 146-fold.

Beans, 9,250 bushels, yield 57-fold. Miscellaneous grains, 7,600 bushels; yield 28-fold.

The neophyte population had fallen to 250 in 1834, but there was no marked loss in live stock or agriculture up to that time.

The ex-neophytes were now to enjoy every privilege of citizenship, even to the founding of families of Spanish name, who were to keep the pueblo populated and loyal to the Mexican Government.

The secularization of Santa Cruz by 1835 was considered more complete than at most other establishment.[10]

The inventory, dated December 1st, 1835, is as follows:

Buildings	$16,940
Furniture, etc.	478
Implements, machinery, etc.	2,163
Huerta, with 1,210 vines and 1,024 fruit trees	2,173
Live stock at the Mission	1,051
Live stock, with tools at rancho	17,581
Effects in store house	3,291
Produce	5,176
Credits	3,338
Total	$52,191
Debt	4,979
Balance	$47,212

Church property as follows:

Church building	8,050
Ornaments, bells, cannons, etc.	23,505
Library of 152 volumes	386
Total	$31,931

The live stock noted above consisted of 3,700 cattle, 500 horses, 2,900 sheep, 18 mules, 10 asses, 28 swine.

The chief debtor was the National Treasury.

---

[10] Bancroft, Cal., Vol. III, p. 696.

During the year 1835, Figueroa had devised a plan for establishing separate ranchos at each Mission for the support of the padre and of public worship. A beginning was made at San Carlos and Santa Cruz, but on his death the scheme was carried no further.

Branciforte and Santa Cruz (or Figueroa) were to form ecclesiastically a parish of the second class, and Padre Real continued as the priest in charge until 1844, or even later.

From this time on the annals are scattered and few, and only serve to show how quickly the hard and faithful work of years may be overturned by the rude grasp of a despoiler in a moment. The rule of Governor Alvarado, from 1836 to 1842, was a period of further plunder and ruin of most California Missions.

When the property was valued in 1835, $47,000 seemed a just inventory. Only $10,000 of this was turned over to the Indians at the time, and there is no further record of distributions, or how the estate disappeared.

In March, 1836, the Governor found it necessary to issue orders that the Indians must comply with their church duties.[11] Already it appears the new Mexican citizens were falling into "Gentile" ways and were again becoming wild. (See Appendix No. 1.)

Mission property and some new produce was regularly shipped off; therefore in 1836 Spear's lighter was running between Santa Cruz and San Francisco, using the beach as a loading and unloading place.

The report dated April 22nd, 1837, gives the live stock as 1,000 cattle, 460 horses, 2,000 sheep, 22 mules, and 16 asses; 70 *fanegas* of grain; credits, $3,040; debits to Russian American Company and N. Spear, $594.

On March 11th, 1839, the receipts since the beginning of 1838 from the sale of hides was $1,120; expenditures for salaries, $1,465; besides cattle and horses, delivered on the order of the Government.

Francisco Soto had succeeded Gonzales as administrator in January, and in October he was ordered to turn over the property to Jose Bolcoff, the *juez de paz,* but did not do so at once.

On October 7th, 1839, *Visitador* William Hartnell, a high-class man, whose duty it was to inspect the ex-Missions throughout the State, found only seventy Indians at the Mission, with perhaps as many more scattered in the Santa Cruz district, and about one-sixth only of the former inventory of stock.

The remaining Indians were fearful of and dissatisfied with the administrator and were clamoring for liberty and a final distribution of the property. They particularly wished to retain Rancho El Refugio and

---

[11] Sta. Cruz Rec. M. S. 6, B. C.

the Mission *huerta,* which the padre also desired. The ex-neophytes became very bitter against the administrator, and Jose Antonio Rodriquez aspired to the position.[12]

There were only 36 cattle, 127 horses and 1,026 sheep left of all the great herds and flocks that had been listed in 1834.

Juez de paz Jose Bolcoff took charge this year (1839) or the next. (See Appendix No. 2.)

Though the Pueblo de Figueroa had come into existence, at least on paper, no records were ever found of the organization of a real pueblo. The Mission of Santa Cruz had passed out of existence, and with it the beneficent influence of the padres on the Indians.

In the same year (1839) the Indians became more unruly. Eugenio Soto was murdered, and the killing by the guards of some evil-doers in Branciforte, who resented being taken to San Juan, started more trouble, which had repercussions in several parts of the State.

The ruin of Santa Cruz Mission had been ostensibly completed in six years; in fact, it had begun long ere 1834, through the unending requisitions of the military and civil authorities, which caused the neophytes to be overworked and resulted in dissatisfaction.[13]

Most of the other Missions had likewise ceased to function as such, or were near disintegration. Had the original ideas of secularization been carried out, little complaint could have been made, for right from the beginning Spain had always insisted that the original children of the soil should be the final beneficiaries of the efforts of the missionaries.

The Mission system had lost accord with the times. It could not be continued as it was operated. It had done very well during the "reduction period," the taming of the wilderness, but now it had become antiquated under the prevailing circumstances. It could not be rejuvenated, for the Colleges had lost their power; they had been stripped of men, property and influence; too many new currents of thought had entered the field. A change had therefore become inevitable, and it was intended to effect the liberation of the Indians, gradually and cautiously, under the guidance of the public authorities, with the advice of their old mentors, the padres.

But ideals are one thing and acts of men on plunder bent are a totally different matter; besides, a certain class of politicians the world over

---

[12] Hartnell Diario, MS. 8, 44.
[13] On December 7, 1843, Father Antonio Real wrote to Father Lorenzo Quijas, Vice *Comisario* of the Missions in the North, a pitiful letter beginning: "Your Paternity is not ignorant of the critical situation in which this poor church and its priest find themselves, since they are without funds and even without an Indian to ring the bells." Engelhardt, "Missions and Missionaries of California," Vol. IV, p. 297.

have never been known to be scrupulous about the disposal of confiscated property, or property in receivership.

The neophytes were now free; that is, free to choose between independence, which for most of these incompetents meant starvation after a short period of squandering and feasting, or dependence on the new landlords, which meant far worse servitude than they had been subjected to at the Missions.

The lay authorities had also to deal with the question of land grants. In the beginning of the Mission period there were no grants of land for the so-called private ranchos. True, the Laws of the Indies provided for settlement of the new countries, and in 1775 Governor Rivera made one grant for a rancho to Manuel Butrón, but this grant was soon abandoned. Afterwards, under Governor Fages, the question was revived and certain grants were made around Los Angeles. Care was taken that no lands were sold off or assigned without the approval of the Friars, who as a rule showed determined opposition, as they regarded it as an infringement on the territorial rights of the Missions, and also as inviting neophyte insubordination through corruption.

The Spanish regime was therefore cautious in the granting of such lands, only twenty being granted up to 1823, and these to select, dependable men, loyal to the Crown and Church.

Under the Mexican rule, after the enactment of the naturalization and colonization laws of 1824 and 1828, a marked change took place. By 1830 there were fifty, and by 1840 six hundred, of these land holdings.

At first the land grantees were men of established families, often of good education and of a totally different class from the colonists who had been sent out by the Governors to the pueblos.

On the Santa Barbara Channel the Ortegas lived on the Rancho del Refugio, where their daughter, Doña Maria, married Don Luis Arguello in 1822; many other prominent families also had acquired important land grants.

These properties were, almost without exception, ranchos where cattle, horses, mules and sheep were raised, and the ranchero was an expert horseman and cavalier, riding among his wild stock. They were a brave, romantic, spectacular lot of men, with little business acumen; quick to take offense, loving equestrian rivalry, bull and bear fights, *matanzas* and rodeos, swinging their *riatas* with consummate skill when on horseback, and when in town draping a *serape* about their shoulders and carrying a sword under the arm. They formed a kind of feudal land owners class.

Births, christenings, betrothals, weddings and what not were the motives for extensive festivities, including barbecues, the graceful Spanish dances, etc.

All work at the town houses and on the ranchos had to be performed by hand, mechanical appliances being almost unknown. The actual household alone, combined with the work of carting, weaving, laundrying, soap making, meat curing, etc., and the extensive entertaining, took a large retinue of servants. The owners and their sons and their relatives and friends did not think of demeaning themselves with work. They had the tradition of the true *gachupines* (wearer of spurs) that a gentleman never soils his hands, and to the Indians fell the lot to provide all the necessary labor.

Perhaps the report which gives us the clearest view of Alta California was written by a young student of Harvard College, Richard Henry Dana, born in Cambridge, Massachusetts, on August 2nd, 1815. His father was a distinguished man of letters, and his grandfather, Francis Dana, had been the first American Minister to Russia, and later Chief Justice of the Supreme Court of Massachusetts. When sixteen years old, young Dana entered Harvard College, but after his third year, an attack of measles affected his eye-sight and further study was impossible. He thereupon decided on a sea voyage and shipped as a sailor from Boston, August 14th, on the brig *Pilgrim,* bound for the coast of California. His experiences covered two years.

After he returned to Boston in 1836, he re-entered Harvard, was graduated, became a lawyer, and in 1840 opened an office in Boston. In 1841 he published his famous book, "Two Years Before the Mast."

Dana had a fresh, and probably entirely unbiased, outlook on the conditions which he found in California. He was remarkably observant, and had the ability of reducing his observations to lucid and simple English. He often goes into the smallest details, and while some of his predictions did not become true, this must be ascribed to the young man's lack of experience. His book shows here and there the generosity of heart with the intolerance of the mind inherent to youth, but his observations give a truer picture of the conditions of California generally, and of the *gente de razon* particularly, in 1834-36 than any other chronicle. He wrote:

"We came to anchor within two cable lengths of the shore, and the town (of Monterey) lay directly before us, making a very pretty appearance; its houses being plastered, which gives a much better effect than those of Santa Barbara, which are of mud color. The red tiles, too, of the roofs contrasted well with the white plastered sides and the extreme green-ness of the lawn upon which the houses—about an hundred in number—were dotted about here and there, irregularly."

He remarks that in this, as in every other town which he saw in California, there were no streets or fences, and that the houses were all one story high.

Before reaching Monterey, Dana had visited Point Conception, coming up from Santa Barbara, and he correctly remarks that Conception is the dividing line between two different faces of the country, northward the country becoming more wooded, having a richer appearance and being better supplied with water, while to the south, as at Santa Barbara, San Pedro, and particularly San Diego, there was very little wood, the country having a naked, level appearance, though still being very fertile.

Among the *gente de razon* at Monterey Dana found several persons who spoke English. They were all English or Americans who had married and settled there. He observed that they had all become Catholics, as that was the only way for them to live peaceably in the country. He tells us that the Californians were notoriously thriftless and improvident, importing all they needed and manufacturing nothing for themselves; that while there was plenty of leather, they had to import their shoes, and while having plenty of grapes, they had to import their wine, and he says that the firm of Bryant, Sturgis & Company, owners of the *Pilgrim,* imported nearly two-thirds of the articles required.

He found that amongst the *gente de razon,* a small part of Spanish blood, if it be only in a quadroon or octoroon, was sufficient to raise a person from the rank of Indians, and that the complexions were various, depending on the amount of Spanish blood they could lay claim to. Those of pure Spanish blood, he says, were far from numerous in California, but were mostly all in official stations, or otherwise on the expiration of their offices, had settled on the property which they had acquired.

Dana observed that they formed the aristocracy and always intermarried, keeping up an exclusive system and speaking the pure Castilian language, and that from this upper class the Californians went down by regular shades and complexions, growing more and more dark and muddy, until one came to the pure Indian, who ran about with nothing on but a small piece of cloth.

He was enchanted by the beauty of the voices and intonations of both sexes, with the dignity of even a ruffian-looking fellow, and with the excessive fondness for dress of the women.

He remarks that no Protestant had any civil right nor could own any property, nor could remain more than a few weeks ashore, unless he belonged to some vessel, and he says that he has heard that all Americans or

English who intended to remain in the country became Catholics, the current phrase being: "A man must leave his conscience at Cape Horn."

He reflects on the laziness of the *caballeros,* stating that the Indians did all the hard work, several of them being attached to each house; that all kept Indian slaves, who only received coarse food, and as clothing, the men wore a piece of cloth and a belt, and the women a coarse gown without shoes or stockings.

It gave him pleasure to note that the chief *alcaldes* in Monterey and Santa Barbara were Yankees by birth, but he says they married natives to allay suspicion and brought up their children as Mexicans, not even teaching them the English language.

With the valor of youth, Dana announces that "nothing but the character of the people prevents Monterey from becoming a great town." Almost one hundred years have passed since then, the people have changed greatly, but Monterey is still a lovely village, while other villages have grown into large cities.

One is left with the impression that the native citizenry of California did not exactly consist of sturdy, industrious families, keen merchants or forward-looking men, but to the contrary, in the sixty-five years which had passed since California had been settled, first by the Spanish and then by the Mexicans, the country as such, except for the efforts of the missionaries, had made exceedingly little progress. Its inhabitants consisted of grand *seigneurs* of Castilian blood, of Mexican or Spanish descent, and of a small number of foreign traders who enthusiastically took advantage of all the rest, of a lazy lot of people of mixed Indian and Spanish blood, of indentured Indians, and of Gentiles or so-called wild Indians.

The nearest rancho to the Santa Cruz Mission was the Soquel Rancho, owned by Martina Castro, a daughter of Maria Antonia Amador and Joaquin Castro, a soldier in the Spanish service, who had come to California, had been pensioned as an invalid and settled in the Villa Branciforte in 1799. He must have been friendly with the padres, for in 1818 he was *majordomo* of the Santa Cruz Mission, and in 1831 he became *alcalde* of the Villa Branciforte.

Following the vogue of the time, Martina had married a foreigner, one Michael Lodge, an Irishman who had come to Monterey in 1822.

In 1833 Mr. and Mrs. Lodge determined to settle down as land owners, and on September 8th they obtained permission from Jose Antonio Robles, the *alcalde* of Branciforte, to erect a home and plant crops on some land near the Soquel River. The land and the prospect of the harvest looked good to them, so they decided to try to get title to the land.

On November 16th, Mrs. Lodge went to Monterey and petitioned Governor Jose Figueroa for a tract of land, situate from the Soquel River to the Canyon de las Borrejas, "for the purpose of placing there her cattle, and to plant, and build a house, and to provide for the needs of her family, which is composed of four children." She made this application in her maiden name, Martina Castro, and the land which she requested was about 1,900 acres.

Governor Figueroa was careful in making such grants, and when the petition was presented he ordered that it be referred back both to the officials of Branciforte and to the priest at Santa Cruz Mission for advice and approval. Inasmuch as the Mission had already been stripped of most of its lands, Father Antonio del Real declared that he had no objection, the tract being no longer under his jurisdiction. The civil authorities at the Villa, to wit, *Alcalde* Robles and *Regidore* Jose Maria Salazar, likewise made no objection, but they reminded the Governor that there might be some settlers living on the land.

The endorsement having been given just three days after being presented, it is safe to assume that the Irish husband of Martina had not neglected to see that a favorable reception would be accorded the petition by the local authorities. At any rate, matters moved with great dispatch, for after another three days (November 22nd) Governor Figueroa gave his approval, with the stipulation, however, that it must be subject to any prior claims of Villa Branciforte and to the final approval of the territorial *diputacion.*

Fortunately, one of the kinsmen of Martina, Jose Castro, was a member of the committee of colonization of this *diputacion.* The other members were Jose J. Ortega, Jose Antonio Estudillo and Antonio Carillo. The committee reported favorably, and on May 17th the *diputacion* gave its formal approval, a copy of the same being issued on August 2nd.

When Martina took possession of her land, she applied to Jose Balcoff, who then was *alcalde* of Branciforte, having succeeded Jose Antonio Robles. The transaction proved to be a delightful family affair, because Boldoff delegated Rafael Robles and Juan Jose Castro to make a survey of the land. It was completed on August 14th, and a report was made.

Some of the leading people at that time were deprived of the most elementary educational qualifications. Bolcoff — a Russian — signed the report, but the two surveyors only placed their marks, and so did the two witnesses, Joaquin Castro and Miguel Ramirez. Even Martina could not write, so five of the six participants in this important transaction were unable even to sign their names.

The matter of transferring title at that time was apparently a good deal the same in California as it had been seven centuries previously in Old England. Bancroft tells us that when Señora Martina went out to the Soquel Rancho that afternoon, she "pulled up grass, threw stones to the four winds, and performed other ceremonies of the act of possession in sign of which she took possession of the land."

The final survey proved that the Soquel Rancho had but 1,668 acres, though request had been made for a tract of land a mile and half long and two miles wide, which would have covered 1,920 acres.[14] However, Dame Martina, guided by her acquisitive husband, obtained a further grant of land—32,702 acres of Soquel Augmentations in 1844—and in 1855 the United States Government confirmed both grants.

Martina Castro's husband was killed by robbers while returning to Santa Cruz from the gold fields in 1849. One of her daughters, Carmelita, married Thomas Fallon, and as Carmel Fallon, became wealthy in Monterey land. A son, Michael Lodge, is still living in a house on the highway between Soquel and Aptos, on land his mother was granted ninety-seven years ago.[15]

---

[14] Land measurements for the Private-ranchos were of rather an informal nature. If prior to 1824 a Californian wanted to become a landowner he addressed himself to the alcalde. Together they would go with two witnesses to the place desired and would erect at a suitable site a pile of rocks or stones. From this starting point the measurements were made on horseback, at a trot or gallop, with a fifty foot riata.

[15] L. Rowland, Santa Cruz News.

THE EPILOGUE

BOOK VI

CHAPTER XXIX

Completion of the Secularization of
the Missions; the California
Arcadia.

BOOK VI

Chapter XXIX

*Completion of the Secularization of the Missions;
the California Arcadia*

WHEN Governor Alvarado took charge in 1836 (he continued to hold office until 1842), the secularization of the Santa Cruz Mission was completed.

As was to be expected, neither the Governor nor his well-meaning associates could keep back the hordes of politicians, grafters, and others who desired to fish in the troubled waters of the transitory conditions and were determined to fatten on the estates now considered public property.

And what magnificent estates they were!

At the beginning of 1832 (there are no official records of 1834), the missionaries reigned over 17,000 neophytes, who tilled their fields, herded their flocks and cattle and increased their wealth. They owned over 151,180 cattle, 16,000 horses and mules, 140,000 sheep, goats and hogs, and raised annually enormous crops. In that year they slaughtered a great many cattle to supply the local demands and that of the traders, and their hides, with the by-products, such as tallow, etc., brought a large sum, though by no means as much as was later reported.

Dwinelle states that the laws, "whose ostensible purpose was to convert the Mission establishments into Indian pueblos, their churches into parish churches, and to elevate the Christianized Indians to the rank of citizens, were often executed in such a manner that the so-called secularization of the Missions resulted in their plunder and complete ruin, and in the demoralization and dispersion of the Christianized Indians."

Hittell comes to the same conclusion, for he says:

"Such were the principles and method adopted for secularization. Though it required some years to finish the ruin of the missionary establishments, this was the commencement of it. As for the Indian pueblos, which were to take their place, there was no success in any of them. Nor was any to have been expected. In other cases it has required hundreds of years to educate savages up to the point of making citizens, and many hundreds to make good citizens. The idea of transforming after barely half a century, the idle, improvident and brutish natives of California into industrious, law-abiding and self-governing town people was preposterous."

349

Governor Figueroa saw and acknowledged this truth. Though the law pronounced the Indians free, he recognized that their unconditional liberty was equivalent to their perdition, and therefore ordered them to be kept in a sort of qualified tutelage under the care and supervision of major-domos; and he directed that in the meantime they should be instructed in the duties of citizenship.[1]

It has been claimed, to mitigate the shameless plunder of the Missions, that as soon as secularization appeared to be inevitable, the missionaries themselves began the work of destruction, slaughtering cattle, uprooting vineyards and orchards, leaving as little to the despoilers as possible.

Some writers later claimed that in 1834 they (the missionaries) slaughtered over one hundred thousand cattle for the sake of the hides in such demand by the traders; and these with the tallow brought them for that year an income of over a million dollars. Inasmuch as the hides only brought $2.00 apiece (see Dana) delivered at seaboard, these range cattle must have been very mountains of walking tallow. Robinson, however, claims that the beef and tallow were allowed to remain rotting on the ground—which makes the contention of $1,000,000 profit still more improbable.

As far as the Mission San Gabriel is concerned we are assured that "over 100,000 cattle in that Mission were slaughtered, and as they were struck down, wherever they happened to be, the hides were taken off and the carcasses were left to rot. For years this region was white with skulls and skeletons; the new rancheros found them useful—for the building of fences."

It reads well, but the facts hardly support the assertions.

The period of secularization and the years immediately following seemed to be filled with many such fanciful tales, which were readily accepted by the enemies of the missionaries.

The wealth of the Missions, though great, has apparently been very much overestimated by Dwinelle, de Mofras, and even Bancroft.

Father Engelhardt has proven from the records[2] that there were far less cattle under the Mission jurisdiction than were reported slaughtered in one year. Then how about the live herds, subsequently confiscated and stolen?

San Gabriel had never more than 17,000 head of cattle.

That some of the Mission Fathers, who had labored the greater part of their lives fostering the interests of the neophytes, were aroused by the

[1] Cal. Archives, M. S. 579; XI 398.
  Hittell, History of California, p. 189, Vol. II.
[2] Father Engelhardt, Missions and Missionaries of California, Vol. III, p. 629.

idea that their herds would fall into the hands of plundering politicians, is likely; that they made contracts with butchers for the slaughter of a much larger number of cattle than usual is also quite likely; that the contractors killed more animals than they accounted for is also plausible; that orchards and vineyards were neglected when the padres realized what would happen to them is but natural, but if in view of all the record evidence, there are still some who cling to the idea that the tremendous slaughter of cattle could have been possible, we must ascribe to them a confusion as to the biological rules involved, which even the salubrious climate of California could not change, for few Missions had more than fifty breeding cattle to start with, of which we may safely assume forty-five were females and five males. It is true that some of the Missions, especially after de Anza's expedition, may have fared better, but these shortly afterwards had to divide their herds with the newer establishments. (See Appendix No. 1.)

It commands admiration for the Mission Fathers that at the time of the secularization of the Missions, the herds were as extensive as their records showed. There being no cattle of any kind in California before the advent of the missionaries, the cattle brought on the long trip from Mexico, were very precious to the Fathers. They thoroughly understood the necessity of carefully nursing the breeding cattle, and in times of privation, they even refused to use this cattle for subsistence, saving all kind of live stock for breeding purposes in order to give the new Missions a start.[3]

Father Junipero Serra expressed this concern in a letter to the Father Guardian on March 31st, 1774, when he wrote from San Diego about the cows "which up to now we have guarded like the apples of our eyes, contenting ourselves with the milk in order that they may multiply, . . . so that our brothers may not suffer hunger at the same time that they suffer inconveniences while they are with us."

Some of the male animals were reserved for breeding, but those not needed for that made the only beef on which the Fathers and their immediate followers, and later the neophytes, the officers and soldiers of the presidios, the non-commissioned officers and soldiers of the *escoltas* at the Missions could depend.

Very wisely the eating of beef was strictly prohibited to the Indians for the first twenty-five years after the founding of the Missions, for if they had once acquired the taste, they would have killed the breeding bulls and cows, as well as the steers. After they had acquired the taste of horse

---

[3] Letter of Father Palou from San Carlos, to the Guardian of the College at San Fernando, dated April 22, 1774. (See also Bolton's Anza's California Expedition, Vol. 5, p. 138.

meat, they stole horses and mules from the various Missions and drove them to the Tulares, slaughtering even the thoroughbreds for their flesh.

During the years when such enormous slaughter was presumed to have taken place amongst the Mission herds, Dana reported (1835) that hides were continuously becoming scarcer and harder to obtain. (See Appendix No. 2.)

The hides exported by no means originated at the Missions alone; a great many came from the private ranchos, where a yearly *matanza,* or slaughter of cattle, occurred immediately after the grand rodeo, or round-up, held for the purpose of counting the stock, apportioning the same to each ranchero, branding the calves, etc. Richman in his "California Under Spain and Mexico" describes the slaughters as follows:

"A band of vaqueros, armed with knives, rode over the fields, selected each an animal, deftly severed a nerve in the nape of the neck, and it fell dead." *Peladores* (flayers) stripped the hide, and the meat was then cut up by the butchers. A great deal of this was converted into dried meat, later known amongst the Californians as jerky, while the offal was disposed of by packs of dogs kept for that purpose.

While hides and tallow were the main property on which the missionaries could realize to provide for the many things required for the operation of their establishments, it is absurd to believe that the secular authorities would have allowed the alleged tremendous slaughter—for what would then have been left for the Governor, his friends, the *comisionados* and their numerous friends?

Of the Spanish and Mexican people living at the Santa Cruz Mission and the Villa de Branciforte little is known, in fact very little is known of any of the more humble white settlers in Alta California or the other Spanish frontier provinces.

Civilians of Spanish blood followed the soldiers and missionaries, as the two latter had followed the *conquistadores.* We do know that these white people, although a very small minority, formed the upper class in every secular pueblo or villa.

There is very little printed literature about any of the civilians and their place in the Spanish conquests. After all, while they belonged to the dominant race, they had no official positions in the new provinces.

The majority of the *gente de razon* could neither read nor write— analphabetes in the Catholic countries were very much more common in those days than at present, and while we hear a good many complaints about them, we do not know what they themselves thought of the country, of their lives, of the Government, the conditions under which they lived, what their moral and mental reactions were, and thousands of other things about which we can only make conjectures, for they have left little or no worth-while communications. All we have are occasional official military records giving the names of the new arrivals under their jurisdictions, so we must depend largely on the annals left us by foreign visitors, although they were subject to the limitations of preconceived ideas and social backgrounds.

Dana, visiting California twenty-five years after his first trip, was so impressed with the lack of independent information that he wrote (in 1859), "When in 1848 a large portion of the Anglo-Saxon race flocked to California there was no other book upon California but mine."

He was mistaken, for Beechey had published his book in 1831, Forbes in 1839, de Mofras 1844, Robinson in 1846, not to speak of others; but there was none by an independent *gente de razon* resident.

We wonder that the Spanish miners, considered the best discoverers of precious metals in the world, did not leave any records. The reason is that there were none of them in California Alta, notwithstanding that the presence of gold was already known during the Mexican period and suspected long before that. This was due to the difficulty of travel. While the Serra and Portola expeditions came by the way of Baja California, it was recognized that this route would have to be abandoned as unpractical. After that San Blas, on the mainland, was established by Galvez as the base for Alta California, but this also was only temporary, for an overland route was the only satisfactory way to transport white colonists to these outlying provinces, the sea route with its storms raging on the gulf, and many shipwrecks, the scurvy and other obstacles being too dangerous and expensive to be anything but a makeshift.

The trouble with the land route was that the Apaches in Sonora were far from being subdued; several times the white settlers had been routed, the pueblos wiped out, and the district of Pimera Alta, between the Gila and Altar Rivers, beyond which California Alta lay, was constantly disturbed by the Moquis. De Anza had established a route via the Gila and Colorado, but the Yuma Indians, first friendly under their chief Palma, and then dissatisfied, arose in 1781 and closed the overland route to California, preventing the prospectors and miners from arriving in any noticeable numbers. Had this route remained open, there would have been a great rush of Spanish miners to California, as there had been a great flow of these men in 1736 to Arizonac, just south of the present southern border of Arizona, where that remarkable silver mine, known as the "Bolas de Plata" or "Planchas de Plata," was discovered, and to Cieneguilla near

Altar, where in 1771 rich surface gold placers were found. (See Appendix No. 3.)

The small number of Spaniards who did reach California Alta, and later the first of the Mexican emigrants, remained either along the coast, or in easy reach thereof, where they were in touch with the ships and the existing establishments. There was no surplus to overflow towards the mountains.

California developed into a semi-modern Arcadia; that is to say, a Spanish Arcadia, as exists today in the district of Andalusia, southern Spain, where under the azure skies a smiling countryside offers a lovely sight of palms, orchards, orange groves, banana groups, olive trees, loaded with fruit, and what not. There the *seigniors* hold sway, proud, courteous, hospitable towards equals and guests, loving to their own families, but often as cold and uncompromising as the *caciques* were in their dealings with "inferiors," and callous as to the latter's poverty and suffering.

While our knowledge of the doings of the early civil settlers in California is very slim, we know more about the actual modes of living of the Spanish and Mexican gentry in the later period. Then they had their graceful dances—the *contradanza,* the *jarabe, el son,* and the waltz. They likewise had *fandangos,* rodeos, neighborly visits, horse races and picnics, not to speak of gambling and sporting in general. The women had their pearls and diamonds, their gold chains, rich clothing of silk, velvet and fine linen, their *rebosos* and gorgeous *mantillas.* But even the houses of the great land owners contained little furniture, for this was too bulky to be brought by the light vessels; and of modern accommodations there were none. The men had their embosesd saddles embroidered in gold or silver, their silver spurs, silk riding clothes and gay *serapes,* their magnificent riding horses, their *sombreros* with brims embellished by silver eagles and other coins, and all that was necessary for the adornment of a handsome *caballero;* they had their Indian serfs or half-slaves, most of them "liberated" from the Missions.

And the women of California, what glorious beauties they were! The middle-aged women, handsome and matronly, far more industrious than their spectacular spouses; the girls, black-haired, small of hand and foot, full bosomed, with deep red lips, were vivacious, but for all that virtuous and religiously devoted; carefully reared by their mothers and lynx-eyed duennas, quick to laugh and quick to anger, and with an abiding respect in their hearts for their elders. All historians are unanimous that those who married Americans, English, German or French husbands made most devoted wives and mothers. They are full of admiration for the *senoritas* and *senoras,* though a lack of enthusiasm in valuing the qualities of the picturesque men-folks is equally pronounced.

De Mofras says: "Their habits are those of the old Spanish colonists in America; the Californians have coarsened the qualities and the faults of their forefathers. Unfortunately, lately a great number of circumstances have contributed to their corruption; the contact with strangers, the introduction amongst them of luxurious habits, has increased their needs, and has only induced them to pillage the Missions; the abandonment of the system of local Spanish militia has diminished bravery; and their natural inclination for drinking has increased to such an extent that one hardly ever meets a Californian who does not have in his saddle bags, mixed with his arms, a bottle of strong spirits; 'the bottle for my friends,' he says, 'the weapons for my enemy.' These men, who are fine-looking, hardly ever go on foot; the first thing they do in the morning is to saddle a horse, which is hitched to the door of the house, and they use this animal even for a distance of one hundred and fifty feet. Their lives float by in complete *dolce far niente.* You will never see a Californian colonist work the earth. When one enters a rancho, one is sure to find the men lying down, smoking and drinking brandy; the women alone occupy themselves a little with agriculture and their gardens; and they succeed in hiring a few Indians to put in small crops.

"The women are in general large, strong and have conserved the beauty of Spanish peasants. Their fecundity is extraordinary; it is nothing unusual to meet those who have ten or twelve children, and this, combined with the numerical superiority of the men, explains the rapid growth of the Californians. Amongst five thousand white inhabitants there are almost six hundred strangers—men who have succeeded and who are preferred by their women over their own countrymen because they are industrious, because they treat them better, and because they take better care of the children; these women lead very active lives; . . . they handle the horses and the lasso with equal dexterity as their husbands, to whom they are very superior in intelligence and moral qualifications."[4]

---

[4] De Mofras, Exploration du Territoire de l'Oregon des Californies, Vol. 3, p. 22.

CHAPTER XXX

The Last Years Under Mexican Rule; the United States Take Charge.

BOOK VI

Chapter XXX

*The Last Years Under Mexican Rule;
the United States Take Charge*

ON January 16th, 1840, an earthquake at Santa Cruz threw down several houses and the church tower, causing a wave which carried away a large quantity of tiles, piled two hundred varas from the shore.

There is no record who the *majordomo* was in 1840. According to the *reglamento,* however, Governor Alvarado was to continue to manage this ex-Mission pueblo, according to circumstances.

In March the Governor ordered the administrator to give up to Padre del Real the garden and distillery with the houses adjoining the church.

In 1842 Jose Bolcoff was again administrator.

In 1841 or 1842 de Mofras (see Appendix No. 1) visited Santa Cruz. He wrote:

"Its (the Mission's) buildings are large and quite well preserved; but it has been robbed of all its goods, the farms have been given away, and the cattle has been divided amongst the friends of the Governor. The Mission owns nothing any more. Instead of six hundred Indians who were formerly grouped around, there are hardly sixty left. . . ."[1]

He finishes with the following statement, which shows his excellence as a prophet:

"In the space which separates the Mission from the Villa of Branciforte are being built new houses, which in due time will no doubt make an important city."

In 1842 Governor Alvarado's health was failing and he asked to be relieved from his many duties. He is generally described as a man of dignity and resource, a good administrator, and a natural leader of men. He had filled many public offices before he finally became the Governor. Born in Monterey in 1809, he was only twenty-seven years old when appointed to that office. His mother was a Vallejo, and he was married to Dona Martina Castro, of San Pablo.

The Mexican Government appointed Manuel Micheltorena in his place; he held sway from December, 1842, to February, 1845. He was a pro-cleric and a reactionary. This new dignitary was presumed to take

---

[1] De Mofras, Exploration, etc., p. 410.

with him to California additional military forces to prepare it better for defense. Unfortunately, the force of three hundred and fifty men consisted of the scourings of Mexican prisons. They arrived ragged and looking like vagabonds, and became a bane to the country.

They were known as the "Cholo Army," and in accordance to tradition, disembarked at San Diego *sans culottes,* for their lower garments were abbreviated to the point of extinction. Alfred Robinson, who witnessed their arrival, wrote: "I saw them land, and to me they presented a state of wretchedness and misery unequaled. Not one individual among them possessed a jacket or pantaloons, but naked and like the savage Indians, they concealed their nudity with dirty, miserable blankets. The females were not much better off, for the scantiness of their wearing apparel was too apparent for modest observers. They appeared like convicts, and indeed the greater portion of them had been charged with the crime of either murder or theft."

These soldiers later filled Monterey with consternation by their thievery, as they had previously done in Los Angeles. They stole not from hunger, but because they were constitutionally unable to do otherwise. They took everything they could put their hands on—household utensils, fowl, clothing, etc. When twelve or them were employed by Don Vicente Sanchez as guards at a Los Angeles dance, they carried off a chest of silver, and then began highway robbery at the point of the sword.

Of course, the result was a war, led by Alvarado and Castro, who mustered two hundred and twenty *caballeros,* while Governor Micheltorena left Monterey on November 22nd, 1844, with a force of one hundred and fifty men. The usual feints, flourishes and fanfares followed, and when the treaty of Santa Teresa was signed, the Governor agreed to send his "Cholos" back to San Blas.

The California patriots were always "at war." Conspiracies, revolts, treacheries, followed one another almost in regular routine. There had been a revolt against Governor Echeandia by unpaid soldiers; against Victoria by an outraged people; against Pico by Echeandia and Zamorano; against Figueroa by the pueblo of Los Angeles; and against Chico by the Monterey people; against Gutierrez by Alvarado, against Micheltorena by Castro and Alvarado, and once more against Pico by Jose Castro.

However, these "wars" did not affect local conditions much, especially at Santa Cruz, which was more an onlooker than a participant.

The central government in Mexico continued to rob the Pious Fund as readily as the local Governors and leading men in California robbed the Missions and the Indians, and the land titles were in chaos.

Under the administrators the remaining Indians were compelled to work much harder than under the padres; they were ill-fed and ill-treated, they worked in gangs under overseers who treated them like slaves, and their right to the land, respected by the padres and military under the laws of Spain, was ignored.

Fray Francisco Garcia Diego, Prefect of the Zacatecans in Alta California, had been appointed Bishop on April 27th, 1840, and had by January 11th, 1842, established his episcopal headquarters at Santa Barbara. He controlled the Pious Fund, and the pro-clerical Governor Micheltorena saw his way clear to oust the wasteful *comisionados,* and on March 23rd, 1843, issued a decree restoring the temporal and spiritual management of twelve Missions (not including Santa Cruz, for this Mission had by that time been thoroughly looted), and declaring that the Governor would not make another grant of land without the consent of the Friars. This *pronunciamento* was the signal for yet another California "war."

In October, 1842, Commodore Thomas ap Catesby Jones, United States Navy, under the mistaken idea that war had broken out between the United States and Mexico, landed one hundred and fifty marines from his squadron at Monterey and lowered the Mexican colors. Next day he realized his mistake, restored the Mexican flag, withdrew his marines, and fired a salute in apology.

By that time the Mission community across the bay from Monterey was entirely broken up, the establishment was united with Branciforte in secular government as well as sacerdotal rule. The whole was now one town called by both names, but usually known as Pueblo de Santa Cruz, the name of Pueblo de Figueroa being no longer in use.

Sir George Simpson (see Appendix No. 2) gives a vivid picture of the state of the Mission:

"I need hardly add that the Mission in question is in the usual state of decay and dilapidation, and in fact, being so close to the seat of government, it was sure to be one of the first to suffer, for a Californian is not likely to advance one step faster or farther than is necessary, even in the pleasant and profitable path of spoliation."

As to the Mission at Monterey (San Carlos) he says:

"With the exception of the church, the immense ranges of buildings were all a heap of ruins. Here again, as in the case of Santa Cruz, the proximity of the ruling powers had hastened the work of destruction, the last tile having been rifled from the roofs and sold to adorn the houses of Monterey."

Josiah Belden, agent at Santa Cruz for Thomas Larkin of Monterey, who was later Consul of the United States, left a valuable record as to the trade in Santa Cruz after the virtual abandonment of the Mission. He was a Connecticut Yankee, and recorded that:

"There were a number of men in the mountains out of Santa Cruz sawing lumber in saw pits by hand. I bought the lumber of them and had it hauled in onto the beach, taking it in exchange for goods, and we sold the lumber down the coast to different points where it was required. This was mostly redwood lumber and was worth $40 to $45 a thousand feet.

"We carried on the usual business, general merchandise, selling goods and taking pay in hides and tallow. A hide was worth $2 and a *botta* of tallow about $1.50.

"We used to have some trade, also, in a kind of soap that was made in the country, taking it from the makers and reselling it around to the people in exchange for hides. Sometimes we delivered some of it to ships in exchange for goods.

"In taking hides from the country people in exchange for goods, we had a rule that all hides must be branded before they were sold, with the owner's brand, to show they had not been stolen. The owners were all known and each had a recognized brand.

"After gathering a quantity of hides, when I wanted to deliver them to a ship, the *alcalde* would always come and overhaul them to see if they were properly branded. If not, they were confiscated.

"I recollect that in one case I had considerable trouble with the *alcalde*. Sometimes a man would bring in a hide and had perhaps forgotten to brand it. There might be several hides collected in that way. The owners would promise to come and brand them afterwards, but would neglect to do it.

"I had a considerable number without brands, and I was expecting to make a shipment which I did not care to have the *alcalde* overhaul. I made arrangement with the ship to have the hides taken away very early one morning. I locked up the store and went away, so that the *alcalde* should not come in and inspect them that afternoon.

"I made arrangements to get the hides down to the beach in carts about daylight in the morning. When I got them down there I found there was no boat to take them off. I did not know what to do, but having a lot of timber there, I had the hides placed in a pile under a bank and covered with lumber, to wait until the boat should come ashore.

"In the meantime the *alcalde* got wind of the hides having gone down and came charging down to the beach, mad as could be. He wanted to know where the hides were. I told him he was too late; that I had to send them down to the ship early, as she wanted to leave.

"After he had stormed about for some time I got the supercargo of the vessel to take the *alcalde* off to the Mission on some pretense, and while he had him up there I got the men to haul the hides out from under the lumber and put them aboard the ship.

"There was no penalty for shipping them without his supervision if we could manage to do it."

Father del Real remained as parish priest until 1844, and Padre Antonio Anzar, of San Juan seems to have officiated here in 1844-45, Santa Cruz meanwhile being without a priest.

The Santa Cruz Fathers came in for their share of blame for acts which they never committed. The poor priest, presiding over what remained of the Mission of Santa Cruz, was ungraciously maligned. On May 29th, 1842, Josiah Belden wrote to his principal, the merchant Larkin, at Monterey, that he had sufficient proof that it was Padre Antonio del Real who had broken into his store and stolen brandy, handkerchiefs and other articles.[2]

It is hard to believe this story, although one might think that even a patient priest might want to get even for the way the Mission had been robbed by others.

Apparently Father del Real was not a favorite with visitors or historians, for Sir George Simpson tells us of the padre, his bottle and his *seraglio* of native beauties."[3] Simpson, however, does not disclose where the Reverend Father, even if so inclined, could have obtained these native beauties. The Indians around Monterey Bay were a peculiarly ugly type, and the Spanish women were famous for their virtue, while the half-breeds were zealously guarded by their men folks, who were quick to revenge with the knife any undue attention paid to their women. Sir George must have been mistaken.

As Father del Real lived to a ripe old age, it would appear that the *seraglio* of dusky beauties was populated by a few female household servants only. If we may believe other chroniclers, this padre had anything but the appearance of a gay philanderer.

The French traveler, Laplace (see Appendix No. 3), visited Santa Cruz about 1840. He devotes several pages of his report to the melancholy picture of the establishment in its state of ruin, poverty and filth,

---

[2] Larkin's Doc. MS. i, 279. See also Belden's Historic Statements, MS. 33-34. From a clipping in the Santa Cruz News by Leon Rowland.

[3] Belden's Hist. Statement MS., pp. 33-34, 1844.

comparing it with its former magnificence. As he apparently grossly exaggerates the magnificence, it is safe to assume that he paints too dark a picture in his comparison. It seems that as a true, gallant Frenchman, he was very happy to find a lovely farmer's daughter, willing to sell him vegetables for an economical price. Laplace was much incensed by the appearance of Father del Real, who frightened away this "California dove," whom the Frenchman evidently admired both for her beauty and for the commercial advantages which barter with her promised. He then proceeds to draw a picture of the padre which would do credit to a pirate from the old Spanish Main. He describes the ecclesiastic as follows:

"Really, it was no wonder that she was frightened, because it would be difficult to find anyone with a more cynical expression, with a more brutal appearance than this unkempt Mexican priest, with his burned face, great black eyes, the whites yellowed, his head covered with a large wide-brimmed hat, the crown dented in the center (Californians on the range still wear this headgear, but it seems to 'have looked sinister to this observer), his Franciscan robes, formerly white (!), now covered with a thousand spots and without a cowl, but raised almost as high as his waist, in order to give sufficient liberty to his lower members. . . ."

There is an old saying that he who comes from strange places tells strange stories, and Monsieur Laplace is an active competitor with his compeer, Dr. John Coulter, for the laurels of the California Munchhausen. This learned doctor wrote a narrative of his adventures on the Pacific, which was published in London; it covers seven chapters of his experiences in California during the year 1834, and is for the most part an account of absurdly impossible personal adventures, with allusions to magnificent ruins and relics of antiquity, of Indians, of robbers and what not. The book appeared in 1847.

The municipal affairs at Santa Cruz were managed by a succession of *juezes de paz* in 1841-43, and *alcaldes* in 1844-45. (See Appendix No. 4.) The successive local chiefs up to 1845 were Bolcoff, Juan Gonzalez, Rafael Castro, Manual Rodriguez, Ramon Buelna, and Bolcoff again.

On February 2nd, 1844, the Government sent an order directing the *alcalde* to treat the Indians, who for some time had been their own masters, just like other citizens, except that he was to give notice to the padre in case of such offenses as pertained to his jurisdiction.[4]

The importance and estate of Santa Cruz Mission had dwindled to such an extent by 1844 that Rt. Reverend Francisco Garcia Diego, Bishop of both the Californias, withdrew Father Antonio del Real from Santa

---

[4] Santa Cruz Arch. M. S., 87-8, B. C.

Cruz, stationing him at Monterey for a short time, and then returning him to the Franciscan establishment in Mexico.

An inventory signed by P. Anzar, Andres Pico and Juan Manso in 1845 is very expressive. The items follow:

Building with 12 rooms (the rest having been sold when Alvarado was Governor), $800.

Garden and 40 fruit trees, $75; one-half league of bad land, $100; total, $975.[5]

In 1845 Roman Buelna and Francisco Soria were *alcaldes*. Buelna was suspended in September, and in October Jose Bolcoff was appointed first *alcalde* in his place, and in December, Macedonio Lorenzana was appointed second *alcalde*.[6]

In May the citizens petitioned for the removal of both *alcaldes,* for drinking, disorder, disobedience and carelessness.

In 1845 that part of Santa Cruz which was originally Branciforte was reported to have 470 souls, to wit, 120 Indians and 350 *gente de razon,* of whom foreigners with their families numbered 80.

Colonel James Clyman (see Appendix No. 5), an American frontiersman, who took an active part in the early history of the West, has left an interesting picture of Santa Cruz and its environs in "His Diaries and Reminiscences,'" which are epics, though he carefully avoids all punctuation:

"Left Monterey and took back northward to Santa Cruz whare we arived in the Evening of (of) the First of August (1845)

"Santa Cruz is likewise an old Mission establishment and occupies a beautiful situation about 2 miles from the coast and has some fine spring of water from which the fathers draw their water to Erigate their gardens

"This place is likewise dignified by the name of a village scattered along the steep bluffs of a small stream   the low grounds have a number of half cultivated gardens as is usual through all Mexican countrys   The Mexicans nor Foreigners never Labour in (the) province Except Mchanicks   All the outdoors labour is performed by the native Indians who are kept in a state of slavery and receive no pay Except what their masters choose to give them   they are a Lazy indolent race and nearly and Quite naked   those who are house servants excepted which if females ware a long chemise the climate indeed does not seem to require clothing

[5] Pico, Miss. Pap. MS., 152, B. C.
[6] Santa Cruz Arch. M. S. 87-8, B. C.
[7] Quarterly of the California Historical Society, Vol. 5, 1926, p. 133.

at this season of the year Except it may be to keep the sorching sun from blistering but in this the natives are proof against any common Heate

"2 and 3 of August remained with the far famed and redoubtable Capt. (Isaac) Graham The hero of Mr. (Thomas J) Farnhams travels in California and in fact the hero of six or seven revolutions in this province and the chivalrous captain has again during the last winter passed through the ordeal of one more revolution and again been a prisoner in the hands of his old Enimy Colonel Castro the Eex governor and has once more returned to his peacable domicil to his heards and his (saw) mill surrounded by impassable mountains about Eight miles from the Landing of Santa Cruz and if report be correct the hardy vetrian is fast softening down and he is about to cast away the deathly rifle and the unerring tomahawk for the soft smiles of a female companion to nurrish him in his old age and here I must say that the captain has all the Philanthropy and Kindness for his country men that has ever been attributed to him Inviting me to return and remain with him free of cost as long as I might find it convenient or as long as I wished to remain in california"

On the fourth of August Mr. Clyman proceeded along "a small difficult bridle way that (led) across a very rugged mountain for Santa Clare and the village Pueblo, (lf San Jose) where we arrived in the Evening Two days previous to our arrival the mountain Indians had made a desent upon Santa Clare killed one and wounded two of the horse guard and stolen a herd of Horses and the inhabitants ware in pursuit of the Murderers in the mountain we had Just passed through we came through however without seeing either party and slept soundly with Mr Weaver (Charles M. Weber) (a german who speaks good Eenglish) in the village of Puebla and in the morning of the 5 we left our kind and hospitable entertaner and bent our course north along that arm of the Bay of San Francisco which communicates with the Mission of Santa Clara"

In the meantime, California, as a whole, had been in constant turmoil, in which the foreign element played no small part. The difficulties grouped themselves, like most other troubles, around definite personalities.

Isaac Graham, an American backwoodsman, was one of the numerous trappers who had found their way across the country into California. He was a freebooter of Tennessee, and settled down at the edge of the forest near Santa Cruz. Not being over-fond of hard physical labor, he began the making and sale of *aguardiente*—a kind of whiskey distilled from wheat. He soon attracted a band of disorderly associates from the near Villa de Branciforte and from far places, and organized and became captain of a company of riflemen consisting of deserters from whalers and merchantmen and backwoodsmen, all of whom were or became expert riflemen and capable of enduring much fatigue and hardships.

When Alvarado started his revolution against Guiterrez, Captain Graham and his men entered Alvarado's employ in an effort to establish an independent government in Alta California.

In 1840 Graham became a distiller at Monterey and his place there became the rendezvous of free-lances who were in the country illegally and without passports. Here he and his associates soon became a thorn in the side of Governor Alvarado, for, considering themselves an important factor in the country, they assumed arrogant airs, rendering themselves exceedingly disagreeable to the authorities. The Governor found himself insulted at every turn by the followers of Graham, and even when walking in his garden they would ride along the garden wall and call out: "Bautista come here, I want to speak to you," and then not seldom made ribald of him.

We read in a proclamation issued at Los Angeles in May, 1840, by Cosme Peña, that the Branciforte ill-doers had resisted the *alcalde* of that place; that the *alcalde* had complained to the Government; that the Government cautioned them, but that instead of obeying they had armed themselves and defied the authorities.

As we have seen, one of them, believing that he was about to die, confessed to Padre Jose Suarez del Real,[8] of San Carlos Mission, that an uprising of American settlers against the Mexican Government was in preparation. It is claimed that the padre notified the Governor, who instructed Jose Castro, the Prefect of the district. One of them, William Chard, when arrested, begged not to be shot and offered to inform on all of his associates. Through the American influence Texas had separated from Mexico four years previously, and fear was felt that the same would happen in California. Castro proceeded with celerity to execute Alvarado's order; surprised Graham and his associates in their houses, and in all one hundred and twenty persons were arrested, of whom forty-six were sent to San Blas in the national bark *Joven Guipuzcoana*. Twenty-six were eventually banished from Mexican territory, the balance were allowed to return, mostly through the good offices of Eustace Barron, the British Consul, who was a partner of Alexander Forbes, and of the United States envoy extraordinary at Mexico City. Amongst them was Graham, who returned with his special associates in 1842 to Monterey. They were sent there in a Mexican vessel and were fitted out in fine style. Of course, they became the sworn enemies of Alvarado. Several of those arrested were from Santa Cruz, to which place most of them returned.

---

[8] A brother of Padre Antonio Suarez del Real at Santa Cruz.

Another interesting figure was Johann August Sutter, native of Kandern Baden, Germany, born in 1803 of Swiss parents.[9] He arrived first in June, 1839, at San Francisco with a company of colonists—twelve men and two women. He was refused admission, but having good letters of introduction proceeded to Monterey, made an excellent impression upon Governor Alvarado and soon went north to erect upon the Sacramento River a settlement called New Helvetia, the nucleus of Sacramento, which in time was to become the capital of the State of California.

Sutter became a Mexican citizen and was made by Governor Alvarado the *Comandante* on the frontier of the Sacramento River. By quitclaim deed, he subsequently obtained all the right, title and interest and personal property of the Russians at Fort Ross, which project, due to excessive slaughter of the seals, had become unprofitable, and so strengthened his position materially. He agreed to pay $30,000, which was underwritten by the Province.

At New Helvetia he owned the usual eleven square leagues of land, had 42,000 cattle, 2,000 horses, 1,900 sheep, and carried on a very profitable fur trade. His influence spread amongst the trappers and Indians, and many early settlers were befriended by him.

Though friendly with Alvarado (then *jefe politico*), he was soon "at outs" with the *jefe militar,* Mariano Guadalupe Vallejo. The latter, a disciplinarian and enthusiastic patriot, deplored the presence of foreigners in Alta California.

Sutter became involved in several political brawls, the principal one being in 1845, when he and Dr. John Marsh, with about one hundred Indians and one hundred riflemen under Captains John Gantt and Isaac Graham, marched southward to assist Micheltorena in subduing a conspiracy against his authority, by Jose Castro and Alvarado, the former Governor.[10] It was, of course, a mistake which he bitterly regretted.

Another prominent American who came to California was Thomas O. Larkin. He arrived in 1832 from Massachusetts, and after twelve years of experience in dealing with the Californians "over the counter," he was made United States Consul, on April 2nd, 1844, at Monterey, where France and Great Britain also maintained Consuls.

In 1845 President Polk appointed Larkin "confidential agent," a position which came very close to that of an *agent provocateur.* Such an arrangement, in view of Larkin's consular position and privileges, was rather peculiar.

---

[9] He died in Washington, D. C., June 17th, 1880.
[10] Dr. George Lyman's John Marsh, Pioneer.

He received instructions to exert the greatest vigilance in discovering and defeating any attempts made by foreign governments (*i. e.,* France or England) to acquire control over California. He was fortified with a promise that if California would assert and maintain her independence, she would receive all "kind offices" as a Sister Republic. Independence by California was to be fostered with a view to acquisition, and the United States wanted it to be made known that if California behaved herself, she would be accepted in the Union.

Larkin did not have an easy task. The land was being occupied very rapidly by lawless hunters, trappers, backwoodsmen, etc., who looked upon the institutions of the United States as antiquated; they wanted to carve out their own destiny. Leading men (Jose Castro especially) gave the new agent to understand that they might not object to the United States, provided, in the transfer of allegiance, they would be assured of their positions and salaries. It seems that Larkin had told Castro that "by adjusting circumstances he could secure himself and his friends fame and honor, permanent employ and pay."

John C. Fremont, brevet captain of topographical engineers, United States Army, had entered California for the first time in 1844. Coming from Nevada, he had stopped at New Helvetia, now Fort Sutter, at Sacramento; thence had traveled via the San Joaquin Valley and the Tehachapi Pass to the Santa Fe Trail, and thence to Utah Lake.

On December 10th, 1845, he reached Fort Sutter again with a surveying party. His party was split in two divisions for reconnoitering purposes, but reunited again at San Jose on February 15th, 1846, about sixty men strong.

Jose Castro, the *Comandante General,* demanded an explanation and was given the elucidation from Monterey, where Fremont had gone meanwhile, that the object was not of a military nature, but that a survey was to be made of a route to the Pacific. Fremont then started across the Santa Cruz Mountains to the Santa Clara Valley. From Mission Hill in Santa Cruz, a peak can be seen which was named for Fremont. He and his men camped in the grove of *Sequoia Sempervirens,* six miles north of the Mission, and one of the big trees is dedicated to his memory.

Urged by the Mexican authorities and United States Consul Larkin, who feared a premature show-down, he left for Oregon, but on May 8th (1846) he was overtaken by Lieutenant Archibald H. Gillespie, U. S. N., and returned to California.

Pio Pico, Micheltorena's successor as Governor, represented the old California families and at once reversed the policy of his predecessor. He took office February 22nd, 1845.

The President of Mexico issued an order to Governor Pico to raise money to defend California against the threatened attack of the United States. The Departmental Assembly, in March, 1846, made the Missions liable to the laws of bankruptcy, authorizing the Governor to sell them to appropriate persons. Governor Pico lost no time in selling whatever he could to anyone ready to pay cash. Though the law demanded public sales, he sold the lands and appurtenances at private sales, disposing of them for small cash sums, or for promises which were never paid. Before he finally left the country he wrote to some of his intimate friends, asking them whether there was anything they coveted, for if so, he would give it to them before his departure.

This was too much to be tolerated by the Departmental Assembly, and one of the last acts of that august body before the United States took charge was to declare all of Pico's sales null and void, thereby adding still more confusion to the land titles of California.

By 1846 revolt was brewing. In June the American settlers, encouraged by the presence of Fremont in the Sacramento and Napa Valleys, seized the town of Sonoma, raised the Bear flag, captured several Californians, and proclaimed the country independent.

On June 19th, 1846, a military force was organized at San Jose under the leadership of Charles N. Weber, a German merchant. Weber sent word to Thomas Fallon, a twenty-seven-year-old Canadian at Santa Cruz, who organized twenty-five armed men in that pueblo to join the insurgents at San Jose, where they arrived on July 11th.

He found that Weber had been arrested by Castro the day before. Fallon took command, and shortly afterwards joined his Santa Cruz forces with those of Fremont. After peace was declared, he became Mayor of San Jose and married Carmel Lodge, a Soquel (Santa Cruz County) girl.

In November, Manuel Castro and some friends raised a force of one hundred men near San Luis Obispo. Larkin, who was stopping overnight at the rancho Los Verjeles with Joaquin Gomez, was taken prisoner.

Commodores Sloat and Stockton, of the United States Navy, were destined to play important roles on the California stage. The former, coming from Mazatlan on his flagship *Savannah,* on the 2nd day of July, had raised the American flag at Monterey, July 7th, 1846. The news was rushed to San Francisco via Santa Cruz.

Leon Rowland has given us an interesting account:

"This was not due to the importance of the Mexican village with its handful of American lumbermen and traders, but was because the messenger, selected to take the word to Captain John B. Montgomery at San

Francisco knew this region, and wanted to avoid San Juan Bautista and San Jose, where he would risk capture by Jose Castro's men.

"The messenger was Job Dye, a forty-one-year-old Kentuckian. He knew the Santa Cruz mountains because, from 1835 to 1840, he had operated a small distillery and trading post in the Zayante Valley.

"Trusted with the message to the American navy vessel at San Francisco, he circled Monterey Bay, passed through Santa Cruz, went up the old Graham grade to Zayante, and kept north along the ridge of the mountains until he came to the sand hills of San Francisco.

"The flag was raised at Monterey early on July 7th. At San Francisco it was raised on July 9th. Presumption is that it was raised there as soon as the message was received, and that Dye had taken only two days and two nights of continuous riding for the trip.

"Word that California was American territory must have reached the Americans at Branciforte and Santa Cruz Mission more than twenty-four hours before San Franciscans were apprised of the fact.

"Job Francis Dye had come to southern California in 1832, probably in the party which included Joseph L. Majors, Isaac Graham and Ambrose Tomlinson. Dye and Tomlinson came to Santa Cruz together and picked the Zayante as their home. Majors came with them or soon afterwards.

"Dye and Tomlinson rented a part of Zayante rancho from Joaquin Buelna and erected a building of split redwood, which they used as a grist mill and distillery. After a year or so, Tomlinson sold his interest to Majors, and in 1840 Dye bought the latter out.

"Dye applied for Mexican citizenship in 1839. In 1840 he was one of the foreigners arrested for exile, but was not sent to Mexico with Graham and the others. His business at Zayante was ruined, however, and he put in a claim for $66,925 against the Mexican Government.

"Perhaps in settlement of that claim, Mexico in 1844 gave him the Rio de Berrendos rancho of 26,700 acres on the Sacramento River, in what is now Tehama County. Despite his status as a landed proprietor, he continued to live in this region and was *regidore* in Monterey in 1846, and when the American naval forces landed, acted as guide for Fauntleroy's dragoons."

On July 7th, Sloat issued a proclamation to the inhabitants of California in which he declared California to be a portion of the United States. On July 23rd, he relinquished command on account of ill health to Commodore Stockton, who proceeded to Los Angeles, and issued there, on August 17th, a similar proclamation. Stockton had issued a previous one on July 29th. The doughty commodore, in leaving his own element to sail the troubled waters of statecraft and politics, seemed unable to maintain an even keel, for the document has been declared "offensive, impolitic, uncalled-for, inaccurate and most undignified." He resigned his Governorship six months later, on January 19th, 1847. In the second proclamation of August 17th, 1846, he had declared himself Governor.

In these six months he had retrieved himself to no small extent. Los Angeles fell into the hands of the Americans; he made two successful expeditions to the south, made Colonel Fremont the military commandant, and drew up a constitution for the civil government.

Colonel Fremont was his successor; his rule lasted only a few months, and on March 4th, 1847, General Kearny assumed command. (See Appendix No. 6.)

Meanwhile Consul Larkins, transferred to Los Angeles, had been liberated.

On January 10th, 1847, a treaty was signed, whereby the Californians surrendered their artillery and public arms, agreeing to serve no more in the war. They received a guarantee of life and property protection and were granted "rights and privileges as enjoyed by citizens of the United States of America."

 Upon the American occupation, Bolcoff was requested to continue in office at Santa Cruz, either alone or with John Hames. He declined, and Joseph L. Majors was appointed in August with William Thompson as second *alcalde,* and Lawrence Carmichael as secretary." William Blackburn and William Anderson followed Majors and Thompson in office.

Rowland writes:

"An unfortunate Californian of Mexican descent by the name of Gomez was the victim of an occurrence of the early days of the American occupation (1847) in Santa Cruz, which is often told by historians as an example of the picturesque if summary justice dealt out by William Blackburn, the first *alcalde* here after the American flag had been raised.

The Virginian cabinetmaker and carpenter received his appointment from Governor Richard B. Mason on June 21st, 1847, and less than sixty days later was confronted with the necessity of dealing with a case of murder.

Felipe Gomez was the culprit, although Bancroft recorded his name as Pedro Gomez. Returning to his adobe cabin in Arana gulch one day he surprised another Mexican with his wife. The other fled to Branciforte with Gomez in vain pursuit.

---

[11] Larkin's Official Corr. M. S. i, 140-141, B. C.

Balked of vengeance, Gomez returned to his cabin and threatened his wife with hanging as a punishment for her alleged infidelity, but compromised by using a knife, with which he unhappily cut too deeply.

Realizing his crime, he made his way hastily through Branciforte, forded the San Lorenzo, and took refuge at the Mission. It was locked, but he thrust his little finger into the key-hole.

American authority, however, disregarded this interpretation of the right of sanctuary and not only put Gomez in the nearby adobe jail, which stood on the site now occupied by the Knights of Columbus hall, but chained him to the wall.

The slaying of Senora Gomez took place on August 14th. The following day he was tried before *Alcalde* Blackburn, who summoned a jury of twelve to back his judgment. One of the jurymen was A. A. Hecox, the sturdy pillar of the Methodist Church, who the following year himself became *alcalde* of Santa Cruz. Another was Don Rafael Castro, patriarch of the Santa Cruz branch of that numerous family and son of Joaquin Castro, who, an *invalido* soldier, had settled in Branciforte in 1798.

The trial lasted only an hour or two. 'Guilty' was the verdict. Don Rafael returned a verdict all his own: 'Gomez is guilty and ought to be shot.'

The trial was Tuesday, and Blackburn, supported by the jurors' decision, fixed Friday for execution of the Mexican who had used his knife to avenge the violation of the sanctity of his marriage.

Thirty single young men were summoned by the *alcalde,* and from their number six volunteered to act as executioners.

Gomez was placed with his back against the adobe wall above the present residence of Elihu Anthony, on the lower end of School Street, overlooking the bluff. Three volleys were fired and a pistol used to make sure the job was thorough.

With the trial and execution completed, *Alcalde* Blackburn reported to Governor Mason at Monterey. Under Mexican law, which provided the Santa Cruz *alcaldes* with their authority until the county was organized, he had a combination of executive and judicial authority, but was nevertheless a subordinate of the Monterey *alcalde* as well as the Governor. Blackburn's jurisdiction stopped short of the power to enforce capital punishment. He should have placed his jury's verdict in the hands of the Governor and awaited his orders.

Instead, *Alcalde* Blackburn reported to Monterey, 'Felice Gomez was brought before me for killing his wife. He was duly tried and sentenced to be shot. He is shot. I respectfully submit the same for your approval.' "

In 1847 a resolution was passed by the *ayuntamiento* that the town lands extended one league in each direction from the Mission.[12]

In the same archives there is to be found an order requiring that all claimants to land within that limit must present their titles for inspection.[13]

Foreigners, and especially Americans, were relatively more numerous here than in any other district, and were largely engaged in lumbering.[14]

When in 1846 Pio Pico had ordered the Mission buildings in California sold, there was not even a bidder for the one at Santa Cruz, or for its lands and orchards.

In fact, there is no record that the Santa Cruz Mission was ever sold or rented, as were several of the other California Missions. Shortly after the American Government assumed control, General Kearney, as Military Governor of California, issued the following proclamation: "That inasmuch as there are various claimants to the Missions of San Jose, Santa Clara, Santa Cruz, and San Juan, and the houses, gardens, vineyards, etc., around and near them, he does hereby decree that until the proper tribunals to be established shall decide upon the same, the above Missions and property appertaining thereto, shall remain under charge of the Catholic priests, as they were when the United States flag was first raised in this territory, it being understood that this decree is not to affect the rights of any claimant, and the priests are to be responsible for the preservation of said Missions and property while under their charge."[15]

The priest (at Santa Cruz) was next to complain. He objected to the *alcaldes* granting land that belonged to the Missions.[16]

On November 24th, 1847, the Governor of California wrote to *Alcalde* Blackburn:

[12] Santa Cruz Arch. M. S. 109, B. C.

[13] Idem., 108, B. C.

[14] Bancroft, Cal., Vol. IV, p. 664.

[15] Supreme Court of the United States. United States vs. Bolton, James R. Appendix to Brief of Appellees, with Exhibits, No. III, p. 81.
Governor Mason, in a letter to Captain Maylee, July 19th, 1847, writes "The United States Government fully recognizes, and will sustain, the rights of the priest at the mission, and to all mission property, against all those who cannot, in due course of law, show a sound and just title." Supreme Court of the United States. United States vs. Bolton, James R., Appendix to Brief of Appellees, with Exhibits, No. III, p. 82.

[16] No *alcalde* in California has the authority to give any legal force whatever to any existing claims or titles to the missions, or other public land in the territory. Supreme Court of the United States vs. Bolton, James R., Appendix to Brief of Appellees, No. III, p. 83a. The Early History of the Santa Cruz Region, Narcissa L. Parrish.

"Headquarters, 10th, Mil. Dept.
Monterey, Cal. Nov. 24, 1847.

Sir:

The Catholic priest of Santa Cruz has this day called upon me and complained that the *alcalde* has been granting or selling certain lots of land belonging to the Mission of that place. By the decree of General Kearney, of the 22nd March last, certain Missions, of which Santa Cruz was one, and all the land, etc., appertaining thereto, were put under the charge of their respective priests. These Missions and Mission lands cannot be in any way incumbered or disposed of by any of the authorities in California. An *alcalde* cannot grant or dispose of lands, unless when a town has been authorized to be laid off by the proper authorities, and the lots are authorized to be sold for the benefit and improvement of the place. If any town has been authorized to be laid off at Santa Cruz, be pleased to furnish me with a copy of such authority and also with a copy of the town plat."

I am, etc.

(Signed)   R. B. Mason,
Col. 1st Dragoons, Governor of California.

Wm. Blackburn,
Alcalde,
Santa Cruz."

It has been impossible to find the answer to this letter, but in deeds made by the same *alcalde,* reference is made to lots 13 and 14 of the map of the aforesaid town, now deposited in the office of the *alcalde.*

It appears that the American *alcalde,* beginning August 1st, 1847, issued and recorded a large number of deeds to lands situate in the pueblo, even before the survey of the town had been made,[18] and finally encroached on the Mission lands proper.

On June 21st,[19] Governor Mason sent his appointment to Blackburn. (See Appendix No. 7.)

In 1848, Governor Mason, upon complaint of the padre, forbade the sale of lots by the *alcalde.*[20]

On March 20th of that year the council resolved that the best and only suitable location for the town was on the beach.[21]

Throughout the year Blackburn and Anderson acted as *alcaldes,* and A. A. Hecox was acting *alcalde* in November.

---

[17] California Message and Correspondence, 1850.   Dec. 17, pp. 383-4.
[18] See p. 38, Book *Alcalde* Deeds, Santa Cruz County Records.
[19] California Message and Correspondence, 1850, Dec. 17, pp. 383-4.
[20] See p. 5, Book *Alcalde* Deeds, Santa Cruz County Records.
[21] Santa Cruz Archives, 108, B. C.

On March 18th, the town council was elected, consisting of Majors, Rodrigues, Haines and Sinnine. Their election was approved by the Governor on the 24th by petition of citizens. The council was to act as an advisory board to Blackburn.[22]

By the treaty of Guadalupe Hidalgo (1848) Mexico ceded Upper California to the United States of America, and on September 9th, 1850, California was admitted as a State to the United States of America.

Local adminisration of affairs had gone on as usual. On Monday, March 4th, 1850, a bill was introduced and passed, changing the name of Branciforte County to that of Santa Cruz County.[23]

Bancroft says that there is no record to show definitely if there was any priest serving the Santa Cruz Mission between 1844 and 1853, though there must have been a priest living at the Mission building, for Ernest de Massey, who came to California in 1850, mentions calling upon the priest. (See Appendix No. 8.)

The following is a translation[24] from his Diary:

"The old Mission built by the Franciscans at Santa Cruz is no longer standing. At one time, however, it was an extensive establishment and under the paternal directions of the fathers owned vast herds of sheep and cattle. Today the church is in ruins. Only the nave, dilapidated both outside and in, is still standing; it is still used for holding services. The tower has fallen, and the bells, fastened to a few crude beams, are lying in the debris.

"The priests' quarters are composed of two main buildings made of adobe, or clay, which are also disintegrating and would have to be repaired to be habitable. The deserted huts of the Indians, who left the Mission to resume their nomadic life when they were given their freedom at the time of the expulsion of the Fathers, are falling to pieces. The lands are lying idle and the herds have been destroyed or lost.

"The destruction has been so complete that unless California had been taken over by the United States this country in another fifty years under Spanish rule would have been turned into a desert. But the Yankees, with their energy, their activity, and the ability to turn their energy to practical account, will soon change the entire aspect of the country.

"The nucleus of a village has already been laid out at Santa Cruz, and several wooden houses have been erected. This section of the country,

---

[22] Santa Cruz Arch., 108, B. C.
[23] Journal of the Cal. Legislature, 1st session, 1850, p. 939.
[24] Translator, Marguerite Eyer Wilbur, Quarterly of the California Historical Society, Vol. 5, 1926, pp. 360-63.

moreover, has rich soil, abundant forests, and a small port suitable for shipping out what the country produces.

"It is not sufficient for a people to resolve to throw off the domination of a country and a ruler that are antagonistic, for to preserve them from utter ruin there must be someone in authority. Nor is it wise to jump from the frying pan into the fire. This is what the Mexicans overlooked when they achieved independence.

"After stupidly ostracizing the Franciscans, confiscating the Missions, and letting personal interests take precedence over religion, the Government through intrigues tried to foster the same prosperity that had existed before the destruction of these budding colonies, which represented half a century of persevering and intelligent labor. All they succeeded in doing was to replace with desert wastes these productive Missions.

"A series of revolutions further weakened the Government and split the country into factions to such an extent that the Mexicans were powerless to check the American conquest. From the day when the Yankees won out and California became a part of the United States a new era dawned for this country, which at the present writing is rich and almost virgin territory. Those who had confiscated the Missions, however, soon had to suffer all the anguish of retaliation . . . their new properties were taken over, in turn, by their lords and masters, the Yankees.

"The town of Santa Cruz is spread out on a large tableland that commands a view of the harbor. Its population is estimated at between five and six hundred residents. Half of these are Mexicans and Californians, one-fourth Americans, and the rest Indians, Jews and foreigners. There are only a few Frenchmen among their number.

"Though the governing of the town still centers in the *alcalde,* whose title and functions are purely Mexican, the control will soon pass over into the hands of three authorities, the judge, sheriff and mayor. The most important, influential person in the village after the *alcalde* is the Franciscan Father, *curé* of Santa Cruz."

De Massey and Dr. Briot, his fellow traveler, went to call at the Mission, taking with them ten ducks which they had shot. (September 10th, 1850.)

He goes on to say that the *curé,* whom he does not once mention by name, was not able to receive them immediately, so they offered the ducks for His Reverence's supper, and talked with Abbe Doubet, an assistant, with whom de Massey had some business. He continues:

"In leaving this inhospitable presbytery—we had not even been offered a glass of water—as our purses were empty and our stomachs hollow, we were sorry we had given our ducks away, for they would have made us two good dinners. Instead we shall have to feast on beefsteak from the hotel, which is invariably tough and expensive.

"We have only met one French family here, the Bacon family. They are newcomers and have opened a bakery. This is a business which before Bacon's arrival had not been established in this budding village, for the American substitutes for baker's bread, little hot biscuits, which are cooked fresh in the oven for dinner, and the Mexican, in place of bread, has *tortillas.* For this reason, up to the present moment the lack of a bakery has not been noticed.

"Upon going to see Mr. Thomas Pallou, who knew the purpose of our trip, he sent us over to see his brother, Mr. Fourcade, a Frenchman from Bordeaux, who married the daughter of a ranchero and who owns property about two leagues from here.

"On the morning of September eleventh we left Santa Cruz."

In 1853 the Rt. Reverend Jose Sadoc Alemany was created Archbishop of San Francisco instead of Bishop of Monterey, and he revived Santa Cruz as a Mission point, sending the Reverend Sebastiano Filoteo there, who was in turn succeeded by Fr. Benito Capdevilla. Fr. Capdevilla was an active and efficient priest and teacher.

CHAPTER XXXI

The Curtain Drops on a Tragedy

BOOK VI

CHAPTER XXXI

The Curtain Drops on a Tragedy

WHEN, on the 7th day of July, 1846, the American flag had been raised in Monterey, Admiral Sloat concluded his proclamation with the assurance that "all persons holding title to real estate or in quiet possession of lands under color of right shall have those titles and rights guaranteed to them."

Innumerable disputes immediately arose about the titles, and the army officers in charge of the different posts in California were driven to distraction. They had to turn out squatters found in the Missions and on the Mission lands without any title at all. They were faced with bills of sale issued by Governor Pico. Conflicting claims arose everywhere until finally General Kearney declared that all land titles would be held in abeyance until the United States Government should pronounce judgment on the same.

How were the titles in Santa Cruz?

At the time of the signing of the Treaty of Guadalupe Hidalgo (July, 1848), Santa Cruz was an established pueblo with the American, William Blackburn, presiding as major *alcalde*.

The *alcalde* books on file with the county recorder of Santa Cruz show that a great many *alcalde* deeds were filed between 1846 and 1850, that in fact practically all the land within the pueblo, not already privately owned, was deeded away during these years. A survey was made of the lands, a map compiled and deposited in the *alcalde's* office; it is impossible to locate this map, but its known existence and the deeds prove that the pueblo lands were disposed of prior to 1850.

Congress having failed to provide a new government for California and replace the existing one, Brigadier-General Riley, Governor of California, issued a proclamation on the 3rd day of June, 1849, dividing the State into districts, the pueblo of Santa Cruz falling under District Five.

In this proclamation a brief summary of the organization of the existing government was given, and reference was made to the *alcaldes* and the *ayuntamientos,* and it was said that the powers and functions of such officials were "fully defined in the original laws of this territory," and were, therefore, in accordance with the law of nations, continued until definitely changed by law.

It was also stated that the *alcalde* and members of the Town Council should continue in office until the first of January, 1850; the pueblo of Santa Cruz was named as one of the places for holding an election, the local *alcalde* and the members of the *ayuntamiento* to act as judges and inspectors of the election.

On October 10th, 1849, the convention called for that purpose adopted the Constitution of the State of California, proclaimed on December 20th, 1849. The pueblo de San Jose was designated as the place for the first session of the Legislature, and it was decreed that all laws, regulations and provisions which from their nature required publication should be published both in English and Spanish. The Legislature was to provide for the organization of cities and unincorporated villages.

The District of Monterey, in which Santa Cruz was located, was allowed to send one Senator and two members of the Assembly to the Legislature. It was provided that these regulations were to remain in force until the Legislature should divide the State into Counties and Senatorial and Assembly Districts.

On April 25th, 1851, the Legislature passed "an Act dividing the State into Counties and establishing the seats of justice therein," and section seven reads:

"County of Santa Cruz. Beginning in the ocean, three miles from land, at a point due west of the head of San Francisquito Creek, and running due east to the summit of the Santa Cruz Mountains; thence in a southeasterly direction along the summit of said mountains to the Pajaro River; thence along the middle of said river to the Bay of Monterey, and three miles into the ocean; and thence in a northwesterly direction parallel with the coast to the point of beginning. The seat of justice shall be at Santa Cruz."[1]

Thus Santa Cruz became the county seat, and has remained so ever since. Even at that time it had already grown into a place of some importance.

By the Act of Congress of the 3rd day of March, 1851, each person claiming lands by virtue of any title derived from the Spanish or Mexican Government was required to present the same to the Board of Land Commissioners for examination, and confirmation if found valid, and all lands for which claims were not presented to the Commissioners within two years after the date of the Act were to be deemed, held and considered as part of the public domain of the United States.

The purpose was to ascertain and settle private claims, and the Act was silent as to land in public use.

---

[1] Statutes of 1850-1853.

All property which had not passed into private ownership under grants of the Mexican *alcaldes* and *ayuntamientos,* and later the American *alcaldes,* before the signing of the Treaty of Guadalupe Hidalgo, but which were still held in possession by the pueblos for the purpose of sale, were open for sale and barter by the successors of the pueblos and for the benefit of the pueblo or town treasury.

Santa Cruz did not avail itself of this right, having disposed of almost all land prior to the American occupation, and therefore having little or no interest in the matter.

Its rights to the streets, plazas, beaches and landing places were safe under the law of nations, and the treaty obligations imposed upon the United States and the State of California.

By State statute of April 22nd, 1850, amended May 4th, 1852, the Bishop of Monterey had become a corporation sole, for the administration of the temporalities of the church.

Joseph Sadoc Alemany, Bishop of that diocese, on behalf of the church, filed his petition on the 19th day of February, 1853, with the Commission at San Francisco. He claimed the confirmation to him and his successors of the title to certain church property in California to be held by him and them for religious purposes.

A decision, covering twenty-two octavo pages of print, was rendered, entitled, "Land Case No. 609, Joseph S. Alemany, Bishop, etc., vs. The United States."

Commissioner Alpheus Felch, an appointee of President Pierce, wrote the decision. It covers churches, cemeteries and gardens which are claimed to pertain to the twenty-one Missions established within the limits of the State of California. It goes into a detailed description of the two kinds of property formerly under the control of the missionary priests: Mission property and church property, the former embracing the large tracts of land which were used for the ordinary purposes of the community, and which were to be divided eventually among the neophytes, to hold in severalty, or granted to the white inhabitants in colonization; and the church property comprising such smaller portions as were separated from the mass, were under the more especial charge of the priests and devoted to the uses of the church, the purposes of worship and the support and comfort of the ministers. This second kind of property was evidently designed to be permanently devoted to such purposes, after the Mission priest would have given place to the ordinary clergy.

The amount of land allowed by the Land Commission varied for the different Missions. For Santa Cruz it confirmed the title to be approximately seventeen acres, described as follows:

"The church and the buildings adjoining the same, constituting the church and Mission buildings of the Mission of Santa Cruz, in Santa Cruz County, together with the land on which the same are erected, and the curtilage and appurtenances thereto belonging and the cemetery as the same is enclosed by its adobe walls, which adjoin said church buildings. Also the premises adjoining said buildings and their curtilage and said cemetery, and situated to the north and east of the same, known as the Mission Garden, and enclosed partly by a ravine and partly by adobe walls."[2]

The Patent from the United States Government to the Bishop of Monterey, which is found in Book 2 of Patents, page 120, et seq., Santa Cruz County Records, is in the following words and figures:

"The United States of America to all to whom these presents shall come Greeting:

"Whereas it appears from a duly authenticated transcript filed in the General Land Office of the United States, that pursuant to the provisions of the Act of Congress approved the third day of March One thousand eight hundred fifty one, entitled 'An act to ascertain and settle the private land claims in the State of California' Joseph Sadoc Alemany, Roman Catholic Bishop of the Diocese of Monterey in the State of California as claimant, filed his petition on the 19th day of February 1853 with the Commissioners to ascertain and settle the private land claims in the State of California, sitting as a Board in the City of San Francisco, in which petition he claimed the confirmation to him and his successors of the title to certain church property in California 'to be held by him and them in trust for the religious purposes and uses to which the same have become respectively appropriated,' said property consisting of church edifies, houses for the use of the clergy and those employed in the service of the church, church yards, burial grounds, orchards and vineyards, with the necessary buildings thereon and appurtenances, the same having been recognized as the property of said church by the Laws of Mexico in force at the time of the Cession of California to the United States, and whereas the Board of Land Commissioners aforesaid on the 18th day of December 1855 rendered a Decree of Confirmation in favor of the Petitioner for certain lands described therein to be held in the same capacity and for the uses set forth in his petition, the lands at the Mission of Santa Cruz, being described in said Decree as follows, 'the church and the buildings adjoining the same, constituting the church and Mission buildings of the Mission of Santa Cruz in Santa Cruz County together with the land on which the same are erected, and the curtilage and appurtenances, thereto belonging, and the cemetary

---

[2] United States vs. Bolton, Appendix to brief of Appellees, with exhibits No. XLIII, p. 132.

as the same is enclosed by its adobe walls which adjoin said church and buildings; also the premises adjoining the said buildings and their curtilage and said cemetary and situated to the North and East of the same, known as the Mission Garden and enclosed partly by the River San Lorenzo, partly by a ravine and partly by adobe walls, the same being the premises delineated on Map No. 16 in the Atlas before referred to and there designated by the term "Orchard" and whereas it further appears from a certified transcript filed in the General Land Office that an appeal from said Decree or decision of the Commissioners having been taken on behalf of the United States to the District Court of the United States for the Southern District of California, and it being shown to the Court that it was not the intention of the United States to prosecute further said appeal, the said Court "ordered that said appeal be dismissed and said appellee have leave to proceed under the Decree of the said Land Commissioners in his favor as a final Decree" and whereas under the 13th Section of the said Act of the 3rd day of March 1851 there had been presented to the Commissioner of the General Land Office a plat and certificate of the survey of the tract of land confirmed as aforesaid and authenticated on the 3rd day of May 1859 by the signature of the Surveyor General of the public lands in California, which plat and certificate are in the words and figures following to-wit:

United States Surveyor Generals Office
San Francisco, California

Under and by virtue of the provisions of the 13th section of the Act of Congress of the 3rd of March 1851 entitled an Act to ascertain and settle the Private Land Claims in the State of California, and of the 12th Section of the Act of Congress approving on the 31st of August 1852, entitled "an Act making appropriations for the Civil and Diplomatic Expenses of the Government for the year ending the 30th of June Eighteen Hundred and Fifty three and for other purposes" and in consequence of a Certificate of the United States District Court for the Southern District of California of which a copy is annexed, having been filed in this office whereby it appears that the Attorney General of the United States having given Notice that it was not the intention of the United States to prosecute the appeal from the decision of the United States Board of Land Commissioners, appointed under said Act of March 3rd, 1851, to ascertain and settle the private land claims in California, by which they recognized and confirmed the title and claims of Joseph S. Alemany, Bishop &c to the tract of land designated as the "Mission Lands of Santa Cruz," the said appeal has been vacated and thereby the said decision in favor of the said Joseph S. Alemany has been final; The said tract has been surveyed in

conformity with the grant thereof and the said decision and I do hereby
certify the annexed map to be a true and accurate plat of the tract of land
as appears by the field notes of the survey thereof made by John Wallace,
Deputy Surveyor in the months of May and December 1858 under the
directions of this office which having been examined and approved are now
on file therein; and I do further certify that under and by virtue of the
said confirmation and survey the said Joseph S. Allemany, Bishop &c is
entitled to a patent from the United States upon the presentation hereof
to the General Land Office, for the said tract of land, the same being
bounded and described as follows to wit: "Beginning at a post marked
'M No 1' where the two walls of the cemetary join and form an obtuse
angle; thence according to the true Meridian the variation of the magnetic
needle being fifteen degrees, thirty minutes East, South seventy six degrees, thirty minutes East at eight chains and eighty links; the South West
corner of Temperance Hall is five links to the left of line, nine chains to a
post marked 'M No 2' Station; thence North seventy one degrees East
forty five links the South East corner of Temperance Hall is five links
to the left of line, one chain and twenty five links to a post marked 'M No.
3' Station; thence North nineteen degrees fifteen minutes East fifty links
to a post marked 'M No. 4' on the right bank of the San Lorenzo River
Station; thence meandering up the right bank of the San Lorenzo River
North forty degrees thirty minutes West seven chains and 10 links to an
Olive tree marked 'M No. 5' Station; thence North nineteen degrees West
four chains and nine links to a° post forty one chains and sixty five links
West of corner to Sections twelve, thirteen, seven and eighteen, township
eleven South Ranges One and Two West six chains and eighty two links
to a post marked 'M No. 6' Station; thence leaving the San Lorenzo River
North thirty six degrees thirty minutes West sixty links to the ruins of
the Old Adobe Wall course South seventy seven degrees West three chains
and forty three links to a post marked 'M No. 7' Station on the South
side of a dry ravine; thence along the edge of said ravine South thirty nine
(39) degrees West one chain and forty links to a post marked 'M No. 8'
Station; thence South sixty one degrees, thirty minutes West at one chain
and sixty links, the ravine bears off to the right of line; a bridge and road
are 50 links to the right of line, six chains and sixty five links to a post
marked 'M No. 9' station at corner to the old adobe wall near the public
road; thence along the old adobe wall, the public road being to the right of
line South twenty eight degrees thirty minutes West one chain and twenty
one links to a post, fifty one chains and ninety links West of corner to
Sections twelve, thirteen, seven and eighteen, Township eleven South

BOUNDARIES

NO.	COURSE	DIST.	NO	COURSE	DIST.
1	S 76½ E	4.00	8	S 61½ W	6.65
2	N 71 E	1.25	9	S 28½ W	4.45
3	N 19¼ E	0.50	10	S 4 W	7.06
4	N 40½ W	7.10	11	S 8 E	1.23
5	N 19 W	6.82	12	N 8½ E	8.00
6	N 36½ W	3.43	13	N 2¼ E	1.94
7	S 39 W	1.40			

PLAT
OF THE
MISSION LANDS
OF SANTA CRUZ
FINALLY CONFIRMED TO JOSEPH S. ALEMANY
BISHOP &c. SURVEYED UNDER
INSTRUCTIONS FROM THE
U.S. SURVEYOR GENERAL
BY JOHN WALLACE DEPT. SURV.
MAY & DECEMBER, 1853.
CONTAINING 16 ACRES.

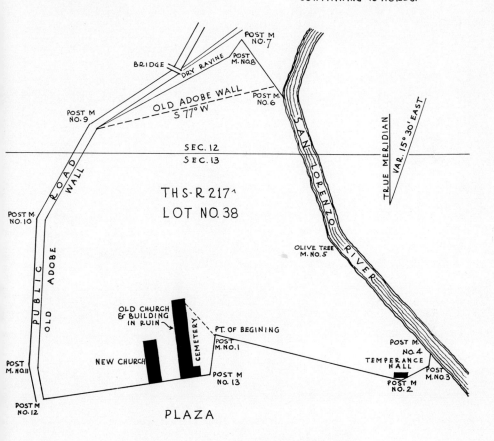

J.W. MANDEVILLE
U. S. SURV. GEN. CAL.

THE FIELD NOTES OF THE MISSION LANDS OF SANTA CRUZ & FROM WHICH THIS
PLAT HAS BEEN MADE OUT, HAVE BEEN EXAMINED AND APPROVED
AND ARE ON FILE IN THIS OFFICE.
U.S. SURVEYOR GENERAL'S OFFICE.
SAN FRANCISCO, CALIF.
MAY, 3, 1859

Range One and Two West four chains and forty-five links to a post marked 'M No. 10' Station; thence South four degrees West, seven chains and six links to a post marked 'M No. 11' Station; thence South eight degrees East, one chain and twenty three links to a post marked 'M No. 12' Station at corner of the public road and old adobe wall; thence north eighty one degrees thirty minutes East five chains and ten links to the South West corner of the New Church five chains and seventy links to the South East corner of the same six chains and sixty links to the South West corner of the ruins of the Old church seven chains and thirty-five links to the South East corner of same eight chains to a post marked 'M No. 13' Station at corner of the cemetary wall and thence along the cemetary wall North two degrees fifteen minutes East one chain and ninety four links to the place of beginning, containing sixteen acres and ninety four Hundredths of an acre and being designated upon the plats of the public surveys as Lot numbered Thirty eight, in Township eleven, South of Range Two West of the Mount Diablo Meridian; In witness whereof I have hereunto signed my name and caused the Seal of the said office to be affixed at the City of San Francisco the third day of May A. D. 1859.

L. S.   Sgd.   J. W. Mandeville
                                                     U. S. Surveyor Gen. Cal.ᵃ"

"Now know ye, that the United States of America in consideration of the premises and pursuant to the provisions of Act of Congress aforesaid of the 3rd March 1851 Have Given and Granted and by these presents Do give and grant unto the said Joseph S. Alemany, Bishop of Monterey and to his successors in trust for the religious purposes and uses to which the same have been respectively appropriated, the tract of land embraced and described in the foregoing survey, but with the stipulation, that in virtue of the 15th Section of the said act, the confirmation of this said claim and this patent 'shall not affect the interest of third party persons':

To Have and to Hold the said tract of land with the appurtenances and with the stipulation aforesaid unto the said Joseph S. Alemany, Bishop of Monterey and to his successors in trust for the uses and purposes aforesaid: In Testimony whereof I, James Buchanan, President of the United States have caused these letters to be made patent and the Seal of the General Land Office to be hereunto affixed:

"Given under my hand at the City of Washington this second day of September in the year of our Lord One thousand eight hundred fifty nine and of the Independence of the United States the eighty fourth.

By the President James Buchanan

(Land)   By J. B. Leonard, Secretary
(Office)   J. H. Granger, Recorder of the
(Seal)   General Land Office

Recorded Vol 2 pages 259 & 259 (?) inclusive
Ex^d J. S. W.

10

Filed for record and recorded July 24, 1874 @ 11 — O'Cl AM @
60

request of C. B. Younger."

The Trustees of the Inhabitants of the Town of Santa Cruz made a subsequent conveyance to Bishop Thaddeus Amat of Monterey and Los Angeles on the 8th day of December, 1866. Glover W. Field, George C. Stevens and Amasa Pray were the signers of the deed, in which they conveyed two parcels of land of .130 acres and 5 acres respectively, both of which parcels adjoined the property conveyed by the United States in the above-mentioned patent. This deed is on record in Vol. 9 of Deeds, page 103, Santa Cruz County Records.

The population of the country in 1850 was 643, the majority living in and around the Mission buildings and in Santa Cruz. By 1860 the population of the town alone had increased to 800, and the other principal village of Watsonville, founded by Judge John Watson in 1852, had 460 more.

The mode of travel to and from the County Seat was still entirely on horseback. The Californian and his wife or sweetheart traveled on one horse, the latter not behind on a pillion as the Colonial dame, but on the saddle, in front of the *caballero,* he holding the reins as well as the lady.

While from 1850 to 1852 there was no appreciable increase in population, the "Mission," as the town of Santa Cruz was then generally called, profited by the efforts of the early American settlers in the neighborhood.

Davis and Jordon burned the first lime ever made in the State in 1841 near Santa Cruz. A tanyard had been established by Paul Sweet in Scotts Valley in 1843; Joseph L. Majors built the first flour mill in the same valley, close to the Mission, in the same year; the first schooner was built in 1846, and called *The Santa Cruz;* two years later William Blackburn

MAP FILED IN COUNTY RECORDER'S OFFICE IN SANTA CRUZ
IN 1845 BY E. ANTHONY

Courtesy of Mrs. Belle Lindsay, County Recorder.

had the schooner *Zach. Taylor* built, and in 1848 Elihu Anthony built one of the first foundries in the State at Santa Cruz.

The inhabitants were mostly Catholic, but already in 1847 Protestant worship was held in the house of John D. Green, and in 1848 Mrs. Case established the first secular school at her residence, and the first "gringo" marriage in the Pajaro Valley was celebrated in 1852, between a Mr. Stockton and a Miss Lynn.

In 1845 a map was filed by E. Anthony in the County Recorder's Office of Santa Cruz County, which is still in existence. A photographic copy is found opposite this page. The map is the oldest one in the Recorder's office, and it is easy to see that it has been much used and is at the present time in a precarious condition. On this map, Pacific Avenue appears as "Main road from mission to the beach;" and the various buildings of the Mission, then still in existence, are indicated.

In 1855 Bishop Alemany again petitioned for one square league of land at each Mission "on behalf of, and for the benefit of the Christian Indians formerly connected with the Mission." This claim was rejected,[2] inasmuch as there had been no grants, or even individual occupation by the Indians, and there was therefore no valid claim before the court. It was unfortunate that neither the Mexican nor the United States Governments made any provision for the Indians by granting lands to be held in trust by the church or lay authorities.

These decisions and the consequences following the secularization were bound to change the nature of the whole settlement on the San Lorenzo. While under the Spanish and Mexican rule the Mission had been the center of the settlement, under the American rule it simply became a part of the new community.

In 1856 the *Pacific Sentinel,* established as a newspaper in Monterey the previous year, was moved to Santa Cruz, its name being changed to the *Santa Cruz Sentinel.* It is still one of the leading newspapers in the county.

Between 1855 and 1860 the Santa Cruz business district began to move down the hill, where Mission Street met Main and Willow (now Pacific Avenue and Front Street), although the old plaza remained for some time the center of much activity transacted in a number of business houses, and in the old adobe court house and jail.

On the morning of January 9th, 1857, occurred one of the coldest snaps ever known in that region, ice forming half an inch thick. An

---

[2] United States vs. Bolton, Appendix to Brief of Appellees, with Exhibits, No. XLIII, pp. 137-138.

earthquake then shook Santa Cruz, which was felt from the northern Sacramento Valley to the Bay of San Diego. It crumbled the front wall of the Mission building proper, which had already passed through an earthquake in 1840, when the tower at one front corner had fallen. On January 20th, another, though less heavy, quake occurred, leaving the Mission buildings which were still standing in a much-weakened condition. Thirty-eight days after the first shock of January 9th, the southwest corner of the old edifice fell at three o'clock in the morning with a crash which awakened the residents around the plaza.

Father Benito Capdevilla, the priest in charge, immediately launched plans for rebuilding, and on July 5th of that year, Bishop Thaddeus Amat came over from Monterey to lay the cornerstone of the new church, preaching a sermon first in halting English and then one in Spanish. A year later, on July 4th, 1858, he returned to dedicate the structure, with Father J. B. Comelias, of Monterey, and Father F. Mora, of San Juan Bautista.

Waters and Beck, Santa Cruz builders, were not only the carpenters who erected the new wooden structure but the architects who designed it, with four Gothic windows on each side and two in front, one on each side of the entrance. The interior was plastered by George Stevens and painted by Robert Lampée, both Santa Cruz artisans. The church was twenty-seven feet to the eaves, thirty-six feet wide and one hundred and ten feet long. The structure cost $8,000 and seated about three hundred and fifty people. It stood on a site at about the west edge of the present Holy Cross Rectory.[4]

What was left of the old rock and adobe Mission building was used for some time thereafter as a store house, and as the adobe crumbled it was walled and roofed with redwood plank from the mills up the San Lorenzo, but finally it had to give place to the modern church now occupying part of the site.

As years passed, the memory of the Old Mission and of the padres became dear to the inhabitants of the old Mission Town—Santa Cruz, the City of the Holy Cross.

If in the beginning Santa Cruz had to forego the prestige and many of the pleasures and benefits enjoyed by its immediate neighbor, Monterey, on account of its not being located on the King's Highway—El Camino Real—it was later to reap some of the benefits of its comparative isolation.

Prior to the rush for gold in 1848 and 1849, when it was estimated that seventy thousand immigrants arrived from the East alone, a great

---

[4] The present brick church was built in 1889, when Father Hugh McNamee was priest.

many Easterners had already filtered into California. Those who came by sea generally settled in the coast communities; those who came overland were mostly men and women who sought land and security of title—the opportunity of making homes. Sutter from his fort, New Helvetia, had for many years watched these immigrant trains coming down the Sierra Nevada trails, and had received them hospitably.

The hunters and trappers were of a different breed. Hardy men, half vagabonds, half nomads, they were on adventure bent and willing to join, outside of the regular hunting season, any undertaking which promised excitement and gain. There were only comparatively few of them, and the Californians of Spanish and Mexican descent, often enough politically turbulent themselves, were able to maintain their Arcadia in comparative safety against the intruders.

But when in January, 1848, James W. Marshall, a wheelwright in the employ of Sutter, found gold in a mill race which he had built, the discovery brought a class of men different in economic ideas, in energies and governmental policies. Many of them were American or European miners, attracted by the lure of the precious metal; they belonged to a rough element and showed a scant respect for the native sons, whom they contemptuously indicated as "greasers;" while the Californians, self-satisfied and convinced of the superiority of their own civilization and ideas, drew close together, showing either an amused contempt or alarmed disdain for the newcomers, whom they classed in one group of "gringos"—sharpers.

The mining communities were soon settled on a basis of every man for himself. Crude local governments were formed, where a rough and ready sort of popular justice was dispensed. The Digger Indians were, of course, free game for everybody. Submissive, unless gathered in overwhelming numbers and acting under great provocation, they submitted to many outrages, without resistance or revenge. It was quite different with the old Californians, who had no idea of yielding to such treatment, and when other measures failed, some of them took to their horses, turned bandits, and inflicted terrible revenge.

While in the Southern States of the Union the rule prevailed that the smallest particle of negro blood made one a "nigger," and placed him beyond the pale, in California the reverse rule was in vogue, for the smallest percentage of Spanish blood made of a *mestizo* a "Spaniard," and gave him an inordinate pride of race and station. They were like *los correctos* one meets today in Mexico, equally proud and ready to take offense.

It was principally this class of the *gente de razon* which drifted away from the coast and into the interior districts; they were treated with contempt by many of the red-shirted miners, who were often offscouring of the water-fronts, run-away sailors, men hiding from justice, broken-down gamblers, shady lawyers, doubtful preachers, and what not. Sometimes the better class of miners had the upper hand, and the outrages stopped, but many a time the other element was in the saddle.

During the frequent altercations the miners endeavored to protect their lives and property with the means at hand, and while many of the guilty were caught and punished, some innocents likewise met their fate— and the "greasers" were the majority of the latter. Public opinion was against them; as long as someone had to hang, and the identity of the guilty party was doubtful, let it be a "greaser"—so the mob reasoned.

Lawlessness always breeds lawlessness, and some of the natives of California and Mexico, especially of the Sonora province, banded together under leaders—at first only for protection and defense. As time went on, they became fired by hatred, smarting under the indignities inflicted on their fierce pride as "Spaniards," exasperated by the knowledge that many of their kindred had been killed though innocent, forgetting the often justifiable provocations which explained the lynchings, and they united under bloodthirsty and capable leaders, attracted to their standards many outlaws, went on the warpath, and exacted a terrible toll of retribution, which finally degenerated into a saturnalia of murder and pillage.

A Mexican from Sonora, of a respected family, was the chief leader of the banditti. His name was Joaquin Carrillo, but later he called himself Murrieta.

In 1845 he had left his native place to go to Mexico City and act as a groom in the stables of President Lopez de Santa Ana. In 1848 he made a trip to San Francisco to hunt for his brother, Carlos. On his return to Mexico he married and once more came to California in 1850; his brother informed him that the gringos had swindled him out of his rancho, which a previous Governor had granted to him. He and his brother went to Sacramento and rode to Placerville, then known as Hangtown, but there his brother was accused of having stolen some horses. The brother and a friend of his, Flores, were seized and hung by infuriated miners.

Embittered Murrieta took his beautiful young bride, Carmen, to the mines in Stanislaus County, where he was attacked by white miners. He was left senseless on the ground, and his wife was assaulted and murdered. Shortly afterwards he was again seized by a mob, tied to a tree, and given a shameful lashing. It was then that he swore vengeance and organized several large bands of his mounted compatriots, who became the terror of the countryside. They roamed from San Diego to the Oregon line, robbing and murdering as they went along.

Murrieta began his operations in 1850, and was finally killed in August, 1853, by a special body of twenty California State rangers under command of the famous bandit hunter, Captain Harry Love, at a spot in the Coast Range where a chain of low mountains divides two great valleys. His head was cut off, preserved in alcohol, and taken to San Francisco, where the reward of one thousand dollars offered personally by the Governor, Colonel Bigler, was paid, and the next year the Legislature, considering that the reward had not been sufficient, made Lowe an additional grant of five thousand dollars. (See Appendix No. 1.)

About the same time the other members of Murrieta's gang were either killed or fled from the State. Pedro Sanchez was killed by Albino Teba, not far from Columbia; Joaquin Blanco was killed near Stockton by Eugenio Corral; the infamous and bloodthirsty Manuel Garcia, nicknamed Jack Three Fingers, the trusted lieutenant of Murrieta, was killed with him.

Santa Cruz, on account of its peculiar location, though in the immediate neighborhood of the bandit-invested countries (see Appendix No. 2), escaped these predatory bands and most of the lawlessness then existing throughout the State, but of course it had a modest share of the latter, especially when the San Francisco Vigilance Committee of 1851, under William T. Coleman, executed a few and drove many more criminal characters out of the city by the Golden Gate. A few of them chose Santa Cruz for their next place of residence, but the new town suffered little from that element.

By 1860 the curtain had definitely dropped upon the Spanish-Mexican scene in California. Though evidences of the Hispano occupation were then, and still are to be found in the names of many of the rivers, mountain ranges, valleys, counties and cities of the State, most of the Mission buildings and presidios were still standing, proud old family names of Iberian origin were still cherished, even as they are honored today, either in *propra personae* or in the names of modern boulevards, streets and parks, large ranchos were still owned by the original recipients of the Mexican grants, or their immediate descendants, but for all that, the stream of modern American life had been steadily rising, sweeping before it all resistance, and burying everything as far as possible under the sediment of its turbulent emotions.

FINIS

Finis

WHEN the curtain dropped at the end of the last act of the drama of the Spanish-Mexican occupation, a great tragedy took place behind the scenes.

The actors stood forlorn—the last representatives in the Golden West of the largest colonial empire that men had ever known, stretching from Porto Rico in the East to San Francisco in the West, from Cape Horn in the South to Canada in the North, and from which realms came two-thirds of the entire continental territory of the United States. They could not know that in the Spanish names of States, of cities, of rivers, mountains and valleys, the history of their countries would be forever impressed on these United States.

They could not foresee that their "Laws of the Indies" would leave on the Western shores a judicial monument, never to be forgotten by lawyers and laymen; that from their national legal system they left us many great, beneficial principles of law, unknown to the Common Law of England, such as the doctrine of water appropriation, instead of the narrow doctrine of riparian rights, the laws declaring community interest of the wife in the property of the spouses, standing in sharp contrast to the Law of England and of the Eastern States, where the husband is the controller, if not the owner, of the wife's property.

But for them there was no applause, nor calls of "bravo" from the pit, nor any demands from the gallery for encores, so dear to the Latin heart. Instead hoots and cat-calls, over-ripe tomatoes and ill-smelling eggs descended in a shower on the lowered curtain, which divided the proscenium from the back stage. The audience arose, growling at the bewildered mummers, huddled together on the boards and filed out of the play-house into "God's free air," making derisive remarks at "those ham-actors who botched the play." The voices from nigger-heaven were of course the loudest, denouncing with vigor "the damned foreigners, the greasers from Spain and Mexico," forgetting that they themselves were the real foreigners in this Land of Promise.

But now we know better, and even those of us who stand outside the temple of the Mother-Church have learned our lesson.

When the jolly padres, some almost supermen, the great majority very good men, and a few of weaker timber, ceased to direct their great estates and many Indian retainers and serfs, like feudal barons; when the chimes ceased ringing out a great welcome to them, when they visited a neighboring Mission; or when their musicians playing lively tunes upon flutes, fiddles, trumpets and other instruments for festivals and Masses, finally silenced their melodies, we are now convinced that there departed with these religious from the California stage a spiritual force of pure ideals and high hopes. It may be, in accordance to some modern viewpoints, that these ecclesiastics erred in their fixed idea that they were bestowing a priceless boon by forcibly bringing salvation to the heathen; still their loss has hardly been compensated by our eloquent Doctors of Divinity, stern-faced and austere divines, our liberal writers, our self-satisfied columnists, our politico-radio diagnosticians, and other "Leaders of Modern Thought."

When the vainglorious caballeros, spectacular, showy, some true patriots, some only patriots *de bolsa*,[1] often lazy, given to gambling, bull and bear fighting, lacking in acumen for the practicality of modern life, finally rode out of the picture on their gaily caprisoned horses, and were replaced by Nordics, cut from sterner stuff, we now appreciate that with these showy gentlemen, slightly ridiculous in our sophisticated eyes, went much fine courtesy, stately friendships, a high point of honor, sometimes, it is true, expressed in rather bombastic language, but noble for all that; and we also realize that this was a great deprivation, which so far has not been replaced in our advanced bankers, able engineers, great merchant princes, prominent lawyers, honest or grafting politicians, bootleggers, hot-dog peddlers and what not.

When the handsome and dignified matrons, who bore and raised many children in a doctorless country, who presided with dignity over homes which lacked modern mechanical devices, who dispensed hospitality to wayfarers as a matter of course, courtesied themselves off the boards, hand in hand with their pleasure-loving, passionate and beautiful daughters, who were often more skilled in throwing confetti or cologne-filled eggshells at the heads of favored suitors at their gay fiestas than in scholastic attainments, we lost much. As they gathered their voluminous skirts and shawls about them to dance gracefully from the stage, lustrous black eyes twinkling coquettishly through the gauzy parts of their Spanish fans, they took with them ideals of motherhood and wifehood, of faithfulness and sacrifice and virtue unsurpassed in any part of the world.

All the modern sanitary hospitals, clever doctors, famous surgeons, devoted nurses, great hotels, modern society leaders, scarlet-lipped flappers, scandal mongers, movie queens and shrinking bathing beauties have hardly been able to compensate us Californians for our loss, though we cherish the idea that they had no unworthy successors in our own pioneer mothers of the West.

---

[1] Purse patriots.

When the final curtain dropped, the finis was written to a play such as never before had been presented, and can never be enacted again, for where will mankind find anew such a magnificent stage setting for so dramatic an array of events?

The play was cast in Alta California, a country of marvelous beauty and unexcelled climate, with a rugged coast, romantic valleys, great plains, towering mountains, mighty rivers, extensive woods, many of which teemed with game, washed by the waves of an ocean abundantly stocked with a great variety of edible fish. All this lay slumbering for centuries, bathed in soft California sunshine, and then suddenly felt the awakening touch of the Spanish knights and padres, who were allowed for three-quarters of a century to prepare this Sleeping Beauty for her nuptials with modern mankind. Thereafter pastoral simplicity and contentment fled the country, when it became subject to the modernized and mechanized civilization of more enterprising races.

It is true that the Mission Fathers did not fully succeed in their purpose of Christianizing the natives—of planting permanently the doctrines of Christ in the minds and hearts of the California Indians. They attempted the impossible; no persons could have ever reached the ultimate goal, short of centuries of sustained endeavor. But how well they wrought!

Physically they left us a conception of architecture which is today one of the few expressions in stone and mortar of the native spirit of the country, surpassing the Dutch and English Colonial styles on the Eastern seaboard. They have pointed out, through the application of irrigation and the introduction of fruits and vines, the untold wealth obtainable from the soil by useful efforts; in this way they never practiced the predatory and destructive methods of other white men opening up a new country.

But they have left us far more than material benefits. They have bestowed a great legacy of high ideals, of devotion to duty and sacrifice; they have left a memory of men of noble purpose and conception—educated men who went into the wilderness, opened up the country and brought civilization to far-away places, where it was utterly unknown before; they have painted a worthy, romantic background for the great country that California is today. No wonder that their memory is still held in affectionate esteem by all Californians, native or adopted, Catholics, Jews, Protestants and Unbelievers.

We are continuously reminded of them even today, for many words of their soft and melodious language, in their original spelling or but slightly modified, are now household words in California, and indeed in most of the States of the Union. We speak of *armada, flotilla, commodore, canoe, tornado* and *hurricane,* of *barricade, grenade* and *guerilla,* of *alli-*

gator, buffalo, merino, canary and *mosquito,* of *duenna, parasol, paragon,* of *sarsaparillo, vanilla, chocolate, cacao, soda,* of *cigar, tobacco,* of *sombrero, fandango, gala, barbecue, potato* and *tomato.* There is no danger that they will be forgotten.

Ave to the State of California, welcomed with a smile by her Sisters in the American Union; we know your march to success has only just started, and we cheer you on your way to your brilliant future; *Vale* to California *Alta y Nueva;* your part we cherish with feelings of love and devotion, and especially gratitude to your *dramatis-personae,* who played so well their different roles on a mighty stage.

If the curtain which fell on your last act could only be raised once more, a thunderous applause would greet them, and a great demonstration of admiration and affection would shake the very dome of the play-house, to gladden the hearts of the departing actors.

This cannot be, but your memory will remain with Californians for generations to come.

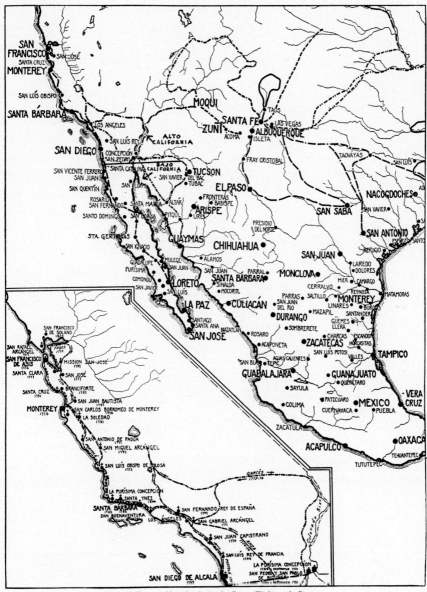

Map of Western New Spain in the Later Eighteenth Century.
(From BOLTON, *Palóu's New California.*)

APPENDIX

APPENDIX

APPENDIX No. 1

Chapter I, Book I

The Seven Cities of Cibola

To some of these fairy tales,—many as old as mankind,—impetus was given by a Spaniard, Cabeza de Vaca, who was found almost naked and half wild in 1536 by a party of scouting Spaniards in the vast, unknown Southwest. He was accompanied by a Moor, Estévanico (Stephen) and a small number of Indians, and had wonderful tales to tell of far away cities of great wealth.

This caused the expedition of Francisco Vasquez Coronado. It was a most ambitious undertaking, the cavalcade including 300 Spaniards, 1000 Indians, 1000 extra horses, droves of live stock and so forth, and the Spaniards carried the best known armaments.

Needless to say the seven cities were never found, and the poor tribes which were visited, apprehensive of this mighty invasion, promptly passed them on "to the beyond" with new tales of wonder; this time it was La Gran Quivira.

Coronada rode on and on, never finding the sought for cities, but only hardships for all and death for many of his followers. When he returned in 1542 and reported that the seven cities were myths, he was not believed!

APPENDIX No. 1

Chapter III, Book I

The Pious Fund (*Fundo Piadoso*) was raised for the purpose of the "reduction" of the Californias. The first subscriptions amounted to 47,000 pesos. A great many gifts were later added to this fund, some of them large amounts, and all donated by devout followers of the Church, who desired to aid the Christianization of the Indians, principally in the Californias.

In 1792 the foundation was in excellent condition, its capital being 828,937 pesos, its yearly income 55,177 pesos.

It was finally confiscated by the Mexican Government in 1842, but subsequently was partly returned to the successor of the first Bishop of Alta California, appointed immediately after the secularization of the Missions.

Full particulars of the founding, the growth and the final disposition of the Pious Fund, as far as California Alta is concerned, can be found in the Report made to the Secretary of State at Washington, D. C., by the Honorable Jackson H. Ralston, LL.D. (now of the Faculty of Leland Stanford University at Palo Alto, California), as Agent of the United States Government and Chief Counsel before the Court at The Hague, in the famous case generally known as the "Pious Fund of the Californias." This American Agent's report is known as Senate Document No. 28, 57th Congress, 2nd Session, and was printed in the Government Printing Office at Washington, D. C., in 1902, and also appears as Appendix No. 2 in Foreign Relations Report of 1902.

In this report, which consists with the transcript of two heavy volumes, it is pointed out that the Pious Fund was first founded at the end of the 17th century, when in the year 1697 Fathers Juan Maria Salvatierre and Eusebio Francisco Kino, Members of the Order of Jesus, presented a Memorial to the King of Spain, asking permission to undertake the conversion of the heathen in California.

Important donations were made to this fund, the total contributions down to 1731 for the development of the Missions of California amounted to $120,000. (See Noticias de la Provincia de Californias, Venegas, Vol. 2, p. 48 et seq.)

In June, 1735, a large donation was made by the Marquis de Villapuente and his wife, Marquesa de las Torres De San Roda. More donations came in but in the year 1767 the Spanish Government took possession of the temporalities of the Jesuits banishing them from the country. The fund was administered under Government supervision, chiefly for the benefit of the Missions in California Antiqua (part of what is now the Republic of Mexico) and California Alta (now the American State of California), although the conversion of the heathen in the Philippine Islands had also been mentioned. In Alta California Missions were established and maintained by the Franciscan Fathers from this Pious Fund, controlled by Spain, until the Revolution, by virtue of which Mexico threw over the power of Spain, and thereafter the Mexican Government assumed the administration of the Fund.

The first Mexican Law regulating this fund was passed on May 25, 1832. (See Transcript of the American Agent's Report, p. 579.)

In 1836 Mexico took under consideration the formation of a Bishopric of California, appointing Francisco Garcia Diego first incumbent of this Bishopric.

In 1842 (October 24th) the Mexican Government incorporated the properties of the Pious Fund into its Treasury and at the same time charged the Public Treasury with an indebtedness of 6% per annum on the proceeds of the sale of the property.

In 1845 (April 3rd) Mexico passed a decree regarding the restitution of the debts and property of the Pious Fund of the Californias. (See Report supra, p. 211.)

Thereafter war broke out between the United States Government and the Republic of Mexico and by the Treaty of Guadalupe-Hidalgo of 1848 Alta California was ceded to the American Republic.

No benefits of the Pious Fund, whatever, were turned over either to the Bishop of Lower (or Antiqua) California, or to the Bishop of Alta California, who on behalf of the Catholic Church were the successors in interest to the Missions and appurtenances.

In 1870 the claim of the Roman Catholic Bishop of the State of California against Mexico for interest, arising out of the fact that the diocese had been deprived of all income created for its benefit on the taking of its property was brought before a Mixed Claims Commission between the United States and Mexico. This claim was severely contested by Mexico but finally referred to the umpire, Sir Edward Thornton, for adjudication. He decided in favor of the United States, giving an award of $904,700.99, on behalf of the Bishop, the amount being one-half of the interest upon the property taken by Mexico. Mexico paid this award and declared that upon its payment she was freed from all obligation to pay any further sum. This the United States contested and insisted that the award of Sir Edward Thornton, based as it was upon one-half of the annual income of the Pious Fund established the amount which was yearly payable to the Bishop by Mexico, and that this obligation extended over all the years after the date of the Thornton award until each successive payment should be made, aggregating 1,420,682.67 dollars Mex.

Finally in 1902 the United States Government succeeded in arranging an arbitration. This case was heard at The Hague, The Netherlands, before a distinguished Tribunal, consisting of Mr. Matsen of Denmark, as President, Sir Edward Fry, Dr. de Martens, Dr. Asser and Dr. de Savornin Lohman, as Judges. The final arguments were made by an array of brilliant counsel. Honorable Jackson Ralston, the Agent and Chief Counsel, who had prepared and submitted all the data and briefs in the case, argued for the United States, and additional arguments were made by Senator William M. Stewart of Nevada, Garret W. McEnerney, Esq., of San Francisco, Maitre Descamps of Brussels and the Honorable Judge William L. Penfield, Solicitor of the Department of State at Washington, while for Mexico the case was fully presented by Emilio Pardo, as Agent and Chief Counselor and assisted by Maitres M. Delacroix and Beernaert, of Counsel. The case was decided in favor of the United States for all the yearly payments then due with a declaration that Mexico was thereafter indebted to the United States on behalf of the (Arch)bishop of California perpetually for an annuity of $43,050.99.

APPENDIX No. 1

CHAPTER V, BOOK I

The true name of the Spanish navigator who is usually mentioned as Juan Rodrigues Cabrillo, was Juan Rodrigues. He visited the coast points now known as San Diego, Catalina Island, San Pedro, Ventura, Santa Barbara, Point Conception, Cuylers Harbor (Island of San Miguel) and went as far North as Fort Ross (38° 31′).

He died on January 3, 1543, while his ship was lying at San Miguel in the Santa Barbara Channel.

APPENDIX No. 2

CHAPTER V, BOOK I

One of the reasons for encouraging the expedition of Vizcaino was the advent of two Dutch fleets which sailed through the Strait of Magellan to the Pacific in 1599 and 1600 respectively. One of them under Oliver van Noort made several captures along the West Coast of Peru and went as far North as the Equator before veering to the West.

APPENDIX No. 3

CHAPTER V, BOOK I

The terms "religious" and "secular" are strongly contra-distinguished in the Catholic Church, which distinctions enter into the written law of Spain. A "Religious" (*religioso*) is one who has taken the habit and the vows of one of the "*Regular* Orders," such as the Franciscans, the Dominicans, the Capuchins, and the like; hence he is also called a "Regular," or one of the "Regular Clergy." Having taken the three vows of chastity, obedience, and poverty, he has renounced the world, and therefore is held to be *Civilly dead*. For this reason he cannot make a contract, nor take or hold property, either by purchase or descent; nor sue or be sued; nor make a will; nor fill any fiduciary or civil office. A "Secular" Clergyman, (also called *clerigo*) who has not taken these vows, is not subject to these disabilities; he can contract, buy and sell; take by purchase or descent; make a will; and hold fiduciary and civil offices. He therefore has still a hold upon "secular" or worldly matters; hence the term "secular." A thing is also said to be "secularized" when it is changed from an "ecclesiastical" use, purpose or control, to a secular one. (*Escriche,* Diccionario de Legislacion; *Religioso, Clerigo, Secular y Secularizacion.*) A Mission is therefore secularized when its temporalities are given in charge to a secular or civil officer, when its Missionary establishment is superseded, converted into a curacy, and given into the charge of a Secular Priest. (See Jones's Report, p. 13, Colonial History of San Francisco, by John W. Dwinelle, p. 21, Par. 27.)

APPENDIX No. 1

Chapter VI, Book I

After Fortún Jeminez landed on the East Coast of the Peninsula near La Paz in 1533, and Cortes in May 1535, four more important expeditions were undertaken to the supposed islands (Las Islas Californias): those of Francisco de Ulloa in 1539, Hernando de Alarcón in 1540, Cabrillo in 1542, and Vizcaino in 1596.

In the following century many official and so-called unofficial or semi-official expeditions were undertaken, some by pearl-fishers, others by adventurers and some by plain buccaneers.

APPENDIX No. 2

Chapter VI, Book I

Father de Salvatierra had crossed the Gulf with five soldiers, a captain and some servants.

Tragedy after tragedy followed. The land was arid and sterile; little timber was available for construction; the land was so broken up that communication was made difficult and many of the natives were hostile.

APPENDIX No. 3

Chapter VI, Book I

A series of depredations took place from 1730 to 1740, when several of the devoted Fathers were murdered in a most revolting way. In the midst of all this turmoil stood Father Sigismundo Taraval, a dauntless priest, who has left us a famous Journal (from 1734-1737). He described with a vivid pen the sacrifices of the religious, the blunders of the military commanders, the loose living of the soldiers, the treachery and cruelty of the natives.

He was a man of prominent birth—an Italian of Spanish ancestry, born in Milan in 1700, his father being Lieutenant Teresa Andrade. He reached the Californias in 1730, where he fearlessly combatted polygamy and the superstitions fostered by the "medicine men," who were sorcerers, sleight-of-hand performers, fakers and scoundrels. He served with great distinction.

In 1751 he returned to Guadalajara, where he died in 1763.

His original journal is now at the Newberry Library in Chicago. See recent publication of the Quivira Society of Los Angeles, "The Indian Uprising in Lower California," described by Father Taraval. (Translated with introduction and notes by Marguerite Eyer Wilbur.)

APPENDIX No. 4

Chapter VI, Book I

In England, about one hundred years later, several men arose who fervently embraced similar doctrines, the principal advocate being John Wycliff or Wicliff. Born in 1324, he entered Oxford College in 1346. He was a contemporary of Chaucer in England, of Jacob and Philip of Artevelde in Ghent, the Low Lands, while Thomas à Kempis was born four years before Wycliff's death, which occurred in 1384.

His was the first general English translation of the Bible. Tyndall's translation of the New Testament appeared in 1526; the Douay Bible and King James Version in 1610, with Coverdale's, Matthew's, Crammer's, Geneva and Bishops' versions between.

He denounced the repulsive practices of the friars, the clergy and their officials, especially of acquiring wealth through abuse of the doctrine of indulgences, which had become almost as gross in England during his life, as it did 150 years later under Tetzel in Germany, arousing Martin Luther.

Wycliff wrote: "It is plain to me that our Prelates in granting indulgences do commonly blaspheme the wisdom of God, pretending in their avarice and folly that they understand what they really know not. They chatter on the subject of grace as if it were a thing to be made a merchandise of selling pardons, the devil having availed himself of an error in the schools to introduce after this matter heresies in morals."

He organized a company of Poor Priests to preach God's Law through England, and many believe that the "Parson" in the Prologue to Chaucer's Canterbury Tales is either a portrait of Wycliff himself or one of his "Poor Priests."

APPENDIX No. 5

Chapter VI, Book I

Serra's birthplace in Petra, near Palma, on the Island of Mallorca, Spain, was recently purchased by the Rotary Club of Mallorca and presented to the City of San Francisco. It was the desire of that organization to preserve the house and make of it a museum and monument to the worthy Padre's great work in establishing the California Missions.

The California Historical Society of San Francisco sent to the Serra Museum a collection of pictures of the California Missions, made from drawings of Mr. H. M. T. Powell, in 1848-1850; they were framed in California redwood (palo Colorado). A similar collection of pictures taken in 1906 and a third collection of present-day pictures of the Missions and the cities which have grown up about the Missions have been included, together with several sets of books, dealing with Father Serra's life and missionary efforts.

The presentation ceremonies were held by the Rotary Club of Mallorca on May 11, 1932, and the wish of that organization expressed that the "City of San Francisco, named for the patron saint of Fray Junipero Serra's order, should be the perpetual holder of title to this memorial." The deed to the birthplace was forwarded to San Francisco, and gratefully accepted by the city.

APPENDIX No. 1

Chapter VII, Book I

The San Jose, which had been specially built for the California voyages, departed from Cape San Lucas, in May, 1770. It was lost at sea, with all men on board.

APPENDIX No. 2

Chapter VII, Book I

Portola dictated a statement to Juan Manuel de Viniegra, former secretary to de Galvez in September, 1773, giving an account of this terrible march. A translation is to be found in Chapman, History of California, The Spanish Period, page 225.

APPENDIX No. 1

Chapter IX, Book I

There were many famines in California Alta. In 1770 when Governor Portola resolutely held out until the supply ship arrived, he and his men on the return trip to San Diego were reduced to a mule diet. He wrote that in order that they might not die meanwhile, they had to kill one of the weak mules at the end of each day. The flesh was roasted or half fried in a hole in the ground, and they had not a grain of salt or other seasoning. He says: "We shut our eyes and fell on to that scaly mule. . . . We ate 12 in as many days. At last we entered San Diego, smelling frightfully of mules."

In 1772 when the supply ships were late in coming, Governor Fages organized a successful bear hunt on a large scale in the neighborhood of San Luis Obispo, and again in 1774 there was famine again, when Viceroy Bucarelli saved the situation.

APPENDIX No. 2

Chapter IX, Book I

San Blas was never a successful port. The harbor began sanding in soon after the base was established and ships often had difficulty in entering and leaving. Moreover the place was unhealthy and supplies easily spoiled there. Many times its abandonment was under consideration but this was never accomplished.

APPENDIX No. 3

Chapter IX, Book I

The first California code was called the *Reglamento Provisional*. It eventually comprised three documents: Echeveste's recommendations, dated May 19th, 1773, the opinion of a junta dated July 8th, making some modifications, and the Viceroy's decree of July 23rd.

One provision aimed at the Colonization of Alta California. The offer made was:—transportation free of charge to San Blas, free supplies for 5 years, wages as a sailor for 2 years. The response, however, was very scant.

APPENDIX No. 4

CHAPTER IX, BOOK I

De Anza set out on March 23rd, from Monterey to explore the site of San Francisco. He chose the present site of Fort Scott for a Presidio and likewise selected a site for a Mission, calling it "Dolores." He made an attempt to explore the Rio de San Francisco (the Sacramento and San Joaquin Rivers) and returned to Monterey, on April 8th, emerging through a pass near the present Gilroy Hotsprings.

APPENDIX No. 5

CHAPTER IX, BOOK I

Viceroy Bucareli issued instructions to Governor de Neve on December 25th, 1776. There were 27 paragraphs, which together with the *Reglamento* of 1773, the Viceroy's previous and only partly executed instructions to Rivera, and the de *Neve Reglamento* of a later day, formed the nucleus of the Spanish regulations governing Alta California throughout the Spanish period.

APPENDIX No. 6

CHAPTER IX, BOOK I

The first effort toward real colonization—with women—had been made by Rivera, who upon going to Monterey to succeed Fages as Governor, had taken with him 51 persons—about 6 families and some unattached persons—from Sinaloa. These colonists reached San Diego September 26th, 1774.

APPENDIX No. 1

CHAPTER XIII, BOOK II

The accused priest was Padre Suarez del Real, who lived at San Carlos. The story goes that Ambrose G. Tomlinson, an American, had become a Mexican, and had adopted the Roman Catholic faith in order to enable him to marry a California woman. He was known as "Tom the Trapper," and had associated with most of the trappers and hunters who had crossed the *Sierra Nevada.* In 1840, believing that he was going to die, he called for the priest to make his confession, and Padre del Real responded. On his death bed he confessed the knowledge that several Americans were conspiring to overthrow Governor Alvarado, the leader being Captain Isaac Graham of Santa Cruz, and that the conspirators intended to turn over the province to the United States Government. By some historians it is claimed that the ecclesiastic at once informed the governor of this confession, although others give quite a different and more plausible explanation. Anyhow, widespread arrests were made, a great many Americans being taken to Monterey and enduring untold suffering in the filthy jail. Afterwards they were deported to San Blas.

The incident intensified the bitter feeling between the American immigrants and the permanent Mexican and Spanish settlers. (See John Marsh Pioneer, by Dr. Lyman, p. 233.)

APPENDIX No. 1

Chapter XIV, Book II

Trowbridge Hall in "California Travels, An Intimate Guide to the Old Mission" writes:

"Most of the Indians profited nothing by being reprimanded and had to be whipped. Curiously enough when whipped they had the choice of a scourge of rawhide or one of stinging hazel twigs, which was applied to the culprit, stretched face downward on the ground. All severe punishments were administered within the guard house, but slight misdemeanors were corrected every Sunday after Mass with six or eight lashes, after which the sinner went in submission to kiss the hand of the padre, who watched from the church door. After being punished one of the Indians is said to have torn off his shirt and flung it at the feet of the priest saying: 'Padre, take back thy Christianity,' but most of them accepted a dozen blows with indifference, absolute, which is hardly to be wondered, considering the extreme torture they underwent as boys, whipped with nettles until their skins were enflamed to rawness, and then carried to a nest of stinging ants and laid on top, where the insects were annoyed with sticks to render them more furious. When able to suffer all this with patience, the boy was considered a man."

APPENDIX No. 2

Chapter XIV, Book II

Cortes caused 200 unarmed Indian warriors to be butchered in their citadel, after promising them a peaceful parley.

Pedro de Alvarado who executed one of the most brutal massacres of the whole conquest was rewarded with Xochimilco, its floating gardens and 30,000 people. (Chase, Mexico, page 96.)

APPENDIX No. 1

Chapter XV, Book II

De Mofras is most enthusiastic. In Volume 1 of his Explorations, p. 384, he says:

"The magnificent results obtained by . . . . the Spanish missionaries here and their success in gathering around their missions in Alta California more than 30,000 neophytes, proves conclusively that it is easy to attract them by offering presents, to make them realize the advantages of labor in moderation and to keep them by kindness. In the most isolated deserts of America, travellers are often surprised to find rude wooden crosses, erected by the natives; these natives from the most remote times of the conquest cherished recollections of veneration for the missionaries. These men in contrast with all the other whites, never did them any harm but only good and continuously protected them; also they were the only nation that did not destroy the Indian, that is to say, who did not employ the methods of the United States towards the Indians of Florida. . . . Amongst such wild tribes, as amongst all known civilized people, military authority alone could never accomplish lasting results.

"The wooden cross of a few poor religious has conquered more provinces for Spain and France than the swords of the popular generals."

APPENDIX No. 1
Chapter XVI, Book III

When Father Francisco Palou left, after turning over to Father Fermin de Lasuen the Presidency of the Alta California Missions, he hoped to enjoy a well-earned rest.

His life had been an eventful one. Prior to coming to California, he had been President of the Sierra Gorda Missions. The Guardian of the College of San Fernando, admiring his zeal, pronounced him especially successful in the reduction of the Indians. He served the Sierra Gorda Missions from 1750 to 1759, and subsequently lived at the college for eight years. He was appointed to Baja California, and arrived at Loreto in April, 1768; he took charge of San Francisco Xavier, and in 1769 became the Acting President. In 1773 he surrendered the southern Missions to the Dominicans and started north. He served in the Missions of Alta California until 1780, when by reason of ill-health and fatigue he asked leave to retire. At first there was no transportation to Mexico; then Father Serra died, and as senior missionary, Palou was called to serve as Acting President, until de Lasuen was appointed in September, 1785. He returned to his college but found no rest, for he was made Guardian in July, 1786, in which capacity he served for a few years. Bancroft says, "I think he died before 1790."

Amongst his writings, the best known are his famous Life of Serra, "Relacion Historica de la Vida y Apostolicas Tareas del Venerable Padre Fray Junipera Serra" (printed for the first time in Mexico City in 1787; a translation of this great work of love and friendship, made by C. Scott Williams, was published by George Wharton James, with notes and introductions, in 1913); and his not less famous "Noticias de la Nueva California," which did not appear in print until 1857, and is considered by many historians as the most reliable source of information of early California history.

(Bancroft, History of California, Vol. I, p. 473-4. Also see Historical Memoirs of New California by Palou; translated into English from the manuscript in the Archives of Mexico by Herbert Eugene Bolton, University of California Press, 1926.)

APPENDIX No. 2
Chapter XVI, Book III

The Padres had never seen the *Sequoia Sempervirens* until they arrived in the fall of 1769 in the country north of Monterey, somewhere in the vicinity of Watsonville, with the Portola Expedition, searching for the Port of Monterey. Father Crespi wrote in his diary: "these trees are unlike anything ever seen in Spain." The Padres called them *Palo Colorado,* (on account of their heavy red bark), or *Palo Alto,* (on account of their great height).

They only grow in a belt along the California coast, between Santa Cruz and the northern State line, about 450 miles long and 30 to 40 miles wide, with the exception of two small groves in Curry County, Oregon, just over the State line. They are found in no other part of the world. They require an altitude of no more than 3500 feet, grow well even at sea level, and demand a cool, humid climate, preferring sheltered locations like mountain basins and protected slopes or gorges. They grow to great heights (some 350 feet), being the highest living things known; they are very graceful when young—up till about 60 or 70 years—and have a very thick, fire resistant bark.

They grow in groups in large forests and the so-called "big trees" amongst them are simply older and larger ones of the same species, which have some way or other escaped death.

The botanical classification was made by Stephen Endlicher in 1847, his original specimen having been taken in Santa Cruz County, California.

The *Sequoia Sempervirens* grow to be very old, some claim 2000 years and more, but the average age seems to be between 500 and 1400 years. Their long life is due to the fact that they are free from insect pests, fungus or other diseases, and their bark being fire resistant, they escape the consequences of forest fires.

APPENDIX No. 3
Chapter XVI, Book III

This grove contains many famous trees, such as the Fremont 285 feet high, 60 feet in circumference and about 20 feet in diameter; the Giant, 306 feet high, 66 feet in circumference; and the Grant, 300 feet high, etc.

Elsewhere in the state the "Save the Redwood League" of California has done good work in preserving these noble living memorials of ancient times from the lumbermen's axe.

APPENDIX No. 4
Chapter XVI, Book III

This grove was first "discovered" by Archibald Mendez of the Vancouver Expedition.

The most notable trees have been given individual names. The Santa Cruz tree is 18 feet in diameter, 3 feet above the ground. The Father of the Forest is 32 feet in diameter, about 90 feet in circumference at the base, 22 feet in diameter 5 feet above the ground, and 285 feet high. The Animal tree (so named on account of several burls at its base, showing likenesses to certain animals) is 330 feet high. The Mother of the Forest is 335 feet high.

An abundance of other trees, with which the Redwoods like to associate, is found in this grove, such as the Tan Oak (*Lithocarpus Densiflora*), Douglas Firs (*Pseudotsuga taxifolio*), etc.

During the season of 1931 (May to November) 225,000 visitors from all over the world visited this grove, many camping there for weeks.

APPENDIX No. 5
Chapter XVI, Book III

This species of *Sequoia,* which the Padres never knew, was first discovered in 1852 by A. T. Dowd, a hunter and trapper.

Of the two branches of the family—both named in honor of Se-quo-yah, a Cherokee Indian, famous for inventing a means of producing thought on paper in the Cherokee language—the *Sequoia Gigantea* is undoubtedly the older and the larger in girth, though not the taller.

There are several groups or groves of these trees, especially in the forests of the Yosemite (Mariposa, Tuolumne and Merced Groves), in the Sequoia and General Grant National Parks, all on the western slopes of the Sierra Nevadas in California, and in elevation from 4000 to 8500 feet.

APPENDIX No. 6
CHAPTER XVI, BOOK III

When Father de Lasuen noted the presence of forests of redwood and pine they were in their pristine beauty, for the Indians took excellent care of them.

Although still beautiful today, the destruction of these forests has been frightful.

By 1843 sawed lumber from the mills in the redwoods of the Santa Cruz mountains were being hauled by ropes from the beach, through the breakers, rafted to ships and delivered to southern ports. Isaac Graham, who after years of adventurous life, had quieted down considerably, established the first lumber mills in Santa Cruz County on Zayante Creek towards the end of 1842.

The little city of Boulder Creek, fifteen miles north of Santa Cruz, was at one time the heart of this lumber industry and as much as 150 carloads a day were shipped away.

APPENDIX No. 7
CHAPTER XVI, BOOK III

That the Santa Cruz environs in the past invariably made a deep impression on visitors—as indeed they do today—is shown by the diary of Fremont, who in February, 1846, travelled from Los Gatos to Monterey. In his memoirs he writes:

"Resuming the work of the expedition, on the 22nd February, we encamped on the Wild-Cat Ridge on the road to Santa Cruz and again on the 23rd near the summit. The varied character of the woods and shrubbery on this mountain, which lay between my camp and the Santa Cruz shore, was very interesting to me, and I wished to spend some days there, as now the spring season was renewing vegetation, and the accounts of the great trees in the forest on the west slope of the mountain had roused my curiosity. Always, too, I had before my mind the home I wished to make in this country, and first one place and then another charmed me. But none seemed perfect where the sea was wanting, and so far I had not stood by the open waves of the Pacific. The soft climate of the San Jose valley was very enticing, and in the interior I had seen lovely spots in the midst of the great pines where the mountains looked down, but the sea was lacking. The piny fragrance was grateful, but it was not the invigorating salt breeze which brings with it renewed strength. This I wanted for my mother. For me, the shore of "sounding sea" was a pleasure of which I never wearied, and I knew that along this coast the sea broke deep against the gold rocks or shining sands. All this I had reason to believe I would find somewhere on the Santa Cruz shore. We remained on the upper portion of the mountain several days.

The place of our encampment was two thousand feet above the sea, and was covered with a luxuriant growth of grass a foot high in many places.

"At sunrise the temperature was 40 degrees; at noon, 60 degrees; at four in the afternoon, 65 degrees and 63 degrees at sunset, with very pleasant weather. The mountains were wooded with many varieties of trees, and in some parts with heavy forests. These forests are characterized by a cypress (taxodium) of extraordinary dimensions, which I have already mentioned among the trees in the Sierra Nevada as distinguished among the forest trees of America by its superior size and height. Among many we measured in this part of the mountain a diameter of nine or ten feet was frequent, sometimes eleven; but going beyond eleven only in a single tree, which reached fourteen feet in diameter. About two hundred feet was a frequent height. In this locality the bark was very deeply furrowed and unusually thick, being fully sixteen inches on some of the trees. It was now in bloom, flowering near the summit, and the flowers consequently difficult to procure.

"This is the staple timber-tree of the country, being cut into both boards and shingles, and is the principal timber sawed at the mills. It is soft and easily worked, wearing away too quickly to be used for floors; but it seems to have all the durability which anciently gave the cypress so much celebrity. Posts which had been exposed to the weather three quarters of a century, since the foundation of the Missions, showed no marks of decay in the wood and are now converted into beams and posts for private dwellings. In California this tree is called the "Palo Colorado," Redwood.

"Among the oaks in this mountain is a handsome, lofty evergreen tree, specifically different from those of the lower grounds, and in its general appearance much resembling hickory. The bark is smooth, of a white color, and the wood hard and close-grained. It seems to prefer the north hill-sides, where they were nearly four feet in diameter and a hundred feet high.

"Another remarkable tree of these woods is called in the language of the country "Madrona." It is a beautiful evergreen with large, thick, and glossy digitated leaves; the trunk and branches reddish colored and having smooth and singularly naked appearance, as if the bark had been stripped off. In its green state the wood is brittle, very heavy, hard, and close-grained; it is said to assume a red color when dry, sometimes variegated, and susceptible of a high polish. This tree was found by us only in the mountains. Some measured nearly four feet in diameter and were about sixty feet high.

"A few scattered flowers were now showing throughout the forests, and on the open ridges shrubs were flowering; but the bloom was not yet general.

"On the 25th of February we descended to the coast near the northwestern point of Monterey Bay, losing our fine weather, which in the evening changed to a cold southeasterly storm that continued with heavy and constant rains for several days.

"The rainstorm closed with February, and the weather becoming fine, on the 1st of March we resumed our progress along the coast. Over the face of the country between Santa Cruz and Monterey, and around the plains of San Juan, the grass, which had been eaten down by the large herds of cattle, was now everywhere springing up and flowers began to show their bloom. In the valleys of the mountains bordering the Salinas plains wild oats were three feet high and well headed. The Salinas River runs through these plains, which are some fifty miles in length.

"Pursuing our course to the southward I encamped on the afternoon of March 3rd at the Hartnell rancho, which is on a small creek bed well out on the plain. We were now passing Monterey, which was about twenty-five miles distant.

"The Salinas Valley lay outside of the more occupied parts of the country; and I was on my way to a pass, opening into the San Joaquin valley, at the head of a western branch of the Salinas river." (Memoirs of my Life—John Charles Fremont, pp. 456-459.)

Fremont must have emerged from the mountains to the coast at a point not far from the Mission, but he does not mention this.

APPENDIX No. 8
CHAPTER XVI, BOOK III

Thousands of carloads and truckloads of lettuce and apples—Belflowers for the domestic market and Newton Pippins for the foreign—are shipped yearly, while its main city, the prosperous town of Watsonville in Santa Cruz County, is the clearing house for trainload after trainload of garden produce, especially lettuce, relished by the eastern consumers.

In the year 1929 there was shipped from Watsonville Junction an average of 72 carloads of produce a day. The principal commodities were lettuce (19,636 cars), apples (2,129 cars), artichokes (1,012 cars), mixed vegetables (587 cars), cauliflower (445 cars), etc., etc. These figures do not include the quantities of apples shipped by truck, nor the enormous tonnage placed in driers, nor the extensive express shipment of fruits and vegetables.

In 1930 this little valley received nine and one-half million dollars in return for its products, the principal ones being lettuce $2,725,000; green apples $2,500,000; dried apples $860,000, berries $559,000; dried and green apricots $250,000, and the balance made up of a great variety of commodities.

In the same year the bank clearings were $20,491,958.35; the bank deposits $8,108,627.97 and the post office receipts $64,575.55.

According to the 1920 census the population of Watsonville was 5,013, and the 1930 census lists 8,344.

APPENDIX No. 1
CHAPTER XVII, BOOK III

A rather curious and fanciful account of the establishment of the Santa Cruz Mission, the accuracy of which we leave to the author, is to be found in Trowbridge Hall's "California Trails, An Intimate Guide to the Old Missions. Mr. Trowbridge writes:

"It was on September 22, 1791, within sight of the singing ocean that Santa Cruz was founded. And when the sun rose, bells were swung over a bending branch and rung in the presence of the tattered savages who stood in no fear of the white man and apparently no terror at the thunder of the guns fired. At the elevation of the cross, it seems as though perhaps the true signification of the holy emblem was somehow known to this primitive fold. As the sign of the cross goes back to a far remote point, and from the earliest time has had a symbolic religious meaning—all evil spirits from the dawn of the world being afraid of the sign. . . . "

"After considerable delay, as the needed church ornaments were not on hand and they could not go ahead until they borrowed them, the cornerstone of the Santa Cruz church was laid with the usual ceremony. A cross was first planted in the ground where the altar was to be, and then salt and water to exorcise the evil spirits were blessed, first taking the salt the priest prays that it may have sufficient influence to destroy the malice of Satan. Next he takes the water, that its virtue, like the salt may be able to destroy the power of the devil and his angels, after which he places the salt in the form of a cross within the vessel of water, and sings 'Set, O Lord, a mark of salvation on this place. Do not suffer the destroying angel to enter into it,' all the while sprinkling the water where the cross stands. Finally addressing himself to God in prayer through the mediation of the particular Saint under whom the church is consecrated, he blesses the cornerstone in the name of the Father, the Son and the Holy Ghost."

Mr. Hall also gives this account as to the acquiring of the Mission bell:

"Henry Fitch, though a young sailor of Puritan forefathers, led the same heedless, daredevil life as most sea folk, and was always in love with some pretty face, but when he met the beautiful Dona Josefa" . . . . a daughter of Joaquin Carrillo . . . . "he wanted to make her his wife."

The story goes that the parents gave reluctant consent, but the Uncle, who was the official witness at the wedding, withdrew his consent. The couple eloped and went to New England, returning after two years with their little child.

"Immediately on arrival Fitch was arrested, as having violated the laws of the territory and his wife was taken to the home of the parents in disgrace. The little pueblo was all agog with excitement. Never before had such a thing occurred, though the law forbidding marriage to foreigners had long been on the statute books. Morning, noon and night, this heretical marriage was the subject of conversation in every household, until it became necessary to convene an ecclesiastical court to pass on the legality of the wedding" (which had been solemnized in Peru). "After a long session with many arguments pro and con, the court decided that the marriage was valid, but considering the great scandal caused by Fitch, he was condemned in penance and as reparation to present a bell to the church.

"Thus the mission got its first bell."

APPENDIX No. 1

CHAPTER XVIII, BOOK III

In accordance with the narrative of a Mission Indian, mentioned elsewhere, bears were bold enough to come very close to the Mission confines, and sit on the hill where the reservoir is now and the residences of Moore, Cowell, Torchiana, Erlanger, and the late Judge J. H. Logan are located, watching for a chance to kill one of the calves of the Mission. The Indians killed bears with bows and arrows and clubs.

Fremont tells us that on his third expedition, in the beginning of 1846, while they were camping on the Cosumne River (in the San Joaquin Valley), a grizzly bear charged the party while at breakfast, scattering the men, driving some in the trees, and holding possession until some of them got hold of their guns and killed him. The bear even succeeded in treeing the Delaware Scouts of the expedition. He had four inches thickness of fat on his back, and on his belly, and weighed a thousand pounds. In April of the same year he had further experiences with these great animals on the upper Sacramento River, for he tells us that at their encampment among oak groves they found themselves in a regular bear garden, and that only with great difficulty they saved one of their number, "Charley Delaware," from being killed by a slightly wounded grizzly. ("Memoirs of my Life,"—John Charles Fremont, pp. 455-456—marked volume I, but only one volume was published.)

De Mofras in the account of his Explorations remarked: "Just like the Santa Inez mountains, those of Santa Cruz abound with bears and deer of several kinds."

A bear was captured near Santa Cruz in November, 1866, which weighed 642 pounds. In the early seventies Mr. Charles McKiernan, known as "Mountain Charley," a large land owner, after whom the Mountain Charley Grade on the old toll road between Santa Cruz and Santa Clara was named, was attacked by a bear which scalped him and fractured his skull. McKiernan killed the bear and was afterwards rushed to the hospital. He survived and lived to a ripe old age.

In 1875, a Mr. William W. Waddell, Santa Cruz County pioneer lumberman, was attacked by a grizzly bear, from which attack he died, and as late as 1880 the "Big Basin," above Santa Cruz, was the hunting ground for these predatory animals, which killed many domestic cattle.

APPENDIX No. 2
Chapter XVIII, Book III

The following tables give lists of the Missions in the chronological order of their founding, with the year; the largest number of neophytes at any one time in each Mission and the year in which this maximum was reached, also the total for each Mission of its baptisms from date of founding up till the disestablishment by Mexico in 1834, likewise the names of the founding Fathers and first missionaries.

Name of Mission	Founded	Max. No. Neophytes	Year of	Total of Baptisms
San Diego de Alcalá	1769	1829	1824	6638
San Carlos Borromeo	1770	921	1794	3957
San Antonio de Pádua	1771	1296	1805	4456
San Gabriel Arcangel	1771	1701	1817	7854
San Luis Obispo	1772	852	1803	2657
San Francisco de Asis	1776	1252	1820	6998
San Juan Capistrano	1776	1361	1812	4404
Santa Clara	1777	1464	1827	8640
San Buenaventura	1782	1328	1816	3876
Santa Barbára	1786	1792	1803	5679
Purísima Concepcion	1787	1520	1804	3314
Santa Cruz	1791	523	1796	2466
Soledad	1791	725	1805	2222
San José	1797	1886	1831	6737
San Juan Bautista	1797	1248	1823	4100
San Miguel Arcangel	1797	1076	1814	2588
San Fernando Rey	1797	1080	1819	2839
San Luis Rey	1798	1869	1826	5591
Santa Inez	1804	768	1816	1372
San Rafael Arcangel	1817	1140	1828	1873
San Francisco Solano	1823	996	1832	1315

Name of Mission	Date of Founding	Founding Frailes and First Missionaries
San Diego de Alcalá	July 16, 1769	Fr. Júnipero Serra Fr. Fernando Parron
San Carlos Borromeo (Carmel)	June 30, 1770	Fr. Júnipero Serra Fr. Juan Crespi
San Antonio de Pádua	July 14, 1771	Fr. Júnipero Serra Fr. Miguel Pieras Fr. Buenaventura Sitjar
San Gabriel Arcangel	Sept. 8, 1771	Fr. Jose Angel Somera Fr. Pedro Benito Cambon
San Luis Obispo	Sept. 1, 1772	Fr. Júnipero Serra Fr. José Cavaller
San Francisco de Asis (Dolores)	Oct. 9, 1776	Fr. Francisco Palou Fr. Pedro Benito Cambon
San Juan Capistrano	Oct. 30, 1776	Fr. Fermin Francisco de Lasuen Fr. Gregório Amurrio
Santa Clara	Jan. 12, 1777	Fr. Tomás de la Peña Fr. José Murguia
San Buenaventura	Mar. 31, 1782	Fr. Júnipero Serra Fr. Pedro Benito Cambon
Santa Bárbara	Dec. 4, 1786	Fr. Fermin Francisco de Lasuen Fr. Cristobal Oramas Fr. Antonio Paterna
Purisíma Concepcion	Dec. 8, 1787	Fr. Fermin Francisco de Lasuen Fr. Vicente Fuster Fr. José Arroita
Santa Cruz	Aug. 28, 1791	Fr. Fermin Francisco de Lasuen Fr. Isidoro Alonzo Salazar Fr. Baldomero Lopez
Soledad	Oct. 9, 1791	Fr. Fermin Francisco de Lasuen Fr. Diego Garcia Fr. Mariano Rubí
San José	June 11, 1797	Fr. Fermin Francisco de Lasuen Fr. Isidoro Barcenilla Fr. Agustin Merino
San Juan Bautista	June 24, 1797	Fr. Fermin Francisco de Lasuen Fr. Magin Catalá Fr. José Manuel Martiarena
San Miguel Arcangel	July 25, 1797	Fr. Fermin Francisco de Lasuen Fr. Buenaventura Sitjar Fr. António de la Concepcion
San Fernando Rey	Sept. 8, 1797	Fr. Fermin Francisco de Lasuen Fr. Francisco Dumetz Fr. Francisco Xavier Uria
San Luis Rey	June 13, 1798	Fr. Fermin Francisco de Lasuen Fr. António Peyri Fr. José Faura
Santa Inez	Sept. 17, 1804	Fr. Estevan Tapis Fr. Marcelino Cipres Fr. António Calzada Fr. Romualdo Gutierrez
San Rafael Arcangel	Dec. 14, 1817	Fr. Vicente Franc de Sarría Fr. Ramon Abella Fr. Narciso Duran Fr. Luis Gil y Taboada
San Francisco Solano (Sonoma)	July 4, 1823	Fr. José Altimira

APPENDIX No. 1
CHAPTER XX, BOOK III

Sal's minute instructions and control of all details is revealed in "A Peep Into The Past" (Bancroft Collection)—"Interesting Reminiscences of Our Early Settlement. Government Order No. 16."

"I remit you enclosed in this a certified order from government, that you, after informing yourself of its contents, may have it strictly complied with, and you will put it up in the accustomed place. By the first mail in the coming month of July I expect you to remit me an account of cigaritos, with proof of the quantity on hand which should not be signed by you, but by two persons, who will by personal inspection and count, certify to the amount as is required by the Regulations. You will also approximate the quantity required for consumption during the next 13 or 15 months, for I have not been sent any cigaritos this year. I send you by the wife of the pensioner Josef Brabo, one piece of cotton goods and one ounce of sewing silk. There are no combs, and I have no hope of receiving any for three years. May God protect you many years.

Hermenegildo Sal.

Monterey, June 3, 1799
To Mr. Gabriel Moraga."

APPENDIX No. 2
CHAPTER XX, BOOK III

There seems to have been some confusion in the records in regard to the number of settlers in Branciforte.

In the State Archives, in the file marked "Census of 1798," can be found two manuscripts. One is signed by Josef Argüello, and reads as follows: "Provincia de Californias: Jurisdiccion de San Francisco. Estado que manifiesta el numero de Indios, y Gente de Razon existiene en dicha Yurisdiccion segur el Padron de fin de 98 con distincion de Hombres, Muyeres, Muchachos y Muchachas.

	INDIOS					ESPANOLES & OTROS.				
	Hom.	muy.	m^{os}	m^{as}	tot.	hom.	muy.	m^{os}	m^{as}	totales.
Presidio de San Francisco						80	44	36	46	206
Villa de Branciforte						20	9	20	13	62
Mission de San Francisco	310	258	27	30	625	2				
" " Sta Clara	568	445	173	179	1385	3				
" " Sta Cruz	196	170	64	80	510	2				
" " San Jose	30	24	30	34	118	2				
	1124	897	294	323	2638	109	53	56	59	277
										2915

(Signed)   Josef Argüello,
(rubric)"

The total population of Branciforte is given as 62.

Another manuscript is signed by Gabriel Moraga, and reads as follows:

"Provincia de California, Jurisdiccion de Monterey.

Estado que manifiesta el numero de Yndios y gente de Razon existiente en dha Yurisdiccion segur el Padron de fin de 98 con distincion de ombres, muyeres, muchachos y muchachas.

	INDIOS			ESPANOLES Y OTRAS CASTAS					
hombres muyeres	muchados muchachas	totales		h	m	m^os	m^as	total	total
Villa de Branciforte	1	1	11	2	4	3	20	21	
Total por fin de 1798	1	1	11	2	4	3	20	21	

(Signed)

GABRIEL MORAGA."

Moraga gives the total population as *21,* which is evidently correct, for in a third manuscript found in the same file the names of 9 pobledores, 6 ynvalidos and 4 others, including Gabriel Moraga, are given. This manuscript is headed:

"Estado que manifiesta el numero de Cabesas de

Ganado, Bacuno . . . . . ano de 1798."

APPENDIX No. 3

CHAPTER XX, BOOK III

THE LAW IN BRANCIFORTE IN 1816

By Leon Rowland of The Santa Cruz News Staff

Villa Branciforte had a population of about 50 when, in 1816, Gov. Pablo Vicente de Sola at Monterey drew up a written code of civil law for the inhabitants of the 19-year-old pueblo.

The regulations for the conduct of Villa Branciforte residents were sent in the form of instructions to Luz Garcia, comisionado of civil affairs and commander of the squad of six soldiers which formed the military garrison.

The instructions, "for the government and direction" of the people, were:

"The first care of the comisionado shall be to maintain peace, goodwill and harmony among the colonists and to be vigilant in maintaining good order.

"Living in adultery, gaming and drunkenness will not be allowed and he who commits such vices shall be punished, as also he who fails to appear and do duty upon public works when so ordered.

Must Go to Church

"He will oblige all persons to attend the celebration of mass on the days fixed by the laws of the church, and to make the responses in a loud voice, and if any person shall fail to observe this without good cause, he shall be put in the stocks for three hours.

"During Easter all persons shall be careful to comply with its annual observance. The comisionado shall remit to the government a certificate of their having done so.

"He will not permit the actual colonists, or any sojourner, to traffic with any Indian, male or female, and much less have illicit intercourse with them. To this end the comisionado will prohibit going to their huts, whether at night or in the day-time. This rule must be rigidly observed.

Will Get Land

"Any individual wishing to become a colonist must have presented to me some person who will vouch for his status and ability; and I will order that he have leave to settle, and will indicate the suertes of land that will be given him.

"No colonist or sojourner shall depart from the villa for the purpose of settling at some place that is populated without first procuring my permission.

All Must Work

"The comisionado will exercise the greatest care to prevent lethargy among the settlers and also sojourners, causing them all to labor and to sow and cultivate the lands that have been given them; and he will provide me with a list of names of those who have sowed and harvested annually, and at the proper time inform me how they are getting along.

"The comisionado will notify the governor what lands are unoccupied up to this date, how much of it is agricultural and how much is pasture belonging to the village, and how much of the land is useful for both purposes and the reason it is not occupied."

(Note: The text of the instructions, given above, is from a translation made by E. L. Williams of Santa Cruz in 1876 from the original document, which is still preserved in the office of the county recorder. The translation was printed in the Santa Cruz weekly Local Items.)

APPENDIX No. 1
Chapter XXII, Book IV

Sir George Simpson who visited the Mission of Santa Cruz in 1842 has this to say about Father Quintana's death:

"In 1823 one Quintana, then a priest of Santa Cruz, forgot one of his vows in the society of a certain squaw, who, through penitence, or indignation, or vanity, or some other motive, let her husband into the secret of her conquest. After watching his opportunity, the man at length succeeded in mutilating the lover in the most brutal manner, leaving him insensible, but was himself dragged to the calabozo, whence, according to common rumor, he was soon afterwards carried off by the Devil for his impiety. Quintana, on the contrary, died with the fame of a martyr, for a long time elapsed before the truth was known through the confessions of a woman who had been privy to the injured savage's fatal revenge."

This version is at variance with the official records, and seems to have been based on local gossip. Furthermore, Sir George's information was incorrect, for he gives the date as 1823, and Quintana was murdered in 1812.

APPENDIX No. 2

Chapter XXII, Book IV

These beautiful vestments are still in existence, and the author was courteously granted the privilege of examining them and the ancient Mission records by the local priest, Father J. P. McGrath, at Santa Cruz. During all the years they have scarcely changed color in any way and are now used at solemn mass on Christmas night. Even to modern eyes, surfeited with beautiful things, they are magnificent. To the Indians they must have been a revelation, and we suddenly realize that the only beauty the Indians ever knew was wrapped up in the religious observances which the Fathers brought them. Color of lovely brocades and the bright paints with which they learned to adorn their churches; melodious sound, an important part of the religious services; new sensations—a bit of the culture of old Spain brought from far, far away to primitive people.

The Mission spirit has by no means died out, for on the evening of the Sunday when kindly Father McGrath had sacrificed several hours of his well-earned afternoon rest, to show the Mission treasures and give the benefit of his opinion as to the Mission period, he telephoned to the author that he had just received intelligence of a serious movement on foot to erect a worthy reliquary for the Mission treasures, in the immediate neighborhood of the Church, thereby eliminating the necessity of transferring them to a fire and burglar proof repository in Monterey. This has since been accomplished by the erection of the "Restored Mission."

APPENDIX No. 3

Chapter XXII, Book IV

For such a fight the pawing bull was first brought into the arena and then a grizzly bear by four vaqueros, holding him lassoed by four legs; the animals were fastened to one another with a chain long enough to allow free action, and after the loosening of the lassos and the withdrawal of the horsemen the fight started.

After the Spanish influence waned, the delight of the population in the bear and bull fights continued, but they were finally suppressed on the agitation of puritanically minded persons. During this period the fight "fans" claimed that the objection of their opponents was based not so much on charity towards the animals, but more on a dislike of the pleasure which the spectators derived from it.

APPENDIX No. 4

Chapter XXII, Book IV

The voyage of the "Rurik" is commemorated by the introduction of the famous California poppy to the gardens of the world. This wild flower of the western plains was called by the Spaniards "El Capitan de Las Flores." Dr. Adelbert von Chamisso, in a book which he published some time later, called it, in honor of his companion-scientist, Dr. Johan Friederich von Eschscholtz, "the Eschsholtzia California," and as such it is botanically known everywhere.

The other books were published as a result of the visit of the "Rurik," one by Kotzebue and one by Louis Choris: a book of lithographic reproductions of his drawings, with descriptions of von Chamisso and others.

APPENDIX No. 1

Chapter XXIII, Book IV

Alexander Forbes was the founder of the house of Barron, Forbes & Co., of Tepic in Mexico. He died in the city of London in the early part of 1863. He wrote "A History of Upper and Lower California, from Their First Discovery to the Present Time," which was published in octavo volume at London in 1839.

He had never been in California prior to the publishing of his book, which was the first printed volume entirely confined to that subject. His partner, Mr. Barron, was British Consul-General at the City of Mexico.

Forbes purchased from General Jose Castro his share in the New Almaden quick-silver mine, and operated the same with considerable financial success. The mine brought him to California in 1846.

A second edition of his book was published in 1919 by Thomas C. Russell, a San Francisco printer, who put a great deal of work and enthusiasm in this endeavor. The edition was long since sold out.

APPENDIX No. 2

Chapter XXIII, Book IV

Los Angeles is at present a great modern city with a population of one and a quarter million.

The University of Southern California, one of the leading Universities of the United States, with an enrollment of over 15,000 students, is located here, and so is the Southern Branch of the State University (at Berkeley).

The University of Southern California was founded as a Methodist College, but is now practically non-sectarian. It is presided over by Dr. Rufus B. von KleinSmid, a scientist and business executive of great ability. He is likewise Chancellor of the University of International Relations of Los Angeles.

In eighty-three years following California's admission to the Union (1850-1933), Los Angeles rose from the obscure, little, battered Spanish-Mexican Pueblo de Nuestra Senora La Reina de Los Angeles to an American city of first rank.

Sir George Simpson gives us a description of the Pueblo in 1842:

"The Pueblo de Nuestra Senora la Reina de los Angeles, about eighteen miles distant (from San Pedro) . . . . contains a population of fifteen hundred souls, and is the noted abode of the lowest drunkards and gamblers of the country. This den of thieves is situated, as one may expect from its being almost twice as populous as the two other pueblos taken together, in one of the loveliest and most fertile districts of California."

APPENDIX No. 3

Chapter XXIII, Book IV

Captain Beechey visited the pueblo de San Jose in 1826 and tells us:

"A beautiful avenue of trees, nearly three miles in length, leads from the mission to the pueblo of San Jose, the largest settlement of the kind in Upper California.

It consists of mud-houses miserably provided in every respect, and contains about 500 inhabitants—retired soldiers and their families, who under the old government were allowed the privilege of forming settlements of this nature, and had a quantity of ground allotted to them for the use of their cattle. They style themselves *Gente de Razon* to distinguish them from the Indians, whose intellectual qualities are frequent subjects of animadversion amongst these enlightened communities. They are governed by an *alcalde,* and have a chapel of their own, at which one of the priests of the mission occasionally officiates."

Five years later the pueblo was visited by Alfred Robinson, who gives the following account of the *pobladores:*

"El Pueblo de San Jose de Guadalupe consists of about one hundred houses. It has a church, court-house, and jail. Its civil authorities are, an *alcalde,* two *regidores,* etc., as in the Pueblo de los Angeles, at the south. . . .

"Many little gardens of fruit-trees are attached to the houses, also some fine fields, where are raised large quantities of wheat and corn. A small stream of water supplies the means of irrigation, and serves as the power to a profitable grist-mill.

"The men are generally indolent, and addicted to many vices, caring little for the welfare of their children, who, like themselves, grow up unworthy members of society. Yet, with vice so prevalent amongst the men, the female portion of the community, it is worthy to remark, does not seem to have felt its influence, and perhaps there are few places in the world where, in proportion to the number of inhabitants, can be found more chastity, industrious habits and correct deportment than among the women of this place."

San Jose, which is the county seat of Santa Clara County, is today a modern city, situate in the highly cultivated Santa Clara Valley with a population of 82,500.

APPENDIX No. 4

CHAPTER XXIII, BOOK IV

The form of the ox-cart is as rude as that of the plow. It is composed of a bottom frame of a most clumsy construction, on which is raised a body of a few bars stuck upright, of a great height, and connected at the top with other slight bars. This cart is usually without lining, but when used for carrying maize, it is lined with canes tied to the upright bars. The pole is of very large dimensions, and long enough to be fastened to the yoke in the same manner as the beam of the plow. (Forbes, Upper California, pp. 250-1.)

APPENDIX No. 5

CHAPTER XXIII, BOOK IV

There was little change in the agricultural conditions between 1821 and 1831. We therefore give the statistics of the last named year.

GRAIN

Names of the Jurisdictions, Missions and Towns	Wheat	Maize or Indian Corn	Frijoles or Small Beans	Barley	Beans Garbanzos and Peas	Total Fanegas
Jurisdiction of San Francisco.						
Presidio of San Francisco..	273	70	40			343
Town of San Jose de Guadalupe	1,657	1,560	191			3,408
Mission of S. Francisco Solano	1,171	200	24	241	24	1,660
Id. of S. Rafael Arcangel ...	774	130	15	388	20	1,327
Id. of S. Francisco de Asis	670	15	9	340	58	1,092
Id. of Sta. Clara de Asis	2,400	60	25		200	2,685
Id. of San Jose.......	4,000	1,000	123	1,100	418	6,641
Id. of Sta. Cruz	160	300	10	386	20	876
Jurisdiction of Monterey.						
Presidio of Monterey	490	332	131			953
Villa of Branciforte......	103	160	80			343
Mission of S. Juan Bautista	840	170	40	225	6	1,311
Id. of S. Carlos Borromeo ..	200			215	62	477
Id. of Na. So. de la Soledad	538	50		243	62	893
Id. of S. Antonio de Padua	955	115	40	568	23	1,701
Id. of S. Miguel Arcangel ...	599	36	9	57	33	734
Id. of S. Luis Obispo de Tolosa ..	350	60	20	20		450
Jurisdiction of Santa Barbara.						
Presidio of Santa Barbara..		300	90			390
Mission of La Purisima Concepcion .	700	100	20	56	17	893
Id. of Sta. Ines	800	400	20			1,220
Id. of Sta. Barbara ...	730	90	50	336	30	1,236
Id. of S. Buenaventura	700	200	160	800		1,860
Id. of S. Fernando Rey de Espana	200	250	40		65	555
Town of La Reina de los Angeles	138	1,758	179			2,075
Jurisdiction of San Diego.						
Presidio of San Diego.....	140	125	5			270
Mission of S. Gabriel Arcangel ...	1,400	400	13		25	1,838
Id. of S. Juan Capistrano .	450	625	30		5	1,110
Id. of S. Luis Rey de Francia	1,800	2,000	200	1,200	15	5,215
Id. of S. Diego de Alcala	2,946	420	80	1,200		4,646
TOTAL FANEGAS	25,184	10,926	1,644	7,375	1,083	46,202

APPENDIX No. 6

CHAPTER XXIII, BOOK IV

DOMESTIC CATTLE

Names of the Jurisdictions, Missions and Towns	Black Cattle	Horses	Mules	Asses	Sheep	Goats	Swine
Jurisdiction of San Francisco.							
Presidio of San Francisco..	5,610	470	40				
Town of San Jose de Guadalupe	4,443	2,386	134				
Mission of S. Francisco Solano	2,500	725	4		5,000		50
Id. of S. Rafael Arcangel ...	1,200	450	1		2,000		17
Id. of S. Francisco de Asis	4,200	1,239	18		3,000		
Id. of Sta. Clara de Asis	9,000	780	38		7,000		
Id. of San Jose	12,000	1,300	40		13,000		
Id. of Sta. Cruz	3,500	940	82		5,403		40
Jurisdiction of Monterey.							
Presidio of Monterey......	5,641	3,310	70				
Village of Branciforte	1,000	1,000	3				
Mission of San Juan Bautista	7,070	401	6	1	7,017		17
Id. of San Carlos Borromeo ..	2,050	470	8		4,400	55	
Id. of Na. Sa. de la Soledad	6,599	1,070	50	1	6,358		
Id. of S. Antonio de Padua	5,000	1,060	80	2	10,000	55	60
Id. of S. Miguel Arcangel ...	3,762	950	106	28	8,999	15	60
Id. of S. Luis Obispo de Tolosa ..	2,000	800	200	50	1,200		24
Jurisdiction of Santa Barbara.							
Presidio of Santa Barbara .	7,900	1,300	220				
Mission of La Purisima Concepcion .	10,500	1,000	160	4	7,000	30	62
Id. of Sta. Ines	7,300	320	112		2,200		50
Id. of Sta. Barbara ...	2,600	511	150	2	3,300	37	63
Id. of S. Buenaventura	4,000	300	60		3,100	30	8
Id. of S. Fernando Rey de Espana	6,000	300	60	3	3,000		
Town of La Reina de los Angeles	38,624	5,208	520				
Jurisdiction of San Diego.							
Presidio of San Diego	608	625	150	58			
Mission of S. Gabriel Arcangel ..	20,500	1,700	120	4	13,554	76	98
Id. of S. Juan Capistrano	10,900	290	30	5	4,800	50	40
Id. of S. Luis Rey de Francia	26,000	2,100	250	5	25,500	1,200	250
Id. of S. Diego de Alcala	6,220	1,196	132	14	17,624	325	
TOTALS	216,727	32,201	2,844	177	153,455	1,873	839

APPENDIX No. 7

CHAPTER XXIII, BOOK IV

Frederick William Beechey (1796-1856), English naval officer and geographer, published in 1828 the results of an overland survey under the title: "Proceedings of the Expedition to Explore the Northern Coast of Africa from Tripoli Eastward in 1821-1822." In 1825, in command of H. M. S. "Blossom," he undertook a long voyage of exploration, especially of Bering Strait, and published a "Narrative of a Voyage to the Pacific and Bering's Strait to co-operate with the Polar Expeditions, 1825-1828," two volumes. During this trip he visited California and left a vivid account of his impressions. In 1854 he became a Rear Admiral and died in November, 1856.

In his "Narrative of a Voyage to the Pacific" he gives a most interesting account of the gentiles in 1826:

"I shall conclude this imperfect sketch of Upper California with a short description of the Indian mode of living, and of the natural productions of the country, derived principally from the information of the priests, and from the journals of the officers who went overland to Monterey. The Indians who enter the missions with which we became acquainted are divided in their wild state into distinct tribes, and are governed by a chief whose office is hereditary, but only in the male line. The widows and daughters, however, though not allowed to partake of this privilege, are exempted from labour, and are more respected than other women. Each tribe has a different dialect; and though their districts are small, the languages are sometimes so different that the neighbouring tribes cannot understand each other. I have before observed that in the mission of San Carlos there are eleven different dialects. Their villages consist of wigwams made with poles, covered with bulrushes, and are generally placed in an open plain to avoid surprise. Like the Arabs and other wandering tribes, these people move about the country and pitch their tents wherever they find a convenient place, keeping, however, within their own district.

"They cultivate no land, and subsist entirely by the chase, and upon the spontaneous produce of the earth. Acorns, of which there is a great abundance in the country, constitute their principal vegetable food. In the proper season they procure a supply of these, bake them, and then bruise them between two stones into a paste, which will keep until the following season. The paste before it is dried is subjected to several washings in a sieve, which they say deprives it of the bitter taste common to the acorn. We cannot but remark the great resemblance this custom bears to the method adopted by the South Sea Islanders to keep their bread-fruit, nor ought we to fail to notice the manner in which Providence points out to different tribes the same wise means of preserving their food, and providing against a season of scarcity.

"The country inhabited by the Indians abounds in game, and the rivers in fish; and those tribes which inhabit the sea-coast make use of muscles and other shell fish, of which the haliotis gigantea is the most abundant. In the chase they are very expert, and avail themselves of a variety of devices to ensnare and to decoy their game. The artifice of deceiving the deer by placing a head of the animal upon their shoulders is very successfully practised by them. To do this, they fit the head and horns of a deer upon the head of a huntsman, the rest of his body being painted to resemble the colour of a deer. Thus disguised, the Indian sallies forth, equipped with his bow and arrows, approaches the pasture of the deer, whose actions and voice he then endeavors to imitate, taking care to conceal his body as much as possible, for which purpose he generally selects places which are overgrown with long grass. This stratagem seldom fails to entice several of the herd within reach of his arrows, which are frequently sent with unerring aim to the heart of the animal, and he falls without alarming the herd; but if the aim should fail, or the arrow only wound its intended victim, the whole herd is immediately put to flight.

"Their method of taking ducks and geese and other wild fowl is equally ingenious. They construct large nets with bulrushes, and repair to such rivers as are the resort of their game, where they fix a long pole upright on each bank, with one end of the net attached to the pole on the opposite side of the river to themselves. Several artificial ducks made of rushes are then set afloat upon the water between the poles as a decoy; and the Indians, who have a line fastened to one end of the net, and passed through a hole in the upper end of the pole that is near them, wait the arrival of their game in concealment. When the birds approach, they suddenly extend the net across the river by pulling upon the line, and intercept them in their flight, when they fall stunned into a large purse in the net and are captured. They also spread nets across their rivers in the evening, in order that the birds may become entangled in them as they fly.

"The occupation of the men consists principally in providing for their support, and in constructing the necessary implements for the chase and for their own defence. The women attend to their domestic concerns, and work a variety of baskets and ornamental parts of their dress, some of which are very ingenious, and all extremely laborious. Their closely wove baskets are not only capable of containing water, but are used for cooking their meals. A number of small scarlet feathers of the oriolus phoenicus are wove in with the wood, and completely screen it from view on the outside; and to the rim are affixed small black crests of the Californian partridges, of which birds a hundred brace are required to decorate one basket,—they are otherwise ornamented with beads, and pieces of mother-of-pearl. They also embroider belts very beautifully with feathers of different colours, and they work with remarkable neatness, making use of the young quills of the porcupine, in a similar manner to the Canadian Indians; but here they manufacture a fine cloth for the ground, whereas the Canadians have only the bark of the birch-tree. They also manufacture caps and dresses for their chiefs, which are extremely beautiful; and they have a great many other feather ornaments, which it would be stepping beyond the limits of my work to describe.

"The stature of the Indians which we saw in the missions was by no means diminutive. The Alchones are of good height, and the Tuluraios were thought to be, generally, above the standard of Englishmen. Their complexion is much darker than that of the South-Sea Islanders, and their features far inferior in beauty. In their persons they are extremely dirty, particularly their heads, which are so thatched with wiry black hair that it is only by separating the locks with the hand that it can be got at for the purposes of cleanliness. Many are seen performing such acts of kindness upon their intimate friends; and, as the readiest means of disposing of what they find, consuming it in the manner practised by the Tartars, who, according to Hakluyt—'cleanse one anothers' heades, and ever as thei take an animal do eate her, saeing thus wille I doe to our enemies' (Hakluyt's Selection of curious and rare Voyages, Supplement).

"Their bodies are in general very scantily clothed, and in summer many go entirely naked. The women, however, wear a deer skin or some other covering about their loins; but skin dresses are not common among any of the tribes concerning whom we could procure any information. The women are fond of ornaments, and suspend beads and buttons about their persons, while to their ears they attach long wooden cylinders, variously carved, which serve the double purpose of ear-rings and needle-cases.

"Tattooing is practised in these tribes by both sexes, both to ornament the person, and to distinguish one clan from the other. It is remarkable that the women mark their chins precisely in the same way as the Esquimaux.

"The tribes are frequently at war with each other, often in consequence of trespasses upon their territory and property; and weak tribes are sometimes wholly annihilated, or obliged to associate themselves with those of the conquerors; but such is their warmth of passion and desire of revenge that very little humanity is in general shown to those who fall into their power. Their weapons consist only of bows and arrows; neither the tomahawk nor the spear is ever seen in their hands. Their bows are elegantly and ingeniously constructed, and if kept dry will discharge an arrow to a considerable distance. They resemble those of the Esquimaux, being strengthened by sinews at the back of the bow, but here one sinew, the size of the wood, occupies the whole extent of the back, and embraces the ends, where they are turned back to receive the string; the sinew is fixed to the bow while wet, and as it becomes dry draws it back the reverse way to that in which it is intended to be used. The Indian manner of stringing these bows is precisely similar to that practised by the lovers of archery in England; but it requires greater skill and strength, in consequence of the increased curvature of the bow, and the resistance of the sinew.

"The religion of all the tribes is idolatrous. The Olchone, who inhabit the sea-coast between San Francisco and Monterey, worship the sun, and believe in the existence of a beneficent and an evil spirit, whom they occasionally attempt to propitiate. Their ideas of a future state are very confined: when a person dies they adorn the corpse with feathers, flowers and beads, and place with it a bow and arrows; they then extend it upon a pile of wood, and burn it amidst the shouts of the spectators, who wish the soul a pleasant journey to its new abode, which they suppose to be a country in the direction of the setting sun. Like most other nations, these people have a tradition of the deluge; they believe also that their tribes originally came from the north.

"The Indians in their wild state are said to be more healthy than those which have entered the missions. They have simple remedies, derived from certain medicinal herbs, with the property of which they have previously made themselves acquainted. Some of these roots are useful as emetics, and are administered in cases of sickness of the stomach; they also apply cataplasms to diseased parts of the body, and practise phlebotomy very generally, using the right arm for this purpose when the body is affected and the left where the limbs. But the temischal is the grand remedy for most of their diseases." (pp. 73-79.)

APPENDIX No. 8
Chapter XXIII, Book IV

John Charles Fremont was born in Savannah, Georgia, January 21, 1813. His father was a Frenchman, his mother a Virginian, member of an aristocratic family. After visiting the College of Charleston he became a teacher of mathematics, and in

July, 1838, a second lieutenant of Topographical Engineers, U. S. A. He made several surveys for the Government.

In 1841 he married Jessie, the daughter of the powerful Senator of Missouri, Thomas H. Benton.

In 1842 he surveyed the South Pass in the Rocky Mountains, through which the American immigration flowed towards the West. A second expedition followed next year to complete the survey across the continent along the line of travel from Missouri to the mouth of the Columbia River. He then reported back on the Great Salt Lake, the Great Basin, the Sierra Nevada Mountains, and the Mexican Province of Alta California.

In 1845 he set forth on a third expedition and he and his party arrived in California in January, 1846.

After meeting with all kind of trouble, especially with General Kearny, he resigned from the army in 1847.

He then made one more (fourth) expedition at his own and his father-in-law's expense, found new passes through the mountains for railroad purposes, and arrived in San Francisco in 1854.

In the meantime he had been elected one of the first United States Senators from California, but as he drew the short term, he had to run again in 1851, and was defeated by his pro-slavery opponent.

In 1856 he ran on the Republican ticket for President, but was defeated by James Buchanan.

In the spring of 1861, he became a Major General in the Union Army, with headquarters at St. Louis, proved inefficient and was removed November of the same year, but was placed in command of the Mountain Department of Virginia, Kentucky and Tennessee. Soon afterwards he retired from active service. From 1875 to 1881 he was governor of the Territory of Arizona, and in 1889, he was by Act of Congress appointed Major General, and placed on the retired list. He died in New York on July 13, 1890.

APPENDIX No. 9

CHAPTER XXIII, BOOK IV

There was constant friction between the secular and religious authorities. For instance, in July, 1797, Father Antonio de la Concepcion Horra became insane, terrorizing the neophytes, the pagans and even the soldiers of the guard. Father Horra thereupon made numerous charges, accusing the friars of cruelty to the Indians in a letter to the Viceroy dated July 12, 1799. (See Cal. Arch. Prov. St. Pap. XVII, p. 91-98.)

Via Governor de Borica, Commandant de Goycoechea received fifteen questions, to be submitted for answer to the Fathers within his jurisdiction. Father Tapis of Santa Barbara made answer, and here we have an illuminating example of this friction:

Question 11 was: Are the Indians permitted to have intercourse with white people? Are they chastised when they visit the presidios, even at the period of their vacation? Answer: . . . . It sometimes happens that the Fathers in the morning . . . . find that some spinners, carders, or weavers are missing. They ask and learn that the absentees are working at the loom of Comandante Felipe de Goycoechea, or that they are washing wool for him. Two neophytes are sent after them, and on arriving at the Mission they receive a few blows with the lash.

APPENDIX No. 1

CHAPTER XXIV, BOOK IV

Judge Logan for a number of years was Judge of the Superior Court of Santa Cruz County, and owned a place overlooking the site of the former Mission. He was a lover of nature, and developed the famous Loganberry. This locality is still known as "Logan Heights." Besides the old Logan home, the brow of this hill is now occupied by several country homes.

APPENDIX No. 2

CHAPTER XXIV, BOOK IV

Alexander Forbes says: "In concluding this sketch of the present state of the domesticated Indians of California, which unquestionably betrays a lamentable want of judgment and sound philosophy on the part of the men who have been the original founders, and are still the strenuous supporters, of the system under which these melancholy results have arisen, it would be extreme injustice not to place in the strongest contrast with their want of judgment the excellent motives and most benevolent and Christian-like intentions by which they have been always influenced. Considering the perfectly absolute and totally irresponsible power possessed by the missionaries over the Indians, their conduct must be allowed to have been invariably marked by a degree of benevolence and humanity and moderation probably unexampled in any other situation. To each missionary is allotted the entire and exclusive management of his mission. He is the absolute lord and master of all his Indians, and of the soil. He directs, without the least interference from others, all the operations and economy of the establishment—agricultural, mechanical, manufacturing, and commercial—and disposes, according to his will and pleasure of the produce thereof. He allots his lands; orders his seed-time and harvest; distributes his cattle; encourages, chastises, and commands all the human beings under his charge—and all this without being accountable to any power on earth, for, by a convenient fiction, this property belongs to the Indians, and the Indians are his slaves. There are, I fear, few examples to be found, where men enjoying such unlimited confidence and power have not abused them. And yet I have never heard that the missionaries of California have not acted with the most perfect fidelity, or that they ever betrayed their trust or exercised inhumanity, and the testimony of all travelers who have visited this country is uniformly to the same effect. On the contrary, there are recorded instances of the most extraordinary zeal, industry, and philanthropy in the conduct of those men." (See pp. 226-227, California, by Alexander Forbes, 1839.)

APPENDIX No. 1

CHAPTER XXV, BOOK V

Father Miguel Hidalgo y Costilla was a true patriot. The Indians loved him; he had done much to better their lot, encouraging them in the old industries of leatherwork, pottery and weaving, and introducing silk and wine culture, though it was prohibited by the government.

In the Mexican-Indian religion there was a virgin, called the Virgin of Guadalupe, who was supposed to have been responsible for many miracles. Father Hidalgo declared allegiance to this virgin, thereby incurring the enmity of the leaders of the Catholic Church.

In Mexico there always has been and is even today a survival of paganism. Stuart Chase, in his recent book, "Mexico" (p. 100 et seq.) tells of witnessing in a yard surrounding a church at Taxco an Aztec dance, a Roman Catholic mass and an itinerant circus, all enacted in the same holy precincts.

"It is impossible to say where idols stop, and the trinity begins," says Anita Brennan, in "Idols behind Altars" (1929), while Dr. Manuel Gamio tries a classification by speaking of Pagan Catholic and Roman Catholic congregations in his "Forjardo Patria."

As a result the observance of many pagan holidays and customs were continued and tolerated, if not incorporated, in the fiestas and services of the church, even as was done by the early Christians in the Roman Empire, many so-called Christian holidays, like Christmas, Easter, etc., being of pagan origin. No wonder Stuart Chase declared: "Meanwhile to this day priests and Indians still carry on their ancient compromise of idols flanking altars, perhaps the strangest and the most colorful religion in the world."

Father Hidalgo, whose appeal was especially directed to the Indians, therefore elected to enlist his parishioners under the banner of an Indian virgin, beloved by all—the Virgin of Guadalupe.

APPENDIX No. 2

CHAPTER XXV, BOOK V

Decree of the 18th of August, 1824, Respecting Colonization

The sovereign general constituent Congress of the United Mexican States has been pleased to decree:

1st. The Mexican nation promises to those foreigners who may come to establish themselves in its territory, security in their persons and property, provided they subject themselves to the laws of the country.

2nd. The objects of this law are those national lands which are neither private property nor belonging to any corporation or pueblo and can therefore be colonized. (*Son objeto de esta ley aquellos terrenos de la nacion, que no siendo de propiedad particular, ni pretenecientes a corporacion alguna o Pueblo, pueden ser colonizados.*)

3rd. To this end the Congress of the States will form, as soon as possible, the laws and regulations of colonization of their respective demarcation, with entire conformity to the constitutive act, the general constitution, and the rules established in this law.

4th. Those territories comprised within twenty leagues of the boundaries of any foreign nation, or within ten leagues of the seacoast, cannot be colonized without the previous approval of the supreme general executive power.

5th. If, for the defense or security of the nation the federal government should find it expedient to make use of any portion of these lands for the purpose of constructing warehouses, arsenals, or other public edifices, it may do so, with the approbation of the general Congress, or during its recess with that of the government council.

6th. Before the expiration of four years after the publication of this law, no tax or duty (*direcho*) shall be imposed on the entry of the persons of foreigners, who come to establish themselves for the first time in the nation.

7th. Previous to the year 1840, the general Congress cannot prohibit the entry of foreigners to colonize, except compelled to do so, with respect to the individuals of some nation, by powerful reasons.

8th. The government, without prejudicing the object of this law, will take the precautionary measures which it may consider necessary for the security of the federation, with respect to the foreigners who may come to colonize. In the distribution of lands, Mexican citizens are to be attended to in preference; and no distinction shall be made amongst these, except such only as is due to private merit and services rendered to the country, or inequality of circumstances, residence in the place to which the lands distributed belong.

10th. Military persons who are entitled to lands by the promise made on the 27th of March, 1821, shall be attended to in the States, on producing the diplomas granted to them to that effect by the supreme executive power.

11th. If by the decree of capitulation, according to the probabilities of life, the supreme executive should see fit to alienate any portion of land in favor of any military or civil officers of the federation, it may so dispose of the vacant lands of the territories.

12th. No person shall be allowed to obtain the ownership of more than one league square, of five thousand varas (5,000) of irrigable land (*de regadio*), four superficial ones of land dependent on the seasons (*de temporal*), and six superficial ones for the purpose of rearing cattle (*de abreradiso*).

13th. The new colonist cannot transfer their possession in mortmain (*manos muertas*).

14th. This law guarantees the contracts which the grantees (*empresarios*) may make with the families which they may bring out at their expense; provided they be not contrary to the laws.

15th. No one, who, by virtue of this law, shall acquire the ownership of lands, shall retain them if he shall reside out of the territory of the republic.

16th. The government, in conformity with the principles established in this law, will proceed to the colonization of the territories of the republic.

APPENDIX No. 1

Chapter XXVI, Book V

Captain F. W. Beechey in his Narrative of a Voyage to the Pacific Coast and Bering's Strait says:

. . . . "The most productive farms are held by the missions of San Jose, Santa Clara, San Juan and Santa Cruz. . . . Santa Cruz is rich in supplies, probably on account of the greater demand by merchant vessels, whalers in particular, who not unfrequently touch there the last thing on leaving the coast, and take on board what vegetables they require; the quantity of which is so considerable, that it not unfrequently happens that the missions are for a time completely drained. On this account it is advisable, on arriving at any of the ports, to take an early opportunity of ordering everything that may be required."

In another part of his narrative he says that vessels go to Santa Cruz for fresh water and supplies of vegetables, neither of which are to be had in any quantity at Monterey.

On a return visit he tells of putting in at Santa Cruz for vegetables, "which were afterwards served daily in double the usual proportion to the ship's company, who benefited so much by the diet that, with one exception, they very soon recovered from all indisposition."

APPENDIX No. 2
CHAPTER XXVI, BOOK V

"Provisional Commander of California.

"In a few days there will come to that landing-place (Santa Cruz) the Russian Brigantine *'Baikal'* (to which permisison has been given by the Commander General) to load wheat from the Mission of Santa Cruz. Being notified, have ready to deliver the thirty loads of wheat and the ten of beans of which you speak in your official letter of the 1st inst. The 1st and 2nd as a part of the already known payment, as well as all the corn that may have been gathered, as I need it for the use of this Presidio. Tell me also the No. of loads that the Englishman G—— owes, that I may collect same.

"God and Liberty, Monterey, Dec. 27, 1826.

"J. M. HERREA.
"*Alcalde* Constitutional of the town of Branciforte."

(Santa Cruz Archives No. 290, Hall of Records, Santa Cruz Co.)

APPENDIX No. 3
CHAPTER XXVI, BOOK V

Captain A. Duhaut-Cilly visited California and the Sandwich Islands during the years 1826, 1827, 1828 and 1829. He was in command of the 370 ton ship the *"Heros."*

His book, "Autour du Monde, principalemente à la Californie en aux Iles Sandwich," was published in Paris in 1834. On the title page the captain is described as: *"Capitaine au Long-Cours, Chevalier de la Legion d'Honneur, Membre de l'Academie d'Industrie Manufacturiere, Agricole et Commerciale, de Paris."* (See Quarterly of the California Historical Society, Vol. VIII, No. 2), p. 130.

APPENDIX No. 1

CHAPTER XXVII, BOOK V

The writing of exaggerated reports seems to have been a fine art in California.

In November, 1826, at the request of the Padres at Mission San Jose, it was considered necessary to make a military demonstration from the Presidio of San Francisco against a tribe of Indians named Casemenes, on the Rio San Joaquin. This military expedition was commanded by Alferez Sanchez, a veteran well acquainted with every part of the country. The Casemenes had objected forcibly to the too aggressive proselyting of armed neophytes from the San Jose Mission, and had driven off their assailants, who left thirty-four of their party in the field.

It appeared that the 20th Troop of Cavalry made an attack on the unfortunate gentiles, who were practically all slaughtered, and 44 women and children taken prisoners. They were at once taken to the Mission and Christianized.

Not one of the brave troops were even wounded in this hour of great battle, except one Jose Maria Gomez, whose own gun exploded, and as the valiant Alferez remarked "this misfortune did not hinder the other brave soldiers from firing."

This ludicrous account of a one-sided murderous expedition was headed by a note of the doughty commander reading: "Written with gunpowder on the field of battle." (Beechey, pp. 27-29.)

APPENDIX No. 2

CHAPTER XXVII, BOOK V

Governor Figueroa's idea of caution was the same as Captain Beechey's, who writing about the plan of secularization, stated:

This philanthropic plan at first sight appears to be a very excellent one, and every friend to the rights of man would naturally join in a wish for its prosperity; but the Mexican Government could not have sufficiently considered the state of California and the disposition of the Indians, or they would have known it could not possibly succeed without long previous training and then it would require to be introduced by slow degrees.

APPENDIX No. 1

CHAPTER XXVIII, BOOK V

Dr. Charles E. Chapman in his History of California, The Spanish Period, described the conduct of the Indians as follows: (pp. 470-471)

"After the death of Figueroa, Alta California suffered for several years from internal convulsions. During all this time the administrators were left to their own devices. Many of them enriched both themselves and their friends; still others were merely incompetent; and a few, perhaps, were both honest and capable. The distributions of property to the Indians were made as each administrator saw fit. The worst feature of the system, however, was the behavior of the Indians. Relieved from mission discipline they refused to work. Despite the provisions of the law, they sold their properties (especially domestic animals) for anything they could bring.

When their own stock of supplies was gone some hired themselves out in a state of virtual slavery to such families as could employ them, others joined the non-Christian tribesmen in horse-stealing and life in a state of barbarism, and still others sank to the uttermost depths of degradation. The missions and the mission system were dead."

APPENDIX No. 2

Chapter XXVIII, Book V

Jose Bolcoff, who was the last Mexican *alcalde,* was a Russian by birth. A native of Kamchatka, he had deserted in 1815 from a Russian sealing vessel which visited Monterey Bay in 1817. At Soledad he was baptized, or at least had his Greek church baptism ratified, becoming Jose Antonio Bolcoff. Immediately after his baptism he settled in Santa Cruz, which was his home until his death in 1866. He was married in 1822 to Candida Castro, a sister of Don Rafael, and in the following twenty-two years they had eleven children.

Bolcoff seemingly had no dealings with the settlement of the Imperial Russian-American Fur Company outpost at Bodega from 1812 to 1841, but he maintained contact with his Russian brethren who visited this coast in sealing vessels from his native town.

The Mexican census of 1829 named Jose Bolcoff, a shoemaker of good conduct and standing as a citizen of Santa Cruz. In 1833 he was naturalized as a Mexican citizen to obtain a grant of land which came to him eight years later as Refugio Rancho, west of what is now Santa Cruz. His naturalization brought him political honors, for in 1834 he served a short term as *alcalde.* Again in 1839-40 and once more in 1845-46 he was *alcalde,* holding that office when the American flag was raised.

In 1839 Bolcoff was put in charge of the buildings and properties of the Santa Cruz Mission.

His land grant was made by Governor Juan Alvarado on April 7, 1841, and confirmed by the United States, but the land had already passed out of Bolcoff's hands. He had become so badly in debt that Augustus L. Plongeon had obtained a judgment against him for $20,561, and the property was sold on the steps of the old adobe court house in Santa Cruz.

This land finally passed into the hands of Moses Meder, one of Sam Brannan's ship load of Mormons from Brooklyn, who landed in San Francisco in 1846. Meder Street, Santa Cruz, was named after the latter owner, who figured in long litigation started by Bolcoff to recover some of his early wealth.

APPENDIX No. 1

Chapter XXIX, Book VI

We have stated elsewhere that the male cattle were allowed to remain unaltered, contrary to more modern practices, but in accordance to the Spanish American custom. This, however, could not have had a tendency to increase the herds, for a surplusage of contending, fighting males has rather a tendency to decrease effective breeding.

It was perhaps on account of the menace of the predatory animals such as bears that the males were allowed to remain bulls thereby giving them greater fighting courage than if made into steers.

APPENDIX No. 2

Chapter XXIX, Book VI

R. H. Dana, Jr., writes: "The ship *California* had been 20 months on the coast and the *Lagoda,* a smaller ship, carrying only 31,000 or 32,000 hides had been two years getting her cargo; and we were to collect a cargo of 40,000 besides our own, which would be 12,000 or 15,000, and hides were said to be growing scarcer."

The hides, dried and stiff as boards, were collected at different places on the coast under a great deal of hardship of surf loading and then taken to the hide houses, mostly situated at San Diego, where they were cured, salted, etc., and prepared to stand the long trip around the Horn. The hides were purchased for about $2.00 apiece.

Dana says: "They have no circulating medium but silver and hides, which the sailors call 'California bank notes.' Everything that they buy (from the ships) they must pay for in one or the other of these things. The hides they bring down dried and doubled in clumsy ox-carts or on mule backs, and the money they carry tied up in handkerchiefs." (R. H. Dana, Jr., p. 96 of the Harvard Classic Edition of "Two Years Before the Mast.")

APPENDIX No. 3

Chapter XXIX, Book VI

The northern miners, on the other hand, who succeeded later in breaking through the grasslands of the far Middle West and crossing the Sierra Nevada mountains, were flowing in ever increasing numbers into the hills and plains of California. A great gold rush took place to the California hills north of Sacramento, in which Americans, English, Germans, French and many other Europeans and even Asiatics participated. A great romance about these mines and miners sprung up, a rich literature on these mining romances was issued, and the types immortalized and idealized by Bret Harte, Clemens, and others, will ever live in the history of California.

APPENDIX No. 1

Chapter XXX, Book VI

Eugene Duflot de Mofras was a young attaché of the French embassy at Madrid in 1839, when he was transferred to the French Legation at Mexico City. He received a mission to visit the Northwestern provinces and report back on the economic conditions and possibilities of extending trade. Arriving in Mexico City in 1840, he soon started upon his mission. In May, 1841, he arrived at Monterey, and in July he visited San Jose and Santa Cruz. During his travels he probably visited every Mission and settlement in California, and managed during his stay at Sonoma to give offense to Vallejo, the *Comandante-General.* On his return to Paris, he published his "Explorations," etc., in two volumes and an atlas. This literary work is generally considered one of much merit.

APPENDIX No. 2

CHAPTER XXX, BOOK VI

Sir George Simpson, governor in chief of the Hudson Bay Territories in North America, sailed from Liverpool in March, 1841, for a trip around the world. He published (London, 1847) a book in two volumes "Narrative of a Journey around the World, 1841, 1842." He devoted 150 pages to California, and it is charmingly written.

APPENDIX No. 3

CHAPTER XXX, BOOK VI

Translation from

Compagne de Circumnavigation

de la Fregate

L'Artemis

Pendant les annees 1837, 1838, 1839 et 1840.

De M. Laplace

Tome Sixieme

(printed at)
Paris 1854

p. 184-5

Nevertheless the colony did enjoy a certain prosperity at this epoch. The missions were multiplied everywhere where the fertility of the soil, a favorable location, or the vicinity of a good anchorage seemed to promise a future. They had generally prospered, but principally in those districts to the North, of which Monterey was the main one, and whose roadstead was so to say the boundary to the South. The largest ones developed on the shore of the ocean; the mission and presidio of San Francisco, both situate on the magnificent bay of the same name, those of Santa Cruz, San Carlos, Santa Barbara, where the travellers, tired from their long voyages, always found a hospitality as generous as insistent, and also provisions in abundance, derived from the towns of San Jose, San Raphael, San Solano, and many others less important, all more or less removed from the shore of the sea.

p. 272 et sec.

. . . . after a very peaceful night, during which we profited by all the little variations of the breeze to skirt the shore at a short distance, the frigate arrived at break of day in the vicinity of the mission of Santa Cruz, only a few leagues distant from Monterey to the north, and we let the anchor drop in the afternoon on a good bottom, near two islets only about a mile from a favorable small cove of white sand, where a small river flowed.

This anchorage, which awakened a desire to procure for the crew, for the ship's officers and myself a provision of fresh vegetables, before leaving California for Peru, is frequented during the summer by the merchant ships and coasters. Many famous explorers have put into port here during the last century; amongst them our illustrious compariot de la Perouse, who, in the account of his voyages made mention of the reception, equally pressing as generous, which he as well as his companions received from the monks of this mission, then the finest, the richest, the best administered of all those in California. The good priests heaped up their cares and the most delicate attentions, and even wanted to furnish gratis all the provisions which they needed to the crews of the two ships of the expedition. It was under the gentle influence of such recollections, the same, however, which had occurred to me when arriving at San Francisco and which had been so painfully dispelled, that I disembarked on the shore near where the frigate had dropped anchor. I was quite enchanted by the lovely views which we had at intervals of the mission with its little white houses and red tiled roofs, its church surmounted by a little steeple, which seemed to appear suddenly from the bosom of a magnificent stretch of green, at the end of which it arose. At the same first view of the picture, there unrolled before our eyes, the fields, which with their color of emerald, one could believe to be cultivated with care, so rich was the vegetation, the charm of which was enhanced anew by the clusters of fruit trees, distributed here and there. Further on and closing the perspective on that side, there arose a ridge of higher elevation, covered from the foot to the summit with a forest of large pines with dark foliage, contrasting in an agreeable manner with the warm colors of the plain, which bordered on the sea. All that was delicious; and yet deceptions awaited me there also and still more painful, for after having completed a walk, quite prolonged under a burning sun, although the afternoon was advanced, a spectacle of misery and of desertion offered itself to my eyes.

The buildings, which from afar had a good appearance, were in ruin and abandoned by their former inhabitants. In vain I searched for some human being in the courtyards surrounded by walls, which we crossed before arriving at the principal part of the lodgings, occupied in former times by Franciscan monks; everywhere a profound silence reigned, in the very places where some years ago a thousand converted Indians, maintained through their agricultural and manufacturing activities an abundance and life and progress. All of that indigenous population has disappeared, decimated by misery, sickness and desertion. The main building, where de la Perouse* had found such a noble and kindly hospitality, did not show a vestige of its former splendor, if I may so express myself. On every side a picture of disorder; and even the apartment of the administrator of the mission was stripped of necessities, bordering on uncleanliness. However, I was agreeably surprised when I discovered in the master of the dwelling, manners and a figure prepossessing, even distinguished, which contrasted singularly with the forbidding aspect of everything surrounding him. He made excuses in very good terms for his destitution, which prevented him from receiving us as he would have desired, and he offered in an amiable way, but not without a certain embarrassment, of which I soon understood the cause, to conduct us through the different parts of the establishment.

In fact with every step we encountered objects of sadness and disgust; the long rows of little huts made of sun-dried bricks, lately occupied by the neophytes of the monks, had no doors or windows and were covered in part by their debris; in a court adjoining the lodging of our guide and contaminated by a thousand sweepings which gave off an abominable odor, we saw several individuals occupied rather in tearing to pieces than in properly cutting up the cadavre of a steer, still palpitant, of which the blood and the entrails lay about upon the ground, and where they would remain until the birds of prey devoured them. The kitchen garden, into which we had

---

* Apparently he confuses Monterey and Santa Cruz. De la Perouse visited California in 1786, therefore several years prior to the founding of the Santa Cruz Mission.

entered by a gate half in ruins, the sill of which covered by rubbish and filth, offered scarcely a space for our feet; it did not have any less repulsive aspect; in a corner were lying several carrion, covered by a myriad of winged insects; the borders— walks of that sort of field—found themselves encroached upon equally by weeds, to which some cabbages, half nibbled by the caterpillars, gave a desperate resistance; the fruit trees, poor exiles of our southern provinces, left to themselves, were exhausted by a mass of tall sprouts and bore only poor fruit. But in the midst of that chaos, nature showing itself always beautiful, always disposed to repair the damage caused by the errors of man, endeavored to hide miserable results of the California carelessness and heedlessness under a magnificent cover of verdure, which had already invaded almost all of the ruins and the surrounding fields.

That reflection, not very flattering to our poor humanity, and which unfortunately I have made only too often in the course of my long role of observer, seems to me even more justified, if possible, when walking over all the parts of that deserted mission, I thought of what it had been and of the state in which I found it now. How many mistakes must have been committed by the men charged with the destinies of that country, before they succeeded in destroying an institution, the creation of which had demanded so much care and so many years of work! On which side lies the blame? Is it on the side of the founders, or is it necessary to blame only the present masters? The monks without doubt were somewhat to blame, just as I stated at the beginning of this chapter; they showed themselves too convinced that in their hands the temporal power should be inherent to the spiritual power. They considered their neophytes perhaps too much as the instruments of fortune and well-being; as unintelligent beings, big children; and in these diverse convictions, equally unfounded, they did not sufficiently exert themselves to develop in these unfortunates, the moral feelings and at the same time the taste for work and the love of the family. The result was that instead of these Indian converts becoming civilized and better, they were completely brutalized, thus justifying the profound contempt in which the whites held them.

The adversaries of the Fathers have equal wrongs to reproach themselves with on this account. They should be taxed with injustice, even with ingratitude, not only because of the prompt forgetfulness with which they have repaid the eminent services rendered to the country by the Franciscans, but even with having made the latter miserable by persecution, by abandonment of the establishments which gave them a living as well as a prosperity which they enjoyed. Nevertheless, let us admit that the Mexican government has, as far as it was able on account of the incessant revolutions with which it has had to battle since the commencement of the century, made efforts to pull the converted indigenes out of the profound degradation in which they were. For a long time it has shown itself their protectors. By its orders, the Indians of the mission, who conducted themselves well and who showed some aptitude for agriculture or the mechanical arts, obtained concessions of land, cattle, implements of irrigation, assistance of all kinds, to exercise their industry; and where more of their kind were aggregated they were aided to form villages under the direction of curates and magistrates. Other advantages were accorded them by the same government, which unfortunately had no more favorable results than the first ones.

The new citizens gave themselves up to idleness and debauchery, in spite of all that could be done to restrain them; some returned to the forests, their primitive residence; others retired to the little villages along the sea, where they found more opportunity to follow their evil inclinations. Is it for this that the severe judgment held against them by their former pastors and adopted a little blindly by the white population, should be considered as just and as applying to the whole race? I do not think so. In the first place, I have heard it said generally, that the Indians, once converted, showed much less cleverness than their free compatriots belonging to the same tribes, who proved in the chase, in war, even in their relations with the colonists, as well as in their industries, coarse as they were, to have a skill, an intelligence, one would almost say a spirit, of which the poor Californian serfs seem to have been entirely deprived. On the other hand, the commandant general of the troops, Vallejo, a resolute man of means, first nephew of Governor Alvarado, seeing that it would be impossible for him to persuade his fellow citizens to take arms to repulse the most audacious assaults of the hordes of savages on the inhabited districts, concluded, as I said above, to form a corps of infantry from the Indians of the missions, to whom he accorded a good pay and whom he treated like Spanish soldiers. The men, seeing themselves so raised in their own eyes, entrusted to carry arms and wear a respected uniform, well nourished, cared for when ill, in fact, loved by their chiefs, have given incontestable proofs of courage, moral capacity and devotion.

I confess, that seeing in that desolate place which I traversed, those few neophytes who were still confined there, so ugly, so dirty, so badly dressed, with such a brutal air, I felt myself quite disposed to range myself amongst their detractors. In fact, they resembled beasts more than human beings; and if the women, instead of the chemise of thick cotton cloth and the covering of wool, which composed the clothing of the men, had not worn a camisole and a short petticoat of a coarse kind of flannel, of reddish color, I would have found it impossible to distinguish between the individuals of the two sexes. Still it was said that occasionally some rather pretty girls were found amongst the families of the indigines, either amongst the Christians or the independents; but I am forced to confess that, despite my most determined researches to verify the truth of such assertions, I did not find anything to justify this contention. I have reason to believe, on the contrary, that the complaints were well founded, which the ships captains expressed generally, when putting into ports of California, regarding the fatal consequences which the debauches of the sailors had with these ugly creatures, a very great many of them being prey to shameful diseases, developed to a really frightful point. No wonder many of the individuals belonging to that unhappy race died from it; and when abortion was added to these guilty and destructive practices, which caused inflammatory fevers, lung and bowel infections, misery naturally followed such misconduct, in fact, such frightful deprivation preyed upon the former subjects of the monks that one is not astonished that they diminished so rapidly since the destruction of the missions.

As the administrator at the Mission of Santa Cruz, knowing that I desired to buy fresh vegetables and fruits for our crew, had warned the proprietors of neighboring farms, we found when we came back to the house several of them awaiting our return. Amongst them was a signora, who, by her fine features, dignified air and gracious figure attracted my attention immediately, although she was no longer very young. Our merchants, showing too exaggerated pretentions, we soon left them, but not without our having sworn many times that in no part of the country, not even at Monterey, had we found any better conditions. Nevertheless, we did not fail to remain to talk to our pretty farmerette, and to speak truthfully, we showed ourselves generally willing to make to her better terms than to her competitors; unfortunately, she was able to satisfy only a small part of our needs; and it is easy to believe that she promised more than her resources permitted, for on the morrow, at the time fixed for the delivery of the commodities, she did not put in appearance.

Notwithstanding we parted on the best possible terms, and the meeting was an agreeable diversion to the painful impressions which I had experienced shortly before, by that certain attraction which women, if gracious and good, always spread about them, and which makes men gentle, influences them, subdues them even often in spite of themselves. What an immense power, what a source of great benefit to society, when exercised with gentleness, good-will and chastity!

At the moment when we were leaving the enchantress, the monk of the mission arrived, whom we had seen on landing, crouching close to the earth, hunting in the fields, and whose presence, I think, hastened the departure of our California dove. Really it was no wonder that she was frightened, because it would be difficult to find anyone with a more cynical expression, with a more brutal appearance than this unkempt Mexican priest, with his burned face, great black eyes, the whites yellowed, his head covered with a large wide-brimmed hat, the crown dented in the center, his Franciscan robes, formerly white, now covered with a thousand spots, and without a cowl, but raised almost as high as his waist, in order to give sufficient liberty to his lower limbs; and finally with a carabine and a shoulder strap which contrived to make his costume somewhat picturesque, recalling to my mind the tableaux in which modern painters have retraced some of the episodes of the Spanish war, where monks, escaped from the monasteries, took up the calling of brigands and guerilla soldiers. Such a one had replaced the last Spanish padre, chief of Santa Cruz, an old man very much venerated, loved in the countryside; and who having founded this mission, was able to raise it to remarkable prosperity which it enjoyed before the several revolutions had commenced, of which Mexico had been the theatre for so long a time: Instead of this prosperity I found ruins, the most profound misery, a priest, unworthy from all reports to fill the so noble and important functions of priesthood. How could a society, so unique, so little advanced in civilization, be able to progress under the direction of such ministers of religion, men as generally disreputable as their predecesosrs were respectable! Otherwise our new acquaintance soon made himself at home with us and acted as a good companion. Having taken us along to his abode, the same which had been occupied by his venerable predecessor, and which we found abandoned to disorder and the most sordid uncleanliness, our host took from the cupboards and placed on the dirty, wobbly table, nearly the only piece of furniture in the apartment, a demijohn of native wine, bread and fruit, and then invited us to partake of his improvised meal; and upon our refusal, he took long drafts, without his head seeming in the least affected.

The sun having set, and since such society did not attract us sufficiently for us to remain longer, I made my adieus to the two authorities of the establishment, thanking the administrator for his friendly reception, and retraced the route which led us to the place on the shore where my captain's gig awaited me.

The evening was lovely; the moon gently lighted the countryside, the heavens scintillated with stars, a light breeze from the land refreshed the atmosphere, still warm from the heat of the day, and brought to us the distant sound of the clock of the mission sounding the Angelus. The path which we followed wound sometimes across a cluster of large trees, under which a superb greensward unrolled, sometimes in the midst of fields covered with a rich vegetation, from which we exhaled sweet, aromatic odors.

Each of us, feeling the influence of such a lovely moment and of the memories which that enchanted spectacle awoke in his soul, marched quietly along, wholly absorbed in his own reflections. I enjoyed one of those moments so rare for a man who has reached the autumn of his life, when the imagination, left to itself, once more beautifies his future, tears away all difficulties, makes us dream again of pleasures which fate often has not reserved for us, or by which perhaps we would not be at all benefited. But these dreams, are they not happiness, compared with the reality of life, so full of deceptions, compared with that satiety of joy, which, like the harpies of Virgil, spoil all that they touch and which impose once more the chances of war and the perils of long sea voyages, upon the very navigator who during previous expeditions has sworn a thousand times that he would never again abandon the dear beings amongst whom he so often had desired to return and pass his life?

APPENDIX No. 4
CHAPTER XXX, BOOK VI

"Prefecto of the 2nd District.

I enclose a copy of the proclamation published by His Excellency the Gov. of the Department relating to the election of Deputies to the Congress General and Assembly of same, so that you may immediately and with order take the official measure, so that in the town at your charge you may proceed with the primary elections of the 11 of the present month.

Notifying the referee of this segregation to be present, Sunday the 18 of this month, before the head of the party of this Port, so as to name two secondary electors who will also be present in the City of Los Angeles the last Sunday of this coming Sept. Conforming to Article 16 of the law of the 19 of June of 1843.

To 1st *Alcalde* of Sta. Cruz and Branciforte."

(Spanish Archives, Hall of Records, Santa Cruz, No. 213)

"Justice of the Peace of the town
of Branciforte and Santa Cruz.

Friday at eight o'clock A. M. you will appear in this tribunal, which is in my charge, to unite with the seven electors, named by the majority of votes, so that the 1st and 2nd *Alcaldes* may be elected.

God and Liberty,

Santa Cruz, 20th of Dec., 1843

RAFAEL CASTRO.

Juan Jose Feliz
En Qu Rancho."

(Spanish Archives, Hall of Records, Santa Cruz, No. 119)

"Prefecture of the
2nd District.

I enclose a copy of the proclamation sent out by his Excellency the Gov. of *Departmento,* dated the 12th of last month, referring to the naming of political authorities, so that you may give it the necessary publication in the town of which you are in charge.

God and Liberty.

Monterey Aug. 6, 1845,

MANUEL CASTRO.

(To)

*Sr. Alcalde Comandante
de Sta Cruz."*

(Spanish Archives, Hall of Records, Santa Cruz, No. 544)

(Seal) "His Excellency the Gov. orders me to tell you to have care that the citizens Jose Aranso & Guillermo Wilkis, shall not clash with each other in the cultivation of the land which has been granted them.

Later the above named are to appear before the government to give the necessary testimonies.

God and Liberty

Monterey, May 30, 1844

MANUEL CASTRO.

(To)
*Sr Alcalde 10
de Santa Cruz."*
(Spanish Archives, Hall of Records, Santa Cruz, No. 182)
Manuel Rodriguez
1st Constitutional *Alcalde*

To the residents of Santa Cruz

So that all may benefit by the usage of the water, I have judged it wise to observe the following.

1. Monday of next week from six to twelve A. M. Nicolas Dodero will use the water to irrigate and from twelve to six P. M. Rafael Castro.
2. Tuesday A. M. Juan Gonzales, and in the afternoon Gracia Rodriguez.
3. Wednesday A. M. Don Antonio Rodriguez and in the afternoon Juan Perez.
4. Thursday A. M. Guillermo Vocle and Roman Rodriguez P. M.
5. Friday all day the water will be used by the gardener of the Mission.
6. The persons above mentioned will under no pretext use the water longer than the time allotted. Any one violating the above order will be fined according to the amount that the 1st or 2nd *Alcalde* will judge right to impose. That it may come to the notice of those interested in the matter, I order this proclamation to be placed where it is customary.

Santa Cruz, May 11, 1844.

MANUEL RODRIGUEZ."

(Spanish Archives, Hall of Records, Santa Cruz, No. 517)

*"Juzgado Constitucional
   de Sta Cruz.*

It being necessary that there should be an auxiliary judge in those ranches, which belong to Branciforte, so that order may be maintained, and a report sent weekly of what has occurred, I have had you named as Auxiliary Judge and *Juez de Campo.* I hope you will fulfill this post to the best of your ability.

God and Liberty

Sta Cruz, Jan., 1846

JOSE BOLCOFF.

To

Sr. D. Isidro Salazar."

(Spanish Archives, Hall of Records, Santa Cruz, No. 110)

"Notice to the Public.

Senor Guadalupe Castro, by the majority of votes, has been elected 1st *Alcalde* of jurisdiction and of Campo of the town of Sta Cruz. No. of votes received 16. Jose Majors 11 votes. Juan Hime (John Hames) 12 votes. The elected will take charge of his office the 3rd of the present month.

Santa Cruz, 1st of August, 1846.

JOSE BOLCOFF."

(Spanish Archives, Hall of Records, Santa Cruz, No. 523)

APPENDIX No. 5

CHAPTER XXX, BOOK VI

Colonel James Clyman was born in Virginia on Feb. 1, 1792. The land on which his father held a life-lease was owned by George Washington. During the 90 adventurous years of his life, beginning in the days of Washington, he crossed the continent three times, pioneering almost every step of the way, and his career ended in California only fifty years ago.

Clyman saw service in the War of 1812 in Ohio, worked as a land-surveyor under a son of Alexander Hamilton, engaged in the early twenties with William H. Ashley as a trapper in the Rockies, enlisted in the army at the time of the Black Hawk Indian War in the same company with Abraham Lincoln, was a homesteader, hunter and storekeeper in Illinois and Wisconsin in the thirties, came to Oregon in 1844 with the great immigration of that year, thence into California (in 1845) as leader of the party in which came James Wilson Marshall, journeyed east over the Sierra in 1846 with Lansford W. Hastings and came overland again as captain of one of the last pre-gold-rush trains of "agricultural" immigrants.

On his first journey to California he saw little that pleased him except the natural beauty of the forests and the hills and the abundance of wild game. He detested the indolent life of the Californians and the slavery in which some of them held the Indians. He seems to have looked a little askance at the attempts of revolution by the foreigners, but after the conquest he was back again with the intention of purchasing a great tract of land where Vallejo now stands—a project which could not be realized.

APPENDIX No. 6
Chapter XXX, Book VI

For some time there was considerable confusion as to the question of authority.

Cutts, in his "Conquest of California and New Mexico" (p. 183), quotes Colonel Cook who wrote on March 12th:

"General Kearny is supreme somewhere up the coast; Colonel Fremont supreme at Pueblo de los Angeles; Commodore Stockton is commander-in-chief at San Diego; Commodore Shubrick the same at Monterey; and I at San Luis Rey; and we are all supremely poor; the government having no money and no credit; and we hold the territory because Mexico is poorest of all."

APPENDIX No. 7
Chapter XXX, Book VI

William Blackburn came to Santa Cruz in October, 1845, travelling over the plains from Independence, Mass. He was a native of Jefferson County, Virginia, and was born in 1814. He and his travelling companions, Jacob R. Snyder, Geo. McDougal and Harvey Speel, stopped on the Zayante Creek, and worked at making roof shingles. They had all been under the Bear Flag in Fremont's battalion, Blackburn being first lieutenant of artillery; Snyder was the quartermaster. They remained in the service until the treaty of Couenga. Afterwards Blackburn went into the merchandising business in an adobe building fronting on the upper plaza, facing the then mission buildings, but now the Catholic church. The store was connected with an open hotel, where any white man received his supper and bed without pay. In 1847 he was appointed alcalde by Governor Mason, and for two years dispensed justice in his own peculiar way.

APPENDIX No. 8
Chapter XXX, Book VI

Marguerite Eyer Wilbur, the translator of the Journal of Ernest de Massey, says:

"One of the younger sons of the French nobility who joined the gold rush to California was Ernest de Massey, a member of a well-known family who had lived for many generations at the Chateau de Passavant on the Upper Saone River near the Swiss border. In his youth, de Massey had prepared for a military life, but had later abandoned this career to become a glass manuafcturer. This venture proving unsuccessful he then tried agriculture.

"In the effort to recuperate the losses sustained in these two unfortunate ventures de Massey decided to join the migration to California."

APPENDIX No. 1

CHAPTER XXXI, BOOK VI

Many tales of the bandit, Murrieta, survived him. For instance, it was believed for a long time that he had died almost sixty years later in Peru at the age of ninety-two; and Captain George Baunton gives even a circumstantial account of the bandit's life in South America.

Similar stories were afloat in regard to John Wilkes Booth, the murderer of President Lincoln, shortly after the close of the Civil War. Notwithstanding that Booth's corpse was fully identified by a surgeon in the United States Army, who had operated on Booth a short time before his demise for an ugly ulcer in the neck, it was still believed that Booth had escaped pursuit, and that he had died only in 1902, in Enid, Oklahoma, where under the name of John St. Helen, he was presumed to have committed suicide. The body of St. Helen was embalmed and afterwards bandied around the country as the corpse of President Lincoln's murderer.

Those who are interested in the life of the bandit Murrieta will find additional data in the sketch written by Mr. Frederick R. Bechdolt, "When the West was Young," and the "Life of Murrieta," translated from the Spanish of Ireneo Paz by Francis P. Belle, or in the account written by John R. Ridge and published by the Hollister Free Lance.

Recently the Grabhorn Press of San Francisco republished Murrieta's story.

The name Murrieta is spelled in half a dozen different ways.

APPENDIX No. 2

CHAPTER XXXI, BOOK VI

In 1851 Governor MacDougal commissioned S. E. Woodworth to raise a company of rangers to capture the horse thieves in Monterey County.

Claudio, a famous bandit, together with six of his men was intercepted in 1853 on his way to Monterey by H. Cocks, Justice of the Peace at Salinas; they were all killed.

Vendettas were also known in and around Monterey, viz., the twelve murders which were committed in the Roach-Belcher quarrel, originating in the settlement of the Estate of Jose Maria Sanchez, who died about 1852, having been shot while in the barroom of the Washington Hotel; Roach who had retired to his ranch near Santa Cruz was assassinated near Watsonville.

Tuburcio Vasquez, who operated somewhat later, but who became as famous as Murrieta, also honored Monterey County with his presence many times, but was finally hanged in Los Angeles.

INDEX